Training and Development: Enhancing Communication and Leadership Skills

Steven A. Beebe

Texas State University–San Marcos

Timothy P. Mottet

Texas State University–San Marcos

K. David Roach

Texas Tech University

PEARSON

Boston   New York   San Francisco
Mexico City   Montreal   Toronto   London   Madrid   Munich   Paris
Hong Kong   Singapore   Tokyo   Cape Town   Sydney

Executive Editor: *Karon Bowers*
Series editorial assistant: *Jennifer Trebby*
Marketing Manager: *Mandee Eckersley*
Composition and Prepress Buyer: *Linda Cox*
Manufacturing Manager: *JoAnne Sweeney*
Cover Administrator: *Kristina Mose-Libon*
Editorial-Production Coordinator: *Mary Beth Finch*
Editorial-Production Service: *Heckman & Pinette*
Electronic Composition: *Publishers' Design and Production Services, Inc.*
Photo Research: *Jennifer Trebby and Amy Giese*

For related titles and support materials, visit our online catalog at www.ablongman.com

Between the time Website information is gathered and then published, it is not unusual for some sites to have closed. Also, the transcription of URLs can result in unintended typographical errors. The publisher would appreciate notification where these errors occur so that they may be corrected in subsequent editions.

Library of Congress Cataloging-in-Publication Data

Beebe, Steven A., 1950–
    Training and development : enhancing communication and leadership skills / Steven A. Beebe, Timothy P. Mottet, K. David Roach.
      p. cm.
    Includes index.
    ISBN 0-205-33243-9 (pbk. : alk. paper)
    1. Training. 2. Communication. 3. Leadership. I. Mottet, Timothy P.
II. Roach, K. David. III. Title.

LB1027.47.B44 2004
658.3'12404—dc21

2003052161

Printed in the United States of America
10 9 8 7 6 5 4   08 07 06

To Sue, Mark, and Matt
S. A. B.

To my loving parents, Carol and Joe Mottet
T. P. M.

To Becky, Lauren, and Lindsey
K. D. R.

BRIEF CONTENTS

CONTENTS

PREFACE

This book is written to be used as the primary text or supporting text for a course to teach people how to design and present a training seminar or workshop. This is not a book just *about* training; it is a book that prescribes *how to do* training.

We often tell our students and clients that if they don't remember anything else about how to develop an effective training program, they should remember this one sentence: *It depends upon their needs.* Embodied in that one sentence is the essential principle of addressing learners' needs when training them to perform a skill. We believe a needs-centered approach to training is so powerful that we tell our students if we ever ask them a question related to training and they are unsure of the answer, they should just say, "It depends upon their needs"—and that will, in all probability, be the right answer.

Increasingly, more colleges and universities are offering courses in how to design and deliver training programs. A significant surge in training and development courses is occurring not only in communication departments but also in education, business, and health care, as well as many other disciplines. Many books have been written about training and development. But there are virtually no resources designed to be used in a university-level course that are theory based, yet help students develop practical skills and methods of designing and presenting training programs. This book is written to fill that gaping hole by presenting a comprehensive, needs-centered approach to training that will help both undergraduate and graduate students learn practical principles and skills of how to develop a training program from start to finish. Although we are all communication professors and emphasize communication skills in the training programs we teach, all of us are also trainers and consultants for a wide variety of clients. This book has been written to be used by instructors in communication, business, education, and a variety of other disciplines that teach students how to design and present training programs.

A Needs-Centered Approach

At the heart of our approach to designing and delivering an effective training program is the philosophy that trainers must meet trainees' needs; this will, in turn, enhance their performance. By its very nature, training has a practical goal of helping trainees learn how to perform specific skills. What should be the guiding force in identifying the skills that need to be taught? We believe trainee needs should be that guiding beacon upon which a trainer should always focus. Training that does not address specific need or job function of a trainee is not effective training.

Training is essentially a communication process of developing objectives, identifying content, selecting methods, and presenting the training message. But our needs-centered training model is also based on the centuries-old wisdom of focusing on the needs of listeners when developing a message. We didn't invent the needs-centered approach; it's been the key principle that speech and communication instructors have used since Aristotle noted in his classic work *Rhetoric* in 333 BC that the audience is central to effective speaking. For over two thousand years, public speaking teachers have stressed the importance of being audience-centered when speaking to others.

At the core of our needs-centered training model (shown below) is the ongoing process of identifying the needs of the organization and especially the specific needs of trainees who will attend the training session. Preparing a training program involves both a rhetorical needs-centered process and a series of steps. Our needs-centered model captures both the continuing process of identifying and meeting trainee needs and the step-by-step sequence of tasks needed to design, deliver, and assess a training program. We first introduce our needs-centered model of training in Chapter 1 and then refer to it in every chapter in which we discuss the nuts and bolts of developing a training program. Viewing the model as a clock, start at "high noon" with the first task of analyzing the training task and move around the model clockwise to "develop training objectives," then " organize training content," and so on. At each step of the training process, however, the training student is reminded that at the core of the process is to analyze the needs of the organization and the trainee. Even when conducting the final step of the training process, "assess training," it's important to note how effectively the needs of the organization and trainees have been met.

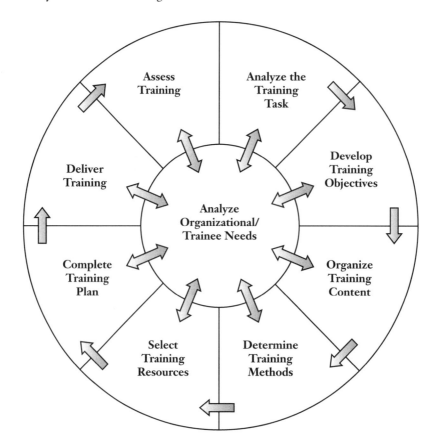

Theory-Based Adult Learning Principles

Our needs-centered approach is anchored in contemporary learning theory. After introducing the needs-centered training model in Chapter 1, we devote Chapter 2 to a discussion of learning theory and principles. We discuss general principles of learning and emphasize the importance of considering the needs of adult learners, bolstered by the latest research findings about adult learning. Andragogy, the art and science of teaching adults, rather than pedagogy, the art and science of teaching children, informs the training techniques and strategies that we present throughout the book. Because adults need to learn what is relevant to them and are problem-oriented learners, our needs-centered model reflects the importance of addressing the needs of adults.

The fact that adults have different learning styles is yet another reason to be keenly focused on the needs of learners. Differences in perceptual learning differences, learning time differences, and information processing differences mean that the effective trainer should be responsive to these various preferred learning styles. We do more than just describe learning differences; we identify specific strategies that can enhance adult learning.

Following our discussion of adult learning theory in Chapter 2, the remaining chapters carefully walk students through the skills needed to design and deliver training programs. Chapter 3 covers the essential skills of how to assess trainee needs as well as analyze the training task. Developing objectives and designing curriculum is the focus of Chapter 4. How to develop training content, including how to conduct research, is presented in Chapter 5. Chapter 6 reviews how to use various training methods and notes advantages and disadvantages of each method. Chapter 7 reviews practical strategies for using technology and presentation aids in training. How to design the training plan or lesson plan is covered in Chapter 8. Chapter 9 not only emphasizes how to deliver a training presentation but also includes applications of the latest research conclusions from the instructional development literature. Even the best-prepared trainer faces challenges. Chapter 10 offers practical tips for coping with challenges in training. Chapter 11 identifies specific techniques of assessing training. The final chapter, Chapter 12, identifies trends and career opportunities in training.

Special Features

We not only do our best to talk about how to be an effective trainer, we model training principles and skills with special features throughout the book.

Learning Objectives: Each chapter begins with clearly articulated learning objectives. Our objectives model our approach to writing objectives that are observable, attainable, measurable, and specific.

Numerous Examples: Each of us has had considerable experience not only as an educator but also as a trainer. We draw upon our experience by providing several examples of good training practice. We've also learned from our mistakes; the wisdom we've learned from our training errors is also reflected in the examples we use throughout the book.

Recap Boxes: Students need to have the key content reinforced. We liberally sprinkle in review boxes that cogently reinforce the learning by highlighting essential principles and skills.

Glossary: Boldfaced terms are not only defined in the text but are also presented in a glossary at the end of the book.

Chapter-End Questions: To help students test their own knowledge and application of principles, we've included questions for discussion and review at the end of each chapter. We want students to do more than recall essential information; we want them to apply what they've learned. To help them accomplish this goal, we've included questions for application and analysis at the end of each chapter. Many of these questions are like mini case studies so students can assess their skill in solving problems related to training.

Useful Support Resources

Accompanying this text is an *Instructor's Manual/Test Bank*, prepared by Sue Stewart of Southwest Texas State University. This supporting material includes detailed chapter outlines; multiple choice, true/false, and essay questions; and numerous activities for use in or out of class. Please contact your Allyn & Bacon representative for details or to receive a copy.

Acknowledgments

Writing a book is a team project. In our case, we benefited from working together as a team of authors bouncing ideas off one another, which we believe strengthens the book. It's a special joy to work together not only as colleagues but also as good friends. In addition to our own synergy, we've had a support team of editors, reviewers, and colleagues who have provided outstanding assistance in helping us write this book.

Karon Bowers, Senior Editor at Allyn & Bacon, provided consistent encouragement from the beginning until the fruition of the project; her legendary support is greatly appreciated. Jennifer Trebby, Editorial Assistant at Allyn & Bacon, was also exceptionally helpful in assisting us manage the myriad of editorial details.

We appreciate the excellent advice and suggestions from our talented group of reviewers who read the manuscript (some more than once) to help us polish our prose and fine-tune our ideas. Reviewers are: Paul N. Lakey, Abilene Christian University; Jeff Hudson, Scott County, Minnesota; Jean M. DeWitt, University of Houston; and Joseph Chesebro, SUNY–Brockport.

David thanks his 4th-grade teacher, Mrs. Hicks; Kenneth and Anita Roach; Kelly Hamby; Chantry Fritts; Rob Stewart; Ed Townsend; Virginia Richmond; and Jim McCroskey—all of whom actively live their beliefs of being learner centered in their teaching and training. He also expresses his deepest gratitude to Becky Roach, who in addition to being his spouse and best friend is also one of the most gifted and talented teachers he has ever encountered and has taught him much about teaching. Most of all, David thanks The Great Teacher, who modeled perfectly how to meet the real needs of people while showing them a better way.

Tim expresses his appreciation to his team of trainers who have invested numerous hours developing him and meeting his needs: Lois Anne Harris, Tom Willett, Marilyn Root, Julia Dobrow, Jim Shanahan, Jim McCroskey, Virginia Richmond, and Steve Beebe. He is truly grateful for the mentoring he has received from these role models and hopes that he can return the invaluable gift by mentoring and developing his own students. Tim would also like to thank his professors at West Virginia University and his colleagues and graduate teaching assistants at Southwest Texas State University for giving him an academic community that allows him to grow as a teacher and researcher. Tim offers a special thanks to Katrina Stone and her crew at "Owens" for giving him a place to write. Most importantly, Tim would like to thank his parents—Carol and Joe—for the love and support they have given him and for giving him a sense of home.

Steve thanks his two decades of training and development students, at both the University of Miami and Southwest Texas State University, for their feedback, encouragement, and ideas, which helped shape the core concepts of this book. Jack Johnson from the University of Wisconsin–Milwaukee is a friend and colleague who was helpful in developing strategies for teaching a course in training and development. Dennis and Laurie Romig, from Performance Resources, Inc., are good friends as well as skilled trainers and consultants who have both modeled effective training and inspired training paradigms that inform the content of this book in several chapters. Nathan Faylor, also a good friend and former student, authored the sample training plan that appears in Chapter 8. Most importantly, Steve expresses his appreciation to his personal grammar queen, musical partner, sometime coauthor, all-the-time soul mate, best friend, and spouse, Sue Beebe, for her enduring wisdom, love, and encouragement.

Steven A. Beebe
Timothy P. Mottet
San Marcos, Texas

K. David Roach
Lubbock, Texas

Training and Development: Enhancing Communication and Leadership Skills

Introduction to Training

CHAPTER OBJECTIVES

After studying this chapter, you should be able to:

1. Define training.
2. Compare training with the processes of education, development, motivation, and consulting.
3. Describe three approaches to consulting.
4. Define and describe the communication process.
5. List skills that are frequently presented in communication, leadership, and management training seminars and workshops.
6. Identify and describe the nine steps involved in designing and presenting a training workshop.

It's been estimated that 98 percent of all our problems boil down to "people problems." In the workplace, if the problem involves people, the solution is often improved communication and leadership skills. According to surveys, scholars who study organizational effectiveness, and management consultants, as well as corporate chief executive officers, the most important factor that contributes to success in today's information-driven marketplace is the ability to communicate and skillfully lead others.[1] Whether it's interacting with customers, clients, or colleagues, the ability to understand and respond to the messages of others is among the most valued strategies in any organization's visionary blueprint for success. Although effective communication and collaborative leadership are practically worshiped by most corporate executives, how to enhance the quality of communication, management, and leadership skills can be a challenge.

This book is designed to enhance the effectiveness of organizations—to develop effective communication, leadership, and management skills by training people to improve their interactions with others. There are many strategies and pathways to organizational effectiveness, such as conducting a communication audit, changing the organizational chart to reduce barriers to communication, or redesigning a communication message system. Courses in organizational communication, management, professional communication, and leadership provide a vast array to tools, techniques, and theories to enhance communication, which, in turn, leads to organizational effectiveness. But if the goal is to help employees possess valued skills such as speaking, listening, relating, collaborating, solving problems, customer service, and managing conflict, then training people to enhance their communication and leadership abilities is an effective method of developing organizational communication effectiveness.

Training is sometimes viewed as a simple panacea to enhance organizational effectiveness. One of your authors remembers being interrupted from his work at the office by a man who brusquely knocked on the door and announced his name followed by his self-assessment that he was a "very important person." Unfamiliar with the gentleman's name or accomplishments, I listened politely while he stated his reason for visiting me. He explained that he knew that I was a communication consultant who had presented communication training seminars for several corporations and organizations and provided one-on-one coaching. After reminding me several times how busy and important he was, he got to his point. He had been told by some of his friends and colleagues that he needed to improve his communication skill. I'll never forget his specific request: He wanted me to *do something to him* to make him a better communicator. (I had a momentary vision that he sought a magic potion, incantation, or some kind of laying-on-of-hands ceremony to instill the communication skills he coveted.) He further explained, "I can pay you very well for your services," which led me to believe he knew something about communication, because he quickly got my attention. I suggested, however, that enhancing communication skill is not something that can be simply "done to" someone by revealing a few techniques or little-known skills. Developing communication and leadership ability takes effort, time, practice, and a personal commitment to enhancing skills and changing behavior.

This book does not offer promises of shortcuts or tidy lists of techniques that will enhance organizational communication and leadership effectiveness. What we do offer is a systematic way to enhance communication, management, and leadership skills by teaching you how to develop and present training seminars and workshops to others. Our approach is relatively straightforward. Regardless of your training objective, keep one thing in mind: *Develop and deliver training that meets the needs of the trainees.* We also emphasize that the training process is essentially a communication process. We therefore draw heavily upon communication as well as learning principles to support our strategies.

In this chapter we'll clarify differences between training, education, development, and consulting; provide a brief introduction to communication fundamentals, noting how training is a communication process; and point the way ahead by providing an overview of the steps involved in designing and delivering a training seminar or workshop.

Understanding Training

When you hear the word *training* what do you think of? Perhaps you envision lion tamers training wild beasts to obey the crack of the trainer's whip. Or maybe you think of a military drill sergeant training fresh recruits in boot camp. Stated simply, to train is to develop skills. ***Training** is the process of developing skills in order to more effectively perform a specific job or task.* Communication, leadership, and management training focuses on teaching people to enhance their skill of relating to others. The short description of these skills is that they are "people skills."

Training in the United States is big business. It's been estimated that over $200 billion is spent annually on organizational training.[2] Conservatively, over one million people make their living involved in some aspect of training.[3] Communication and leadership skill training occupies a large chunk of the training business; it's not surprising that enhancing these skills is so important. The largest part of virtually any organization's budget is for personnel costs. People make organizations function. What is the number-one valued skill for employees? Effective communication takes that spot, followed closely by the ability to lead and manage others.[4]

Central to our definition of training is the focus on developing skills. A **skill** is an ability to *do something* as opposed to knowing something. If you are skilled you are competent to perform some behavior or act. A skilled communicator is one who is able to effectively and appropriately deliver a presentation, listen empathetically, manage conflict, facilitate a meeting, or conduct a performance appraisal interview. Similarly, a skilled leader is one who can develop a collective vision and help the organization work collaboratively to make the vision a reality. It is true that each of these processes, communication and leadership, involves knowledge (understanding concepts) as well as skill. The essential element in making something a skill, however, is the proficiency of performing some behavior or task. We're not suggesting that skills are the only or even ultimate reason for studying communication and leadership strategies. We are suggesting that the goal of communication training is the performance of an observable and measurable skill that can be assessed in some way. To clarify our definition, we'll compare the training function to four related processes: education, development, consulting, and motivation.

Training and Education

Education is the process of imparting knowledge or information. People can educate themselves by reading, or they can have someone teach them what they want or need to learn. Training, on the other hand, focuses more on skill development and behavior change. John Kline, who is both an expert educator and trainer, made some useful distinctions between training and education that clarifies how these two processes can be distinguished from one another.[5]

Training emphasizes doing, and education emphasizes knowing. As we have already noted, to train is to focus on seeing a behavioral change, while education typically focuses on learning information. Although it's true that the information learned may influence behavior or skill, if the primary outcome is learning definitions, concepts, principles, and theories, then that's an education process.

Training emphasizes achieving a certain level of skill attainment, and education often evaluates mastery by comparing one student to another. When you train someone, you want that person to be able to successfully perform a behavior or a set of behaviors. Teaching someone to drive a car is an example of training. Before you hand your car keys to someone, you want to make certain that person has attained a level of car-driving skill that will permit him or her to successfully navigate the highways and byways of your community. There is a clearly specified level of skill attainment. In many education settings, such as college classrooms, you may be evaluated in comparison to others. You might be graded "on the curve." You don't know what grade you will receive until all the other tests or papers have been graded. A score of 85 could be an A, B, or C, depending on how the grades are curved. Training is less concerned with evaluating you in comparison to others; training emphasizes whether or not you can perform the skill.

Training is more a closed system, whereas education operates more as an open system. By "closed system," we mean that there are certain right and wrong ways of performing a skill based not on external constraints but on simply performing the skill properly. Regardless of outside interference, there is a preferred way to achieve the desired results such as operating a complex computer program or running an electronic personal organizer. When applying principles in education, you may be able to be more creative in solving problems and achieving results. As described by Kline, education occurs when "Learning is continuous with no cap or ceiling on how well the graduate may be prepared to handle new responsibilities."[6] In education there is less emphasis on finding the "right answer"; the focus is typically on finding the best answer.

Training emphasizes requirements to perform a specific job linked to a specific job duty, whereas education is often less linked to a specific job. You might receive training to fry hamburgers so that each hamburger is always cooked the same way each time. Training, as in this hamburger example, is linked to performing a specific job with certain specifications. Education emphasizes knowledge with less application to a specific job. When you take history, math, or music, you are less focused on applying the information you learn to a specific job description; you learn to use the information in less precisely defined ways. In a public speaking class, you may be educated to give speeches in a variety of to-be-specified situations; in a corporate sales seminar, you may receive skill-development training to help you polish closing a sale in your on-the-job duties.

Training is more likely to offer a comprehensive list of the skills required to perform a specific behavior; education is less likely to provide a complete summary of all information on a specific subject. When you receive effective training, someone has thought through the various steps involved in performing the task. To be trained in operating a microwave oven is to receive information about how to operate all of the features the oven offers. When being educated, you're less likely to hear your teacher say, "This is everything there is to know on this subject." Scholars and educators are always discovering new knowledge.

Training and Motivation

Have you ever heard a motivational speaker either on TV on in person? If so, you know that the goal of a motivational speaker is to persuade you to take some positive action such as working harder, setting goals, spending more time with your family, or losing weight. Motivational speakers often use strong emotional appeal by presenting personal stories or drawing upon the lives of others to encourage people to take action to improve their lives. Some trainers also work as motivational speakers. **Motivation** is an internal state of readiness to take action or achieve a goal. Motivational speakers attempt to tap that internal state of readiness by encouraging listeners to achieve a worthwhile goal.

Trainers and motivational speakers have some things in common but also use significantly different methods to achieve their goals. What do they have in common?

RECAP

Comparing Training and Education

Training	Education
Training is the process of developing skills for a specific job or task.	Education is the process of imparting knowledge or information.
Emphasizes doing	Emphasizes knowing
Emphasizes achieving a specific level of skill attainment	Emphasizes achieving often in comparison to the knowledge level of others
Emphasizes a closed system perspective: There are specific right and wrong ways of performing a skill.	Emphasizes an open system perspective: There are often many ways to achieve the goal; creativity and critical thinking are encouraged.
Emphasizes performance levels in order to perform a specific job	Emphasizes knowing information not necessarily linked to a specific job or career.
Emphasizes a comprehensive listing of the skills required to perform a specific behavior; each step in the process is prescribed.	Emphasizes an open-ended approach to achieve a goal; not every step in the process is always prescribed.

They both seek to bring about change in their listeners. They differ in that trainers are more likely to seek individual and organizational change by teaching *skills;* change happens because the listener now has a new repertoire of tools and behaviors that he or she didn't have before. Motivational speakers strive to change people by stimulating emotions and attitudes; the assumption is that if emotions are heightened and attitudes are touched, change will follow. **Emotions** are feeling states that often result in behavior change. **Attitudes** are learned predispositions to respond favorably or unfavorably toward something.

Zig Ziglar, one of the best-known motivational speakers in America, started his career as a door-to-door vacuum cleaner salesman. Zig's stories of endurance and common-sense advice told with humor and wit have made him a popular motivational speaker. Another well-known motivational speaker, Anthony Robbins, has provided advice to people in many vocations, including former U.S. presidents. The success of motivating people just by telling stories, using humor, and providing inspirational anecdotes is evidence that motivational speakers have a role in influencing organizational dynamics. There is some question, however, about the staying power of motivational messages. After the emotion fades, the listener may still need strategies and skills to enact change.

Training and Development

The concept of development is a process often linked to both training and human resources. You may have seen the phrase "human resource development" or "training and development." The word *development* added to other terms suggests a broadening of the behaviors or strategies to achieve a goal. But what precisely is development?

Development is any behavior, strategy, design, restructuring, skill or skill set, strategic plan, or motivational effort that is designed to produce growth or change over time. Organizations seek positive change, not just change for the sake of change. Positive change includes such things as making more money if the organization's goal is to turn a profit for the owners or shareholders. If the organization is a hospital, the desired change is to make people healthy (while simultaneously not losing money or even making money if the hospital is a for-profit health facility). Educational institutions seek change to enhance student learning. You get the idea. Development is a process of helping the organization or individuals in the organization do their jobs more effectively. Development involves a set of strategies that can help an individual or organization change to perform more effectively in achieving individual or corporate vision, mission, and goals.

How does development differ from training? Development is a broader, more encompassing function. Training is narrower in focus. There are a variety of organizational or personal intervention strategies that may be used to develop an organization; training (teaching people skills to perform a specific job or task) is but one of the methods used to effect change. Similarly, educating people (imparting knowledge) is another strategy that may be used to develop people and organizations. So when the word *development* is linked to the word *training*, it suggests that training is designed to achieve a broader function than just performing a specific skill. Training and development suggest that the goal of the training is to facilitate the transformation of the organization—to bring about positive change not just for one person, but to have a larger impact on the organization.

The model in Figure 1.1 shows the relationship among the functions of training, education, and development. The outer circle, development, encompasses both education and training. Training and education are methods of developing individuals and organizations. Education is a more general function than training; that's why the "education" circle is larger than the "training" circle. Training is typically a component in a broad-based education program, which ultimately is designed to develop an organization. Don't get the idea that training and education are the only ways to develop an organization. They aren't. Courses in organizational communication discuss several strategies (such as analyzing and diagnosing communication message flow) that are designed to enhance organizational effectiveness by developing the organization in positive ways.

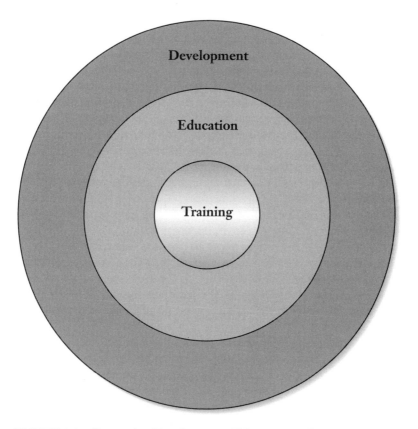

FIGURE 1.1   Comparing Development, Education, and Training
Development—encouraging growth and change—is a more comprehensive process than education and training. Education is broader in scope and purpose than training. Training focuses on enhancing skills to perform a specific job.

Training and Consulting

Another process related to training, education, and development is consulting. Perhaps you have heard of people who do communication or management consulting for an organization in your community. While you may have a vague idea of what consulting is, you still may be uncertain as to precisely what a consultant does. A consultant is often a person brought in from outside the organization, department, or program area to help solve a problem. A consultant offers insight, advice, wisdom, and research- or experienced-based intervention strategies that may help an organization more effectively achieve its goals by solving problems. The goal of consulting is personal and corporate development. A consultant may be external, from outside the organization, or internal, someone who works for the organization. Many organizations have a department, sometimes called "organizational effectiveness," within the human resource development division that specializes in providing internal consultant services.

A communication or management consultant, then, is a person who provides advice about some aspect of communication or leadership to enhance organizational effectiveness. A consultant could provide training services or could offer an analysis of a communication problem and suggest that training or education may be one of the strategies that could enhance organizational effectiveness. Consultants are problem solvers. They help by offering a set of skills or services that augment or compliment those already resident within the department, program, or organization.

According to organizational development specialist Edgar Schein, there are three typical types of consulting approaches: purchase, doctor–patient, and process.[7] The **purchase** approach to consulting is often associated with training. A member of the organization already has diagnosed the problem and seeks to purchase a solution from a consultant. Say, for example, a manager has decided that people in her department have difficulty leading and participating in meetings. The manager may decide to hire a consultant to provide training to members of the department to improve meetings.

The **doctor–patient approach** to consulting places greater emphasis upon the consultant to diagnose the problem in the organization. The manager or director may know that something is wrong without having developed a specific recommendation on what the problem is or how to manage the problem. You can undoubtedly see the analogy to a doctor and patient situation. The patient knows he's not feeling well but isn't quite sure what the problem is or what to do about it. The physician, after running a series of tests, figures out what is needed and prescribes a treatment program to achieve health.

Finally, the **process approach** to consulting involves an even greater involvement of the consultant to diagnose a problem and offer recommendations. The organization may not even yet be aware that there is a problem. The process consultant uses a variety of assessment measures to determine the overall vitality of the organization and then recommends strategies for improving organizational effectiveness. Many organizations have a team of process consultants who work for the organization to enhance the well-being of the organization. Or an external process consultant may be hired and retained to assess the organization's effectiveness. In Chapter 12 we will dis-

---

RECAP

Comparing Three Approaches to Organizational Consulting

Purchase Approach	Doctor–Patient Approach	Process Approach
Someone in the organization has determined what the organization needs (e.g., training) and seeks a consultant to provide the service to meet the needs of the organization.	A consultant is hired to help diagnose an organizational problem and then prescribe strategies for managing the problem.	A consult is hired and retained to spend considerable time analyzing the organization and joining with members of the organizational management team to identify problems and obstacles to organizational effectiveness.
There is little consultant involvement in diagnosing the problem.	There is some consultant involvement in diagnosing the problem.	There is considerable consultant involvement in diagnosing the problem.

---

cuss specific career opportunities related to consulting as well as training and human resource development.

Understanding "Soft" Skills: Communication, Management, and Leadership

There are two broad categories of training skills—soft and hard. Soft skills are those skills that focus on managing people, information, and ideas, such as management training and leadership training. Technical training, such as computer programming or Web page design, is often called "hard" skill training. It's called "hard" skill training not because the skills are necessarily hard to learn, but because the technical skills that are taught typically have specific right answers or precise procedures to follow. *This book focuses on soft skills training.* Communication and leadership skills are essential soft training skills that are valued in the workplace.

Just what soft skills are in the most demand in today's organizations? We assume you've already had some coursework, training, or educational background in communication. You may have also completed coursework in management, organizational communication, or industrial psychology. We don't intend to provide a comprehensive summary of communication and leadership principles, skills, and strategies in this chapter. We will, however, remind you of some of the fundamental principles of communication that may help you sharpen your focus on communication-related training issues. A better understanding of the definition, characteristics, and models of communication can also help you in both designing and delivering communication training programs. *Training others is, in essence, a communication process.*

Communication Defined

Defining communication is controversial. Communication scholars often don't agree on the exact definition of communication. Researchers counted over 150 definitions of communication when they studied the issue several years ago.[8] There are, however, some general perspectives about which most scholars agree. In the broadest sense, **communication** is the process of acting upon information.[9] Expanding on this definition, we suggest that **human communication** is the process of making sense out of the world and sharing that sense with others by creating meaning by verbal and non-verbal messages.[10] Effective communication focuses on the needs of the receiver of the message. Meaning is ultimately created in the mind and heart of the listener. In the context of communication training, the trainer's job is to help people see how we make sense out of what we experience and develop strategies and skills that accurately and clearly express thoughts, ideas, and emotions to others. By focusing on the needs of the trainee, the trainer can craft a training lesson that achieves the objectives of the training.

Communication has several distinct characteristics. Understanding these fundamental attributes of human communication can help diagnose problems and enhance communication among others. Classic communication characteristics include:

- *Communication is inescapable.* Communication is ever-present in our lives. You spend up to 90 percent of your day involved in purposeful communication activities.[11] In an organization, regardless of your specific job description, primarily what you do is communicate with others. Communication training, therefore, is of vital importance to contemporary organizations.
- *Communication is irreversible.* Once words leave your mouth you can't take them back, even if you'd like to. You can tell others to discount what you've said, but if your message is something you regret, the damage has already been done. Even if you try to brush off your offhand comment as a joke you didn't mean, many people believe the maxim: Much truth's spoken when you're only jokin'.
- *Communication is complicated.* As we noted earlier, even though trainees would like trainers to "do something to them" to make them better communicators, it really is not that simple. Communication is often messy. A skilled trainer should be wary of offering simple explanations or quick bromides to solve entrenched communication problems.
- *Communication emphasizes both content and relationships.* The content of a message focuses on the new information, ideas, or suggested actions the speaker wants to express. Relationships involve more implicit cues about feelings, emotions, attitudes, or power involved between the communicants. The content of a message refers to *what* is said. The relationship aspect of a message often refers to *how* something is said.

- *Communication is governed by rules.* Rules are followable prescriptions that indicate what is appropriate or acceptable. Communication training often involves teaching others appropriate rules for managing conflict, giving presentations, and achieving other communication goals.

A Model of Communication

Communication instructors like models. Almost every book about communication includes models to explain the relationships among the many variables or components of the communication process. A model is simply a visual, verbal, or tangible way of representing something else. Just as a model airplane represents the actual plane, a model of communication shows what the parts of the process look like. Reviewing some of the key elements of communication as depicted in a basic communication model is an effective and efficient way of describing and understanding the complicated process of making sense out of our world and sharing that sense with others.

Most contemporary models of communication view communication as a transactive process in which both the sender and receiver of a message *simultaneously* express and respond to messages. As illustrated in Figure 1.2, the sender of the message is also receiving feedback (responses) from the receiver. At the same time the receiver is hearing or seeing a message expressed by the sender, the receiver is also actively responding to the message. Because of the nature of this dynamic process, it's been said that you cannot not communicate. Even if you nod off to sleep while the sender of the message is communicating with you, your slumber communicates something (perhaps not what you intended) to the speaker. Communication is not as sluggish as a tennis ball being batted back and forth; messages to do not bounce hither and yon, but rather we make sense out of messages and respond to messages at the same time we are hearing and seeing a message. The same arrow in the model in Figure 1.2 illustrates the message and feedback, because the source of a message is also simultaneously the receiver of the message. Meaning is created when words and nonverbal messages are expressed and interpreted by others.

The key elements in most basic communication models include the following:

- *Sender:* The originator of the message—usually a person, but in today's technological society it could be a machine.
- *Receiver:* The person who decodes or makes sense out of the message.

FIGURE 1.2 A Model of Communication as Transaction.

- *Message:* The written, spoken, and unspoken elements of communication to which we assign meaning.
- *Channel:* The pathway through which messages are sent, such as a TV cable or the vibrating air that carries the spoken message of another person in your presence.
- *Noise:* An interfering message that decreases the accuracy of the communication of the message. The noise could be literal (the loud roar of a motorcycle) or psychological (thinking about being on vacation while listening to a trainer lecture).
- *Feedback:* A response to a message.
- *Context:* The physical and psychological communication environment.

An Overview of Communication, Management, and Leadership Skills

As you review the model of communication in Figure 1.2, you may be left with the question, "So what does this have to do with training?" Our answer: a lot. Trainers are communicators, and they also teach communication.

A trainer is a communicator who prepares and delivers messages to enhance the skills of the trainees. A communication model helps us understand how communication works or doesn't work. For example, the goal of a trainer is to eliminate noise, both psychological noise and literal noise, so that the message is understood and achieves its intended effect. Although our depiction of communication is relatively simple, it provides a beginning place to diagnose communication problems in organizations.

Communication, management, and leadership training are designed to teach people specific skills that will enhance the quality of messages and human relationships. Returning to the assertion that opened this chapter, communication and leadership skills, especially collaborative leadership skills, are often the solution to problems that arise in organizations. When messages are poorly expressed or misinterpreted, the result can be hurt feelings, missed orders, lost customers, colleague conflict, and lost opportunities for organizational success; lost opportunities translate into losing money or not achieving the goals of the organization. Helping people enhance the quality of communication is a positive, direct way of helping an organization become more effective.

As we emphasized earlier, the training process is a communication process. People don't learn simply because someone teaches something. Learning happens when the learners make sense out of what they've experienced. Learning happens best when the focus remains upon the needs of the trainees. In many respects, the trainees determine what should be taught; skilled trainers know how to assess trainee needs and are aware of how to meet those needs. This book helps you both enhance your communication with trainees and teach communication skills to others.

Communication is how we make sense out of our experiences and share that sense with others. Stated another way: Information is not communication. We are awash in information. Giving people information in this information age does not mean that the information will be useful or acted upon. "Didn't you read the memo?", "Haven't you read the policy?", "Didn't you go to the training session?" Just pronouncing a message does not mean others will get it. Communication training is not as easy as simply telling people what to do or how to behave and then expecting complete understanding. Trainers can't simply "do something" to others and expect learning to occur. As we've seen with our model of communication, the communication process, as well as the training process, has many components (source, message, channel, receiver, noise, feedback). Just because someone has been to a training session does not mean that skills have been mastered. Yet because of the value of effective communication, even if it may be challenging to develop those skills, communication and leadership training remains an important goal of most organizations.

Effective communication involves the receiver of the message in an active rather than a passive way. Therefore, training programs should also actively engage the trainee. It was Confucius who said:

> *What I hear, I forget.*
> *What I see, I remember.*
> *What I do, I understand.*

When viewing the training process as a communication process, the trainer should build in strategies that engage the learner. Bob Pike, a well-known trainer of trainers, suggests that at least every eight minutes participants should have an opportunity to internalize what they are learning; don't just keep piling on more information.[12] Learners need to have experiences to help them make sense out of the information and skills presented.

What are the typical kinds of communication, management, and leadership skills that are taught in training seminars? Here's a sample:

- How to improve listening skills.
- How to become more assertive.
- How to avoid issues of sexual harassment in the workplace.
- How to use and interpret nonverbal messages of customers.
- How to manage conflict.
- How to deal with angry customers.
- How to develop a collaborative team.
- How to solve problems and make decisions in groups and teams.
- How to lead and participate in meetings.
- How to deliver a sales presentation.
- How to use computer graphics in a business presentation.
- How to persuade a customer to purchase a product.
- How to manage time and be more productive.
- How to present a briefing, report, or presentation.
- How to improve the quality of employee communication.
- How to communicate the leadership vision to an organization.
- How to communicate with people from a culture different from you own.
- How to more accurately interpret nonverbal messages of others.
- How to lead others by being collaborative.
- How to develop a cooperative management style.

- How to train the trainer to prepare and deliver a successful training program.
- How to conduct an employee appraisal interview.

The list could continue, but we think you get the idea. Each of these topics involves not just one skill but usually a set of skills or behaviors that lead to enhancing the quality of human relationships and work quality. In virtually every instance, these training topics evolve from our understanding of communication as a transactive process where it can be a challenge to make sense out of the messages expressed by others. If communication was not a problem, there would be no need for communication training.

Understanding the Training Process

Thus far we've defined what training is and how it is similar to and different from other methods of developing an organization (such as educating, developing, motivating, or consulting). We've also defined communication and sketched some basic principles of how it operates and noted how the training process is a communication process. But how, you may wonder, do we get about the task of training others? What do trainers do? What are the steps involved in translating skill and knowledge about human communication to others? The rest of this book answers these questions.

In the chapters ahead we will offer strategies and suggestions for designing and delivering communication training programs. Here we will briefly introduce the major steps in the process. Figure 1.3 presents our needs-centered model of training, which we will use to anchor our discussion of training. It's called a needs-centered model of training because of our belief that the primary purpose of any training program is to respond to the learning needs of the trainee. Training that does not address a need or specific job function of a trainee is not effective training. Following are the major steps of the training process that we will amplify in much greater detail throughout the rest of the book.

Analyze Organizational and Trainee Needs

At the center of the model is the process of identifying the needs of the organization and especially the specific trainees that will be present in the training session. How do you know what trainees need? You ask them—or at least that's one way to assess their needs. In Chapter 3, we offer several specific strategies for conducting surveys, questionnaires, or interviews and a host of other methods for determining what trainees need. If you've had a course in public speaking, you know that analyzing your audience was an early and essential method of beginning to plan your message. The process of identifying trainer needs is quite similar to analyzing your audience when delivering a presentation. Analyzing trainee needs is so central to the process of training that it is in the center of the model; every other aspect of designing and delivering a training presentation depends upon the needs of the trainees. In addition to analyzing the needs of individuals, it's also important to consider the needs of the organization. To analyze the needs of an organization, consider what the organization needs in order to achieve

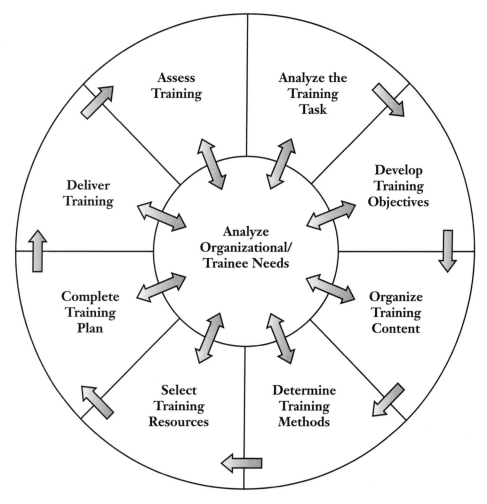

FIGURE 1.3   The Needs-Centered Training Model Focusing on trainee needs drives every step of designing and delivering a training presentation.

its mission. Does it need skilled workers? Or does it need competent leaders and managers? After considering the needs of the organization, you'll then need to determine how training can help address those needs.

Analyze the Training Task

Viewing our model as a clock, after noting that the heart of the model is focusing on the needs of the trainee, begin at the top of the clock and work your way around clockwise to explore the steps of designing and delivering a training presentation. After you've figured out what trainees need (for example, skill in listening or conflict management), an early critical step in designing a training program is to thoroughly analyze the specific task you want the trainees to perform. You conduct a task analysis. A task analysis is a detailed, step-by-step description of precisely what the trainee should do and know in order to perform that desired skill. If you are going to teach someone how to give a sales presentation, as the trainer you first need to know what those steps are before you teach them to others. A task analysis is performed to provide a comprehensive outline of what you would be teaching others if you had unlimited time. You may only have three or four hours to teach a skill, so you may have to focus on only the most critical steps. Developing a task analysis lets you discover what the essential elements of the task are. Our needs-centered training model is really a task analysis of how to train someone. Each piece of the model represents an essential step in the process. We'll review the details of conducting a task analysis in Chapter 3.

Develop Training Objectives

After you have figured out what are the steps of the skill you are teaching, it's important to develop objectives or learning outcomes that you want your trainees to accomplish. We emphasize, and will emphasize again in Chapter 4 when we go into detail about how to write training objectives, that it's vital that you specify the precise behavior you want trainees to perform at the end of the training. What do training objectives look like? We begin each chapter in this book with learning objectives. Reviewing those objectives will give you an idea of the format and style of writing training objectives.

Organize Training Content

Once you have your precise training objectives in hand, you now begin work on drafting the information that trainees need to know and describing the behaviors that they will be expected to perform. When teaching people skills, there are several specific principles to keep in mind. We'll present those principles in Chapter 5 as we describe strategies to help you conduct research and organize what you will say to trainees.

Determine Training Methods

Training is not synonymous with lecturing. Adult learners do not like to sit and hear a three- or four-hour speech. That's not good training. You'll need to develop effective methods of presenting information to your trainees. You may decide that, rather than lecture, it would be better to have trainees participate in a role-playing situation. Or you may decide to have them discuss a case study or brainstorm solutions to a problem that you pose. We will review a variety of training methods in Chapter 6 and offer suggestions to help you determine which methods are best, depending upon your training objectives and the needs of the trainees.

Select Training Resources

Perhaps you've discovered an excellent video that masterfully illustrates the skill you want to teach. Or maybe you've decided to use a small-group method, and you want trainees to respond to discussion questions. Whether you're using a video, discussion questions, or other types of resources, you'll need to decide what you'll need to prepare to present your training presentation. In most training sessions, trainees will expect to see overhead transparences or PowerPoint presentation slides to illustrate your message. These resources take time to develop. We'll talk about how to develop these tangible resources in Chapters 7.

Complete Training Plans

After you've developed your objectives and have settled on what you will say, the methods you will use to present your message, and the resources you need, it is important to develop a comprehensive written plan that describes how you will present your session. A training plan—sometimes called a lesson plan in educational settings—is nothing more than a written description of how you will organize and present your training session. There are many different formats, which we will present in Chapter 8. Most training module plans include a description of the objectives, methods, training content, and training resources needed, along with an estimate of how much time you will need to present each part of the lesson.

Deliver Training

Armed with a well-crafted plan, you now bring the training presentation to life. You not only deliver your training by planned lectures, videos, and activities, but you also need the skill of facilitating class discussion by asking good questions. A training presentation should be much more interactive than a speech. Although the elements of effective speech delivery such as eye contact, good posture, effective gestures, and varied vocal inflection are essential when training others, we will review skills and strategies of how to ask effective questions in Chapter 9. Sometimes the trainer may encounter specific problems in interacting or motivating trainees; we will present an overview of how to manage those issues in Chapter 10.

Assess the Training Process

When the training session is over, a trainer's job is not complete. Competent trainers evaluate how effectively their training was received—did trainees like it?—and, even more importantly, did they learn it? The ultimate test of a training session is: Did they use it? Did the training make a difference in how they now communicate with others? We'll talk about how to determine if your training was successful when we discuss how to assess the effectiveness of training in Chapter 11.

In addition to presenting the nuts and bolts of designing and delivering a training session, we will also review principles and assumptions of how people learn, focusing on adult learning theory in the next chapter. We conclude the book by noting trends and career opportunities in training in Chapter 12.

What do trainers do? Each piece of the needs-centered model of training gives you a glimpse of the essential elements in what a trainer does. Trainers first and foremost focus on the needs of the learners and then carefully develop a training program that meets those needs.

Summary

Training is the process of developing skills in order to perform a specific job or task. In this chapter we have described what training is and compared training to other methods of enhancing the effectiveness of an organization. Education is the process of imparting knowledge or information to others. Training is more skill focused than education. We have not suggested that training is always superior to education. There are many instances in which skill development is not needed; people need to learn principles and concepts. But when specific tasks are to be performed, training is the strategy to teach people how to do critical job functions. Motivating others, trying to tap an internal state of readiness to take action or achieve a goal, is another strategy to bring about behavior change. Training may draw upon methods of motivating trainees. Development is any behavior, strategy, design, restructuring, skill or skill set, strategic plan, or motivational effort that is designed to produce positive organizational or personal change. All educational, training, and motivational efforts are part of the larger process of development. Consulting is the process of offering insight, advice, wisdom, research, or experienced-based intervention strategies that can help an organization more effectively achieve its goals. Consultants are problem solvers. We discussed three approaches to consulting. The purchase approach occurs when an organization already knows what it needs and decides to implement a training program or other intervention strategy to solve its problem. The doctor–patient approach occurs when the consultant is brought in to help diagnose the problem; the organizational leaders may know that the organization needs some help, but the leaders are not sure precisely what help is needed. The process consulting approach is used when organizational leaders seek more comprehensive help in assessing the needs of an organization.

We have presented an introduction to basic communication definitions and principles. At the most elementary level, communication is the process of acting on information. We defined human communication as the process of making sense out of the world and sharing that sense with others by creating meaning by verbal and nonverbal messages. During communication, messages are sent and received simultaneously.

We concluded the chapter by introducing the needs-centered model of communication training. At the heart of the model is the critical step of analyzing organizational and trainee needs. All training should be directed at addressing specific needs. The other steps in the process include: Analyze the training task, develop training objectives, organize the training content, determine the training methods, select the training resources, complete the training plan, deliver the training, and assess the training process. In the chapters ahead we provide the essential details to help you develop the skill to design and deliver effective communication training programs.

QUESTIONS FOR DISCUSSION AND REVIEW

1. What is training, and how does it differ from education, development, motivation, and consulting?

2. What are three approaches to communication consulting?

3. Why is it important for a communication trainer to understand a basic definition and model of communication?

4. How is the training process like the communication process?

5. What are typical communication training topics for a communication or leadership training seminar?

6. Describe the underlying assumption for the needs-centered model of training on page 17.

7. How does the needs-centered model of training help clarify what trainers do?

QUESTIONS FOR APPLICATION AND ANALYSIS

1. Mark is having difficulty developing training programs that focus on specific training skills. He tends to develop training programs that include too much lecturing, discussions about theory, and conversation about principles rather than emphasizing communication or leadership skill development. Why do you think Mark may be having such difficulty making the transition from education to training? What suggestions would you offer Mark to help him make his training sessions more skill development than information sharing?

2. Wendy is the director of Human Resource Development for a midsized electronics manufacturing company. Based upon comments from supervisors in the company, she senses that workers have the technical skill to adequately perform their jobs but that they may need some additional skill in collaboration, teamwork, and conflict management. Should Wendy approach someone who has expertise in training or consulting? How might Wendy begin to develop a strategy to diagnose and manage the problems that she senses exist?

3. Alicia has been a high school English teacher for 10 years and has decided to pursue a career in corporate training. She is a skilled writer and would like to make the transition from education to corporate training. She has asked you to tell her some of the differences between teaching and training. What would you tell her? How could you use the needs-centered training model on page 17 to give her an overview of the differences and similarities between teaching and training?

2 How Adults Learn

General Laws of Learning
Law of Effect
Law of Frequency
Law of Association

Andragogy versus Pedagogy
Adults Need Relevant Training
Adults Bring Experience to the Classroom
Adults Are Internally Motivated to Learn
Adults Know What They Need to Learn
Adult Learning Is Problem Oriented

Learning Styles
Perceptual Learning Differences
Learning Time Differences
Information Processing Differences
Kolb Learning Style Inventory
Recommendations for the Training
Practitioner

Summary

Questions for Discussion and Review

Questions for Application and Analysis

CHAPTER OBJECTIVES

After studying this chapter, you should be able to:

1. Define and explain learning.
2. List and explain the three general laws of learning.
3. Differentiate andragogy from pedagogy.
4. List and explain the five principles of andragogy.
5. Define learning style.
6. Differentiate visual, aural, and kinesthetic learners and explain how trainers can accommodate these types of learners.
7. Differentiate reflective and impulsive learners and explain how trainers can accommodate these types of learners.
8. Differentiate whole–part and part–whole learners and explain how trainers can accommodate these types of learners.
9. Differentiate divergers, assimilators, convergers, and accommodators and explain how trainers can accommodate these types of learners.
10. Differentiate the matching, bridging, and style-flexing approaches to training.

Learning is no longer the mystery that it once was. This chapter explores how adults receive and process information so that trainers can be more effective in developing and presenting training programs that produce change in their trainees. The chapter is divided into three sections. The first section examines three general laws of learning or principles of learning that are directly relevant to the training practitioner. The second section presents a theory of adult learning known as andragogy. The third and final section examines learning styles. After discussing each of the three sections, we emphasize how you can use and apply this information to your training programs. Before delving into the first section, which examines the laws of learning, begin with a working definition of learning. What exactly is it?

There are a number of definitions for learning. Here's one that we like. "**Learning** is a change in individuals, due to the interaction of the individuals and their environment, which fills a need and makes them more capable of dealing adequately with their environment."[1] The key words and phrases in this definition include *change, fills a need*, and *makes them more capable of dealing adequately with their environment*. Once trainees have learned something, trainers should be able to recognize changes in the trainees' behaviors and attitudes. This change fills a need or takes care of a problem that trainees have been experiencing, which is at the center of the training model introduced in Chapter 1. In other words, we don't train for the sake of training. It's too expensive and time consuming. There has to be a reason for training. There has to be a need. Finally, this change in behavior and attitude allows trainees to more effectively manage their environment. For example, training customer service employees how to handle irate customers makes them more effective on the job. It makes them more effective in managing their work environments.

Now that we have a working definition of learning, we're going to introduce the three general laws of learning that are applicable in the training classroom. These three laws provide a foundation for this chapter on adult learning.

General Laws of Learning

A **law of learning** is a statement that describes the conditions that must be met in order for trainees to learn. We will review three general laws in this section, including effect, exercise, and association, and suggest a number of ways that you might be able to use this information in the training classroom to enhance learning.

Law of Effect

The **law of effect** states that people learn best under pleasant and rewarding conditions.[2] Here are a few ways you can use the law of effect in your training programs:

- *Create a pleasant physical environment.* The physical environment remains critical to successful learning. Let's start with the training classroom. Classrooms that are well lighted, temperature controlled, and clean promote learning.[3] Consider the way the training classroom is arranged. Classrooms that contain desk/chair units that are arranged in the traditional classroom format do not always encourage interaction and remain cramped for trainees. Large tables and chairs that are arranged in a horseshoe or a circle invite and encourage interaction and allow trainees ample room to spread out and arrange their training materials.

- *Accommodate trainees' work schedules.* If possible, try to accommodate trainees' schedules and give them scheduling options. For example, you obviously would not want to schedule customer service training in a department store during the holiday season. Trainees, especially those on commission, would resent your taking them off the sales floor for a training program. If possible, allow them to choose from a list of training times. This way they feel as though they have some control over their training.
- *Schedule appropriate breaks.* Another scheduling issue concerns how long trainees can remain attentive before needing a break. Don't punish them by making them sit too long in any single training program. The general rule of thumb is to take a break at least every 90 minutes. Most trainees need a break and a change of scenery after being in training for 90 minutes. Providing refreshments during breaks is also a way to make the training program more rewarding.

Law of Frequency

The **law of frequency** suggests that the more often you practice a trained behavior, the more likely you will continue using the desired behavior accurately.[4] Teachers refer to it as "D & P," or drill and practice. It's one of the oldest teaching techniques around. It may be old fashioned, but it still works. Athletes and musicians understand fully the law of frequency. Coaches and directors require their players to practice until they get it right. Practice does make perfect. Here are a few suggestions for how you can use the law of frequency in your training programs:

- *Make sure trainees are practicing the correct skill.* In other words, practice makes perfect *if* practice is perfect. The law of frequency can do more harm than good if the trainee is practicing the wrong skill. If you've ever learned something incorrectly, you know how hard it is to unlearn it. Relearning the appropriate behavior can be challenging. For example, when making business presentations, many people insert "vocal interrupters" or vocal fillers into their messages, such as "uh" and "ok." This habit has a tendency to erode a speaker's credibility. Training business professionals to unlearn this poor speaking habit is quite challenging and frustrating for both the trainer and the trainee.
- *Use "plus-one" mastery technique.* The **plus-one** technique is when you learn a process one step at a time while adding each new step to the preceding steps you've mastered. For example, when training others in how to deliver business presentations, break the presentation down into its smallest parts: introduction, body (first main point, second main point, third main point), and conclusion. Have trainees start by delivering the introduction. Have them repeat the introduction until they've mastered it. Then have them complete the introduction

plus one additional step, which would be the first main point in the body of the presentation. Once this is mastered, they add the second main point of the body and so on until all steps are mastered.

■ *Have trainees train the trainer.* After you teach a particular skill to a group of trainees, switch roles and have them train you on the same skill, or train each other. Knowing how to do a skill is one thing, but training someone else in how to do a skill is quite different and challenging. Trainees believe they know how to do a skill until they are asked to teach others. They then realize what they don't know. Asking trainees to train others not only emphasizes frequency but also enhances their depth of understanding of the particular concept or skill.

Law of Association

The **law of association,** our third and final general law or principle of learning, suggests that every new fact, idea, concept, or behavior is best learned if we can relate it to or with something we already know.[5] One of your authors was quite relieved to learn that the Paris subway system was very similar to the system in New York City, his home at the time. Even though he was in a new city where English was not commonly spoken, he felt confident in his ability to navigate the subway system because of his familiarity with New York's subway. Training remains a simpler process when we help trainees associate new information with something they already know.

Another example would be training others in how to group problem solve after training them in how to manage interpersonal conflict. Many conflict management models are very similar to the group problem solving process. Rather than starting over at the very beginning, a trainer would simply ask trainees to recall the interpersonal conflict management model and build on what they already know. Here are a few suggestions for how you can use the law of association in your training programs:

■ *Use analogies.* Steve Jobs and his associates at Apple computer understood the law of association when they were developing and designing the first desktop computer. They referred to the computer screen as a "desktop." They used language that trainees were familiar with such as filing cabinets, folders, trashcans, and "cut and paste." Because trainees were familiar with the language of the office, they learned how to use the computer more easily. Jobs and his associates made the computer more approachable to office workers who were not computer science majors, and they ultimately revolutionized the way we train others in how to use the computer.

■ *Compare and contrast with other familiar processes.* As with using analogies, comparing and contrasting familiar processes helps adults learn. For example, when training others how to make presentations, trainers usually begin by teaching the principles of informative speech making. Once trainees understand this process, it's easier for trainers to teach them how to make persuasive presentations. Trainers simply compare and contrast the two different types of presentations, pointing out similarities and differences.

RECAP

General Learning Laws and Putting Laws into Practice

Learning Law	Definition	Putting Laws into Practice
Law of effect	Trainees learn when the conditions are pleasant and rewarding.	Create pleasant physical environment. Accommodate trainees' work schedules. Schedule appropriate breaks.
Law of frequency	Trainees learn when they practice a skill or behavior.	Insure trainees are practicing correct skills and behaviors. Use the "plus-one" mastery technique. Have trainees train the trainer.
Law of association	Trainees learn when every new fact, idea, concept, or behavior is related to or with something they already know.	Use analogies. Compare and contrast with other familiar processes.

Andragogy versus Pedagogy

As a student, do you ever get upset with a teacher who treats you as though you were still in high school? How about a teacher who doesn't give you enough credit for what it is you already know and bring to the classroom? Some trainers do the same thing. Teaching and training adults is not the same as teaching and training children. Adults and children learn differently. This section of the chapter focuses on how adults learn best by examining the principles and practices of andragogy, a term coined by Malcolm Knowles, a leading author in the field of adult education. **Andragogy** is the science and art of teaching adults.[6] An andragogical approach to learning is self-directed rather than teacher-directed and is based upon the Greek word *aner*, which means "adult." **Pedagogy**, on the other hand, is the science and art of teaching children. It refers to a teacher-directed approach to learning that is based on the Greek words *paid*, which means "child," and *agogus*, which means guide.

At this point in the chapter it's important to clarify what we mean by the adult learner. For example, what about the traditional-age college student? What about young adults? Are they considered adult learners from the trainer's perspective? It's not so much about chronological age as it is about maturity. **Maturity** is the degree of experience that a trainee brings to the training classroom.[7] Not all young adults are inexperienced or immature, and not all adults are experienced and mature.

Andragogy is based on five assumptions. These assumptions may help you differentiate andragogy from pedagogy. The *first* assumption focuses on the relevance of learning. Adult learners need to know "why" they're learning something. It needs to be meaningful and directly related to their lives and the problems they experience on a daily basis. Children learn for learning's sake. They don't often ask, "Why is this important?" They might assume it's important because the teacher is asking them to learn it. Adult learners remain more critical of what they are asked to learn.

The *second* assumption focuses on the role of the learner's experience. Adult learners bring many years of life and work experience to the classroom. They're not blank slates. They want to use the information they have learned from their experiences in the classroom. With adult learners, trainers don't often have to start at the very beginning of a training program. Rather, trainers can begin with what their trainees already know. Children, on the other hand, have limited life experience. Teachers have to be more thorough and cannot assume what a child might and might not know. Although teachers use children's experiences in the classroom, their experiences remain more limited, and teachers have to create experiences for the children.

The *third* assumption focuses on the motivation of learners. Adults tend to be self or internally motivated. Many children learn because they know that learning or getting all good grades on a report card will be externally rewarded by others in the form of praise or financial rewards from parents. Adults are internally motivated to learn because they get a sense of personal satisfaction and accomplishment. They're less motivated by what others will think of them and more motivated by how they'll personally feel about themselves once they learn. Adults understand fully that learning is one thing that no one can ever take from them. Once you learn something, it can be yours for a lifetime. Adults are motivated to learn because they know that learning will enrich their lives, making their lives more meaningful.

The *fourth* assumption focuses on the learner's level of self-direction. Adults know their own deficiencies, and they know what they need to learn in order to become successful. Many adult learners return to the training classroom in order to cope with life-changing events such as obtaining a new job, a job promotion, or perhaps losing a job because of cutbacks or downsizing.[8] They know what questions they need answered, and they seek out the answers on their own. Many children, on the other hand, have not yet discovered their deficiencies or what will hold them back in terms of personal development. They don't know what questions they need answered and remain dependent on teachers for what it is they "should" know.

The *fifth* and final assumption focuses on orientation to learning. Adults remain task- or problem-centered in their learning. Unlike children, who approach learning subject-by-subject (math, language arts, science), adults prefer to learn problem-by-problem. Some of these problems might include not being as productive on the job as employees would like to be because they lack particular skills or not being eligible for promotion until they acquire additional knowledge and skills in a particular area.

RECAP
Pedagogical and Andragogical Assumptions

Assumptions about:	Pedagogy	Andragogy
Relevance of learning	Learning for learning's sake	Learning must be relevant.
Role of learners' experience	To be built on more than used	A rich resource for learning
Motivation of learners	External rewards and punishments	Internal incentives, curious
Level of self-direction	Dependent personality Depends on others for what he or she "should" know	Increasingly self-directed organism; knows what he or she needs to know
Orientation to learning	Subject-centered learning Learning how to learn	Task or problem-oriented learning

We're now going to show you how you can apply each of these five assumptions or principles to the training classroom.

Adults Need Relevant Training

Relevance remains critical to adult learners. From our own professional experiences, too many employees leave training programs asking, "What was that all about?" and "Why do we have to know this stuff?" Employees have limited time and energy on the job, and they resent attending training programs they perceive to be of little relevance to their lives and work. It's not uncommon to hear, "Not another training program!" Your intentions may be good; however, employees sometimes perceive training to be a waste of their time. They learn to resent training and trainers rather than the content of the training program.

In order to make training useful, you will need to conduct a needs assessment, which will be discussed at length in the next chapter. A **needs assessment** is the process of identifying what learners do not yet know or the important or necessary skills that they can't yet perform. Said more simply: Train employees for their in-baskets. Almost every employee has an in-basket. These baskets sit on top of desks and contain various action items that require immediate attention. Most employees can process their in-baskets in minutes; however there are always a few items that remain challenging for the employee to process. As a trainer, identify these challenges and train employees for their in-baskets. A needs-centered training program helps employees process their in-baskets.

Adults Bring Experience to the Classroom

Unlike children whose life experiences are more limited by virtue of their age, adults bring to the training classroom a rich array of life experiences. Many adult learners are seasoned. They have done and seen it all, or so they think. Trainers must recognize and use their trainees' experiences to facilitate the learning process. We bring the training content to the classroom, but it's the trainees who must not only learn the content, but also learn how to apply it to their jobs and personal lives.

One of the general rules of training is that *"it's always better to get a message out of someone rather than put one in them."* If you're training a class in how to handle customer complaints or how to process a conflict, ask your trainees how this training content could be applied immediately to their jobs on the front line. For example, assume you're training a group of airline customer service employees about how to manage and resolve customer conflict. You might ask the ticket agents how they see the training content being applied in the airport. You might ask the reservation agents how the content could be applied while talking to a customer over the phone. You might also ask flight attendants how this training content would work in the cabin of an airplane. This way, trainees learn from each other. Additionally, they learn multiple ways to apply the training content.

There are also potential disadvantages to drawing upon trainees' life experiences. Some adult learners have had positive experiences on the jobs and remain receptive to new communication skills that will improve their effectiveness. Others, unfortunately, have had less-than-positive experiences on the job and are not always receptive to training. For example, assume you're training flight attendants in how to handle air rage, or passengers who become irate once they're airborne. It would not be uncommon to hear some flight attendants saying, "You know this is never going to work, because from my experience . . ."

To what degree do you want trainees sharing negative experiences in the classroom? It takes a skilled trainer to use employees' negative experiences in a positive way. Here are a few suggestions:

- *Acknowledge their less-than-positive experiences and empathize with trainees, but don't dwell on their negative experiences.* For example, you might say, "I realize you have had some unfortunate experiences, and I'm sorry that you have had to experience them, but this training is designed to help you."
- *Acknowledge the fact that negative experiences are inevitable and that the job of training is to reduce the number of negative experiences.* For example, you might say, "Training is not going to solve all of your problems, but the skills that this training program addresses and develops will hopefully minimize some of the negative experiences."
- *Ask trainees how new training content might address some of these negative experiences.* For example, you might say, "How do you see this training content or these new skills helping you through the negative experiences on the job?"
- *Place the negative experiences in context.* Many times, isolated employees have single experiences that remain negative. There is a tendency to generalize to all

employees and to increase the frequency of negative experiences. You will hear, "It's happening to all of us all the time!" Ask for additional information and then help trainees place the experience in a meaningful and more accurate context. For example, you might say, "I realize a group of you had an unfortunate experience, but let me provide you with some additional information that might allow you to see how that unfortunate experience was limited and isolated."

Adults Are Internally Motivated to Learn

Adult learners are usually internally motivated to learn, whereas many children remain externally motivated to learn. Here's the difference. Adult learners tend to be motivated by internal drives such as increased job satisfaction, self-esteem, their sense of accomplishment, and quality-of-life issues. Again, they are often motivated to learn by life-changing events such as job promotions or possibly losing a job. Their drive to improve their own condition in life comes from within. They reward themselves. Children are usually motivated by external drives such as a better-paying job, prestige and status, and pleasing others. Their drive to improve their own condition comes from outside. It's not what's necessarily good for them, but it's perceived to be good, and therefore others reward them. They do it for others rather than for themselves.

One example might be the less-*mature* college student's motivation for attending college. Some less-*mature* students attend college not because they necessarily want to, but because it's what they perceive others wanting them to do. In order to obtain the rewards of college (good job, status) and to avoid the punishers of not attending (being perceived as a deadbeat), they go through the college experience lacking interest and direction. They're there to please others and not because of their intellectual curiosity or to better themselves.

The adult learner returns to the college classroom for some of the same reasons that a traditional-age student will attend college (good job, status), but also for different reasons. Here are a few suggestions for how you might use this principle of adult learning:

- *Take advantage of the internal motivation.* Challenge your trainees and keep them focused and on task. Encourage them to keep moving forward, because the momentum doesn't always last. Adult learners encounter numerous roadblocks. Many times they are discouraged from returning to school because it remains disruptive to their already-complicated lives. For example, many adult learners have to find alternative arrangements for family obligations or they have to negotiate with their employers for getting off work early to attend class.
- *Set realistic expectations.* Trainers must develop reasonable expectations for trainees given the amount of training time coupled with trainees' abilities and work experiences. Trainees must feel as though they can successfully learn. Whether they are learning information or skills, trainees must feel as though they can be successful in the training classroom. Provide constant support, praise, encouragement, and constructive feedback.

Adults Know What They Need to Learn

Unlike some less-mature learners who don't know what it is they need to learn, adult learners know and understand their deficiencies. They have a readiness to learn. Many adult learners are at a roadblock in life or with their careers and cannot move forward until they obtain additional information or develop new skills. They know where they're deficient and need options and alternatives that will allow them to pursue their deficiencies. Here are a few suggestions for how you can apply this principle of adult learning to your training classroom:

- *Make training "needs-based" or "learner-centered."* As introduced in Chapter 1, all training must be learner centered rather than trainer centered. Training is not about us. It's about our trainees. If our trainees ask, "Why do I have to learn this stuff?" then we have failed them. You will learn how to conduct a needs assessment in the next chapter.
- *Encourage self-directed learning.* Allow your adult learners the freedom to pursue their own deficiencies. A one-size-fits-all training model doesn't always work for the adult learner. Research suggests that adult learners prefer self-directed and self-designed learning projects to group learning projects.[9] It should also be noted that self-directed learning does not mean that adults learn in isolation. Self-directed learning projects involve a variety of individuals who serve as resources for the adult learner including guides, experts, and encouragers. The flexibility to be self-directed allows adult learners to target their specific problems and allows them to control start/stop times, which are important since most juggle numerous other obligations.
- *Make training timely.* With **just in time** (JIT) training, trainees receive just the right amount and type of training exactly when it's needed. Unfortunately, many trainees receive "single shot" training, which is a one-time training program that includes all the information and skills trainees will need to perform their jobs. A single dose of training usually results in information overload where important information is not retained and where skills are never developed to the proficiency that is needed for trainees to succeed in their jobs.
- Unlike single shot training programs, just in time training is chunked into smaller training programs and given to trainees only when they need it. For example, training customer service employees in how to handle irate customers is not as effective during normal operations as it is during times of turmoil such as in labor disputes, mergers, product recalls, or holiday rushes. Similarly, airline customer service employees are more receptive to learning about how to recover service deficiencies and manage customer complaints and anger when they know that a strike is pending or when winter and numerous snowstorms are imminent rather than during normal summer operations. Employees remain more receptive to training and more self-directed in their learning when the training program is timely and fills an immediate need. What you don't want to hear from your trainees is, "Where were you six months ago when I could have used this information?" Instead, you want to be "just in time" by anticipating their needs and by providing training that they perceive to be immediately relevant.

■ *Coach trainees through mistakes.* Trainees have a readiness to learn when they're making mistakes or when they're "stuck." For example, when training others in how to make presentations, many trainees get stuck in the same place each time they practice the presentation. They find a particular part of the presentation difficult to explain. This is where you can be most effective as a trainer. This is where you can coach them through the difficult part. You provide and demonstrate strategies for how they can make this particular part of the presentation more clear. It's important to note that many adult learners take errors and mistakes personally and are more likely to let these mistakes affect their self-esteem.[10] As a trainer, you are encouraged to coach trainees through the process by making the training classroom as safe as possible, by recognizing the trainee's strengths, and by addressing the trainee's performance deficiencies using specific behavioral and descriptive terms rather than general evaluative terms. "I hear you having difficulty explaining your sales figures from last month" is an example of the former, and "Your presentation is not good" is an example of the latter.

Adult Learning Is Problem Oriented

Finally, adults have a problem-centered orientation to learning, whereas children and less mature adults have a subject-centered orientation to learning. Remember, adult learners bring prior knowledge and experience to the training classroom. They know what they need to know. Rather than starting from scratch, trainers can oftentimes bypass the basic knowledge and jump into how to process and handle specific problems.

Here are a few examples that highlight the differences between subject and problem-centered orientations to learning. When training inexperienced young adults in how to be effective leaders, trainers oftentimes spend considerable time discussing the vocabulary associated with leadership and the characteristics of effective leaders. When training experienced adults, trainers may be able to skip the introductory vocabulary and characteristics associated with effective leadership and jump right into solving their leadership problems.

Another example might be managers who have a difficult time leading and motivating their employees. The managers attend a weeklong training program and soon realize that the program focuses on the principles of human communication, which they already understand, and not on how to use communication to motivate. In other words, they understand the subject of communication. What they don't understand is how to use communication to solve their problem of employee motivation. Managers who have considerable leadership experience and knowledge of human communication need a troubleshooting guide or a set of strategies for how to resolve particular motivational issues using communication. Here are a few of our suggestions for how you can make your training more problem oriented:

■ *Group your trainees.* Survey your trainees to determine how many years of work experience they have and to determine the types of problems they have experienced. Based on this information, divide the training class into groups based on years of experience and types of problems experienced. Provide training that is group specific.

- *Ask trainees to forward their specific problems ahead of time to the trainer.* Take time to develop training programs that address these problems or find ways to address these problems in current training programs.
- *Provide trainees with a bibliography or a set of resources.* Remember, adult learners are self-directed and internally motivated. If you provide them with direction and resources, they'll seek out answers to their problems.
- *Provide trainees with a series of training classes.* Just as with a college curriculum, some students "test out" of the more basic classes and are placed in advanced classes. Training curricula should offer similar options to trainees. Some of these classes should be basic, while other classes should address job-related problems that are more complex.

RECAP
Andragogical Principles and Training Applications

Principles	Training Applications
Adults need relevant training.	Conduct a needs assessment. Train employees for their in-baskets.
Adults bring experience to the classroom.	Recognize trainees' work experiences. Ask experienced trainees for their assistance in applying new training content. Give experienced trainees the opportunity to train less experienced trainees.
Adults are internally motivated to learn.	Take advantage of the trainees' internal motivation. Keep trainees focused on task. Use the momentum to pull trainees through the roadblocks and obstacles that adult learners face. Set realistic expectations.
Adults know what they need to learn.	Make training needs-based or learner-centered. Encourage self-directed learning. Remain timely. Coach trainees through their mistakes.
Adult learning is problem oriented.	Survey trainees and group by years and type of experience. Ask trainees to forward problems they would like training to address. Provide trainees with a bibliography or a set of resources for self-study. Provide trainees with a series of training programs.

Thus far, we have examined three general laws of learning and five principles of adult learning, along with how training practitioners can apply these laws and principles to the training classroom. The third and final section of this chapter takes these laws and adult learning principles one step further and examines individual learning styles. Understanding individual learning styles is just another way you can adapt your training to enhance adult learning.

Learning Styles

A **learning style** is the way an individual perceives, organizes, processes, and remembers information. Some people are flexible in how they learn. Others remain more limited and have a preferred learning style or a preferred mode of processing information. In fact, Howard Gardner at Harvard University argues that individuals learn differently because they possess different intelligences and that some of these intelligences go beyond the purely cognitive such as processing information. He argues that individuals possess linguistic, musical, mathematical, spatial, bodily kinesthetic, and/or interpersonal forms of intelligence.[11] How do you prefer to learn? The author of this chapter is considered a whole–part learner or a "splitter." Perhaps you're the same. Read on to learn more about your learning style. We're going to first summarize the research literature by examining perceptual, learning time, and information processing differences. Second, we're going to review Kolb's Learning Style Inventory, which classifies learning styles. Finally, we will discuss how you can apply this information to your training classroom.

Perceptual Learning Differences

Some individuals learn by reading and through observing others. They're referred to as visual learners. Some learn by hearing and speaking. They're the aural or auditory learners. Still others learn by doing and touching. They're the kinesthetic learners. These perceptual learning differences are referred to as modalities. Some learners have a single modality preference, others are comfortable perceiving in two modalities, and yet others are considered mixed and remain comfortable learning in all three modalities. Research suggests that the most common modalities are visual and mixed (visual, auditory, kinesthetic) with each accounting for 30 percent of the U.S. population. The research also suggests that about 25 percent of the population prefers learning using the auditory modality, and approximately 15 percent prefers using the kinesthetic or tactile modality.[12]

Visual learners learn by reading and viewing. They remain visually oriented and need to see what they're learning. Visual learners need to see how the pieces fit together. Oftentimes they will stop what they're doing, look into space, and visualize what it is they're learning. They are easily distracted by visual disorder and movement and become impatient when extensive listening is required. Trainees who are visually oriented learn from reading prepackaged training materials and from trainers who outline content using flip charts, chalkboards, or electronic presentation software (i.e.,

PowerPoint). They appreciate handouts that contain graphic representation of ideas and concepts along with space to jot down notes and follow-up questions.

Visually oriented trainees also learn by modeling other people's behaviors. With **modeling,** people acquire knowledge, attitudes, beliefs, and values and learn how to perform certain behaviors by observing others who model the behavior. Many parents refer to this type of learning as "monkey see, monkey do." Here are a few suggestions for how to motivate the visual learner using modeling:[13]

- *Set realistic expectations for trainees.* They're more motivated to learn if they perceive themselves as actually being able to imitate the modeled behaviors. Don't set them up for failure. Once trainees experience initial success imitating simple modeled behaviors, then continue developing more complex behavioral processes with them.
- *Model "real" behaviors.* Trainees are more motivated to learn and perform behaviors they perceive to be "true to life" and "real" than behaviors they perceive to be "canned" and "artificial." Trainees are more motivated to model behaviors that they know they're going to have to demonstrate in future situations and encounters.
- *Praise models for their behavior.* Trainees are more motivated when they see models (who are oftentimes experienced trainers) being rewarded for appropriately demonstrating the behaviors. For example, if you have two models demonstrate how to manage interpersonal conflict by role-playing the appropriate communication behaviors, reward them for their nice work in front of the other trainees.
- *Use models that are similar to trainees.* Students appear to be more motivated when they see models who are like them demonstrating the appropriate behaviors. For example, it's not uncommon to hear older trainees saying, "I could never do that." However, once they see a model of similar age, they quickly change their minds and become motivated.

Aural learners, sometimes called auditory learners, learn through hearing and speaking. Auditory-oriented learners need opportunities to articulate what they're learning. They clarify their thinking by making the words come out of their mouths. Have you ever tried explaining a concept or an idea to a friend to find out that once the words left your mouth, you really didn't know what you were talking about? This happens to teachers quite frequently. You think you know something until you try conveying your knowledge to others and then soon realize that you don't know the idea or concept as well as you thought. Aural learners need opportunities to articulate their ideas to others. They also learn from hearing others speak. They prefer processing the spoken word rather than the written word. They do well in traditional lectures or in training contexts where new information is delivered as a series of oral presentations. They learn well from listening to audiocassettes, sound tracks, and peer presentations.

Kinesthetic learners learn from touching and doing. Kinesthetically oriented learners remain tactile and prefer to be engaged in movement. They are partial to action and have a tendency to express emotion in physically exuberant ways. Kinesthetic learners prefer a hands-on approach to learning. They enjoy involving themselves in

RECAP

Perceptual Learning Differences and Training Applications

Learning Style	Definition	Training Application
Visual learner	Learning by reading and viewing	Observe appropriate behaviors in others or models. Use prepackaged materials, handouts, flip charts, chalkboard, and electronic presentation software.
Aural learner	Learning by hearing and speaking	Use peer presentations, lectures, audiocassettes, and sound tracks.
Kinesthetic learner	Learning by touching and doing	Engage learners by using simulations, case studies, role plays, and demonstrations (see Chapter 6).

the training content and do well by participating in training simulations, case studies, and role play activities. They develop an appreciation and value for training content not by reading or hearing about it but by actually doing and experiencing it.

Learning Time Differences

Another way to approach learning styles is to examine the time it takes individual trainees to learn. **Reflective learners** tend to work carefully and with precision. They take time to process information. Once they have a persuasive argument prepared for their sales presentation, they go back and review their evidence carefully to ensure accuracy. When rehearsing their sales presentation, reflective learners take the time to carefully deliver each section, working out the rough spots, before moving on to the next section. They take time to videotape and review their presentation before presenting it before the actual audience. Reflective learners are often referred to as plodders, meaning that they plod along, slowly but surely. Research suggests that some adult learners tend to compensate for being slow in some behavioral or psychomotor learning tasks by being more accurate and making fewer trial-and-error mistakes.[14]

Impulsive learners tend to work quickly and with less determination. Producing a perfect learning product remains less important to them. When developing, organizing, and rehearsing a sales presentation, they rarely go back and work out the rough spots. In fact, it's rare that they would even rehearse their presentations. Impulsive learners might put together a sketchy outline and then wing the rest of the presentation. They're less concerned with how polished a sales presentation is and more concerned with just getting the presentation over and out of their way. These individuals are often referred to as sweepers, meaning that they sweep through their work quickly and with less precision.

It's important to consider learning time differences when training others. Unfortunately, our culture rewards speed more than accuracy. Reflective learners are often working from a disadvantage simply because it takes them more time to complete a learning task. Additionally, the accuracy of their work is not always rewarded. Most training programs accommodate the impulsive learner simply because time remains a scarce resource in most organizations. From this author's personal training experience, trainers also approach training programs with instructional objectives that are not realistic. They bite off more than they can accomplish effectively in the allotted time. When developing training curricula, trainers need to remain sensitive to the amount of time it takes learners not only to process the training content, but also to complete the various learning tasks requested by trainers.

Information Processing Differences

Another approach to learning styles focuses on information processing differences. Some trainees grasp abstract concepts easily, whereas others need to see concrete applications. Some trainees learn well step-by-step, while others need to see the big picture before they can make sense out of the separate parts. One program of research refers to learners as either whole–part or part–whole learners.[15]

Whole–part learners, also referred to as top-down processors, prefer having the big picture before moving into the details of the concept or idea. For example, if you're

---

R E C A P

Learning Time Differences and Training Applications

Learning Style	Definition	Training Application
Reflective learner	Learning by taking time to process information; more concerned with accuracy and precision	Allow ample time for trainees to complete work. Set realistic learning objectives.
Impulsive learner	Learning by quickly processing information and completing tasks; less concerned with accuracy and precision	Discourage impulsive learners by not rewarding quantity over quality. If quantity remains more important, then encourage this learning style by limiting time.

training midlevel managers on a model of group problem solving, whole–part learners prefer having the big picture before moving into the details. They want to know what effective group problem solving is going to look and sound like before examining the various stages of the group problem solving communication model. When trainers prematurely jump into the details before offering the larger concept or model, whole–part learners become a bit anxious.

Whole–part learners need a **schema** or a way to organize the big ideas before they're ready to receive the detailed information. One way to help trainees develop a schema is by giving them a handout or an outline that depicts the model of group problem solving with each stage of the model being labeled and placed in the appropriate order. Once whole–part learners have the big picture or a schema, they're ready to process the details. Trainers refer to these individuals as lumpers because they have difficulty splitting the parts out of the whole.

Part–whole learners, also referred to as bottom-up processors, prefer examining the big picture in terms of its smaller parts. They don't necessarily need the big picture before examining the various smaller parts that comprise the larger picture. For example, part–whole learners feel comfortable learning the individual stages of the group problem solving communication model. They don't need the big picture in order to understand the various parts or components of a model. Once they have the pieces, they have the ability to synthesize the various stages into a working model of group problem solving communication. Trainers refer to these individuals as splitters because of their ability to analytically examine the big picture in terms of its smaller parts.

R E C A P

Information Processing Learning Difference and Training Applications

Learning Style	Definition	Training Application
Whole–part learner	Learning the big picture first, then the small parts or details comprising the big picture	Show the trainee what the product will look like when completed, then break down the product into its various parts. Use demonstrations and/or other visual representations.
Part–whole learner	Learning the small parts or details first, then the big picture	Show the trainee the various parts that when put together will make the product. Use demonstrations and/or other visual representations.

Kolb Learning Style Inventory

The Kolb's Learning Style Inventory is a diagnostic instrument that integrates much of the aforementioned learning style research and remains popular with many professional trainers.[16] This diagnostic instrument identifies one of four learning style preferences: divergers, assimilators, convergers, and accommodators.

Divergers prefer observing a situation rather than taking action. They tend to be innovative, imaginative, and concerned with personal relevance. They have a need to know how new information relates to prior experiences before they're receptive to learning new information. Here are a few suggestions for how to work with divergers:

- *Use buzz groups.* **Buzz groups** encourage small group interaction and usually include five to ten people who discuss a chosen or selected topic.
- *Facilitate brainstorming sessions.* When problem solving, the **brainstorming** technique encourages creativity among group members in addition to a free flowing of solutions offered without any group member evaluating or judging the ideas. Often, group members will piggyback off each other's ideas to create new solutions.
- *Promote mentor/mentee relationships.* Pair inexperienced with experienced trainees, forming mentor/mentee relationships. These relationships allow inexperienced trainees the opportunity to shadow more experienced trainees on the job. Divergers have a sensitivity to other's experiences and learn by taking perspective with others. Through the relationship, divergers will get answers to their questions such as "What happened to you? Tell me about your experiences," "Why do you feel that way?" and, "Why do you think our attitudes and beliefs are so different?"

Assimilators value sequential thinking and trust expert opinion. They enjoy collecting data and then organizing it or assimilating it into a concise, logical form. Unlike divergers, assimilators remain less interested in learning from others' concrete experiences and are more interested in learning from the experts who have done the actual work. Here are a few suggestions for how to work with assimilators:

- *Present traditional lectures.* In a **lecture,** teachers or trainers use oral messages to impart large amounts of prepared information to students or trainees using one-way communication. The lecture contains information that is presented in a logical or sequential order. The lecture training method will be discussed more thoroughly in Chapter 6.
- *Invite experts to address trainees.* Assimilators value expert opinions. If experts are not available, then trainers must become proficient in the training content area and must be perceived as being credible or believable in the content area.
- *Assign individual research projects.* Rather than working in pairs or small groups, assimilators prefer working individually on projects. Ask trainees to conduct research projects where they collect, process, and present their findings to others.

Convergers are always looking for the utility in ideas and theories. They approach learning from a problem-solving perspective. Convergers prefer analyzing problems and testing theories to find solutions to problems. Here are a few suggestions for how to work with convergers:

- *Introduce new problem-solving processes.* Convergers enjoy learning about new approaches or protocols to problem solving.
- *Demonstrate new problem-solving processes.* Convergers have a need to understand and see how new problem-solving processes work. Through demonstrations, trainees can see, first hand, how these processes work.
- *Use problem-based training methods.* After learning and seeing how new problem-solving processes work, convergers prefer a hands-on approach to learning. They prefer problem-based training methods such as case studies, simulations, and role plays, which will be discussed in Chapter 6. All of these training methods encourage trainees to apply problem-solving processes to real problems.

Accommodators learn primarily from hands-on field experience and by trial and error. They enjoy carrying out plans and involving themselves in challenging experiences. The students who blew up the chemistry sets in your high school science class were probably accommodators. Unlike convergers, who remain more logical in their analysis of events, problems, objects, and events, accommodators rely more on their gut instincts. And unlike convergers, who rely more on their own technical analysis when solving a problem, accommodators are more likely to seek out others for their opinions and knowledge. Here are a few suggestions for how to work with accommodators:

- *Conduct experiments.* Involve your trainees in experiments where they test ideas. For example, when training others about the expectations we have for others' nonverbal behavior, ask trainees to violate others' nonverbal expectations and then to report on their findings. For example, ask trainees to walk into an elevator, stand too close to another person in order to violate that person's spatial expectations, and then report on the findings.
- *Place trainees in the field.* Accommodators prefer learning on the job or in the field rather than in a formal training classroom. They learn from their mistakes and by trial and error.
- *Organize internship programs.* Rather than investing money putting accommodators through formal training programs, place them in internship programs where they learn on the job with some supervision. Ask them to complete a journal or a log of their experiences. Ask them to identify the skills they need to develop further.

Recommendations for the Training Practitioner

We've reviewed a variety of learning styles and suggested a few ways that training practitioners can use the information. Some of these learning styles included perceptual, learning time, and information processing differences, including Kolb's learning

RECAP

Kolb's Learning Styles and Training Applications

Learning Style	Definition	Training Application
Divergent learner	Learning by observing rather than taking action; learning from other's experiences	Use buzz groups. Conduct brainstorming sessions. Promote mentor/mentee relationships.
Assimilating learner	Learning by listening to the experts rather than from other's experiences; learning by sequentially ordering information into logical forms	Present traditional lectures. Invite experts to address trainees. Assign individual research projects.
Convergent learner	Learning by doing the work themselves; approaching learning as problem solving; finding solutions by thinking logically through problems	Introduce new problem-solving processes. Demonstrate new problem-solving processes. Use problem-based training methods.
Accommodating learner	Learning by doing and by working in the field with others; solving problems based on gut instinct and discussions with others rather than through logic	Conduct experiments. Place trainees in the field. Organize internship program.

inventory. All of this information can be a bit overwhelming to new training practitioners. At times, some training practitioners feel defeated before they ever get started. We don't want this to happen to you. We want you to use the information. It's of no value unless you use it. To help you apply this information, we're going to explain what we do when we're developing and presenting training programs:

- *Don't assume that everyone learns as you do.* We have a tendency to train others in ways that we prefer to learn. If you're a kinesthetic and an impulsive learner, don't assume that the rest of the training class learns this way.
- *Don't always train in the manner you were trained.* Trainers have a tendency to train others in the way they were trained or taught in school. This doesn't remain a problem if you were fortunate enough to have a good trainer or teacher. Unfortunately, not all trainers remain effective. Be careful not to model or imitate ineffective trainers' behaviors.

- *Use a variety of training techniques and methods to tap into all learning styles.* Because it's rare that most trainers have the opportunity to survey their trainees ahead of time to find out their learning styles, it's important to develop and deliver training programs that tap into all learning styles. Review the training applications and techniques listed above for each of the learning styles in addition to training methods, which is the focus of Chapter 6. Using a variety of techniques and methods will allow you to reach the visual, aural, kinesthetic, impulsive, reflective, whole–part, part–whole, divergent, assimilating, convergent, and accommodating learners.

Our final recommendation focuses on being aware of how you approach training. You can approach training in a way that will tap directly into trainees' learning styles, or you can approach training in ways that will help trainees broaden how they learn. Three approaches to training that we would like you to become familiar with include matching, bridging, and style-flexing. Here's how they work in practice.

The *first* approach to training focuses on **matching.** In a matching approach, trainees are instructed in their own preferred styles. This approach requires some type of large-scale assessment where all future trainees are surveyed or assessed in order to identify preferred learning styles. Once learning style preferences have been identified, trainees are grouped, and then instruction is presented in a manner that matches learning style preferences.

This approach remains logistically complex because it first requires an identification of learning styles; and, second, it requires the development of a number of training programs that are tailored to the various learning style preferences. Remember, a one-size-fits-all approach to a training curriculum is not always effective. The matching approach may require several different training programs, all focusing on the same content but tailored in different ways to accommodate learning preferences. Although this approach has been shown to be successful, especially in specialized training environments or special education classes,[17] it has also been criticized for failing to teach trainees how to learn in ways that are less preferred. Being successful in life requires learning how to adapt oneself to one's environment and learning how to accommodate others.

The *second* approach to training focuses on **bridging.** As a bridging technique, trainers instruct trainees using their own preferred training style; however, when an individual student has difficulty, the trainer accommodates the student's learning style preference. With this approach, students are not assigned to training classes based on learning style preferences. Instead, trainers bridge or find ways to adapt training content so that it makes sense to individual trainees who are experiencing difficulty with the content.

The *third* and final approach to training focuses on **style-flexing,** a process of teaching trainees in a manner that both accommodates and challenges their learning styles. Trainees learn not only the training content but also how to learn in ways that are different from their preferred learning styles. The goal is help trainees become flexible in how they learn and to increase their confidence with learning in a variety of ways. With style-flexing, trainers develop modules where trainees' learning styles are

---

RECAP

Approaches to Training

Training Approach	Description
Matching	Trainee learning styles are accommodated.
Bridging	Trainee learning styles are accommodated only when having difficulty learning.
Style-flexing	Trainee learning styles are both accommodated and challenged.

---

matched at one point and stretched at others. Curriculum developers and training practitioners may find the 4Mat system, designed by McCarthy, useful in the training classroom.[18] McCarthy's system remains a modification of Kolb's learning style inventory where divergers are referred to as innovative learners, assimilators are referred to as analytic learners, convergers as common sense learners, and accommodators as dynamic learners.

Summary

In this chapter, we have examined how adults learn. We started by first discussing the three general laws of learning. These laws included the law of effect, the law of frequency, and the law of association. Next, we reviewed the differences between andragogy, which is the science and art of teaching adults, and pedagogy, which is the science and art of teaching children. An andragogical approach to learning suggests that adults need relevant training, bring experience to the classroom, are internally motivated to learn, know what they need to learn, and approach learning from a problem orientation.

Finally, we discussed learning styles, which are the ways individuals perceive, organize, process, and remember information. Three classifications of learning styles were examined, including perceptual, learning time, and information processing. Finally, four quadrants of Kolb's Learning Style Inventory were examined, including divergers, assimilators, convergers, and accommodators. Suggestions for how trainers can apply this information to the training classroom were also reviewed extensively.

QUESTIONS FOR DISCUSSION AND REVIEW

1. Define and explain learning.

2. List and explain the three general laws of learning.

3. Differentiate andragogy from pedagogy.

4. List and explain the five principles of andragogy.

5. Define learning style.

6. Differentiate visual, aural, and kinesthetic learners and explain how trainers can accommodate these types of learners.

7. Differentiate reflective and impulsive learners and explain how trainers can accommodate these types of learners.

8. Differentiate whole–part and part–whole learners and explain how trainers can accommodate these types of learners.

9. Differentiate divergers, assimilators, convergers, and accommodators and explain how trainers can accommodate these types of learners.

10. Differentiate the matching, bridging, and style-flexing approaches to training.

QUESTIONS FOR APPLICATION AND ANALYSIS

1. You're a member of a training team who is preparing a training module for new nontraditional students, or students who fall outside the 18-to-22 age range. Rather than going immediately into college from high school, many nontraditional students went into the workforce instead. Using the andragogical assumptions in addition to the andragogical principles and training applications reviewed in this chapter, show how your team would develop a module that trains nontraditional students in how to study and in how to manage time. How would your training module differ if you were teaching seventh graders about study skills and time management?

Identify your learning style. Are you primarily a visual, aural, or kinesthetic learner? Are you primarily a reflective or an impulsive learner? Are you primarily a part–whole or a whole–part learner? Now, recall a moment when you had difficulty learning. Jot down what you can remember about this difficult learning moment. What were you trying to learn? What was the concept? How did the teacher teach the concept? Knowing your learning style preferences, what *specific* advice would you offer this teacher that might have eased your learning of this particular concept?

3. You're a member of the same training team referenced in the first question above. You're developing a training program for nontraditional college students. You and your team are developing a module that will train nontraditional students in how to study and in how to manage time as a student. Your challenge now is to show how your training module would be modified to fit each of the four Kolb learning styles: divergers, assimilators, convergers, and accommodators. How would you develop and present your training module to ensure that all four of the Kolb cognitive learning styles were accommodated?

3 Conducting a Needs Assessment and Task Analysis

CHAPTER OBJECTIVES

After studying this chapter, you should be able to:

1. Explain why a needs assessment is crucial to developing a successful training program.
2. List, describe, and compare and contrast the affective, cognitive, and psychomotor domains of learning.
3. Develop a well-worded needs assessment survey.
4. Conduct interviews to assess learner needs.
5. Use appropriate observation methods to assess learner needs.
6. Describe and use appropriate assessment tests to identify learner needs.
7. Write an effective task analysis of a skill appropriate for training.

The two words *needs* and *assessment* are almost self-defining. A need is some deficiency or lack of something. To assess is to evaluate or identify whether something is or is not present. Hence a **needs assessment** evaluates what is lacking. Conducting a training needs assessment is the process of identifying what learners do not yet know or the important or necessary skills that they can't yet perform. A needs assessment also seeks to determine what skills and information learners already possess. If you are presenting a team-building seminar, before you present the training program it would be useful to know what the learners already know about team building. It would not be productive to spend your time on principles and skills that trainees already know.

Why conduct a needs assessment? Because understanding your trainees' needs is at the heart of developing an effective training program. Assessing trainee needs is also the primary way to ensure that the skills and information you present will enhance both the individual and the organization. Identifying trainee needs can help solve problems that either individuals or organizations may be experiencing. Most problems boil down to something you want more of or something you want less of. To solve the problem of lagging sales, you assess salespersons' needs to determine if they lack sales skills. To help manage conflict, you assess workers' abilities to manage conflict, tension, and disagreement. According to master trainer Mel Silberman, assessing trainee needs is the primary way to: (1) pinpoint the problem, (2) confirm that a problem really exists, and (3) develop solutions that may involve training to help manage the problem.[1]

The needs-centered training model (Figure 3.1) that we introduced in Chapter 1 depicts "Analyzing Organizational/Trainee Needs" in its center; this centrality suggests that *every* step or process of designing and presenting a training program revolves around assessing learning needs. From the outset of designing a training program it's important to consider the overall needs of the organization while also barreling down on the training needs of the people who will be in your training session. We defined training as the process of teaching people skills for a specific job. How can you teach people skills for a specific job if you don't know what they need to know or do to perform that job? The short answer to that question is: You can't. You cannot effectively teach people skills if you don't know what skills the trainees need to learn.

Closely linked to the process of identifying learning needs is the pivotal process of conducting a task analysis. As we will describe in detail later in this chapter, a **task analysis** is a step-by-step outline that describes the skills you are teaching. The task analysis goes hand-in-hand with the needs assessment process; you may first need to know what the details of the task are before you assess what trainees know or don't know about the task. For example, before you can teach someone the steps of problem solving, you need to know what those steps are.

The purpose of this chapter is to present the initial steps in the process of designing a training workshop. We'll start by describing how to assess the needs of trainees in the three primary domains of learning—cognitive, affective, and psychomotor. We then present the nuts and bolts of how to conduct a needs assessment and conclude the chapter by helping you conduct a task analysis of the skills you are teaching.

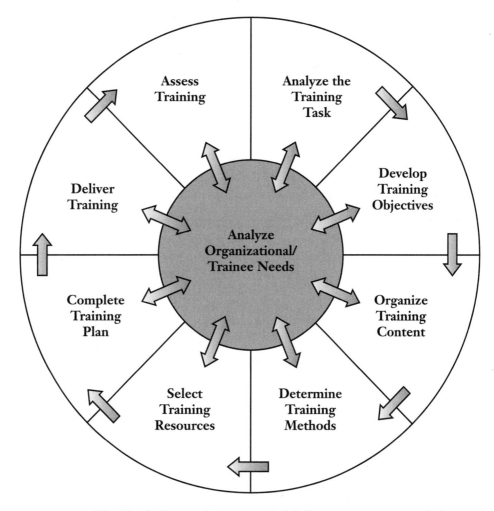

FIGURE 3.1   The Needs-Centered Training Model Focusing on trainee needs drives every step of designing and delivering a training presentation.

Domains of Learning

Training primarily emphasizes teaching people skills—specific behaviors. An effective training needs assessment is designed to identify which specific skills learners can and can't perform. Besides skills or behaviors, there are two other general categories or domains of learning. As a prelude to assessing needs, we'll first describe each of these three learning domains.

In some college and university classes, such as sociology or psychology, you primarily learn facts, theories, and principles. In a course such as public speaking, voice and diction, or physical education (for example, golf or bowling) you learn to perform certain behaviors. In yet other courses where you also learn facts or skills, you are encouraged to develop a greater appreciation of what you are learning. Courses in music and art appreciation have a primary goal of teaching you to value and enjoy great music and art. These different kinds of course reflect the different domains of learning. Based on the work of Benjamin Bloom and his colleagues, we will discuss the three types of learning domains: cognitive, affective, and psychomotor.[2] We introduce these domains of learning here and will reintroduce them in Chapter 11 when we discuss how to evaluate or assess the effectiveness of training programs.

Cognitive Learning

The **cognitive domain** of learning emphasizes remembering facts, knowledge, principles, and theories. When you memorize dates in history class or theoretical principles in a business management course you are focusing on the cognitive domain. In some training sessions there are times when principles are presented, facts are listed, and information is offered. As we learned in Chapter 1, if the primary goal is to present information rather than develop skills, it's more an education process than a training process. But even while learning skills, it is typically necessary to present information. It would be difficult, for example, to learn how to improve listening skill without describing the listening process or identify some general principles of listening. The essence of cognitive learning is presenting facts, information, principles, and theories.

Affective Learning

The **affective domain** of learning focuses on changing attitudes and feelings and enhancing motivation; the affective domain also emphasizes enhancing the value or appreciation for something. A speaker who seeks to inspire workers to work more efficiently is an example of affective learning. Teaching employees to value cultural diversity is another training topic that typically falls in the affective domain. Some people may have considerable knowledge and even be able to perform the desired behavior, such as delivering a dazzling PowerPoint presentation, but if they lack motivation or the desire to perform the skill they probably won't. While all training incorporates some aspect of motivation, many specialists become motivational speakers whose primary goal is motivating or inspiring others. Offering encouragement or empowering others by inspiring listeners to draw upon their untapped potential can be an important part of training. However, training has teaching people skills as its goal. The affective domain of learning is important to ensure that trainees are motivated to perform the skills that you are teaching them.

Psychomotor Learning

The psychomotor domain of learning focuses on teaching people behaviors or skills. If you are teaching someone how to do something new or better, you're focusing on the psychomotor domain of learning. The operative word in the last sentence is *do*. The psychomotor domain emphasizes how to perform or put into action the ideas, strate-

---

RECAP

Domains of Learning

Cognitive domain	Affective domain	Psychomotor domain
Focuses on knowledge and factual information	Focuses on changing attitudes and feelings and enhancing motivation	Focuses on skills and behaviors

---

gies, and suggestions you present. In communication or management training the goal is often to enhance listening skills, teamwork skills, speaking skills.

What do the three domains of learning have to do with conducting a needs assessment? If you are assessing learning needs, it's important to first know whether you are assessing the trainees' knowledge (cognitive domain) , motivation (affective domain), or skill (psychomotor domain). The essence of conducting a needs assessment is to ask trainees what they need to learn or to find out what they can and can't do in order for you to design a training program that best meets their needs.

How to Conduct a Needs Assessment

We've stressed several times the importance of meeting trainee needs, but precisely how do you actually conduct a needs assessment? There are a variety of methods, but all of them have as their goal finding out what learners don't know or can't do that they should know or do in order to perform their job. The essence of conducting a needs assessment is to ask workers what they need, ask others what they need, or observe their work so you can enhance their skills. You ask questions to find out what people know or don't know. We'll discuss the following four needs assessment methods: surveys, interviews, observation, and assessment tests. Although you can get a graduate degree emphasizing psychometric theory, the scientific study of educational assessment, our goal in this chapter is to give you enough information to get you started.

Surveys

The most efficient way to identify learner needs is often by surveying your trainees. A **survey,** also called a **questionnaire,** is a series of written questions or statements for which you seek responses from others to learn about their knowledge, attitudes, or behavior related to your training topic. You've probably responded to dozens of surveys in school, at work, and in other organizations. Surveys and questionnaires are increasingly being distributed electronically via e-mail or the Internet. Electronic surveys have the advantage of speed of return; software programs can be designed to quickly summarize the data received.

Surveys and questionnaires have an advantage of being tailor-made to suit your specific needs assessment purpose. If, for example, you are designing a training program about teamwork, your needs assessment survey would seek to discover how much the trainees knew about teamwork. You might also want to ask what some of their current practices are to assess their behavior rather than just their knowledge or attitudes. You would use the information you glean from your survey to guide you in deciding what information to emphasize (information they didn't know or skills they could not perform) or to deemphasize (if they already knew how to perform a skill).

Regardless of the content of the survey, the most important task in designing the survey is to develop clear, unbiased questions. If respondents aren't sure what you're asking, then it will be difficult for them to answer your questions and for you to get the information you need. There are several formats you can use to gather the information you seek. Formats we'll discuss here include: Likert scale, check lists, yes and no questions, rank order, forced-choice, and open-ended questions.

Likert Scale.   A **Likert scale** item first offers a statement and then asks to what degree a respondent agrees, is undecided about, or disagrees with the statement. Here's an example:

> This course in training and development is an excellent course.
>
> Strongly agree   Agree   Undecided   Disagree   Strongly disagree

By noting the intensity of agreement or disagreement with this item you could assess the attitude a respondent has toward the course. Or, if the respondent circled "undecided," you'd know that although there was no liking or disliking of the course, the respondent was somewhere in the middle.

Likert scale items can be designed not just to tap attitudes but also to assess the behavior or skill level of respondents. Here's an item that seeks to identify specific behavior:

> I always prepare an agenda for each meeting I chair.
>
> Strongly agree   Agree   Undecided   Disagree   Strongly disagree

If respondents circle "strongly agree" or "agree," then you'll know something about what the respondent does. Even if the respondent isn't sure of his or her behavior or may not know what an agenda is and circles "undecided," you know that this may be information or skill that the respondent needs. And if "disagree" or "strongly disagree" is circled then you have evidence that the respondent probably needs to learn this skill or the importance of this skill.

Checklists.   Another format for gathering survey data is to provide a list of skills and knowledge and ask respondents to check those items where they may have little need, some need, or a great need to learn information about. As shown on page 53, most checklists should not be too long. In fact, any needs assessment instrument should not be overly lengthy or detailed. You're likely to get more responses to your survey if it does not take too long to complete the assessment instrument.

Yes and No Responses. You could be very direct and ask respondents a question in which the only response is "yes" or "no." Although most survey designers suggest that it's better to seek a range of responses to questions you pose, there may be times when you want to know a direct yes and no response. Examples of "yes" and "no" questions you may ask include: Have you completed high school? Do you have a college degree? Have you completed a training seminar on the topic of listening?

Rank Order. Yet another method of assessing needs using a survey is to ask respondents to rank skills or behaviors in their order of importance to them. It's usually best not to ask respondents to rank order a list that's too long; ranking six or seven items should be the limit. Note the examples below of how to structure a rating scale or a rank order type of survey question.

"Train the Trainer" Checklist

This questionnaire is designed to help the coordinator of an upcoming "Train the Trainer" workshop to determine your needs and interests. All responses are confidential.

Directions: Please indicate, by checking the appropriate column, the degree of need you have for gaining additional skill or information.

	Great Need	Some Need	Little Need
How to write training objectives	_____	_____	_____
How to conduct a needs assessment of trainees	_____	_____	_____
How to prepare a lesson plan	_____	_____	_____
How to motivate trainees to listen and respond	_____	_____	_____
How to use audio/visual resources in training	_____	_____	_____
How to deliver a training workshop with skill (e.g., good eye contact, gestures, etc.)	_____	_____	_____
How to use a variety of instructional methods in training sessions	_____	_____	_____
How to ask appropriate and stimulating questions	_____	_____	_____
How to make information interesting to trainees	_____	_____	_____
How to facilitate group discussion	_____	_____	_____
How to design an effective training session	_____	_____	_____
How to deal with problem training participants	_____	_____	_____
Other: Please specify	_____	_____	_____

(continues)

Rating Your Training Skill

Rate your training skill using a 1–10 scale, on which 1 = low skill and 10 = high skill.

	Today	Desired
1. I effectively identify and assess what trainees need to learn using effective needs assessment tools.	_____	_____
2. I perform a well-organized task analysis of the training skills I teach.	_____	_____
3. I can write training objectives that are specific, measurable, attainable, and achievable.	_____	_____
4. I effectively organize the material that trainees need to learn.	_____	_____
5. I use a variety of effective training methods during a training session.	_____	_____
6. I use effective training resources such as overhead projectors and computer-generated graphics.	_____	_____
7. I develop and use high-quality lesson plans and facilitator guides.	_____	_____
8. I use effective delivery skills when training.	_____	_____
9. I systematically and effectively evaluate training I conduct.	_____	_____
10. I use adult learning principles when designing and delivering training.	_____	_____

Assessing Your Communication Skill

Rank order the following communication skills in order of importance to your job. Place a 1 in front of the most important item, a 2 in front of the second most important item, and so on. Your least important skill will be ranked 7.

_____ listening

_____ note taking

_____ team problem solving

_____ persuasive speaking

_____ informative speaking

_____ participating in meetings

_____ leading meetings

Multiple-Choice Questions.   Another format for assessing needs is to ask a question and offer only a limited number of choices for a respondent to select. In classes you've undoubtedly taken many multiple-choice tests. The challenge in writing a good multiple-choice question is to write a clear stem, the question or statement to which you want respondents to select their responses. The other challenge is to write realistic foils; these are the alternative choices that follow the stem of the item. Here are some examples of multiple-choice items:

1. For every meeting I lead, I usually
   A. develop a clear, written agenda and distribute it before the meeting.
   B. develop a clear, written agenda and distribute it at the meeting.
   C. develop a meeting agenda by asking participants what they want to discuss at the beginning of a meeting.
   D. do not develop or distribute an agenda for meetings.

2. When preparing a persuasive sales presentation, I usually
   A. develop written notes and rehearse my presentation.
   B. rehearse my presentation but do not prepare written notes.
   C. develop written notes and do not rehearse my presentation.
   D. do not develop written notes or rehearse my presentation.

Open-Ended Questions.   Sometimes the best way to determine what people's needs are is just to ask them an open-ended question. An **open-ended question** is a question in which you provide no structure for the respondent's response. You just ask for information and leave a space for the respondent to write his or her answer. Here's an example:

1. What are the most important challenges you experience when you make a sales presentation to a customer?

Here's another example:

2. What skills would you like to learn in the upcoming training seminar about how to deal with angry customers?

Both of these questions are designed to solicit a wide range of responses that could give you information about the issues and needs in designing a customer service training presentation.

Ideally, you should invite all participants who will be attending your seminar to complete and return a survey to you. Sometimes it is not practical or possible. Designing and administering a needs assessment survey takes time and money. Having a representative sample of participants complete a survey would be better than receiving no survey responses.

360 Survey Method.   A survey technique that can be especially effective in conducting a training needs assessment is called the **360 survey method.** The 360 method seeks information not only from the employee but also from the employee's colleagues and those who may be subordinate to the employee, as well as the employee's supervisor. It's called 360 because information is gathered from all perspectives, or at 360 degrees (which is the circumference of a circle). When comparing responses from the employee and his or her boss, as well as colleagues, a more accurate picture of perceptions of strengths and skill level occurs.

Perhaps you want to assess how an employee manages conflict. Using a 360 survey method, you could design a questionnaire that includes specific Likert-scale items designed to describe how an individual manages his or her emotions, clarifies misunderstandings during conflict, tries to develop collaborative goals, and generates multiple options to try to resolve conflict. First the employee would complete the items evaluating his or her own perception of how well he or she managed the conflict. Second, the employee's colleagues would complete the same questionnaire assessing the identical items; not every colleague may be asked to complete the questionnaire, but just five or six coworkers who know the employee fairly well. Third, the employee's supervisor could also evaluate the employee. Finally, if the employee works with customers or clients, they could also be asked to complete the questionnaire. After the questionnaire has been administered to the various people who work with the employee, the results are compiled and shared with the employee. Usually charts and graphs are prepared to summarize how others evaluated the employee compared with the employee's own evaluation. Sometimes the results of the 360 evaluation are shared with the trainee during the training session, or the results may be shared with the employee a few days before the training.

When using a 360 questionnaire or any type of needs assessment instrument, it is vital that all responses be kept confidential. Although the employee will see how the supervisor evaluated him or her, the employee should not be able to determine which coworker made specific evaluative comments. As a trainer you should never reveal the results of the needs assessment with others unless given specific permission to do so by the persons completing the needs assessment instrument. Breeched confidentiality will decrease the likelihood that you will be able to obtain honest results from others in the future; it's also unethical. Your own credibility will suffer from such an ethical lapse in judgment.

Interviews

Rather than distributing surveys to trainees before a training session, you may decide it would be best to interview all or some of the participants prior to the workshop. An interview is a form of oral interaction structured to gather information. Interviews often include two people—the person asking the questions and the person responding—but interviews could include more than one respondent; it's possible to interview a group of people.

A group interview is usually called a **focus group** interview. One person usually acts as the moderator or facilitator, asks open-ended questions, and then gives group members a chance to share their views on the questions asked.

Methods of Survey Design

Likert scale	A statement that asks to what degree a respondent agrees, is undecided, or disagrees with the statement
Checklists	Offer a list of skills or behaviors and ask responds to check those skills in which they either do or do not need training
Yes and no responses	Asking respondents direct questions that could be answered by either a "yes" or "no" response
Rank order	Trainees indicate which of a list of skills, behaviors, or information is most important, second most important, and so forth
Multiple-choice questions	Respondents are asked a question or given a statement and have a fixed number, usually four, options from which to respond
Open-ended questions	Respondents are asked a question with no fixed structure for the answer
360 questionnaires	Respondents are asked to complete items to assess their skill; coworkers, supervisors, and, if appropriate, customers and clients also evaluate the trainee to gain a comprehensive assessment of how the trainee is perceived in comparison to self-perceptions
Interview	A form of oral interaction that is structured to gather information

Interviews can often yield richer, more detailed information because you can ask follow-up questions and probe for more detailed explanations. Many trainers prefer the interview method of needs assessment to other methods because of the enhanced quality of information that can be gathered. The primary disadvantage to interviews is that they are more time consuming to administer. Another problem is that, if the same questions aren't asked of all respondents, it may be difficult to identify consistent themes in the responses. Also, it takes considerable skill to interview others. An effective interviewer needs to first establish rapport with the interviewee and then ask appropriate questions and have good listening skills. Distributing a survey is much more efficient than asking each participant to respond to a set of standard questions.

You can use some of the same question formats used for surveys and questionnaires. You may seek some basic information such as job description, the amount of time the person has been performing the job, education level, amount of previous training, and other general questions. Interviews are probably best used, however, when you can ask open-ended questions.

Before designing a written survey or questionnaire you may decide to interview employees to get a general idea of the issues you want to explore and questions to ask in a survey. Sometimes during interviews the interviewee may make candid comments about a superior; in all cases, ensure the interviewee complete confidentiality.

Most interviews, like a speech, have a beginning, middle, and end. During the opening of the interview, put the person at ease; establish rapport by engaging in general conversation rather than immediately firing questions at the interviewee. The middle of the interview consists of getting to the essence of the information you seek. You will probably want to take notes. You may also decide to record the interview, but the presence of a tape- or videorecorder may make the interviewee uncomfortable; you may not yield as much honest information if the respondent knows his or her interview is being recorded. It is unethical to record an interview without telling the interviewee that the interview is being audio- or videotaped. Toward the end of the interview you can signal that the interview is over. You may want to give the respondent a chance to provide any other general comments about the topic or ask questions about the process or the training program.

If it's not possible to interview the trainees who will be attending the seminar, you may want to interview their supervisors. Asking for supervisor input about the kinds of skills and information trainees need can often provide important clues about the essential content that you need to present at the training seminar.

Observation Methods

Besides asking trainees to respond to written questions with a survey or interviewing them, another strategy for determining what trainees need to learn is to watch them work. No, we don't mean that you have to hide behind a potted plant or use hidden cameras to observe workers. You can, however, observe them performing some of the skills you plan to include in your training session. If you're going to be presenting a seminar about improving meetings, attend one of the trainees' meetings. Or, for a customer service seminar, spend some time watching the trainee working with customers. If you're delivering a seminar on giving sales presentations, watch the trainees interact with a customer; or, if that's not possible, ask the trainee to videotape his or her sales presentation and share a copy of the tape with you.

An indirect way of observing trainees would be to examine reports, sales records, attendance records, job descriptions, or other documents that might give you insight as to the skill level of the trainees. Noting the number of customer complaints or congratulatory comments from clients may provide important information about the competence level of the trainees.

Assessment Tests

Many organizations, especially large ones, have formal assessment centers. An **assessment center** is a room or suite of rooms where employees are given performance tests to identify proficiencies and weaknesses in their job skills. A person interested in a computer technician position may be given a computer problem to solve. Besides assessing technical skills, assessment centers may also be designed to identify the strengths and weaknesses of someone who is seeking a sales or managerial position.

A classic assessment center activity for someone seeking a management job is an "in-basket" exercise. To assess how someone handles routine work, an employee or potential employee is given a stack of material that typifies what he or she might find on an average day on the job. The employee is told to sort through the papers and information and organize them from most to least important. This kind of activity assesses an individual's triage skills—the ability to identify what's most important or what's least important information in the stack. Assessment centers might also invite people to work on a group or team problem and then observe how effectively the group approaches the problem or how skilled team members are in managing conflict or coming up with a quality solution. Assessment centers can be effective in training needs assessment because of the focus on observable behavior rather than just asking for self-report information, which is the case with surveys or interviews.

How to Assess Needs without a Comprehensive Needs Assessment Process

As we repeatedly emphasize, conducting a needs assessment is essential to developing an effective training program. But we're realistic. Conducting a comprehensive needs assessment takes time and costs money. Many training events are scheduled without the benefit of pretraining surveys, interviews, observations, or assessment tests. How can you develop an effective training program if you or your client has not invested in a thorough needs assessment process? Consider the following strategies:[3]

1. Make your first training event of your training session a needs assessment activity. Develop a worksheet asking for information and background about the trainee's experiences. For example, let's say you were presenting a workshop on improving listening skills. Consider developing a worksheet that includes the following questions: (1) What are the characteristics of someone who has excellent listening skills? (2) What are the characteristics of someone who has ineffective listening skills? (3) What skills would you like to learn that would enhance your listening skills? (4) Why are good listening skills important? After the trainees have responded to these four questions, put the trainees in small groups to discuss their responses. Then, have groups report on their results. In just a short time, you will learn quite a bit about what the trainees already know about listening, what they'd like to learn, and why they think listening skills are important.
2. Prior to the workshop, phone or e-mail some of the participants to introduce yourself and ask them what they would like to learn in the upcoming workshop.
3. Phone or e-mail the person who invited you to present the workshop. Seek as much detailed information as you can about the needs, skills, interests, and attitudes of the trainees.
4. As participants arrive for the workshop, talk with them about their backgrounds and interests in the topic. For example, you could ask them if they have had any previous training about your topic. Or ask why they have come to the seminar.

Even if they say "It's required," you've learned something about the attitudes of whom you will be training.

5. After introducing yourself, just ask participants what they would like to learn and why they are attending the seminar. Write their responses on a flip chart, overhead transparency, or whiteboard. At the end of the seminar, go back to the list that you compiled and note how you have attempted to respond to the specific questions they had at the beginning of the workshop.

6. Develop a presession questionnaire.[4] Before the training begins and as participants are filing into the room, give each participant a brief needs assessment questionnaire that you could review either before the session starts or during the first break. Such a questionnaire could ask for information about the participant's current job, educational background, and previous training on the topic, as well as the specific objectives that the participant has for the workshop. Of course it would be better if you could have distributed the questionnaire and reviewed the results several days or even weeks before the workshop begins. But a short immediate presession questionnaire may at least help you customize that material in ways that you could not have done without gathering such information.

Each of these techniques will call for you to be flexible in presenting your training content. Based upon your impromptu needs assessment, you may need to expand certain portions of your program or condense other sections. It's always advisable to conduct an extensive needs assessment *before* each training session. But when you can't, some effort at needs assessment is better than no needs assessment. It is better to meet trainee's needs than present irrelevant information. Adapt, adjust, and revise training content to help trainees master the material they want to master.

How to Analyze the Training Task

How can you teach someone a skill unless you know how to perform the skill yourself? You can't. A key component of designing any training program is to identify the specific skills and information that you are going to teach the trainees. To do this you need to prepare a task analysis. As we noted at the beginning of the chapter, a task analysis is a step-by-step outline of the behaviors and knowledge that are needed to perform the desired behavior. Not only do you need to specify what the skills are, but it's important that you organize the skills you're teaching in the order in which they need to be taught. Think of the task analysis as a detailed blueprint of what trainees should do or know to be competent. If, for example, you are teaching someone how to give a persuasive sales presentation, the task analysis would be a list of all of the skills and information that the trainee should be able to do to effectively make a sale.

Although we've discussed the mechanics of preparing a needs-assessment survey prior to our discussion of developing a task analysis, it may be useful to prepare the task analysis first so that the list of skills and information can help you design your needs assessment methods. Clearly, the preparation of the task analysis and the needs assessment procedure go hand in hand.

How to Prepare a Task Analysis

How do you prepare a task analysis? You start with making sure that you are knowledgeable about the skill you are training. How do you learn the steps and procedures for teaching a skill? You conduct research. You read. You gather information from research, research summaries, and books. Especially helpful for analyzing communication skills are communication textbooks. Textbooks are useful because they often have descriptions of how to perform a skill organized in a step-by-step manner. You could also visit with experts who have considerable skill and experience about your training topic.

After you've immersed yourself in research and reading, you then begin the process of laying out the steps in performing the skill you are teaching. It's often easier to develop a task analysis for a technical skill such as operating a piece of machinery or using a computer program than it is for a "soft" skill such as listening, managing conflict, negotiating, or preparing for a meeting. Technical or "hard" skills often have very clear steps and procedures; if the procedures aren't followed, it will be impossible to perform the behavior. There are very clear right and wrong ways to perform the skill. For example, in teaching someone to drive a car, it's obviously imperative that you show someone how to turn the car on before teaching them to shift into the proper gear. There's a clear right way to structure the performance of the behaviors.

Our understanding of social skills, including communication, management, and leadership, is less precise. Therefore there will likely be some variation in a soft skills task analysis such as giving a sales presentation, developing an appropriate leadership style, or being a supportive, confirming communicator. There is more than one agreed-upon series of steps to enhance communication skills.

After reading books and articles about the skill you are teaching, you will need to begin to develop a sequence of what a trainee needs to know first, second, and so forth. One technique to help you develop a sequence is to brainstorm the various components or steps in performing whatever skill you are teaching. Get a sheet of paper and just start writing down the steps, or write your list of skill steps on your computer. Because this is a training program that emphasizes skills, begin each step with a verb; verbs denote action. Because training is about doing rather than only knowing something, pay careful attention to your use of action verbs in identifying the sequence of behaviors that should be performed. Of course, there is information that trainees need to know as well as skills that they should perform, so you may have references to information trainees need to acquire. But even if it's information you want them to have, use an action verb to describe what trainees should be able to do with the information. Action verbs such as list and define, describe, state, and explain are good ones. If, for example, you are designing a training program about how to give an informative briefing to a supervisor, your list might look something like this:

Develop a content outline.
Conduct research.
Analyze the needs of the supervisor for information.
Describe the purposes of an effective briefing introduction.
Gather supporting examples and illustrations.
Determine your purpose and specific objective.
Rehearse the presentation.
Deliver the presentation.
Prepare appropriate visual aids.

Once you've started to list the major steps in the process, you then arrange the steps in the order in which they should be performed. As you will note when you research your topic, such as how to deliver an informative briefing, there may be differences of opinion in what should be performed first. Some experts suggest you should first think about your presentation goal, others suggest your should first analyze your listener's need for information, some suggest you begin by doing some general reading and research.

It's ultimately your job to determine what the best sequence of events are in your particular trainees. We recommend that, as the driving force for all decisions you make in designing and presenting a training presentation, you consider the needs of your trainees. In essence, your trainees determine what should be presented and the order in which it should be presented, based upon their needs. If you consistently consider the needs of your trainees, you'll be on the right track in designing your training presentation.

In our example of designing and presenting an informative briefing to a supervisor, your next step is to return to the steps you've identified and then put the steps in the appropriate order. You may decide that the proper sequence is as follows:

I. Analyze the needs of your supervisor for information.
II. Determine your briefing purpose and specific objective.
III. Conduct researeh.
IV. Develop an outline.
V. Gather supporting examples and illustrations.
VI. Describe the purposes of an effective briefing introduction.
VII. Prepare appropriate presentation aids.
VIII. Rehearse the presentation (if time permits).
IX. Deliver the presentation.

Now that you have the major steps of the process identified, you're ready to add more details and flesh out the outline. You need to add substeps under each major step; you may also need to add further steps underneath the substeps that you list. Your task analysis will begin to look like a traditional outline using Roman numerals for major ideas, capital letters for substeps underneath the major ideas, and numbers underneath the capital letters if you need further detail. Here's a sample of a complete, detailed task analysis:

Task Analysis of How to Present an Informative Briefing to Supervisors

I. If appropriate, analyze the needs of the supervisor for information.

    A. If several supervisors are present, conduct a demographic analysis of the supervisors (audience for the briefing).

        1. Assess the culture, ethnicity, and race of the audience.

            a. Design a questionnaire to assess demographic characteristics of the audience.

            b. Administer the questionnaire to assess demographic characteristics of the audience.

        2. Assess the education level of the audience.

        3. Identify to whom the supervisors report.

    B. Conduct an attitudinal analysis of the audience.

        1. Assess attitudes, beliefs, and values audience members have toward your general topic.

        2. Assess attitudes, beliefs, and values audience members may have about you, the speaker.

    C. Conduct an environmental analysis of the speaking situation.

        1. Assess the size of the room in which you will be speaking.

        2. Assess the furniture in the room in which you will be speaking.

II. Determine your specific objective of your informative briefing.

    A. Write a one-sentence thesis sentence for your presentation.

    B. Write a behavioral purpose statement for your presentation.

        1. Write a behavioral purpose statement for your speech that is measurable.

        2. Write a behavioral purpose statement for your speech that is clear.

        3. Write a behavioral purpose statement for your speech that is observable.

        4. Write a behavioral purpose statement for your speech that is attainable.

III. Conduct appropriate research for your briefing.

    A. Gather information from the World Wide Web.

        1. Access the Web using appropriate search engines.

        2. Evaluate Web sources.

            a. Evaluate the accountability of the Web source.

            b. Evaluate the accuracy of the Web source.

            c. Evaluate the objectivity of the Web source.

            d. Evaluate the recency of the Web source.

            e. Evaluate the usability of the Web source.

    B. Locate the sources that you need for your research.

    C. Take appropriate written notes.

            a. Make notes legible.

            b. Make notes easy to retrieve.

            c. Organize notes.

    D. Identify possible visual images or PowerPoint images that you might use to integrate with your verbal forms of supporting material.

IV. Develop a briefing outline.

    A. Write a preparation outline for your briefing.

        1. Write your preparation outline in complete sentences.

    2. Write your preparation outline using standard outline form.

    3. Write and label your specific purpose at the top of your preparation outline.

    4. Write appropriate signposts and internal summaries in your outline.

  B. Write an appropriate delivery outline for your briefing.

    1. Write your outline using as few words as possible.

    2. Write notes summarizing your introduction and conclusion.

    3. Write examples of illustrations.

    4. Write your outline using standard outline form.

V. Gather, when appropriate, supporting examples and illustrations.

  A. Gather appropriate illustrations.

    1. Use illustrations that are directly relevant to the idea or point they are supposed to support.

    2. Develop illustrations that are vivid and specific.

    3. Develop illustrations with which your listeners can identify.

    4. Incorporate appropriate personal examples.

  B. Develop appropriate descriptions and explanations for your briefing.

    1. Keep your descriptions and explanations short.

    2. Use specific and concrete language.

    3. Do not overly rely upon descriptions and explanations.

  C. Develop appropriate definitions for your presentation.

    1. Use a definition only when needed.

    2. Use definitions that are clear.

  D. Develop appropriate analogies for your presentation.

    1. Use literal and figurative analogies correctly.

    2. Do not use figurative analogies to prove a point, only to illustrate a point.

  E. Use statistics appropriately.

    1. Round off numbers to make your numbers memorable.

    2. Use visual aids to present your statistics.

    3. Interpret statistics accurately.

    4. Make your statistics understandable and memorable.

  F. Use expert testimony and opinions appropriately.

    1. Identify your sources.

    2. Cite unbiased authorities.

    3. Cite opinions that are representative of prevailing opinion.

    4. Quote from your sources accurately.

    5. Use literary quotations sparingly.

VI. Describe the purposes of an effective introduction.

  A. Develop an introduction that gets the supervisor's attention.

  B. Develop an introduction that introduces the subject.

  C. Develop an introduction that gives the audience a reason to listen.

  D. Develop an introduction that establishes your credibility.

  E. Develop an introduction that previews your main ideas.

VII. Describe the purposes of an effective conclusion.

  A. Develop a conclusion that summarizes the main ideas.

     B. Develop a conclusion that reemphasizes the main ideas in a memorable way.

     C. Develop a conclusion that provides closure.

VIII. Prepare appropriate visual illustrations for your presentation.

     A. Prepare polished visual aids.

     B. Do not use dangerous or illegal visual aids.

     C. Make visual aids easy to see.

     D. Make your visual aids simple.

     E. Select the appropriate visual aid.

     F. Rehearse with your visual aids.

     G. Establish eye contact with your audience, not your visual aid.

     H. Explain your visual aid; don't just show it.

     I. Do not pass objects among your audience during your presentation unless it is necessary to achieve your presentation objective.

     J. Use handouts effectively.

         1. Don't distribute handouts during the presentation unless your listeners need to refer to the information during your presentation.

         2. Keep your listener's attention focused on the appropriate pages of the handout material.

     K. Time your visuals to control your audience's attention.

     L. Use technology effectively.

         1. Use PowerPoint when appropriate.

            a. Use no more than two font styles.

            b. Do not put too much information on one slide.

            c. Use the same template for the entire presentation.

         2. Bring appropriate hardware, power cords, and other necessary technical support materials with you when you present.

 IX. Deliver the briefing.

     A. Use an appropriate extemporaneous delivery style.

         1. Don't memorize the presentation word for word.

         2. Don't read the presentation.

     B. Use appropriate gestures.

         1. Use gestures naturally.

         2. Be definite when gesturing.

         3. Use gestures that are consistent with your message.

         4. Use a variety of gestures.

         5. Don't overuse gestures.

         6. Use gestures that are appropriate to your audience.

     C. Use effective eye contact.

     D. Use effective posture.

     E. Use effective vocal delivery.

         1. Speak loudly enough to be heard.

         2. Use appropriate pronunciation.

         3. Use appropriate articulation.

         4. Use appropriate variations in pitch.

         5. Use appropriate variations in speaking rate.

         6. Use appropriate pauses for emphasis.

What we've presented here is a *detailed* task analysis. You may decide your task analysis need not be as specific as the example we've provided here. Yet an effective task analysis should provide a comprehensive review of the essential tasks to complete the skill. Our task analysis has emphasized the *skills* or *behaviors* that the trainee needs to perform in order to be proficient in the task. You may also find that you need to include knowledge or information that the trainee should learn. Definitions, concepts, and principles could and should be included in a task analysis. However, if the task analysis includes too many elements of the cognitive domain, you're moving into the area of education rather than training. Education may be what the trainee needs rather than skill training. We suggest that you evaluate your task analysis to ensure that you are emphasizing skills if training is what the trainees need.

What if your training workshop is only two hours in length? You certainly could not present all of the information we've included in our example of a task analysis in that time period. You're right. So how do you determine what actually is presented in the seminar? Answer: *It depends upon the needs of the trainees.* You would present those portions of the task that are most relevant to what trainees need to be able to do. How do you know which skills that trainees need? You conduct a needs assessment—administer a survey, interview, observe, or use another technique that we've discussed in this chapter. The needs assessment and task analysis are closely related to one another. Before designing your survey or other needs assessment method, you may first prepare your task analysis to help you determine what questions you need to ask when assessing needs.

Summary

Meeting the needs of the trainees is at the heart of an effective training program. In this chapter we have discussed how to conduct a needs assessment as well as a task analysis. A needs assessment is a method of identifying what trainees need to learn in order to perform their job. A task analysis is a detailed, step-by-step description of the skills and behaviors the trainees should perform and the information the trainees should learn in order to perform their job.

As a framework for discussing needs assessment and task analysis, we identified the three domains of learning. The cognitive domain focuses on knowledge and information. The affective domain emphasizes changing attitudes and feelings and enhancing motivation. The psychomotor domain emphasizes skills or behaviors. Effective training will focus on the psychomotor domain but may also emphasize cognitive as well as affective domains of learning.

There are several methods of conducting a needs assessment. The most typical methods include: surveys, interviews, observations methods, and assessment tests. The goal of any needs assessment is to identify the skills and knowledge that a trainee does not possess in order to do his or her job effectively.

To conduct a task analysis, it is first important to be personally knowledgeable about the information and skills necessary to perform the task. Essential to the process of preparing a task analysis is to describe, in some detail, the steps or sequence of events needed to perform the task.

QUESTIONS FOR STUDY AND REVIEW

1. What are the cognitive, affective, and psychomotor domains of learning?

2. What is a needs assessment?

3. What are methods of conducting a needs assessment?

4. What are tips and suggestions for conducting an interview as part of a needs assessment program?

5. What is a task analysis?

6. What are the steps involved in conducting a task analysis for a training task?

QUESTIONS FOR APPLICATION AND ANALYSIS

1. Deonna is scheduled to teach a training session about how to enhance assertive communication skills. She is uncertain what level of knowledge and skill her trainees possess. Which needs assessment method or methods would you suggest Deonna use? Explain your choice.

2. Zach is having difficulty developing a needs assessment questionnaire to assess listening and paraphrasing skills. What should Zach do to help him know which questions to ask to assess listening and paraphrasing skills?

3. Sue works as a training consultant for the Southern Water and Technical (SWT) company. The SWT director of training has asked her to develop a comprehensive needs assessment to determine the need for sexual harassment training. What needs assessment methods should Sue use?

4. Jake is scheduled to present a half-day workshop on the topic of how to manage angry customers. Unfortunately, the organization who hired Jake has not conducted a comprehensive needs assessment to determine the precise content of the workshop. What can Jake do to best ensure that his workshop will meet trainees' needs?

4 Developing Objectives and Designing Curriculum

CHAPTER OBJECTIVES

After studying this chapter, you should be able to:

1. Write training objectives that are observable, measurable, attainable, and specific.
2. Organize a training curriculum according to the principle of chronological order.
3. Organize a training curriculum according to the principle of teaching simple skills before more complex skills.
4. Teach a skill by telling, showing, inviting, encouraging, and correcting.
5. Perform a set induction for a training session.
6. Use examples of stimulus variation.
7. Provide closure to a training lesson.

Do you know which direction north is? Stop reading this book for a moment and point north. If you're reading this with friends or family nearby, ask them to humor you by pointing to where they think north is. You'll probably get different answers from almost each person you ask. The point of this odd activity? If you don't know which direction you're headed, you're not likely to get there. When training others, the way to figure out where you are headed is to prepare clear objectives. Training objectives, based upon the needs of the trainees and the task that is to be performed, provide the direction for the training presentation. In addition to knowing which way you're going, you also have to figure out how to get to your destination. Most people achieve their objectives by methodically mapping out the route and then taking one step at a time; this may not be flashy, but if you know where you're going and develop an organized plan for getting there, you will achieve your objective. Determining your objective and mapping out a strategy for achieving your objective are also important when designing training.

In this chapter we discuss the importance of developing clear training objectives and teach you how to write them. Once you have written your objectives, you're ready to start organizing your training content and plotting the overall structure of your training; you need to construct your training **curriculum.** The training curriculum consists of your training content and how you organize and arrange the information you present to achieve the training objectives. In this chapter, we'll identify basic strategies to help you organize your curriculum as well as discuss specific strategies to help you teach a skill. We conclude the chapter by presenting three techniques to ensure that your training will keep your audience attuned to your objectives.

How to Write Training Objectives

A **training objective** is a concise statement that describes what the trainees should be able to do when they complete the training. Because training emphasizes the psychomotor or behavioral domain, we place the emphasis on what trainees should be able to *do* (as opposed to know or feel).

Some people use the terms *objectives* and *goals* interchangeably. Is there a difference? When we use the term *objective* we mean a more specific, precise outcome that you are attempting to achieve. A **training goal** is a more general statement of what you would like to accomplish.[1] Your goal might be to have someone appropriately respond to a hostile customer complaint. The precise objectives involved in achieving that goal could include effectively managing the emotional climate of the conversation, how to paraphrase, how to identify common goals, and how to identify options to manage the problem. The specific objectives are necessary to achieve your overall goal. Both goals and objectives state desired outcome you'd like to achieve at the conclusion of the training. Objectives are simply more specific statements of the outcome you'd like to achieve. Robert Mager was instrumental in developing contemporary approaches to writing clear and useful objectives.[2]

How do you decide which behaviors should be objectives for your training program? In order to make that decision, you'll need to return to your task analysis (the

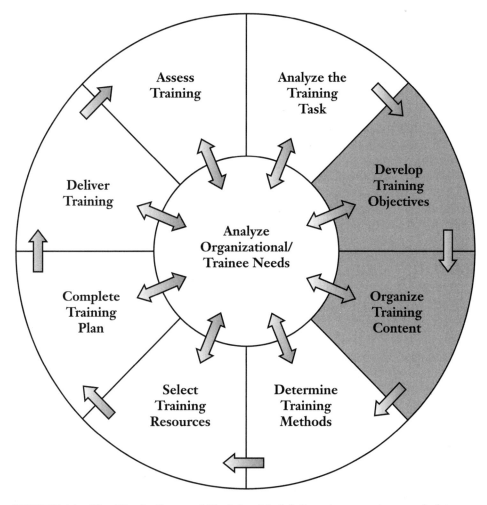

FIGURE 4.1 The Needs-Centered Training Model Focusing on trainee needs drives every step of designing and delivering a training presentation, including the development of training objectives and the organization of training content.

comprehensive list of specific behaviors to perform the task you are teaching) and your needs assessment (the comprehensive analysis of what trainees currently can and can't do). As you see in Figure 4.1, everything revolves around the specific needs of the trainee. If results from your needs assessment suggest that trainees are not able to perform a particular skill, then you'll want to develop a training objective and make that objective part of your training. For example, assume your task analysis indicates that most of the trainees have difficulty managing the emotional climate during a hostile customer complaint. Based on this needs-assessment information, you should develop a training objective that would look like this:

> At the conclusion of the workshop, trainees should be able to perform three emotion-management skills that would improve the emotional climate during a hostile customer interaction.

If your needs assessment suggests trainees can't perform the necessary skill, then they need to learn it. You then need to develop a learning objective reflecting the specific behavior the trainee should perform. The list of behaviors that a trainee should demonstrate should be found in your detailed task analysis. If you have not developed your task analysis, it will be a challenge to write well-worded, specific training objectives. In addition, you won't know which components of your task analysis you'll need to translate into training objectives until you conduct a needs assessment to identify what trainees can and can't do.

At this point in designing the curriculum, you need to be mindful of how long your training program will be. In most cases you won't have unlimited time to present a training program. Although some training programs last several days or weeks, most training is presented in the shorter time periods or modules. A training module is a specified time allotment for a given training topic. The typical time frame for communication training sessions is a half-day (four hours) or a full day (eight hours) of training; some training sessions may last two hours. Obviously, if you have a shorter time period for your training, you will have to be more selective in how many training objectives you use in the training.

A well-worded training objective should adhere to four criteria. It should be observable, measurable, attainable, and specific.[3]

Objectives Should Be Observable

A well-written training objective should specify some type of behavior that you can literally observe in some way. For example, you can observe whether a trainee accurately used the paraphrasing skill in a role play activity. You could not, however, accurately observe whether they *appreciated* learning this skill. Here's an example of a behavior that is observable:

> At the end of the training session, the trainee should be able to accurately paraphrase a one-minute statement by a customer.

Here's an example of an objective that is *not* observable:

> At the end of the training session, the trainee should be able to feel good about understanding what a customer says.

Although you could observe nonverbal behavior of the trainee and make some inferences about how he or she feels about responding to a customer, it would be difficult to validly and reliably assess the trainee's emotional state. The best training objectives state the desired behavior in a way that someone could verify whether the behavior occurred or did not occur.

Objectives Should be Measurable

In addition to being observable, the objective should also be measurable. By measurable, we mean that you should be able to assess how accurately or effectively the behavior was performed. If you can't measure how effectively the trainee performed the objective, you will have no way to determine whether the training was successful. You might, for example, be able to observe a trainee deliver the opening three minutes of a persuasive speech. In order to determine whether the trainee performed the opening three minutes successfully, you need to build in to the objective ways of measuring the success of the performance. Here's an example:

> At the end of the training session, trainees should be able to write a training objective that includes each of the four criteria of a well-worded objective.

By specifying that each trainee should be able to write an objective using all four criteria, it is then possible to measure whether the trainee did or did not achieve the objective. Here's an example of an objective that is *not* measurable:

> At the end of the training session, trainees should know how important it is to develop training objectives.

The use of the word *know* severely limits the clarity of the objective. How could you measure whether someone knows something? They could demonstrate whether they know something by being able to define, state, list, describe, and compare and contrast the idea with another idea. A key to writing well-worded objectives is to use an action word that is both observable and measurable. Here are some other nonobservable words to avoid in writing training objectives:

> To learn
> To appreciate
> To use good judgment
> To understand

Table 4.1 presents a list of words that are good verbs to use in writing training objectives.

Objectives Should Be Attainable

Besides being observable and measurable, the objectives should be realistic. By realistic, we mean that the objective should be achievable given the trainees' background and ability. If the trainees can't perform what you're asking them to do because it's too difficult or not appropriate for their current job, then you've not written an effective objective. Perhaps you've heard the expression, "Never teach a pig to sing. It wastes your time, it doesn't sound pretty, and it annoys the pig." Don't write unrealistic training objectives. Although it is reasonable to expect someone to use the paraphrasing skill in a training session, it may be unreasonable to expect a trainee to go back to the

TABLE 4.1   **Appropriate verbs to use in training objectives.**

administer	correspond	furnish	proceed
adopt	defend	identify	process
advise	define	illustrate	promote
analyze	delegate	implement	propose
answer	deliver	improve	provide
anticipate	demonstrate	indicate	recognize
apply	describe	initiate	recommend
arrange	design	inspect	relate
assemble	determine	instruct	report
assess	develop	interpret	represent
assign	devise	investigate	research
assist	diagnose	issue	respond
authorize	differentiate	itemize	review
calculate	direct	justify	revise
choose	discuss	list	schedule
circulate	dispose	monitor	secure
cite	disseminate	name	select
clarify	distinguish	negotiate	specify
classify	distribute	note	state
collaborate	draft	notify	stimulate
collect	employ	observe	submit
compile	endorse	obtain	suggest
compose	enumerate	operate	summarize
conduct	establish	organize	supervise
confer	estimate	outline	support
consolidate	evaluate	participate	trace
construct	execute	perform	train
consult	exercise	place	transcribe
control	expedite	plan	use
coordinate	explain	practice	verify
correlate	formulate	prepare	

office and solve long-standing conflicts just because the trainee attended one four-hour training session.

Here's an example of a realistic, attainable training objective:

> At the end of the training session, the trainee should be able to list and describe the four characteristics of providing effective feedback to an employee during an appraisal interview.

Here's an example of an unattainable training objective:

> At the end of the two-hour training session, the trainee should be able to deliver a 30-minute persuasive sales presentation from memory.

Although this objective is observable and measurable, it is not realistic to expect someone to memorize a half-hour speech in a two-hour training session.

— Identify Terminal behaviors

Objectives Should Be Specific

There are two ways to ensure that your training objectives identify specific rather than vague or general outcomes. First, make sure you have a well-chosen verb (see Table 4.1). Verbs such as to "know," "feel," "appreciate," and "understand" are not only *not* measurable, or observable, they also offer no specific behavior for the trainee to perform. Another away to ensure that your objectives are specific is to identify the precise actions that you expect the trainee to be able to perform. Do you expect the trainee to be able to recall all five elements of a well-presented speech introduction? Or do you only expect the training to remember three out of the five? Including descriptions of how well the trainees perform the skill is a way to build in specificity. Such specificity will also help you measure how effectively the trainee performed the skill.

You can add specificity to an objective by building in the criteria for successfully mastering the behavior you specify. **Criteria** are standards for an acceptable outcome. Being able to list eight elements out of a list of possible ten is a way to clarify the criteria of the objective.

Here's an example of a specific, criteria-based objective:

At the end of the training session, the trainee should be able to list, describe, and illustrate each of the five steps of providing an assertive communication response.

Note how the objective specifies what the trainee is supposed to be able to do (list, describe, and illustrate) for each of the five steps of providing an assertive communication response. It would be relatively easy to determine whether the behavior was performed properly.

Here's an example of a poorly written, nonspecific objective:

Trainees should understand how conflict can happen in the workplace.

The word *understand* is troublesome in that it does not specific precisely what the trainee should be able to do. There also are no criteria for determining how well the behavior should be performed.

Once you have developed objectives that are observable, measurable, attainable, and specific, you have begun the task of developing your training curriculum. As we noted earlier, the curriculum is the overall content of the training program. Your objectives provide the direction (the "compass") to tell you what should be included in the curriculum. But before you can begin to work on the training plans, the detailed description of how to present each segment of the training program, you will need to make some decisions about the overall structure of the curriculum.

RECAP

Criteria for Well-Worded Training Objectives

Criteria	Question to help you assess the criteria
Objectives should be observable.	Could you actually see the trainee perform the skill?
Objectives should be measurable.	Could you collect data to document whether the skill has been performed?
Objectives should be attainable.	Could the trainees perform the skill, given appropriate practice and feedback, in a reasonable amount of time?
Objectives should be specific.	Does the objective include criteria that provide precise guidelines for describing what the trainee should do?

How to Design Curriculum

To design the training curriculum is to design the essence of what the trainer presents to trainees. Training curriculum consists of the essential content that is included in a training program—it's the over-arching plan for presenting the information and teaching the skills in your training program. In what order do you sequence the training objectives that you've developed? What do you teach first, second, last? These are questions of curriculum design. If you have used your task analysis in developing your training objectives, it may be easier than you think to structure the content of your training session. We'll consider two general principles that can help you organize your training curriculum. First, we'll discuss the importance of teaching skills in chronological order. And, second, we will note the value of presenting simpler, easier material before teaching more complex skills and concepts.

First Things First: Teach Skills in Chronological Order

This principle is a simple one: Teach people how to perform the skill in step-by-step chronological order. **Chronological order** organizes information in a time sequence. What a person performs first, teach first. In essence, you will follow the sequence of the task analysis that you have prepared, because the task analysis should be arranged chronologically. In teaching someone to perform a technical task such as how to use a computer or operate a mobile phone, you teach someone to do first things first. You wouldn't, for example, teach trainees the function of how to "cut and paste" information in a word processing program before you had taught them to draft new information using the program. Nor would you teach someone how to store names and phone numbers in a mobile phone before learning how to turn the phone on. As we said, the principle is a simple one, yet surprisingly often overlooked when teaching communication, leadership, or management skills. Although the state of research does not permit us to make definitive declarations as to what must be taught first in teaching someone to be a leader, there are nonetheless some ideas, concepts, and skills that should be learned before others. Logically thinking through the order in which material should be learned will help organize the training content. Most skill training follows a chronological order.

Easy Does It: Teach Simple Skills before More Complex Skills

An exception to the teaching "first things first" principle are those times when you need to teach simpler or more elementary skills and concepts before teaching more complex material. For example, it would be useful to teach the skill of listening before teaching someone how to manage emotional conflict. Or it may be easier to teach trainees the basics of presenting an informative presentation before teaching them how to design and deliver a persuasive presentation. The rule of teaching material in chronological order does not really apply to what you teach first, informative speaking or persuasive speaking. Teach what is simpler to perform first.

How to Teach a Skill

We have discussed how to establish training objectives and looked at two principles to help you sequence the objectives. Another key element in designing training curriculum is to organize the training content and methods that are appropriate for teaching skills. As we've emphasized, training is essentially about teaching skills. **Training methods** are the procedures you use to present information and demonstrate the behaviors you want the trainees to learn. We'll discuss training methods such as how to organize group participation methods, structure role plays, and encourage discussion during lecture in more detail in the next chapter. Our focus now is on the specific strategy for organizing training content when your goal is to teach a skill. There are five steps in this process. To teach a skill you should, (1) *tell* them, (2) *show* them examples, (3) *invite* them to practice the skill, (4) *encourage* them by pointing out what trainees are doing well, and (5) *correct* errors in their performance.[4] Whether teaching someone how to tie a shoe, drive a car, or learn negotiation skills, these five steps offer a way to structure effective skill training.

Tell

The first step, **tell,** is practically self-describing. The first task to do when teaching a skill is to tell trainees what you want them to do. Most of the time you will tell or describe the skill by giving a short lecture. Other ways to tell trainees what to do are to have them read about the skill or to have an expert describe how to perform the skill.

What works best is to describe how to perform the skill in either chronological order or from simplest to more complex sequences. In most cases, your task analysis—the detailed step-by-step description of how to perform the skill—will serve as your guide for describing the skill. Most trainers include the tell step when teaching a skill. The problem occurs, however, when trainers tell trainees what to do and then immediately invite them to perform the skill. Trainers need to do more than use words to describe the skill they want the trainees to master; they need to show trainees how to perform the skill.

Show

The **show** step involves demonstrating how to perform the skill. Learning theorists tell us that behavior modeling (discussed in Chapter 2), which is nothing more than *seeing* a skill performed, is a basic and powerful learning strategy.[5] When growing up, many children just naturally emulate their parents. Younger brothers and sisters often look to their older siblings for examples of how to navigate through school or other life challenges. As shown in Figure 4.2, we learn more when we see how something is done rather than when we just hear about it. For example, when teaching someone the active listening (paraphrasing) skill, it would be better for the trainer to provide an example of how to listen actively before inviting the trainees to perform the skill. The show step need not be lengthy, but it should not be omitted.

Methods of showing trainees how to perform the skill will, of course, depend upon the specific skill you are teaching. In teaching the paraphrasing skill, for example, you could ask for a trainee to do a short role play with you in which the trainee tells a short story and you, as the trainer, demonstrate how to accurately and appropriately paraphrase. More complex skills may be more effectively demonstrated by showing a short video clip. For example, if you are teaching the skill of how to facilitate a group meeting, you could show a video example of someone performing the skill correctly. You could also, if you think it's necessary, show a bad example so that the trainees will avoid performing the skill the wrong way. Usually, however, positive skill demonstrations work best.

Invite

After you've told trainees what to do and have shown them an example, you're ready to **invite** them to perform the skill. The method you use to invite them to practice the skill will depend on the specific skill you are teaching, the complexity of the skill, and the number of trainees in your class. Usually, the smaller the number of trainees in the class the easier it is to organize and invite them to perform the skill. With a large class, you'll have more difficulty ensuring that every trainee understands the task and how to perform it.

One of the typical ways to invite trainees to perform the skill is to plan a role play. Provide a brief scenario and ask participants to demonstrate the skill. For example, you could have participants role play a situation to have them practice the paraphrasing skill. One person could read a statement or extemporaneously describe a

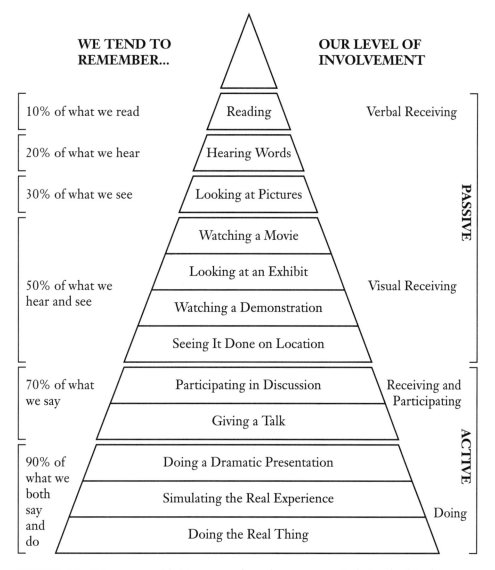

FIGURE 4.2 We are more likely to remember when we are actively involved in the learning rather than when we only read about an idea or hear someone tell us about how to perform a skill. (*Source:* Bruce Hyland, "Developing Student's Problem-Solving Skills." *Journal of College Science Teaching, 13*(2), 1989.)

problem, and the other person could practice paraphrasing what he or she just heard. Even with a very simple role play or simulation activity, it is a good idea to provide written instructions to the trainees. Write out step-by-step instructions for participating in the activity, even if you've orally gone over the instructions with the trainees. While people who learn best by hearing something may understand the instructions if they just hear the trainer explain the activity, visual learners will appreciate having the instructions written down.

Other methods for inviting trainees to practice the skill include using case studies and simulation activities, giving the group a problem to solve in which they practice the skills, or just asking participants to perform the skill individually. For example, if you are teaching the skill of preparing an agenda for a meeting, you could invite each participant to draft an agenda for his or her next meeting using the skills that you've taught them. Or, if you are teaching the skill of offering nonjudgmental feedback, you could use a structured worksheet in which you provide sample dialogue and then ask the trainees to select the best alternative nonjudgmental response to the dialogue. Regardless of the method that you use, if you're teaching trainees how to perform a skill, it's important to have them practice the skill during the training session. Trainees especially appreciate it if you invite them to perform a skill that directly relates to their needs (their in-basket); they like working on projects that directly link to their work—such as having them develop an agenda for their next meeting. Fictional simulations and case studies can be effective, but it is even more effective to have them work on an actual project such as preparing a speech or dealing with a real personnel problem. (If you have trainees work on a real work-related issue, structure the activity so that the identities of workers are protected.) The more realistic the practice, the greater the motivation for the learner and the more likely that the skill training will transfer to the job. We discuss training methods in more detail in Chapter 6.

When inviting trainees to perform a skill, remember our suggestion of moving from the simple to the complex. The first skill you have them practice should be an easy one. After they have gained confidence, you can then increase the difficulty of the skill rehearsal. For example, you may first have them practice the conflict management skill on a fictional case study problem and then move to a real conflict situation that they are struggling with.

Encourage

Catch trainees performing the skill the right way. Most people like and need encouragement. In providing feedback to trainees, first offer encouragement by pointing out what the trainees are doing right rather than first telling them what they are doing wrong. Especially if trainees are performing their skill where others can see them, such as in a role play situation, find ways to point out what they are doing correctly.

Remember this important training principle from Chapter 2: *It's better to get a message out of someone than it is to put a message in them.* Have the trainees tell you what they are doing well. Simply ask, "What did you do well when you performed this task?" Trainees may avoid this question and start telling you what they did that was wrong. If they list a litany of what was wrong, gently steer them back to asking them what they did right. If they come up blank, you could provide honest feedback about what you observed that was good about the performance. We emphasize that the feedback should be honest. We're not suggesting that you patronize trainees with overly positive praise. Unless the trainee was unmotivated or is trying to sabotage the training by purposely performing the skill inaccurately, you can usually find something positive about the training. In addition to asking the trainee what he or she did well, you can also ask other participants for positive feedback about the skill performance of their colleague. Feedback about what the trainee did well need not be lengthy, in fact it shouldn't be too long; overly verbose praise often leads adult learners to suspect that you're trying to sugar-coat your feedback.

Correct

After offering praise, you should follow up with specific suggestions for improving the performance. Rather than phrasing your feedback as what they did wrong, phrase it as a suggestion for improvement the next time they perform the skill. Again, if time and circumstances permit, ask the trainee for his or her own evaluation of the skill; ask, "What would you do differently to improve if you were to perform this skill again?" Adult learners want to know what they can do to improve. But in offering suggestions to correct their performance, don't make your list too long. Focus on just a few behaviors for improvement. Overwhelming a person with a plethora of suggestions may only confuse him or her and leave the trainee bewildered as to what to focus on. Sometimes less feedback is more.

If the group is large, it will be difficult for the trainer to provide detailed feedback to each trainee; you may have to be creative to ensure that each trainee receives both encouragement and corrective feedback. One technique to ensure that each trainee receives feedback is to assign a trainee to be an observer while one or more trainees are performing the training task. For example, when inviting trainees to perform the paraphrasing skill, assign person A to offer a statement (either read or extemporized) to which person B listens and responds with an appropriate paraphrase. Person C could be assigned to observe and provide feedback. Ask person C to first offer encouragement; ask the observer to note what person B did well. Then ask person C to offer feedback that would improve the performance. To help structure the feedback, give person C a checklist of behaviors to observe (e.g., Was there appropriate eye contact? Was the paraphrase accurate? Did the nonverbal message support the verbal message?) One way to enhance the quality of the feedback that person C provides is to provide a brief training session as to how to offer appropriate encouraging and corrective feedback before you conduct the activity. You could tell them what to do and then show them how to provide proper feedback by offering examples of appropriate encouraging and corrective feedback.

Another technique for ensuring that all trainees receive feedback is to ask trainees to write examples of what you are teaching them to do on a chalkboard, flipchart, overhead projector, or sticky notes. Let's again use our example of teaching trainees to provide proper paraphrasing skill. As the trainer, you could read a statement or offer extemporized comments and ask each trainee to write a paraphrase of your message on a sticky note. Then, ask trainees to post their notes on the wall. After the notes are posted, trainees could be assigned to review four or five paraphrases and offer written feedback on an additional sticky note; their assignment could be to offer one encouraging or positive comment and one suggestion (if appropriate) for improving the paraphrase. After the paraphrasing comments have been evaluated, the author of the paraphrase could retrieve the note and read the feedback. It is worth the time and effort in training to ensure that each trainee receives both encouraging and corrective feedback. The bottom line of learning is when the learner receives confirmation that the skill is performed well or receives additional suggestions for enhancing the skill performance and is given another try to perfect the skill.

In summary, when providing corrective feedback to trainees, keep the following suggestions in mind:[6]

1. *Be descriptive:* Identify what you saw the trainee do.
2. *Be specific:* Provide enough detail so that the trainee is aware of what he or she could do to improve.
3. *Be positive.* Even while providing suggestions for improvement, give the trainee hope that he or she can improve.
4. *Be constructive.* Provide honest suggestions that the trainee can put into practice; don't overwhelm the trainee with details that will be a challenge to implement.
5. *Be sensitive.* If you think the trainee may be overly disappointed and dismayed at his or her performance, be considerate of how the trainee is feeling: Be gentle with your corrective comments, monitor your tone of voice and your facial expression, and express empathy and concern.
6. *Be realistic.* Provide feedback about areas in which the trainee can improve rather than about behaviors that he or she cannot control.

How to Make Every Lesson Successful

We've discussed the overall strategy for structuring skill training. Develop clear objectives, consider the overall pattern for organizing the objectives (chronological or from simple to complex), and then map out the general strategy for teaching a skill (tell, show, invite, encourage, correct). We next turn our attention to specific techniques that help you design a specific lesson.

We offer three techniques that, if used effectively, can enhance learner motivation, help you gain and maintain attention, and enhance learner recall of the information and skills you present. The underlying premise of each of these three techniques is this principle: *Learning is more likely to occur when learners are actively involved in material that directly relates to them.* First, we'll describe how to get learners ready to receive your lesson with a technique called set induction. Then we'll describe how to keep trainee's attention by using stimulus variation strategies. Finally, we'll describe how to enhance retention by using the closure technique.[7]

Set Induction: Establish a Readiness to Learn

Set induction is a technique that helps get your trainees ready to learn. Have you been to a track meet and watched what happens when the runners line up for the race? The race manager usually first calls out, "On your mark." When this is said, the runners line up and begin to focus on the task at hand—running the race. But it is the next pronouncement that really gets the runners focused: "Get set." When this is uttered, the runners freeze, arch their backs, and are poised to attack the track. They are all ears waiting in anticipating of the starting gun, which signals them to "Go." A training set induction is the equivalent of telling the learners to "get set." You know you have effectively achieved set induction when the training room gets quiet and the learners lean forward in their seats, maybe picking up a pen or pencil to write down what you will tell them. Like the runners, they are poised to conquer the material you're about to share. How to you achieve "set"? Here's how.

First, determine what their needs are. Sound familiar? As our needs-centered model of training illustrates, virtually every aspect of quality training revolves around meeting the trainee's needs. To induce set, you have to know what will motivate listeners to learn. The runners poised to run the race are motivated by winning; they need no special coaxing; they are ready to be first out of the starting block. What will induce your trainees to focus on winning their "race"? If, for example, you're teaching a seminar about conflict management, and your needs assessment suggests that most of the trainees have work-related conflicts they'd like to manage, you have some powerful information to help you get their attention. Note the following example of a set induction:

> How many of you currently have or have had a conflict with someone you work with? Do you remember what it's like to have a conflict that saps your mental energy and grinds on you like a dentist's drill? Would you be interested in learning strategies that will help you manage those personal conflicts? Would you like to learn what conflict manage research suggests is the *best* technique for dealing with angry coworkers? Stay tuned. That's the focus of today's seminar.

The technique of asking rhetorical questions embedded in this set induction is designed to have the trainees "get set" and focused on the material you're about to cover. The goal of an effective set induction is to have the trainees either verbally or mentally respond, "Yes, I'd like to learn that skill!"

The steps in establishing set are relatively simple: First get the trainee's attention. But inducing set is more than about getting trainees focused on the lesson. When the race starter says "On your mark," attention has been gained. What's needed next is something that establishes set. You do this by saying or doing something that will motivate them to learn. Remember the definition of set induction is to establish a readiness to learn. What motivates is a sincere promise that you can and will meet the trainees' needs. Identifying with their needs and pointing them toward a solution that will solve their problems, conflicts, and hassles is at the core of getting them ready to learn.

There are a host of other strategies to get attention and motivate learners to focus on your message. Consider the following set induction techniques:

- *Demonstration:* Use dominoes to show that what happens to one person in an organization affects others.
- *Analogy:* Blow up a balloon and then pop it to show what can happen if change in an organization occurs too quickly.
- *Story:* Tell a story, either true or hypothetical, that describes a problem the trainees may have and then illustrates how the problem can be solved.
- *Quotation:* Begin with a well-chosen quotation that dramatizes the issue you will be presenting.
- *Cartoons:* Cartoons clipped from the newspaper or a magazine and enlarged on an overhead may help you make your point about the importance of the skill you are teaching. (*Note of caution:* If you plan on reproducing a cartoon in the participant's manual, you'll need permission from the copyright holder of the cartoon.)
- *Statistic:* Use a statistic to show the significance of a problem the trainees may face.
- *Rhetorical question:* Ask trainees a question that focuses their attention on a problem or issue that directly affects them.

So far, it may seem that the only time you use the set induction technique is at the beginning of a lesson. Yes, we think you should always use a set induction strategy to begin a lesson. But set induction can be used any time during a lesson when you find attention waning and motivation flagging. You can use a set induction technique as you move from one lesson to the next. Or you could reach for a set induction in the middle of a lesson if you see less eye contact with you, trainees slumping in their seats, or several trainees talking to their neighbors. Here's a technique that experienced trainers use: Keep a file of stories, statistics, and cartoons that can be used to help spark attention and motivation when you need it; think of this file as your "emergency set induction kit." Seasoned trainers are always scanning the audience watching to see if the trainees need a call to "get set."

Stimulus Variation: Change Methods to Maintain Interest

Once you establish attention and provide a motivating readiness to learn, the challenge is to keep trainees' attention. You do this by making sure you provide a mix of activities and levels of involvement, monitoring your training delivery style, and being mindful of how long trainees have been subjected to any single activity or method. Active learning is the key. You **vary the stimulus.** As a general rule of thumb, we suggest you should move to a different activity or learning method at least every 20 minutes. You should be especially sensitive to the length of your lectures (the tell step); training is about teaching people skills, not overly emphasizing information (cognitive learning). The essence of stimulus variation is to make sure you change the mode of delivery you are using to impart information. How do you do this? Note these strategies:

- *Movement:* Simply changing where you stand can offer a visual stimulus change for the learner. We're not suggesting that you randomly shuffle around the room as you speak or demonstrate a skill. But moving at an appropriate transition or moving closer to learners when you're telling something personal is a way to vary the visual stimulus for learners.
- *Verbal focusing:* Telling your listeners, "This next point is one of the most important points of the seminar," can be an effective way to highlight or focus attention on key ideas. Don't over-use this skill. But used appropriately (as with italics or boldfaced words on the printed page), it can be used to emphasize what's important and to help maintain attention and motivation.
- *Nonverbal focusing:* Pointing to key words or phrases on your overhead with a laser light pointer or just using your hand to direct eye contact can help vary what listeners look at during a presentation.
- *Interaction style:* Vary who talks to whom. For example, some of the time you can talk to the entire group. At other times, you can have the trainees talk to each other. Or encourage trainees to interact with you. Seek ways to change the focus and direction of who is addressing whom.
- *Pause:* Silence can be an important way to emphasize a point. Pausing before you say something important or after you say something significant can help add emphasis to what you're saying.
- *Reading:* Rather than giving a lecture about a topic, have trainees read a short passage in their participants' manuals. Or follow up inviting them to read about a topic (the tell step) by having them write questions over the material that they've read.
- *Visual aids:* We'll discuss the use of visual aids in more detail in Chapter 7, but consciously consider using visual aids as a strategy to vary the visual stimulus of what trainees are looking at.
- *Audio aids:* Using music at appropriate times during training can provide a change of pace and offer variation to the training program. Music before or after a training session can help set or sustain an upbeat mood.

The key to maintain interest in any lesson is variation. Constantly monitor the nonverbal cues of the trainees (their eye contact, posture, and verbal and nonverbal responsiveness) to determine if you need to vary the stimulus.

Closure: Tie a Ribbon around the Lesson

To provide **closure** is to provide a conclusion to one element of the lesson and point the learner to what's next. Lesson closure includes three steps. First, summarize what has been discussed; explicitly state the key points you've covered. Think of it as a brief recap of the lesson. Saying, "Today, we've learned the four steps of managing conflict. First, manage emotions; second, manage communication; third, manage the goal of the conflict; and finally, manage the number of options you're using to seek agreement" is an example of a brief summary of the major points you've covered. Rather than you providing this summary, you could ask the trainees to summarize the key points. Or tell one trainee at the beginning of the session that you'd like for her to summarize the key points at the end of the lesson. But closure is more than a mere summary of the lesson content.

RECAP
How to Make Every Lesson Successful

Technique	Description	Example
Set induction	Establish a readiness to learn by tapping into the learner's needs and desires for success.	"One of the biggest problems in meetings is an over-verbalizer. When leading a meeting, have you ever noticed how some people may dominate the discussion? Would you like to learn a technique that would help manage the over-talker? In the next few minutes, we will talk about a method of curbing the meeting dominator."
Stimulus variation	Change methods of presenting information; vary the learners' focus.	After a short lecture, show a video and then have trainees read a short story to illustrate a point.
Closure	Tie a ribbon around a lesson by summarizing the training content, describing how the skill can be used, and pointing the trainee toward what's next.	"Today, we've discussed the power of paraphrasing, and we've identified the two reasons why paraphrasing is useful: First, it can enhance communication accuracy; and, second, paraphrasing helps manage emotions during conflict. Armed with this skill, you can dramatically improve your understanding of your colleagues and avoid communication misunderstandings. But you may still have questions about how this skill relates to managing personal conflict and dealing with angry customers. Those are the skills we discuss right after our break."

Second, provide a psychological conclusion to what has been learned. Help the learner not only to remember what was learned but also to value this new knowledge and show how the new information and skill can be beneficial in the future. Closure is equivalent to tying a ribbon around the lesson. For example, ask a trainee how this new skill or information can help him on the job. If the training is effective, you can involve the trainees in helping you describe how this new skill will be beneficial. Another technique of providing psychological closure is to refer to your set induction. If you began by asking the trainees if they would like to learn how to solve a work-related problem, end by telling them (or better yet, having them tell you) how they can now solve the problem or enhance the quality of their work life.

Finally, the third step of providing lesson closure is to point the trainee to the next phase of the training. Show or describe how the completion of one objective can logically lead to where you are heading next. An effective technique for pointing the way to the next step is to ask a rhetorical question. Here's an example:

> We've not talked about how to manage conflict in typical conflict management situations. But what do you do when you are faced with a particularly rude or disagreeable person? What are some specific strategies that can help you deal with people who have no desire to collaborate with you? Those are the skills we'll talk about next.

Here the trainer has provided a link between what was just learned and what additional skill might be helpful in building upon the information just presented. Closure can be effective as a transition at any time during a training session when you're moving from one objective to the next or one skill or concept to another one. Think of it as a technique that can be sprinkled throughout a training session, not just used at the conclusion of the workshop.

Summary

This chapter discussed how to prepare training objectives and take the first steps in organizing the training curriculum. Training objectives are statements that describe what the trainees should be able to do at the end of the training session—they describe the outcome behavior that is the focus of the training content. Well-written training objectives should be observable, measurable, attainable, and specific.

The first step in designing curriculum is to identify the sequence in which the training content should be presented. The task analysis provides foundational direction for the steps in presenting training material. There are two guiding principles in designing training curriculum. First, consider teaching skills in chronological order— presenting the content in the order in which the behavior should be performed. Second, teaching simple skills before presenting more complex skills.

Teaching a skill involves five steps. First, *tell* the trainees what they need to know or be able to do. Second, *show* them how to perform the skill; model the skill for them. Third, *invite* the trainees to practice the skill. Fourth, offer *encouragement*.

Provide sincere, meaningful praise for behavior well performed. Finally, *correct* errors in performance.

To ensure success in designing curricula we concluded the chapter by describing three useful techniques that help trainees focus on the lesson, maintain their interest, and summarize key information. Set induction is the training skill of establishing a readiness to learn by first catching learners' attention and then motivating them to focus on the lesson. To maintain interest, we suggested stimulus variation; use a variety of methods and techniques to present a lesson. Finally, to end a lesson or help clinch learning at any point in a training session, we discussed the training skill of closure—summarize key content and note how the new skill and information can be used on the job.

QUESTIONS FOR DISCUSSION AND REVIEW

1. What are four characteristics of a well-written training objective?

2. What are two principles for designing curriculum? Illustrate each principle with an example.

3. What are the five steps in teaching a skill? Develop an original example to illustrate each of the five steps.

4. What are various techniques for providing set induction for a training lesson?

5. Describe the rationale behind incorporating stimulus variation in a training lesson.

6. What are the key purposes of the closure training technique?

QUESTIONS FOR APPLICATION AND ANALYSIS

1. Janice is teaching trainees how to develop skills rather than just giving a lecture about her training topic. She knows she needs to organize her session by telling, showing, inviting, encouraging, and correcting, but she is having difficulty differentiating between these five steps of teaching a skill. How should she organize a training session (pick any skill) using these five categories?

2. Phil knows the following training objectives do not meet the criteria of being observable, measurable, attainable and specific. Rewrite Phil's objectives so that they achieve all four criteria:

   A. After training, the trainees should know how to make an angry customer feel listened to.

   B. All trainees should appreciate the importance and value of using the paraphrasing skill during periods of interpersonal conflict.

C. At the end of the training session, the trainees should be able to understand what transformational leadership is and its several defining characteristics.

D. After the training session, trainees should list, describe, memorize, and give an example of the 25 reasoning fallacies that were presented in the training session.

3. Damon is presenting a training session about how to more accurately interpret the nonverbal messages of customers. He's having difficulty thinking of a set induction for his training session. What could Damon do or say to establish set induction for his training session?

CHAPTER

5 Developing Training Content

CHAPTER OBJECTIVES

After studying this chapter, you should be able to:

1. Identify and locate credible sources of training topics, content, and materials.
2. Identify criteria to evaluate training resource material obtained from the Internet.
3. Explain advantages and disadvantages of internal and external content sources.
4. List and describe implications for training about copyright laws, citing sources, and how to obtain permission for information used in training sessions.
5. Develop a content outline for a training session.

Whether you are a beginning trainer or are exploring a new area as a seasoned trainer, this chapter is designed to help you develop a systematic process to find and develop information for your training sessions. Sometimes the hard part is just getting started. You may have such questions as, "Where do I find training content?" and "Where do I start looking for information and skills for my training session?" As emphasized in Chapter 1, the needs of the trainees should guide you in choosing training content. So first and foremost, consider the needs of your trainees. If you've completed your task analysis (a detailed outline of the steps and skills to achieve the training goal) as well as developed training objectives, you already have a scaffolding on which to build your training content. The objectives, which address the needs of the trainees, are your guide.

In this chapter we offer tips and strategies for using your training objectives as a starting place to help you develop the core content and skills you'll present to the trainees. Two general categories of sources for training material are internal sources (your own experiences and background) and external sources (such as the Web, library sources, and experts). Careful and systematic exploration of these information sources can lead to productive results in developing training content. (See Figure 5.1 for how this chapter's emphasis fits into the overall needs-centered training model.)

Internal Sources of Training Material

Internal sources of training material consist of examining what you already know—your experiences, ideas, and knowledge. Your own practical knowledge about the skills you are teaching is a rich source of training content. If, for example, after assessing trainee needs you conclude that workers need to learn how to motivate work teams, you could ask yourself, "What do I already know about motivating work teams that would be useful material for a training workshop?" If you've worked as a manager before becoming a trainer, you will have some ideas of the problems, issues, and needs managers face when motivating teams. You undoubtedly have life skills stemming from experience that have the potential to enrich your training programs. Such experiential expertise not only provides more confidence and credibility but also serves as a rich source of content.

In a training context, personal experience can serve as a supplement or as the main source for content development. Personal experience is also a great resource for formulating new ideas, theories, and practices in a given area. It's important to process and assess your internal sources for practicality, relevancy, and organizational need.

External Sources of Training Material

Personal experience, although it's a rich initial source of content and illustrations, does have its limitations. It may be a useful place to start, but it should not be your only source of information. Your experiences may be unique to you, limited in scope, atypical, or not relevant to your trainees. Or you may simply have little or no experience in a training area that you are required to develop and present. Whether you have personal experience or not, the second major avenue for content development is the use of **external sources.** External sources include research, knowledge, and experience that you don't already have. The question then becomes, "Where can I find good content material on, for example, motivating work teams, other than my own experiences?" Fortunately, there are many places where you can find high-quality material on various training topics. Other people have knowledge and experiences that you

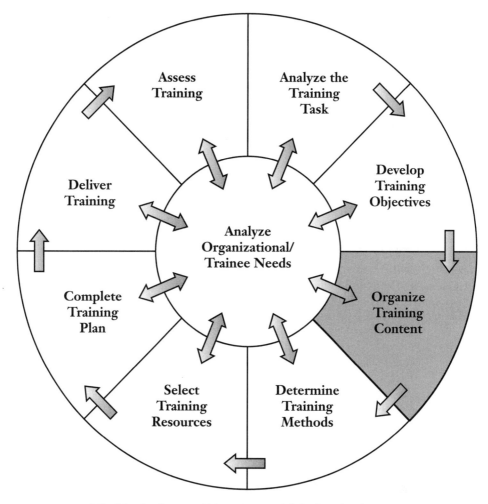

FIGURE 5.1 The Needs-Centered Training Model Before developing training content, assess the organizational and trainee needs as well as completing a task analysis and developing training objectives. Use your objectives to serve as a guide for developing the training content.

may not possess. The Internet, the library, experts, and commercially published information are external sources that can help you acquire the information you need to develop a quality training program.

Internet Sources

In the last few years, the Internet has become a technological highway for a significant part of the population. Information on a variety of topics is at your fingertips. For example, initiating an Internet search using the words "building teams in organizations" will yield a long list of potentially relevant "hits," including relevant books, consulting organizations, specialized topical Web sites, other related topics, and specific essays or bodies of content in this area. Sometimes the Internet is too rich a source of information; the challenge is to find the specific information you need for your training program.

To begin an Internet search you typically start with a director or search engine such as Yahoo!, Google, Alta Vista, or Lycos. Whether you're an expert Web surfer or have not yet explored the vast resources of the Internet, becoming familiar with search engines is the point of departure in developing your Internet research skills.

There are many training associations and corporations that maintain public Web sites full of relevant training information. The American Society for Training and Development (ASTD), available online at www.astd.org, is a professional association for trainers and thus is a very rich source for training topic and content information. Their Web site has many useful sources for trainers, including lists of conferences, publications, services, research, learning communities, job opportunities, featured books, "Webinars," magazines, resources, projects, and shared trainer experiences. In addition, there are many other Web training sites that can provide useful information and ideas for trainers who are seeking to develop training programs (for example, check out The Training Oasis at www3.sympatico.ca/thetrainingoasis).

You must be cautious, however, when considering the credibility and potential bias of information you find on Web sites. Just because information is posted on the Internet does not mean the information is accurate, truthful, or objective. A site with a ".com" suffix, for instance, is likely to be a business trying to sell products and services. Material from such a site is not necessarily objective or research-based. Some sites are specifically developed to advocate a product, idea, or service. Even though a Web site may be impressive and contain dazzling images, the information may be less than credible.

When using Internet information, it is wise to critically evaluate the information presented on the Web site. Knowing the author of the site, the credentials of the author, the type of site (e.g., .edu [education], .org [nonprofit organization]), the institution or organization with which the author is associated, or the recency of the information on the site are important considerations in ascribing credibility to the information presented on the site.[1]

To evaluate Web sites, consider the following criteria:

1. *Accountability:* Who "owns" the Web site, and to whom is the Web site accountable? Find out what individual or organization is responsible for the Web site. If the Web site is unsigned, you may be able to find who is responsible for developing the site by examining the header or footer of the site. Or perhaps there is a hyperlink at the top or bottom of the page that will lead you to the developer of the material.

2. *Accuracy:* Is the material contained in the Web site accurate and reliable? This criterion is closely linked to the issue of accountability. If the site contains information and data without identifying the source of the information or providing hyperlink documentation as to where the information was obtained, be cautious in using the information.

3. *Objectivity:* Is the information biased or objective? As noted previously, if the Web site is linked to a product or service (including consulting services), you should be wary of the objectivity of the information presented.

4. *Date:* Is the information recent? A quality Web site will be maintained frequently. At the bottom of many sites you can find a statement that indicates when the site was last maintained. A hyperlink on the Web site may also lead you to the date the site was last updated. If you don't find the date on the Web site, click on the "View" menu at the top of your screen and go down to "Page Info." When you click on "Page Info," you will find a screen that indicates a "Last Modified" date.

5. *Usability:* Is the information presented in a format that is easy to use? Fancy images and graphics may be impressive to look at but may also slow down the time it takes to load the information on your computer. Some sites offer the option of a "text-only" or "nontables" option that allows you to view information and data without images and photos; this option may speed your search and review process.

In addition to these general criteria, there are many useful Web sites that provide information and additional helpful guidelines on how to evaluate Web sites. You may wish to explore the following Websites to help you evaluate the results of your Web research:

mason.gmu.edu/~montecin/web-eval-sites.htm
www.lib.vt.edu/research/evaluate/evalbiblio.html
www.lib.berkeley.edu/TeachingLib/Guides/Internet/EvalQuestions.html
www.lib.lfc.edu/internetsearch/evalweb.html
manta.library.colostate.edu/howto/evalweb.html
www.pace.edu/library/instruct/webevalworksheet.htm
www.library.kent.edu/internet/evalform.html

Overall, most professional researchers suggest that you should not be overreliant on Web sources alone. There are many rich sources of information that have not yet made it into cyberspace. Do your legwork and make sure you consider, in addition to Web-based sources, more traditional research sources such as those found in the library.

Library Sources

A productive place to search for current research and information on training topics is the library. The Internet surfing skills that you used to access information online can also help you navigate today's library holdings. Many libraries are online and can be accessed from your computer. Some libraries even have electronic collections that can be perused from the comfort of your office or home. Regardless of whether you access them on line or actually go to the library building, there are several places to start as you begin searching for training materials. Most libraries now have computerized lists of holdings and computerized search engines. Typically most libraries will have an assortment of sources that could be potentially useful for you:

- Books
- Periodicals
- Full-text data bases
- Newspapers
- Reference Resources
- Government Documents

Books. Using the library search screen, you can do quick searches in these sources on your chosen topic. When searching for books, you will go to the part of the library search page that deals with their book collections. The screen prompt will ask you to enter a subject, title, or author in the space provided. When you hit "enter," the search will reveal a screen of how many hits your search produced. Frequently, the hit screen will also show you if this particular library has the book in its holdings or if you need to fill out an interlibrary loan form to obtain the book from the holdings of another library. Books are good, but typically they are not the most current materials on a given topic. On the other hand, they do tend to provide more breadth and depth of information on a given topic than you might find in other sources.

A rich source of information for training programs is textbooks. Especially valuable are textbooks that focus on the development of communication, leadership, and management skills. Courses in public speaking, interpersonal communication, group and team communication, conflict management, listening, interviewing, business writing, and business and professional communication typically use textbooks that present research-based techniques, strategies, and principles that focus on the development of specific *skills*. Because training is about skill development, skill-oriented textbooks offer a wealth of information appropriate for training sessions. Many textbooks also offer digests of theory and research principles; the information about skills will be more valuable than theoretical postulates.

Periodicals. Another important source of materials is in the **periodicals** section of the library. Periodicals are cyclically published works like magazines and research journals. These come out on a periodic basis (such as twice a year or quarterly); hence the term *periodicals*. Because they are published several times a year, periodicals are very likely to have more current information than do books. Finding the right journal with the information you need is not difficult if you know where to look. Rather than pulling all the periodicals off the shelf and exhaustively thumbing through them to find relevant articles, it is much better to use indexes. An index is a listing that allows you to search many periodicals at once to find articles on a certain topic. Using various periodical indexes (such as *The Reader's Guide to Periodical Literature, ERIC, Psy Lit, Social Science Abstracts,* and *CommSearch*), you can quickly find current and relevant articles and research reports on your topics in many different magazines or journals. The periodical index will include date, article title, author, periodical name (e.g., *Newsweek*,

Training and Development Journal, Communication Quarterly, Journal of Applied Communication, Training Directors Journal, The Academy of Management, Small Group Research, or *American Psychologist*), page numbers, and even the call number for the periodical.

Full-Text Databases. A full-text database is an electronic depository of information found on the Web or a CD-ROM that provides not only bibliographic data but also full texts of articles or information that you need. Periodicals are the most common type of resources available in full-text format, but some newspapers and government documents can also be found in this format. Among the most popular full-text databases are *LEXIS-NEXIS, CARL UnCover, ERIC, ABI/Inform,* and *Periodical Abstracts.* Your librarian can help assist you in locating and using these full-text databases.

Newspapers. If you can relate your training to events that are happening now, you can give your training immediacy and focus the attention of your trainees on the relevancy of your training. Most libraries have only the latest newspapers in their racks available for immediate use. Back issues are typically transferred to microfilm or available on CD-ROM or another electronic database. To help you locate news stories in newspapers, consult the *National Newspaper Index* and *NewsBank;* these indexes will help you locate information in a number of medium-to-large newspapers.

Reference Resources. Perhaps you need a statistic, definition, quotation, or other piece of information as an attention-catching set induction for your training. If so, you'll be likely to find what you need by consulting the many different types of references resources available in most libraries. Increasingly, many reference resources are available on the Web or from CD-ROM sources. Here's a brief description of the typical reference resources you can find in the library or on line.

- *Encyclopedias:* An encyclopedia may be just what you need to come up with a quick description of a term, concept, or process. The *Encyclopedia Britannica* and *Encyclopedia Americana* are popular encyclopedias that are available in most libraries. An online version of the Encyclopedia Britannica is now available at www.brittannnica.com/.
- *Dictionaries:* The classic *Oxford English Dictionary* (often simply called the *OED*) is the most comprehensive dictionary of the English language. You'll find it on the Web at www.oed.com/. *Webster's Collegiate Dictionary* or *The American Heritage Dictionary* are popular dictionaries for desktop use.
- *Books of quotations: The Oxford Dictionary of Quotations* and *Bartlett's Familiar Quotations* are two of the most popular books of quotations. An early edition of *Bartlett's* is available online at: www.bartleby.com/100/.
- *Almanacs and yearbooks:* When you need a statistic or fact to clarify or support an idea, you'll probably find it in one of many almanacs and yearbooks. *The Statistical Abstract of the United States* is published annually by the Census Bureau and includes statistical profiles of virtually every aspect of American life; it's available online at www.census.gov/statab/www/. *The World Almanac* is another rich source of statistics and data.

Government Documents.   The federal government publishes information on almost every subject you can think of. Documents published by the government are usually located in a specific area of the library called the government-document section. *The Catalog of U.S. Government Publications*, available online at www.access.gpo.gov/su_docs/locators/cgp/index.html, is the most important index of government documents. Using this index can help you find precisely what you need.

Expert Resources

Besides the vast amount of information available from the Web or library sources, another helpful external route to obtaining training content is to talk with educators and professionals. Practitioners and educators who are encountering organizational problems on a daily basis can give you cutting-edge knowledge of current training topics and can provide problem-based strategies for specific training content. One option available for gaining this type of information would be to contact CEOs, managers, and supervisors in corporations or nonprofit organizations. Names, positions, and contact information can be easily obtained by visiting corporate Web pages, calling main corporate offices, or actually visiting corporate headquarters. Attending public corporate meetings or conferences would also be helpful in gaining access to these individuals. Another option would be to contact corporate training offices, consultants, or scholars who are hired by corporations to deal with training and development. These people will have great insight into current training topics and materials and corporate training needs.

Commercial Sources

Another rich source of training content and materials can be found in current published training books and manuals or even training Web sites. Bookstores and online book business sites will have a wealth of listings that may prove useful to you as you search for training content. Many training or publishing companies have books, packages, workbooks, and videotape series they want to market and sell on various training topics. An afternoon at the local bookstore, on the Web, or in the library will be extremely fruitful in locating materials for your training topic.

When reviewing published training materials, make certain that the information and skills presented are based on research and not based only on the "armchair reflections" of the author. How can you tell if the information and conclusions you're reading are based on research? Note whether the author of the material includes footnotes or references to the source of information presented. A book that presents lists of skills, techniques, and strategies but includes few if any references to support the prescriptions should not be used to develop training content. As with any external source of information, consider the credibility and accuracy of the information you use.

Another search option for external sources would be to take a glance at the various training advertisements or outlines of commercially prepared training material that can be found in training mail-outs, airplane magazines, and training magazines. This can provide a good overview of the types of general and specific training topics that are currently on the market. Typically the most popular training materials and topics advertised will be the ones that corporations need (and thus are paying for). A review of current business literature or perhaps business needs from contemporary business publications can provide not only content but also ideas for the organization thereof as well. Taking a training session yourself on a particular topic of interest can provide you a good idea of the typical content covered (and even its usefulness). Just a caution: If you use this option, you need to make very sure that you do not take the material from such a session and adopt it as your own for presentation. This would be unethical and could result in a lawsuit. More considerations on ethical and copyright issues will be discussed later in this chapter.

Processing External Materials

Once you have assembled a large collection of information for your training session, you must sort and process it. Material in its bulk, raw form needs to be refined and assessed. The next step is to evaluate the quality, credibility, and usability of the material you've gathered.

Evaluating the Material

To evaluate the quality of the material you've gathered, consider whether the material relates to your objectives, is appropriate for the amount of time you have to train, is appropriate for the cultural background of the trainees, and is at an appropriate level for the trainees.

Relevance to Objectives.   One of the most important considerations is whether the information you've gathered helps you achieve the training objectives that you've developed. You may have found some interesting information to present, but if it does not help you achieve your training objectives, which were based upon the needs of the trainees, don't be tempted to use it simply because it's available.

Appropriateness for the Training Time Period.   Deciding what material to use in developing your training content also depends upon how much time you have for your training session. You'll obviously have to be much more selective in using material you've gleaned if you're presenting a one- or two-hour training session. Does your personal experience narrative fit well in a particular section, given the topic or the time constraints of the session?

Appropriateness for the Cultural Background of the Trainees.   It's important to consider whether the information and skills you plan to present are appropriate for the culture and background of your training group. Sometimes management and productivity strategies (such as "quality circles") may work well in some contexts (e.g., group-oriented Japanese organizational culture) and not work well in others (e.g., individualistically oriented U.S. organizational culture).

Appropriateness for the Intellectual Background of the Trainees.   In addition to considering the cultural background of the trainees, it's also useful to consider whether the information is appropriate for the knowledge and educational levels of the trainees. Scholarly research summaries are often too technical for your intended trainee audience. You may need to "translate," summarize, or apply information you've gleaned into a form that is useful and understandable to your training group. Scholarly information may be good, but you may simply not want to use it.

Information from pop or junk magazines or publications found in the grocery store checkout lines lacks sufficient credibility or documentation to be used as resource material. The key is that you want to find and use content that is understandable, credible, useful, based on sound research, and relevant to your specific group of trainees. Table 5.1 provides a rating scale to help you evaluate training materials.

Though most libraries are automated with intuitive tools for locating information, if you are unsure how to search for sources or have questions about the credibility of a source, don't forget to ask the friendly reference librarian for help. Librarians are trained professionals and can show you how to search for your topic of interest as well as evaluate the appropriateness and credibility of the research you gather.

Considering Copyright Laws

Once you've conducted your research, another important issue to consider is whether the material you've gathered is protected under copyright laws. If it is, you've got more work to do before you can use it in your training program. Typically, if someone has published an article, book, cartoon, speech, software, music, or poem and you want to use it in your training session, you have to acknowledge the author as the originator and use the published material with the written permission of the copyright holder. The copyright holder will often charge a fee for using the information or material if you are using the information to make a profit. The court battle in the 1990s between the Microsoft corporation and the Macintosh Computer corporation over the "computer desktop" idea and construction was a prime example of a product format from one company that was different but close enough to another company's idea and product that a lawsuit ensued. As a trainer, it is advantageous to play it safe. When in doubt,

TABLE 5.1   Evaluating External Materials

To what degree:	Low				High
1. Is this material relevant to your training purpose?	1	2	3	4	5
2. Is this material relevant to your trainees in their context?	1	2	3	4	5
3. Is this material from a credible source?	1	2	3	4	5
4. Is this material documentable?	1	2	3	4	5
5. Is this material useful?	1	2	3	4	5
6. Is this material understandable to your audience?	1	2	3	4	5
7. Is this material in usable form?	1	2	3	4	5
8. Is this material relevant to the training objectives?	1	2	3	4	5
9. Is this material relevant to the needs of the trainees?	1	2	3	4	5

write to the copyright holder for permission. Even if you just use part of someone else's material, you still have to obtain permission. Usually, if you are using over 250 words from someone else, you need to obtain permission. And even one line of poetry or a brief line from a song is protected under copyright laws.

Most training corporations that produce commercial material for use in training seminars will require you to purchase their materials for each trainee in your training group. For example, if you want to use a copyrighted case study, you will be required to purchase a copy of the case study and materials to debrief the case study from the copyright holder for each person you train. Some educational materials can be used with written permission from the author(s). But there are key differences in copyright restrictions with respect to the type of training sessions you intend to present. There are many materials and ideas that you can freely use and share in academic settings, such as university classrooms (with appropriate source citation, of course), that you simply cannot use in a professional training context where you are being paid a consulting fee. For example, The Personal Report of Communication Apprehension instrument—an evaluation tool constructed by communication scholars James McCroskey and Virginia Richmond—can be used in nonprofit educational settings such as a college classroom.[2] You just need to properly cite the source and give credit to the authors. If you are making money from a training product or the training itself, or are conducting the training for a for-profit organization, a new light is cast on materials you use in the sessions. In such a situation, you should use only public domain materials (materials that are not copyrighted or materials for which the copyright has expired), develop original materials yourself, or obtain legal written permission, which may involve paying royalties to the original sources of the material.

What's the procedure for obtaining permission for materials you wish to use? You write to the person or publishing company who holds the copyright to the material. You'll find the name and usually the address of the copyright holder on the title page of the material you are using. If you do not know the address of the material owner, contacting the publisher of the material is a good place to search for this information. If the owner is willing to grant permission, the normal procedure is for you to get a signed release form to keep in your files. The publisher of the book you are now reading, Allyn & Bacon, offers suggested wording for a release form. Here is an example based on their suggested wording that could be used to secure permission for training materials:

> May I have your permission to include this material in my distribution of materials for training seminars that I will present? These rights will in no way restrict republication of your material in any other form by you or others authorized by you. Should you not control these rights in their entirety, would you please tell me who does? . . . The undersigned hereby represents that the undersigned has the right to grant the permission requested herein and that the material does not infringe upon the copyright or other rights of third parties. The undersigned is the owner/author of such materials.

A space is provided at the bottom of the statement for the signature and date. Though this seems like a great deal of effort, you would certainly want someone else to do this for any training materials you develop. Editors and publishers of the materials you want to use can also be very helpful in providing guidelines for how you can use their materials in your training sessions.

Citing the Material

It is important that you do not use material that was authored by someone other than yourself without giving proper credit. This includes ideas, drawings, photographs, charts, and cartoons. To give credit means that you footnote or clearly reference the source of the information. **Plagiarism** is the use of ideas, words, and work of others as if it was your own. Using someone else's materials as if they are yours is theft. If you are unsure about any materials you want to use, you should not assume it is acceptable to use them. Employ the principle: "When in doubt, check it out" or "When in doubt, cite." Similarly, when in doubt, seek written permission to use the materials in your training session. At a minimum, you must always cite the source of your information. Normally, however, you cannot stop here. It is important to get written permission for any materials you want to use.

Citing external sources has another dimension in training. Keeping in mind the audience, you must make sure to cite your sources in an audience-centered manner.[3] Trainee audiences are characteristically different from college students. In an academic journal, the essay is generally heavily sprinkled with names, dates, and page number

---

RECAP

Processing External Materials: What to Do

1. Evaluate the quality, credibility, and usability of the material, especially with your audience in mind. Determine the following:
   - What is the source of the material?
   - What is the authority and credibility of the source?
   - Is the source biased?
   - Can this material be applied in the trainee context?
2. Discover who owns materials you want to use in your training sessions and what the use restrictions are for these copyrighted materials.
   - Check the bibliography of the source.
   - If the author cannot be determined from this information, write to the publisher of the materials.
   - Ask the publisher about the restrictions for copyrighted materials.
3. Follow procedures carefully for soliciting and obtaining permission to use copyrighted materials.
   - Contact the publisher and author (by letter, fax, or e-mail).
   - Tell them who you are and what material you would like to use.
   - Tell them why, how, when, and with whom you want to use this material.
   - If the copyright holder agrees to grant permission for you to use the material, ask him or her to sign a release form granting permission and return the form to you (sometimes the publisher has a release form that could be used).
   - Keep your letters and signed release forms on file.

citations or footnote references. This format is appropriate for an academic audience. Scholars want to know instantly while reading where various ideas and concepts originate and want to be able to quickly cross-reference and check them. Academic readers need to be able to look up sources and compare perspectives with other scholarly sources. Trainees, however, do not have the same mindset and need when reading a training manual. Trainees are focused on learning the new skill to help them with their job. They need to be able to digest and apply new concepts quickly in ways that will produce a practical outcome. They are less concerned about citations than is an academic scholar. Constantly running into citation after citation in the training material is likely to frustrate and bore typical trainees. You need to make the citations available but unobtrusive for trainees in training material. Using footnotes within the text and including a bibliography page at the end of your training materials will be the most audience-friendly way to cite sources for trainees. You may also put the bibliographical citation in smaller print at the bottom of the page of material.

Sample Training Content Outlines

As you begin to assemble your need-centered training content and activities, we've noted that it is important to review what already exists in the training market. What skills and content are typically covered in a training session on your topic? In what order are they presented? You'll find that many training programs cover similar concepts, but do so from different perspectives and in different ways. Though there are similarities between training programs on a given topic, there will generally be something unique to every program. Typically what makes a training program unique is its adaptation to the special needs of the trainees. After reviewing existing program outlines, identify what is missing or what is not being addressed. Most importantly: *What skills and content are missing that your trainees need?*

The following brief outlines are designed to illustrate typical training content outlines. In many cases, a training content outline resembles a task analysis that we discussed in Chapter 3; it presents an overview of the steps needed to enhance the skill being taught. The difference between the training content outline and the task analysis is that the content outline may not be as detailed as the task analysis. But, similar to a task analysis, *training content outlines should emphasize skills, not theory.* Because we've stressed the importance of meeting trainees' needs, we recommend that you always customize your training content to your specific training situation. The sample outlines we include in this chapter should be used as a point of departure for developing training content. Specifically, outlines are provided on the topics of improving listening skills, conflict management skills, and skills for conducting effective meetings.

Improving Listening Skills

People are likely to receive more training about speaking than listening. Sometimes the results of listening deficiencies or bad habits are merely annoying in a business context. Other times, the results are disastrous and cost the individual and company much in time and money. The following outline presents content and skills that are typically covered in a listening skill-building training program.

Improving Listening Skills
The need for effective listening
Why don't we listen well? How to identify barriers to effective listening
    Identifying **physical barriers**
    Identifying **semantic barriers**
    Identifying **psychological barriers**
How to overcome bad listening habits
    How to avoid formulating a response while someone is talking
    How to avoid interrupting others
    How to avoid multitasking while someone is talking to you
    How to avoid mentally finishing sentences and concepts for the person before he or she does
    How to avoid focusing on external factors (e.g., speaker appearance) rather than the message
How to improve listening skill
    How to assess current listening strengths and weaknesses
    How to promote awareness of strengths and weaknesses
    How to overcome barriers to effective listening
    How to focus all attention on the speaker while he or she is speaking
    How to be objective and open to what the other person is saying
    How to engage in active listening
How to improve empathy skills
    How to tune out distractions and focus on the other person
    How to increase awareness of nonverbal cues
    How to comprehend spoken messages
    How to imagine what others may be feeling
    How to check perceptions
How to improve feedback skills
    How to provide responses that are accurate
    How to provide responses that are timely
    How to provide responses that are supportive

Conflict Management Skills

One of the most popular and most frequently requested training topics is that of managing conflict. Contemporary perspectives suggest that conflict serves a constructive purpose if managed properly. Without an understanding of conflict, how it operates, where it comes from, and, more importantly from a training standpoint, how to manage it, problem situations that arise can damage employee morale, slow productivity, cause employee turnover, and effectively slow or halt the achievement of organizational goals. The following outline provides initial ideas for the skills that are covered in conflict management training sessions.

Conflict Management Skills
How to identify causes of conflict
How to identify types of conflict
    Intrapersonal conflict
    Interpersonal conflict
    Role conflict
How to identify conflict stages
    Prior conditions
    Frustration awareness
    Active conflict
    Resolution
    Follow-up
How to identify effects of conflict to make conflict constructive
    Strategies for identifying destructive conflict
    Strategies for identifying constructive conflict
How to identify and assess conflict styles
    Assessing the nonconfrontational style
    Assessing the confrontational style
    Assessing the cooperative style
How to manage conflict cooperatively
    How to manage emotions
    How to manage communication
    How to manage goals
    How to manage issues and problems

Managing Meetings

Most business employees have participated in unproductive meetings. Frequently employees will think (and sometimes actually say out loud) "Why in the world do I have to be at this useless, droning meeting when I could be back at my desk actually getting some work done?" Given all the unproductive meetings most people have attended, participating in a well-conducted meeting is like receiving a cup of cold water in the desert. Good meetings do not happen by accident. They are planned and carefully facilitated. The following outline includes classic content for enhancing the quality of meetings.

Skills for Conducting Effective Meetings
How to identify purposes for holding meetings
    Disseminate information quickly
    Brainstorm solutions for group problems
    Obtain information from group members
    Assessment and evaluation
How to avoid common problems for meetings
    Insufficient cause or need
    Unclear communication of purpose, time, and necessary preparation

Physical and psychological distractions in meeting location
Bad timing for meeting
Starting and ending late
No clear meeting agenda
Meeting does not accomplish purposes
Topics not on agenda take over the meeting
Interpersonal problems in the meeting
Lack of participation from meeting attendees

How to plan a meeting
Make sure that there is a definite need for a meeting
Pay careful attention to date, time, and place
Notify all group members in advance
Notify all group members of information or considerations they need to have in preparation for the meeting
Send reminders for the meeting

How to develop the **meeting agenda**
Determine the meeting goal
Determine the information that needs to be presented to achieve the goal
Develop a sequence of agenda items to achieve the meeting goal

How to facilitate an effective meeting
Start on time
Provide an orientation to the agenda
Preview the planned duration of the meeting
Preview the objectives or desired results/goals for the meeting
Get into the "body" of the meeting quickly
Facilitate participation
Keep things moving; don't allow the meeting to stall
Don't allow one person to dominate the discussion
Deal politely but effectively with problem people
Move effectively from section to section

How to conclude the meeting
Review the purpose of the meeting
Summarize meeting activities
Review action steps
Preview future action/meetings
Adjourn on time

Summary

When you develop content for a training program, it is wise to have a strategic and systematic plan of approach. First you need to find relevant and current sources of content for your topic. There are many sources of information in yourself, on the Web, in the library, and from experts. Next, all of these materials need to be screened and processed. What is relevant? What is useful? How can this material be processed and used in a way that would work in a training program? You need to make sure that you cover all bases completely when it comes to copyright and permission considerations. Make sure to give credit where credit is due and gain permission to use materials when they are not your own.

Your next task is to assemble your concepts and skill steps into a training content outline that is tailored to your specific training audience. As a trainer, there are many creative and effective training approaches, materials, and activities that you can create yourself. Once you gather and create all of your materials, you need to carefully consider how to put all of your materials together in a fabulous training program, making sure to consider the range of audience needs as you do so.

QUESTIONS FOR DISCUSSION AND REVIEW

1. What are four external sources of training material? Evaluate their usefulness in developing content for a training program.

2. What are criteria for evaluating Web sources?

3. Describe at least three library sources that can help you develop training information. What are the relative strengths of each source?

4. When is it advantageous and useful to use internal sources for developing training material? When is it disadvantageous?

5. When is it necessary to obtain permission to use copyrighted material?

QUESTIONS FOR APPLICATION AND ANALYSIS

1. Sean has a draft of a training session outline, but the Internet sites he is using to provide content for his session are questionable. Develop a checklist of Internet evaluation criteria to present to Sean, so he can evaluate all of his sources and upgrade.

2. Imagine that you are being paid top dollar to present training sessions for middle management in a prestigious accounting organization. You want to assess the communication styles of your trainees and have found a useful evaluation instrument that does this nicely. Should you only cite where you got the instrument in the training booklet, or should you obtain author permission to use this instrument in your training? Discuss the steps needed for each approach.

3. Bethany is doing training on nonverbal communication for a large shipping firm. She has found a Web site that provides "research" on how people respond to men with facial hair or to men without facial hair. How does she know if the research has been conducted scientifically? How should Bethany evaluate this Web site and its information and decide whether or not to use this information in her training session?

CHAPTER

6

Using Training Methods

CHAPTER OBJECTIVES

After studying this chapter, you should be able to:

1. Recall the strengths and weaknesses of the lecture, experiential activity, and facilitated group discussion training methods.

2. Explain each of the following concepts and demonstrate how you would develop and present a lecture/discussion using each of the concepts: relevance, organization, schema, redundancy, immediacy, and engagement.

3. Compare and contrast the following types of experiential activities: case studies, simulations, role plays, and demonstrations.

4. Describe what occurs in each of the following stages when conducting an experiential activity: planning, preparing, presenting, and unpacking.

5. List and explain the four stages of the unpacking process including experience, description, inference, and transference.

6. List prompts or probing questions that will help trainees unpack the description, inference, and transference stages of the E*D*I*T process.

7. Provide examples of the following types of questions: leading, factual, direct, general, controversial, provocative, redirect, yes/no, and why/how.

8. Describe what occurs in each of the following stages when facilitating a group discussion: presenting stimulus, setting ground rules, and facilitating group interaction.

9. Demonstrate how the threaded and round robin techniques are used when facilitating a group discussion.

10. Recall and explain the significance of the four questions a trainer must answer in order to determine which training method is most appropriate.

"I cannot believe we have to do this" is a statement that many trainees mumble under their breaths when trainers ask them to participate or get involved in the training content. Some instructors ask their trainees to role-play scenarios or to work through simulations. Others ask their trainees to demonstrate a process or to make formal presentations. What some trainees don't understand is that most trainers have a method to the madness they create in the training classroom.

Most professional trainers simply do not walk into the training classroom, "work their magic," and "poof!" learning occurs. It's not that easy. What many trainees don't see is the many hours of preparation that it takes a trainer to remain effective in the training classroom. As a trainee, if you learn something new and the learning was fun and somewhat effortless, you can be assured that your trainer invested *numerous* hours out of the training classroom making it happen. Most of this time was in developing a training method, which is the focus of this chapter.

A **training method** is the procedure you use to present the training content (discussed in Chapter 5) to demonstrate the behaviors you want trainees to learn. Many trainers use a variety of methods not only to convey their content, but also to get trainees involved with the training content. Some professional trainers open a training session with a short lecture and then move into an activity where trainees are asked to use the training content. Once this is finished, trainees are then placed in small discussion groups where they're asked to apply the training content to different situations. What most trainees don't see is that all this activity is a carefully orchestrated training method designed to enhance their learning.

There are several different types of methods that trainers use in the training classroom. We're going to discuss three of the more popular categories of methods: lecturing, conducting experiential activities, and facilitating group discussions. While reviewing each training method, we will discuss the advantages and disadvantages of the method and then show how you can develop and use the method. This chapter concludes with our recommendations for how to select the best method for your training program.

Lecturing

Lecturing remains one of the most popular training methods among trainers. Being a student, you're quite familiar with the lecture method. Many professors use the lecture in their courses. In a **lecture,** trainers use oral messages to impart large amounts of prepared information to trainees using one-way communication. Trainers are the source of the information, and trainees are the receivers of the information.

Advantages of Lecturing

Here are a few of the reasons that professional trainers use the lecture as the predominant training method.

Lecturing Is Economical.   As a trainer, you will quickly learn that you never have enough time with your students. Time is always your enemy. With the lecture, you can cover a lot of new information in a short amount of time, because the lecture method doesn't encourage feedback from or interaction with trainees.

Lecturing Gives the Trainer Control.   Trainers have command of what occurs in the training classroom. Because the lecture primarily involves one-way communication, trainers can manage the flow of information with greater precision. They know what to expect. When you conduct an experiential activity with your trainees, which is the second category of methods we're going to review, you never quite know how it's going to work. You never know how your trainees will react to the activity. With the lecture method, your uncertainty is reduced considerably. To many new trainers, this reduction in uncertainty is comforting.

Lecturing Is Flexible.   The lecture training method can be used for any size of training class. You're not limited to a particular number of students. You can lecture to a small group of five just as well as you can lecture to a group of 400. As the size of the group increases, most lecturers enhance their lecture presentation by adding appropriate audio and visual aids.

Disadvantages of Lecturing

There are also a number of disadvantages when trainers use the lecture method poorly.

Lecturing Can Become Trainer-Centered Rather than Trainee-Centered.   Because the lecture remains economical and is controllable, many trainers simply "talk at" their students rather than "communicate with" their students. Do you remember Charlie Brown's schoolteacher, Ms. Othmar, who "talked at" her students? To Charlie, her lecture sounded like "Whaaaaaawhawhawhawha." He never understood what she was saying. Lecturers who "communicate with" their students are more trainee-centered and invest time monitoring trainees' verbal and nonverbal feedback behaviors to check for understanding. They ask trainees for feedback to see if their lectures make sense. If trainees express confusion, effective lecturers adapt and make the necessary adjustments.

Lecturing Can Fail to Engage Trainees.   Poor lecturers also fail to engage trainees in the learning process. If you'll recall from Chapter 2, the more active adult learners become in the learning process, the more likely they are to remember the information.[1] If you will recall from Figure 4.2 in Chapter 4, we tend to remember more of what we've learned as we become more involved with our learning. We retain 10 percent of what we read, 20 percent of what we hear, 30 percent of what we see, 50 percent of what we hear and see, 70 percent of what we say, and 90 percent of what we both say and do.[2] Clearly, training methods that encourage active involvement enhance learning outcomes. And just because you're lecturing doesn't mean that your trainees have to be passive learners. There are a number of ways to engage them while presenting a lecture. We'll discuss these engagement strategies later in this chapter.

Lecturing Can Become Boring to Trainees.   If you're like most students, you can only listen to someone lecture for so long. Based on a study by the U. S. Department of Health, Education, and Welfare, we retain only 20 percent of what we hear.[3] If you want your trainees to remember your training content, they must first pay attention to it. Research suggests that our ability to pay attention is limited, and we can only attend to a few things at once.[4] In fact, there are a number of stimuli in training environments that compete for our attention. Sometimes trainees pay attention to the trainer's lecture. At other times, they pay attention to the handsome man or woman in the third row. Learning how to capture and recapture trainees' attention is addressed in the next section, which focuses on how to develop and present a lecture.

Developing and Presenting a Lecture/Discussion

Even though the lecture has a number of strengths, it's usually ranked low in terms of popularity by students and with good reason. Many trainees complain that the lecture remains too trainer focused and doesn't allow trainees to interact and discuss the content. Although these complaints are valid in many training rooms, it's usually the *lecturer* and not the *method* that remains problematic. A lecture doesn't have to be boring. The traditional lecture can be modified in ways to take advantage of its strengths and minimize its weaknesses. The modified lecture, or what we're referring to as the lecture/discussion, focuses on conveying a lot of new and prepared information to trainees in a short amount of time, but the information is presented in a manner where it is *perceived* as being interactive or as a discussion between the trainer and trainees. The important word here is *perceived*. It's not really an interactive discussion, because it's next to impossible to have a discussion when you have a number of trainees and time remains limited. But you can modify a lecture so that it's more focused on the needs of the trainee. Following are a few strategies for how to modify the traditional lecture to make it more interactive. Many of these strategies were introduced in Chapter 2, which examined how adults learn, including relevance, organization, schema development, redundancy, engagement, and immediacy.[5]

Create Relevance.   Effective trainers make lecture content relevant or useful for trainees. Trainees should never be asking, "Why do we have to know this stuff?" or "Why do we have to do this?" Let your trainees know up front why the training content remains important to them and their work. Or better yet, ask them why they should be interested in your topic. Remember, it's always better to get a message out of your trainees rather than putting one in them, so to speak. If you're having a difficult time convincing your trainees that your training is valuable, then you need to ask yourself if the training is really necessary. Many trainees resist change unless they're convinced that a new procedure or set of behaviors will make their work easier. It's your job to show them *how* the training content will improve their work life.

Organize Content.   For North American trainees, effective trainers develop and present lectures that are well organized and chunked. An effective lecture tells a story. There's an introduction, body, and conclusion. In the introduction, trainers stimulate trainees' interest by leading off with a story, using an interesting visual aid, presenting a relevant case problem, or asking a provocative question. Before leaving the introduction and moving into the body of their lecture, trainers **preview** their lecture, or let trainees know what's ahead. In the body of the lecture, trainers organize or chunk their content around three or four main points or ideas. To help orient trainees, trainers are encouraged to use signposting and internal review/previews. A **signpost** is a message that trainers use to help trainees know where they are within a lecture. An example of a signpost might be, "The first point is . . . The second point is . . . The third point is . . ." An **internal review/preview** is a message that trainers use to let trainees know where they've been and where they're going within the lecture. In the conclusion, trainers provide a **review**, which is a summary of the lecture content, letting trainees know where they've been.

Effective lecturers also help trainees remember information by chunking information into manageable and meaningful units. If you're training others on how to resolve conflict, find a way to break the conflict resolution process down into steps or stages that can be easily processed. You're also encouraged to use **mnemonic** devices, also known as memory aids or memory shortcuts. An acronym is an example of a mnemonic device, where each letter in the acronym stands for something, such as "TGIF," or "Thank God It's Friday."

Develop a Schema.   Effective trainers teach their trainees how to interpret or understand training content by developing either new schema or by tapping into a trainee's existing schema. If you will recall from Chapter 2, a **schema** is an organization system or a "category" of information. One way to develop a schema for students is to provide them with a partial outline of your lecture notes. For example, if you're teaching trainees how to develop and deliver a persuasive presentation, and they've never had any formal instruction in public speaking, it will be necessary to give them a blueprint for how to take notes during your lecture. Without a schema, trainees invest too much time trying to figure out how to organize their lecture notes. When they do this, they miss the lecture content. Your partial outline not only helps trainees take notes better, but it also keeps them engaged by filling in the missing pieces of the outline.

For some training topics, trainees might already have an existing schema. Using the same example from above, assume that your trainees have already had a training seminar in how to prepare and present an informative speech. They understand the speechmaking process. They have an existing schema for speech making. With an existing schema, show trainees how persuasive speaking differs from informative speaking. When trainees have an existing schema in place, trainers can cover more content in less time.

Build in Redundancy.   Remain redundant. Effective trainers repeat and reiterate information as well as highlight important information. Not all students understand your message the first time they hear it. **Repeating** happens when you restate the content in the same exact way. With **reiteration,** you restate the content, but in different ways. You use different examples to illustrate the training content. Anticipate where your trainees are going to get confused and have multiple examples available to illustrate your concepts and ideas.

Also, because lectures have a tendency to be "information rich," which means that you cover a lot of information in a short amount of time, it's necessary to highlight important and critical information. If you don't highlight critical information, trainees may fail to discriminate between what's important and what's less important. Keep focused on your learning objectives. What is critical that your trainees understand in order to complete a particular task? One way to highlight information is by using a **feedforward message** or a message that informs the trainee of how the information is to be processed. "If you don't understand this stage of the conflict management process, then you're not going to be successful in managing conflict in your life," or "What I'm about to tell you is incredibly important," are examples of feedforward messages that highlight information.

Be Immediate.   Effective trainers deliver lectures using an immediate delivery style. **Immediacy,** as we will discuss in more detail in Chapter 9, is a perception of physical or psychological closeness and is created by using certain verbal and nonverbal messages.[6] We are attracted to those who are immediate, and we have a tendency to avoid those who are nonimmediate. For example, we can enhance our attractiveness to others by using people's names, leaning forward, nodding our heads, using appropriate gestures, and looking people in the eyes when communicating with them. When these behaviors are conveyed using an appropriate level of enthusiasm, people pay attention. When lecturers fail to remember our names, lean backward, remain stiff, cross their arms, and fail to look us in the eyes when communicating with us, our attention spans wander. In fact, we perceive these trainers to be cold, chilly, and uncaring. They lack the warmth and closeness of immediate lecturers.

Other ways to be perceived as immediate is by appropriate self-disclosing who you are to your students[7] and by telling personal stories and using appropriate forms of humor.[8] This personalizes the information and makes you and the information you're sharing with your trainees real. In your lecture, show students how you use the information and/or why the information has meaning to you. This will help them see the relevance of the lecture content, all the while making you an individual that they might identify with rather than just a lecturer or someone from the training department.

Engage Trainees.   An **engagement strategy** is any type of communication message that encourages trainees to reflect on or to interact with the information they're receiving. Remember, adult learners want to take an active role in what they learn. They bring experience to the classroom, and they know what they need to learn. Effective trainers find ways to engage their students in the lecture/discussion. They find ways to apply the principles of andragogy, reviewed in Chapter 2, into the lecture/discussion. Two weaknesses that trainers have to overcome when using the lecture method are (1) keeping students' attention focused on the training content and (2) finding ways to get students interacting with the training content, with each other, and with the trainer. Your job is to keep trainees from mentally "checking out." Here are a few of our suggestions:

- *Use stimulus prompts:* A **stimulus prompt** is a partial statement or question that requires trainees to complete the statement or answer the question. "Listening is a five stage process that includes _____, _____, _____, _____, and _____," is an example of a stimulus prompt statement. "Will someone review for us the listening process?" is an example of a stimulus prompt question. Using stimulus prompts throughout the lecture keeps trainees engaged in the lecture process and keeps them interacting with the lecture content. It makes the lecture more interactive. They hear each other's voices. It gives the impression that the lecture is really a discussion.
- *Ask rhetorical questions:* **Rhetorical questions** are questions that don't require answers. Rhetorical questions are usually provocative and sometimes personal; they ask trainees to reflect on their lives and work experiences. For example, a trainer who is conducting a communication workshop for new management trainees might ask "What do you not like about your current manager's communication style?" The trainer doesn't necessarily want a verbal response to this question, but instead wants management trainees to think about what it is about their current manager's communication style that bugs them. Trainers will then use this mental state as a springboard to begin the lecture or to transition into a new idea within the lecture.
- *Ask trainees to complete a personal thought inventory, or a PTI: A **PTI** not only is an engagement strategy but also gives trainers feedback on how they are doing in the training classroom. Whenever you sense a lull in the lecture, or you feel as though you're losing your students, ask them to pull out a half sheet of paper and respond to the following three questions that relate to a concept discussed in the lecture: (1) What is the concept? (2) Why is the concept important? and (3) How do you see yourself using the concept? If time permits, ask for volunteers to respond to the questions in class. If time doesn't permit, ask trainees to turn in their PTIs at the end of the lecture. Again, the PTI serves a couple of purposes. The first is that it gets trainees engaged and interacting with the lecture content

and its application; and the second is that it allows the trainer to get some much-needed feedback from trainees. It allows trainers to assess how they're doing and gives them the opportunity to make the necessary adjustments the next time the lecture is presented.

- *Ask trainees to engage in seatmate discussions:* Ask them to discuss their responses to their PTI with a seatmate or ask trainees to discuss with their seatmate how they might apply a particular concept to the workplace.
- *Ask trainees to journal:* Journaling works especially well with training programs that focus on interpersonal communication. One way to remember this engagement strategy is the formula: journal, lecture, diagnose, recommend. Here's how

RECAP
Developing and Presenting a Lecture/Discussion

Technique	Definition	Explanation
Create relevance.	Making training content useful	Show trainees how training content will improve their performance.
Organize content.	Telling a story with your training content	Use introduction, body, and conclusion. Chunk the body of the training content. Use previews, reviews, and signposts.
Develop a schema.	Developing an organizational system for trainees to help them receive and process training content	Give trainees a partial outline or an incomplete diagram that they complete while completing the training program.
Build in redundancy.	Restating training content	Use multiple examples to illustrate the same training concept or idea. Repeat your ideas.
Be immediate.	Creating physical and psychological closeness with trainees	Be nonverbally expressive and animated. Use appropriate self-disclosure and humor; reveal personal anecdotes.
Engage trainees.	Communicating in a way that causes trainees to reflect on or interact with training content	Use stimulus prompts, rhetorical questions, personal thought inventories, and journaling.

you can apply this technique. Before lecturing on conflict management, ask trainees to *journal*, or write about a conflict they recently encountered. Ask them to describe the conflict and how the conflict was processed. Ask them to detail the communication behaviors that were used. Now, present a *lecture* on how to resolve conflict constructively. Next, ask trainees to apply the lecture content to their journal entry and ask them to *diagnose* their conflict encounter. What worked, and what did not work? Why? They can add this to their journal entry, or they can discuss it with their seatmate. Finally, ask them to make *recommendations* for their next conflict. What behaviors do they want to continue using? What behaviors do they want to change? Again, this can be done through journaling or through a seatmate discussion.

Conducting Experiential Activities

An **experiential activity** is any training activity that requires trainees to involve themselves physically and/or psychologically in the training content. In other words, trainees experience first hand what it is you're training them to do. Examples of experiential activities include case studies, role plays, and demonstrations. Unlike these experiential activities, which require group training, it's also important to remember **on-the-job training,** otherwise known as OTJ, where trainees receive individualized training and coaching that is job specific while performing the actual job. Although some consider on-the-job training to be a superior experiential training method, many trainers do not have the time to coach trainees on an individual basis. Conducting group experiential activities is one way to meet the time crunch that many trainers face. The following paragraphs review some of the more popular types of experiential activities: case studies, simulations, project-based learning, role plays, and demonstrations.

A **case study** is a narrative or short story about some organizational issue where a problem, the history of the problem, and the characters involved with the problem are described in detail. Case studies are usually taken from the daily headlines and describe actual problems that exist in organizations. Trainees are then expected to put themselves into the case study and solve the problem. Here is where students apply the content they have been learning in the training program. Most case studies address organizational problems and are effective in helping trainees apply problem-solving models. One case study resource that may be useful to new communication trainers is Peterson's *Communicating in Organizations.*[9] This resource contains a variety of case studies showcasing organizational communication problems along with questions that guide trainees through the case studies.

In a **simulation,** trainees are given a set of circumstances and are asked to play or enact certain roles in order to resolve a communication-related problem. Like case studies, simulations are beneficial in helping trainees apply training content. Unlike the case study method, where trainees usually read and respond to a particular study, simulations take a bit longer and are more involved. With simulations, trainees involve themselves more thoroughly in the decision-making process. Many simulations are conducted using sophisticated computer software programs where trainees see how their decisions affect other aspects of organizational life. They learn that all decisions have positive and negative consequences. Simulations also help trainees evaluate the quality of decisions.

Project-based learning, or what many trainers refer to as PBL, is similar to the case study and simulation experiential activities; however, trainees process actual work-based problems rather than hypothetical case studies or simulations. With PBL, trainees learn by taking the principles and skills they're receiving in the training classroom and applying them immediately to projects and problems they face on the job. This type of experiential learning can be time consuming and works best in a training program that has several sessions to it or several follow-up meetings. The advantage to this type of learning is that it remains incredibly relevant to the trainee.

A **role play** encourages a trainee to act out a particular part in a communication transaction. Many simulations might include role plays; but, unlike simulations, which are oftentimes prepackaged, role plays are written and enacted by trainees. They remain more authentic and personal to the trainee. Role plays have been shown to be effective in developing trainees' conflict management skills. Trainees learn by developing their own role plays and then acting them out with other colleagues. We recently developed a conflict management model for one of our training programs where trainees developed a role play, structuring it using the PUGSS model. The P represents describing the *problem,* the U achieving *understanding,* the G identifying *goals,* the first S brainstorming *solutions,* and the final S selecting the best *solution.* For each part of this model, trainees integrate communication behaviors that have been shown to be effective in resolving conflict, such as descriptive versus evaluative language, paraphrasing, perception checking, and nonverbal responsiveness. Once scripts have been written, trainees enact their role plays while other observers evaluate the enactment of the PUGSS structure and the integration of communication behaviors.

In a **demonstration,** a trainee or pairs of trainees show the class how certain communication behaviors can be used and applied. It's a form of team teaching. Rather than the trainer demonstrating the application of training content, trainees demonstrate how they see the content applying to their work units.

Advantages of Conducting Experiential Activities

There are a number of advantages to conducting experiential activities; however, only three are discussed here.

Experiential Activities Engage Trainees.   Remember, we retain 10 percent of what we read, 20 percent of what we hear, 30 percent of what we see, 50 percent of what we see and hear, 70 percent of what we say, and 90 percent of what we say and do.[10] Experiential activities require active trainee involvement. This type of engagement stimulates trainees' senses and gets them involved in the training content, both of which conditions are necessary for learning.

Experiential Activities Increase Trainees' Self-Confidence.   With many well-planned and organized experiential activities, trainees come away from the experience with an increased level of confidence. You'll hear them say, "I can do this." Most experiential activities provide a safe environment for trainees to practice communication skills. In many experiential activities, trainees also receive immediate feedback from trainers and other colleagues. This type of immediate feedback helps modify trainee behavior and allows them to succeed with the experiential activity.

Experiential Activities Help Trainees Transfer Training Content.   Having trainees participate in experiential activities allows them to see how the training content can be transferred from the training classroom to the workplace. This remains a problem in many training classrooms. The training content is informative, but many trainees ask, "How can I use this?" Well-developed and managed experiential activities are authentic and allow trainees to see real-world applications. This real-world application also enhances their motivation to participate in the experiential activity.

Disadvantages of Conducting Experiential Activities

There are also a number of disadvantages to conducting experiential activities. We're going to discuss four of them.

Experiential Activities Can Be Underdeveloped.   What appears to be a simple activity is always a bit more complicated than what most trainers anticipate. We all learn the hard way. We try to wing an activity, and it usually fails to meet the learning objective. Many activities lack clear direction. They lack organization. For example, when it's time to conduct the activity, you realize that you forgot many of the instructional supplies needed to pull off the activity. When this happens, you usually run out of time. The next section of this chapter will walk you through how to conduct an experiential activity and addresses how to avoid many of these problems.

Experiential Activities Can Be Gimmicky.   When an experiential activity is not "unpacked," or processed, trainees might say, "That was fun, but I don't get it. What was I suppose to learn?" Remember, many of your trainees are adult learners. Experiential activities must be unpacked or processed. You must help trainees see not only the value in the activity but also how the experience relates to them and their work lives. If activities are not unpacked, and many times they're not because of a lack of time, trainees may perceive it as all fun and games and a waste of their precious time. They may even grow to resent you and training in general. We will discuss how to unpack or process an experiential activity in the next section of the chapter.

Experiential Activities Can Be Artificial.   Limited training budgets make it next to impossible to re-create real workplace environments in a training classroom. We recommend you make the activity as true to life as possible but also address, up front, that all training activities have a degree of artificiality to them.

Experiential Activities Can Be Perceived as Threatening.   Many trainees do not want to participate in experiential activities for fear of embarrassment or fear of losing face in front of subordinates and superiors. The general rule of thumb is to never ask your trainees to do something that you would not want to do. You must be willing to jump in and participate in the experiential activity that you're asking your trainees to do. It's important that you create a safe environment for your trainees. The safer they perceive the training classroom to be, the more willing they are to risk losing face in front of their colleagues.

Having reviewed the advantages and disadvantages of the experiential activity training method, we're now going to show trainers how to conduct a training activity.

Managing Experiential Activities

There are five stages to conducting an experiential activity, including planning, preparing, presenting, unpacking, and assessing. The assessing stage will not be discussed in this chapter, because Chapter 11 is devoted to the assessment process.

Planning.   In this stage, you want to review your learning objectives for the training program or module. Where are you going? Your learning objectives keep you on track. Remember, learning objectives must be observable, measurable, attainable, and specific, and they address the following questions:

- Who is to perform the desired act?
- What will trainees be asked to do to demonstrate that the objective has been mastered?
- Under what conditions, with what limitations and constraints, will the behavior be performed?
- What standards will be applied to evaluate whether or not the trainee's performance is an acceptable indication of mastery?

Once you have your learning objectives, it's time to prepare.

Preparing.   In this stage, you begin brainstorming possible experiential activities. What is it that your trainees could do or experience that would help them master the learning objective? There are a number of resources available to trainers that contain teaching ideas and activities.[11] Many of these were discussed in Chapter 5. Take advantage of the library in your training and development office. Ask other more experienced trainers for some of the experiential activities they have conducted to bring about similar learning objectives. From our training experiences, most professional trainers have a repertoire of activities that are tried and true. They're usually more than willing to share their training ideas with new trainers.

Once you have an activity in mind, what is it that your trainees will need in order to accomplish the activity? Most experiential activities will require a clear set of instructions and a variety of other instructional materials such as paper, markers, videos, handouts, and the like. Clear instructions remain vital to the success of an activity. Spend time developing your instructions. It's not uncommon for trainees to get underway with an experiential activity and then find out that they forgot to tell their trainees one simple important step. This one simple important step could either make or break the activity. A number of experiential activities fail not because of uncooperative trainees, but because of underprepared trainers.

Make sure you have all of the instructional materials you'll need in order to conduct the activity. Some experiential activities are complex and require a number of instructional materials. Other activities are simple and require none. Prepare a list of the training supplies you will need to take with you to the training site. Some of the more common training supplies include: videos and VCR player, compact disks and player, overhead transparencies, preprinted handouts, flip-chart paper and markers, white-board markers, chalk, tape, and writing paper. Many professional trainers have a permanent training supply kit that contains many of these items. They take the training kit with them to every training job site.

Now, you're ready to present.

Presenting. Set the stage for your trainees. How do you set the stage? First, make sure your instructions are clear and understood; and, second, make sure your trainees have all of the instructional materials they will need for the activity. Let's begin with a few suggestions for clear instructions. Too many times, trainers get their trainees involved in an activity to learn that their instructions were not clear. The experiential activity bombs as a result of unclear instructions.

Here are a few suggestions for making your instructions as clear as possible. Write them out step by step and make sure all trainees get a copy of your instructions. Once they have a copy, ask them to read the instructions. Highlight the important parts and then see if any of the trainees have any questions. Now, ask a trainee to paraphrase your instructions in his or her own words. This will allow you to check for appropriate understanding. Because time can get away from you very quickly with experiential activities, you are encouraged to provide trainees with time guidelines. Where do they need to be, in terms of time, with each step of the activity? If your experiential activity involves group work, we recommend that you place trainees in groups first before reviewing instructions. If you don't group them first, trainees will be more concerned about self-selecting into particular groups than listening to your instructions. You will compete for their attention and lose.

Once you get your trainees involved in their experiential activity, don't kick back and take a coffee break. Manage the activity. Much can go wrong. Walk around the training room and make sure that all are on task. Monitor their group work to ensure that your instructions were clear. As you move about the room and watch your trainees engage in the activity, you will realize that you need to refine some of your instructions. Make the necessary adjustments.

Now, it's time to unpack.

Unpacking. Once the activity is completed, it's time to process or "unpack" the activity with your trainees. Unpacking is when you ask your students to make sense out of the experience. You ask a series of questions to help them interpret their experiences. You want them to be able to answer: "What just happened here?" and "What does it all mean to me and my life?" Unpacking is probably one of the most important steps in conducting experiential activities. If activities are not unpacked or processed properly, your trainees may never make the important training connections. You'll hear trainees ask, "That was fun, but what was I supposed to learn?"

Leave time for unpacking your experiential activities. We recommend you allot 25 percent of your total activity time to the unpacking process. One way to unpack experiential activities is by using the E*D*I*T process.[12] **E*D*I*T** is an easily remembered acronym that represents a natural flow of activity from E, engaging in an experiential activity; to D, describing or talking about it; to I, making some generalizations or inferences beyond the activity; and finally to T, transferring the experience from the training context to other contexts such as the workplace, school, or home. The E*D*I*T process is actually a guided discussion that you have with your trainees. The next several paragraphs walk you through the E*D*I*T unpacking process by providing you with a series of questions that you can ask to help facilitate the guided discussion.

- *Experience:* Trainees participate in the experiential activity. Again, this usually takes up 75 percent of the total activity time. Reserve another 25 percent of the time to process the describe, infer, and transfer stages.
- *Describe:* This is the actual first stage of the guided discussion. During this stage you might want to ask your trainees some of the following questions to force them to describe the experience:
  - "What did they see, hear, think, feel, touch, and/or taste?"
  - "I'm blind; paint a vivid picture for me of what you saw."
  - "Rather than telling us about what happened, show us what happened."
  - When your trainees say, "I saw Tina tensing up. She had a bad attitude," ask them, "What does tensing up look and sound like?" and, "What does a bad attitude look and sound like?"

Here's what you can expect during this stage of the unpacking process. First, trainees will want to evaluate ("This was scary") rather than describe ("I saw Tina tensing up. Her body and posture became rigid and tight."). Limit the discussion to description. Second, they'll want to make inferences ("Oh, I get it. So I need to change this behavior to prevent Tina from getting defensive."). They always want to jump ahead. Keep them on track. The purpose of engaging students in this discussion is to sharpen their attention. It helps focus their attention on important details that are oftentimes ignored and that ultimately play an important role in the perception and communication processes. You (or a designated student) may want to place some of the descriptive details on the chalkboard.

- *Infer:* During this stage of the guided discussion, you want your trainees to explain what they have learned from the activity rather than from their own life experiences. "What have you learned from this experience?" is a typical probing question. You might also want to ask, "What do you know now that you did not know before this training activity?" Please limit trainees' comments to what they have learned from the experiential activity rather than from their life experiences. Ask your students to connect their experiences from the experiential activity to other training content they have been learning. When they make a claim or a statement, follow up with some of the following probes, which will help them make the necessary inferences or connections to other training content:
  - "How do you know this?"
  - "Where in the training seminar have we discussed or examined this behavior?"
  - "Based on this experience and from the other content we have been discussing, what can you now predict will happen in similar situations?"
  - "If this happens, then what else is likely to happen? Why? How?"

These probing questions allow them to see how their new knowledge, which was yielded from their experience, is grounded in training content and allows them to make informed decisions about future events or occurrences. Again, you may want to place some of these inferences on the chalkboard.

- *Transfer:* During this stage of the guided discussion, you want your trainees to transfer their experiences and new knowledge and behaviors to their personal and professional lives. Sometimes new knowledge and behaviors that are developed in training classrooms remain in the classroom and never make it to the job and home. Your training program is of no use unless we help trainees transfer their newly acquired knowledge and behaviors to the front lines of home and work. Here are a few probing questions that may help trainees with the transfer stage:

  - "How do you see yourself using this information or behaviors in your life?"
  - "When someone comes to you for advice about this issue, how will you advise or consult him or her?"
  - "What is one thing you would like to change immediately in your personal life or on the job, and how are you going to make this change?"
  - "How has this experience aided your understanding of what is happening in your own life, and what changes, if any, need to occur in order to enhance the quality of your life?"

Again, we recommend your placing some of the answers to these questions on the chalkboard. Although the E*D*I*T unpacking process may seem lengthy, with practice you can process the guided discussion and unpack an experiential activity in ten or fewer minutes. Remember, if the experiential activity is not unpacked, many trainees

---

RECAP

Unpacking an Experiential Activity Using E*D*I*T

Unpacking Stage	Unpacking Objective	Unpacking Prompts
Experience	Trainees participate in activity.	
Describe	Trainees will use descriptive versus evaluative language.	What did you see, hear, feel, taste, and touch? Rather than tell us, show us.
Infer	Trainees will connect activity with training content.	What do you know now that you didn't know before the activity? How does the book help us understand what just happened? Now, if this is true, what else can we predict?
Transfer	Trainees will explain how they will use new knowledge or behavior out of training classroom.	How do you see yourself using what you just learned? How would you inform others of what you have just learned?

will question the point of the activity and will fail to make the appropriate learning connections. Some will see it as fun and games, and others will see it as a waste of their time.

To review where we've been, we have planned, prepared, presented, and unpacked our experiential activity. Now it's time to assess, which is our final stage. When you assess your experiential activity, you want to determine if you reached your learning objectives, which were developed in the first stage of conducting experiential activities. We referred to this stage as the planning stage. Rather than going into detail here about how to assess your activity, we would like to refer you to Chapter 11, which is strictly devoted to assessing your learning objectives. If you want, jump ahead and read this chapter on assessment. If not, wait until you get to Chapter 11. Next, we're going to examine our third and final training method, which is facilitating group discussion.

Facilitating Group Discussions

A **facilitated group discussion** includes a group of three to ten trainees who interact with the assistance of a facilitator who manages the interaction and guides the discussion toward specific learning objectives. As a group facilitator, your job is to ask probing questions and then to ensure that all group members participate equally in the discussion. The discussion is guided rather than free flowing. Your job is to bring out differences of opinion, to note areas of agreement and disagreement, and to provide internal summaries. Your job is to help the group remain on task and to help the group make sense of the varied opinions. Ultimately, it's your job to lead your trainees to your learning objectives through the discussion.

Instructional research shows that one of the most effective ways to create attitudes, change attitudes, or modify attitudes is to provide a safe and open forum where individuals are allowed to voice their opinions.[13] Trainees learn more about their attitudes and beliefs by hearing themselves talk and by fielding questions from others. They learn firsthand what opinions are shared and not shared. As a result of an effective facilitated discussion, group members not only learn about their own attitudes and beliefs, but they also develop an appreciation for varied opinions and for opinions that are shared and not shared.

For some learning objectives that focus on the affective dimension of learning, a facilitated group discussion may be the most appropriate training method. For example, many of today's corporations invest huge sums of money sensitizing employees to cultural and gender diversity issues in the workplace. Many employees lack understanding of what it means to be a minority in the workplace, and others remain insensitive when it comes to sexual harassment-related issues. Learning objectives that focus on changing employees' attitudes require training methods, like the facilitated group discussion, that foster safe environments and training classrooms where communication is free from evaluation.

Advantages of Facilitating Group Discussions

Similar to the lecture and experiential activity training methods, the group discussion training method has a number of advantages and disadvantages. Let's start with three advantages.

Facilitated Group Discussion Involves All Trainees. It remains an active form of learning. As a result of everyone sharing, a variety of experiences, attitudes, values, and beliefs are discussed. This is particularly useful if your learning objectives are affectively based such as sensitizing trainees to diversity and gender-related workplace issues.

Facilitated Group Discussion Allows Trainees to Learn from Other's Experiences, Attitudes, Beliefs, and Values, Which Is Preferred among Adult Learners. They learn, firsthand, what works and what doesn't work. Through a facilitated discussion, group members can learn from each other how to transfer what they're learning in the training classroom to their job sites or workplaces. They learn which of their attitudes, beliefs, and values are shared and not shared by group members. This learning may cause some group members to question their belief system, which may be one of the learning objectives of the training program.

Facilitated Group Discussions Are Perceived as Safe. Not all trainees feel comfortable communicating in front of others. The smaller group discussion may cause some trainees to feel more comfortable encouraging them to make contributions. If it weren't for the small group discussion, we would never hear from the more shy or communication-apprehensive trainee.

Disadvantages of Facilitating Group Discussions

Three of the larger disadvantages to group discussion all stem from not having skilled facilitators. Because of the pressures facing many training departments (time and money), training managers sometime fail to train facilitators properly. Here are some common facilitation problems.

Some Facilitators Have a Difficult Time Keeping the Discussion Focused on Learning Objectives. Everyone might be engaged and enjoying the discussion; however, the discussion is off task and unrelated to the learning objectives. Trained facilitators find ways of keeping group members on task, probing and directing the flow of communication, ensuring that the learning objective will be met.

Some Facilitators Have a Difficult Time Making Sure That All Group Members Participate Equally. Sometimes we hear from only a few members of the group. These group members dominate the discussion and shut others out of the discussion. Other times, facilitators find it difficult to bring out the more shy or communication-apprehensive trainee. Trained facilitators know how to use specific communication strategies to ensure equal participation from all group members. Some of these strategies and techniques will be discussed in the next section of this chapter.

Some Facilitators Have a Difficult Time Managing Group Members' Emotions. Because the group discussion training method encourages honest and open communication, not all group members are going to be pleased or satisfied with what they hear from their fellow colleagues. We can hope that they're going to hear a variety of attitudes, values, and beliefs that run counter to what they believe. When this happens, some group members may become emotional and defensive. Trained facilitators know how to diffuse emotions that can become destructive.

Managing Group Discussions

Like any teaching method, managing a group discussion must begin with a learning objective. Remember, a facilitated group discussion is most appropriate when the learning objective focuses on creating, changing, or modifying trainees' attitudes and beliefs. One example might be an organization that wants to sensitize its employees to sexual harassment-related issues. This type of objective would be considered an affective learning objective.

Although all facilitated group discussions are different and require different types of preparation, all require a **stimulus,** which is used to provoke a reaction in trainees. Two popular stimuli include media and/or trigger questions. Media have been particularly effective in provoking discussion. Many professional training and development departments have media libraries that contain numerous videos, films, television programs, newspaper or magazines articles, and music (song lyrics), to name just a few.

Trigger questions are also useful in stimulating or provoking a discussion. **Trigger questions,** which usually remain controversial, are those that deal with claims of value (What is right and wrong, good and bad?), policy (What *should* be done?), and process (*How* should we do it?) Trigger questions cannot be answered with a simple yes or no answer. Your questions must ultimately tap into your learning objectives. Your facilitated discussion will be only as good as the questions you ask.

As a way to illustrate the use of a mediated stimulus and trigger questions, assume that you're presenting a training program and one of your objectives is to train managers in how to use effective decision-making processes. Before training others in the process, you want to first sensitize them to the effects of poor decision making. One way to do this is by showing them clips from the film *12 Angry Men.* For those who are not familiar with this film, it depicts 12 jurors who have to decide someone's guilt or innocence in a court of law. It exposes those of us who have never served on a jury before to how hastily some life-altering decisions are made. Possible follow-up trigger questions might include:

- *Value:* What *values* did you see these men using to make their decision? Was this right or wrong, good or bad? Why?
- *Process: How* was consensus reached among members of this jury?
- *Policy:* How *should* consensus be reached among members of a jury? Why?

Once you have a stimulus, you're ready to begin the three-part facilitation process: exposing trainees to stimulus; setting ground rules and making sure they're followed; and facilitating group interaction.

Expose Trainees to Stimulus.   Here are a few of our suggestions for how to process this part of the guided discussion using a mediated stimulus:

- Present trainees with a set of trigger questions that will guide their viewing of the mediated stimulus such as a film clip, video, or the like.

- Review the questions with the trainees and ensure their understanding of what it is you are asking them to look for and listen to while viewing the mediated stimulus.
- Ask trainees to view, read, and/or listen to the stimulus and then reflect on what it is they experienced.
- Ask trainees to journal their responses to your trigger questions.

Set Ground Rules and Make Sure They're Followed. Here are a few of our suggestions for setting ground rules to create a safe environment before the discussion begins:

- Do not interrupt others.
- Remain respectful of others' opinions.
- Describe rather than evaluate what it is about others' opinions that you find problematic.
- Self-disclose how others' comments and opinions make you feel.
- Remain nonverbally responsive to others.
- When you disagree, ask questions to achieve understanding.
- Realize that you can understand another's point of view without necessarily agreeing with it.
- Monitor defensive verbal and nonverbal behavior such as using evaluative language, crossed arms, rolling eyes, and deep sighs.

Facilitate Group Interaction. Here are a few of our suggestions for how to facilitate the group discussion along with verbal prompts and probes:

- Ask additional trigger questions. Usually, these are the same questions that guided the trainees' viewing of the video. Other trigger questions might include: Where did you see yourself in this video clip? Do you agree with what just happened in this video clip? Why? Why not?
- See that all group members contribute to the group discussion in a safe manner. "Remember, all comments are respected and valued."
- Provide internal summaries whenever and wherever needed. "Let me review what's been discussed thus far . . ."
- Probe students' comments and raise additional questions. "How do you know that?" "What did you see and hear that led you to that evaluation of your coworker?"
- Continually redirect conversation in order to meet learning objectives. "Great discussion! Now, let me bring the discussion back to our learning objective."
- Monitor other's nonverbal communication behaviors so you can pull out those who disagree with what others are saying. "I can tell you might disagree. We would love to hear from you."
- Carefully, pull out those who are reticent or those who do not hold the majority view. "We have not heard from some of you, and some of you may completely disagree, which is good. Would you care to share?"
- Carefully, shut down those who are too willing to communicate—those who dominate the group discussion. "Hold that idea just for a moment so we can hear from others." "How about the rest of you, we would like to hear from you."

■ Provide a final summary and a debriefing that ultimately lead to your learning objectives. "Let me review or paraphrase what I have been hearing you say is the problem. Please correct me if my understanding is not accurate."

Above we mentioned that a facilitated group discussion is only as good as the questions a trainer asks. There is a certain art in asking questions, and good trainers practice this art, which allows them to reach their learning objectives. Before delving into the various types of questions, it's important to understand Benjamin Bloom's Taxonomy of Cognitive Learning,[14] represented in Table 6.1.

A **taxonomy** is a way to classify information. This taxonomy is useful in that it helps trainers formulate questions. For example, questions that tap into lower-order cognitive learning, such as knowledge (identifying information exactly as it was learned), comprehension (identifying information in general terms), and application (relating

TABLE 6.1   Bloom's Taxonomy of Cognitive Learning

Cognitive Level of Learning	Sample Questions
Evaluation: Determining the value of something based upon learned criteria. Judging whether something is good or bad, useful or unuseful, correct or incorrect based upon a learned set of standards.	What were the strengths and weaknesses of the sales presentation?
Synthesis: Creating something new based upon information and principles learned.	Can you create your own model of communication using the following elements and parts? Do you understand how the various elements and parts are related?
Analysis: Breaking information learned into separate parts. Identifying interrelationships among components.	Can you identify the various elements and parts in the model of communication?
Application: Using information learned to solve a problem or to relate information learned to a new context.	How can you use these communication principles, on the job, to enhance your managerial effectiveness?
Comprehension: Summarizing information in a way other than how it was originally learned to confirm that the information was understood.	In your own words, what does communication mean?
Knowledge: Recalling information as it was learned; recalling facts, dates, names, and definitions.	Can you recall the definition of communication?

Adapted from: Benjamin S. Bloom, *Taxonomy of Educational Objectives: The Classification of Educational Goals Handbook I: Cognitive Domain.* New York: McKay, 1956.

information or principles to a new context) usually stifle group interaction and conversation. These questions are called **closed questions,** or questions that require the recall of specific information. There is a right and wrong answer to the question. "What are the three steps to processing a customer complaint?" is an example of a closed question. When the trainer asks a lower-level closed question, trainees may be more reluctant to respond unless they are confident they have the correct answer.

Questions that tap into higher forms of cognitive learning, such as analysis (breaking a process or event into parts), synthesis (creating something new based upon what was learned), and evaluation (assessing whether something is good or bad) often engender group interaction and conversation, especially if the trainer asks open questions. **Open questions** are more ambiguous and usually don't have a single correct and incorrect responses. These questions usually require additional probing and follow-up questions. "Based on your own experiences, what do you consider to be good customer service?" is an example of an open question. Another example might be, "Would someone break down the process of quality customer service? What are the various parts to quality customer service that you have experienced?" Open questions usually require additional probing, such as "Why do you think this way?" or "How do you know this?" Table 6.2 illustrates the various types of closed and open questions that trainers use when facilitating a discussion that tap into the broad spectrum of Bloom's taxonomy.[15]

In addition to the various types of questions, consider these suggestions when asking questions:

- Allow ample wait time after asking a question. Good questions require thought. Don't expect immediate responses. Become comfortable with silence.
- Don't answer your own questions. Many trainers are not comfortable with silence and, rather than waiting for trainees to respond, they answer their own questions. Remember, it's better to get a response out of a trainee rather than to put one in them.
- When appropriate, probe. Follow up trainees' responses with "Why do you think this is so?" "How do you know this?" "Do you agree? Why? Why not?"
- Accept and dignify responses. Some answers are wrong, and these need to be recognized as wrong; however, nearly every answer to a question can be used in some way. If a wrong response is given, the chances are great that it is due to misunderstanding, unclear instruction, or faulty prior learning. Dignify the response by tentatively accepting it and working with it to see why it was given. Make sure the trainee knows why the response was not 100 percent accurate and why the correct response is accurate.

There are a variety of facilitation techniques that trainers use. Three common techniques included threading a discussion, conducting round robins, and using computer-mediated communication. The first is what is referred to as a threaded discussion. A **threaded discussion** is one in which you ask a question and then integrate carefully all responses and additional follow-up questions into a meaningful and coherent conversation. To thread a discussion, you ask an open question and then wait for someone to respond. Once you get a response, you make the response your next

TABLE 6.2   Question Types

Question Type	Definition or Explanation	Example
Leading	Question suggests the answer	"Would you agree that training is important?"
Factual	Seeking facts, data, information	"What does it cost to process a customer complaint?"
Direct	Directed at a specific person	"What are the three Cs to customer service, Gary?"
General	Directed at entire group; anyone can answer	"What does good customer service mean?"
Controversial	Two or more answers	"Are leaders born or made?"
Provocative	To incite to answer	"What do you think of the statement 'Most supervisors drive their employees too hard'?"
Redirected	Directed at facilitator, but returned to group	Group member: "What is good customer service?" Facilitator: "Let me ask you the same question, what is good customer service to you?"
Yes and no	Calls for a yes or no response	"Did you attend the training program?"
Why and how	Follow-up probes for yes or no responses.	"Why was it important that you attend the training program?" "How do you know this?"

question, redirecting this question back to the same person or to another group member. A threaded discussion might look like the following:

TRAINER: What does sexual harassment look and sound like in the workplace?

SUE: To me, it's someone viewing porn sites on the Internet.

TRAINER: Why is viewing porn sites on the Internet considered sexual harassment?

GARY: Because it makes me uncomfortable.

TRAINER: Why does it make you uncomfortable?

GARY: Because it's distracting, and I can't get my job done?

TRAINER: How is it distracting?

CAROL: I feel pressure to participate?

TRAINER: Describe the pressure.

CAROL: They want me to view the sites with them. If I do, I'm going against what I consider to be appropriate workplace behavior. If I don't, they think I'm too rigid, tense, and uptight.

As you can see from this set of questions, the trainer simply took the response and threaded it back to the group members by making it the next question.

The second facilitation technique is the round robin. In the **round-robin** technique, the facilitator asks a question and then goes around the group asking each member for his or her response. If a particular group member is not ready, he or she simply passes until all have spoken. This technique is useful when it's important that all group members participate.

The third facilitation technique is not so much a technique as it is a channel or medium for facilitating a group discussion. We refer to this communication medium as computer-mediated communication, or CMC. In **computer-mediated communication,** you participate in a facilitated group discussion using a computer terminal. Rather than communicating face-to-face, facilitators can effectively lead group discussion using a series of computer terminals that are all linked together using the Internet or some other networking platform.[16] An example of a facilitated group discussion using computer-mediated communication would be an on-line chat room.

In this section of the chapter, we have focused on facilitating group discussions. We have discussed some of the obvious advantages and disadvantages of this training method in addition to demonstrating how you go about facilitating a group discussion. Having reviewed the three training methods of lecturing, conducting experiential activities, and facilitating group discussion, our final section of the chapter offers some advice on how to select the best training method for your training program.

R E C A P
How to Develop and Facilitate a Group Discussion

Discussion Stage	Example
Present stimulus.	Show mediated stimulus. Ask trainees to reflect on the stimulus. Ask trainees to write out answers to trigger questions.
Set ground rules.	Do not interrupt others. Describe rather than evaluate. Remain nonverbally responsive.
Facilitate group interaction.	Use threaded discussion. Shut down those who talk too much and bring out those who talk too little. Provide summaries.

Selecting the Best Training Method

After reading about the three training methods of lecturing, conducting experiential activities, and facilitating group discussions, you're asking, "Which training method is best?" There is no simple answer to this question. In fact, the answer is, "It all depends." We know that's not the response you were looking for, but it's true. The answer depends on a lot of different variables including your trainees, your learning objectives, the advantages and disadvantages of each training method, and your level of comfort with the various training methods.

Consider Your Trainees

All decisions we make must begin with our trainees. The needs-centered training model introduced in Chapter 1 and illustrated in Figure 1.3 reminds us of how central our trainees are to our success as a professional trainer. Who are they? What are their experiences? What makes them unique and unlike other groups of trainees? Where do they come from? What are their average age and years of work experience? Answers to these questions will help you gauge better their reactions to your training methods. For example, some experiential activities are fine for college-age men and women, but not for the working professional. If you're working with a group of men and women who have extensive work experience, the group discussion method may be more appropriate because the trainees can learn from each other's work experiences.

Consider Your Learning Objectives

Review your learning objectives. If the learning objective is cognitive (i.e., "My students will *understand* interpersonal conflict"), then the lecture training method would be the most appropriate. If the learning objective is behavioral (i.e., "My students will know *how* to resolve interpersonal conflict"), then an experiential activity such as a role play may be the most appropriate. If the learning objective is affective (i.e., "My students will *value* and *appreciate* interpersonal conflict and how to resolve conflict"), then a facilitated guided discussion may be the most appropriate training method.

Consider Advantages and Disadvantages

As discussed above, each training method has its advantages and disadvantages. Do the advantages outweigh the disadvantages? Although the experiential activity training method can be artificial, it does give trainees some experience developing the communication skill. For example, training others how to resolve interpersonal conflict using the role-play experiential training method may be better than just lecturing to them. At times, however, the lecture may be more appropriate, especially when trainers have minimal training time. It's always important to weigh the advantages with the disadvantages. There's never enough time or money for a trainer to conduct the "ideal" training program. Trainers must make the best decisions possible given a certain set of circumstances.

TABLE 6.3   Advantages and Disadvantages of Training Methods

Training Method	Advantages	Disadvantages
Lecturing	Lecturing is economical. Lecturing is controllable. Lecturing is flexible.	Lecturing can be trainer centered. Lecturing can encourage passive learning. Lecturing can bore trainees.
Conducting experiential activities	Activities can engage all trainees. Activities can increase trainee self-confidence. Activities can increase trainees' ability to transfer content.	Activities are often times underdeveloped. Activities can be gimmicky. Activities can be artificial. Activities can be perceived as threatening.
Facilitating group discussion	Discussions encourage group members to share and participate. Discussions encourage group members to learn from each other. Discussions can be a safe environment for sharing different opinions.	Discussions can easily lose their focus. Discussions can become dominated by a particular outspoken trainee. Discussions can become emotional and destructive if not managed well.

Table 6.3 summarizes the advantages and disadvantages for each of the training methods reviewed in this chapter.

Consider Your Level of Comfort

Although trainers are encouraged to become comfortable using all training methods and are encouraged to use a variety of training methods within a single training program, not all new trainers feel comfortable with each of the training methods. For example, new trainers are oftentimes more comfortable lecturing than they are facilitating group discussion or conducting experiential activities. With the lecture, trainers have a sense of control over the training content. They know where they are, and they know where they need to go. When facilitating a group discussion, trainers never know for sure if they will be able to summarize or thread the group discussion in such a way that it will allow them to reach their learning objectives. Similarly, when conducting a new experiential activity, trainers never know if the activity is going to work until after they have tried it at least once.

Summary

In this chapter, we examined the three popular training methods of lecturing, conducting experiential activities, and facilitating group discussions. We reviewed the advantages and disadvantages of each method and explained, in some detail, how to develop and conduct each of the training methods. When developing and presenting a lecture/discussion, trainers are encouraged to create relevance with the training program, organize and chunk training content, develop appropriate schema for trainees, build redundancy into the lecture, present the lecture/discussion using appropriate immediacy behaviors, and involve trainees in the lecture/discussion by using appropriate engagement strategies.

When conducting experiential activities, trainers are encouraged to plan, prepare, present, unpack, and assess their experiential activities. Trainers write learning objectives during the planning stage. During the preparing stage, trainers develop the appropriate activity, write out the instructions for the activity, and pull together all of the instructional materials needed for the activity. Trainers conduct the activity during the presenting stage. Here they present the instructions, and ask trainees to engage in the activity. In the unpacking stage, trainees process the activity using the E*D*I*T process. Trainers complete the activity by assessing their activity to ensure that it met their learning objectives.

When facilitating a group discussion, trainers are reminded to begin with a clear learning objective. Trainers then present a stimulus or trigger question to the group to get the discussion going. Trainers remind trainees of the ground rules that must be followed to ensure a safe discussion environment and then begin the facilitation process, making sure that all group members participate equally.

We concluded the chapter by suggesting ways trainees can select the best training method. Trainers were asked to consider their trainees, their learning objectives, the advantages and disadvantages of each training method, and their level of comfort with each of the training methods.

QUESTIONS FOR DISCUSSION AND REVIEW

1. Recall the strengths and weaknesses of the lecture, experiential activity, and facilitated group discussion training methods.

2. Explain each of the following concepts and demonstrate how you would develop and present a lecture/discussion using each: relevance, organization, schema, redundancy, immediacy, and engagement.

3. Compare and contrast the following types of experiential activities: case studies, simulations, role plays, and demonstrations.

4. Describe what occurs in each of the following stages when conducting an experiential activity: planning, preparing, presenting, and unpacking.

5. List and explain the four stages of the unpacking process, including experience, description, inference, and transference.

6. List prompts or probing questions that will help trainees unpack the description, inference, and transference stages of the E*D*I*T process.

7. Provide examples of the following types of questions: leading, factual, direct, general, controversial, provocative, redirect, yes/no, and why/how.

8. Describe what occurs in each of the following stages when facilitating a group discussion: presenting stimulus, setting ground rules, and facilitating group interaction.

9. Demonstrate how the threaded and round-robin techniques are used when facilitating a group discussion.

10. Recall and explain the significance of the four questions a trainer must answer in order to determine which training method is most appropriate.

QUESTIONS FOR APPLICATION AND ANALYSIS

1. Describe, evaluate, and prescribe advice to one of your teachers about his or her style of lecturing. To protect the confidentiality of this teacher, please use a pseudonym. Specifically, you will need to complete the following:

   ■ *Describe* how the teacher lectures using the concepts from this part of the chapter.

   ■ *Evaluate* how the teacher lectures using concepts from this chapter as your criteria.

   ■ *Prescribe* advice to this teacher about how he or she lectures.

2. Describe, evaluate, and prescribe advice to one of your teachers about how he or she conducts and unpacks experiential activities. To protect the confidentiality of this teacher, please use a pseudonym. Specifically, you will need to complete the following:

   ■ *Describe* how the teacher conducts and unpacks experiential activities using the concepts from this part of the chapter.

   ■ *Evaluate* how the teacher conducts and unpacks experiential activities using the concepts from this chapter as your criteria.

   ■ *Prescribe* advice to this teacher about how he or she conducts and unpacks experiential activities.

3. Describe, evaluate, and prescribe advice to one of your teachers about how he or she facilitates group discussions. To protect the confidentiality of this teacher, please use a pseudonym. Specifically, you will need to complete the following:

   ■ *Describe* how the teacher facilitates group discussion using the concepts from this part of the chapter.

   ■ *Evaluate* how the teacher facilitates group discussion using the concepts from this chapter as your criteria.

   ■ *Prescribe* advice to this teacher about how he or she facilitates group discussion.

7 Using Technology and Presentational Aids in Training

CHAPTER OBJECTIVES

After studying this chapter, you should be able to:

1. List and explain four purposes for using presentational aids.
2. Discuss and implement five strategies for using presentational aids.
3. List and describe two advantages and two disadvantages for using the following types of presentational aids: handouts, posters and flipcharts, dry-erase boards, overhead projectors, video, and the Internet.
4. Discuss two advantages and two disadvantages regarding the use of the Internet in presentational aids.
5. Describe three strategies for designing and delivering computers to generate presentational aids.

Marketing professionals are familiar with a basic law of marketing: How attractively a product is packaged influences how easy or difficult the product is to sell. Consumers are often influenced to purchase a product based only on the shape, color, and external attributes of the box or container. Similarly, restaurant managers know that in addition to the quality and taste of the food, the arrangement and look of it on the plate are important to customers; appearance counts. Though packaging and arrangement says nothing about the quality of the product, they do significantly affect the consumer perception of and response to the product.

The same principle is true with the use of presentation aids in training presentations; the appearance of a message influences how people attend and respond to the message. **Presentational aids** are things such as objects, models, people, drawing, photographs, maps, graphs, charts, videotapes, audiotapes, pictures, sounds, and compact disks that are used to help communicate ideas to trainees. Poor presentational aids may detract from and potentially influence trainees to reject good training material. Trainers should seek first to develop high-quality training content and then to package and deliver it effectively using high-quality presentational aids.

Significant advances in technology in the last few years have made it possible for trainers to use a vast array of media while training. Gone are the days when trainers were limited to a few mimeographed handouts, a flannel board, and a flip chart. Today, trainers have access to an impressive assortment of presentational aids that are relatively easy to use and can be integrated easily into any training program. In fact, trainers may lose credibility if they are still relying on old presentation technology.

This chapter takes an in-depth look at using technology and presentational aids in training. First, we focus on why trainers should use presentational aids in their training programs. Second, we introduce you to some of the basic principles for using presentational aids. The third section examines the various types of presentational aids providing you with suggestions for how to use them well in the training classroom. The fourth section discusses computer-generated slide presentations by describing how to design and deliver them. The fifth and final section focuses on the Internet as a presentational aid.

Purposes for Using Presentational Aids

Before discussing the types of presentational aids or how to use them well in the training classroom, it's important for trainers to ask themselves why they would even want to use presentational aids in the first place. Professional trainers will tell you that visual aids can be your best friend and, at the same time, your worst enemy. A well-presented training presentation with high-quality presentation aids should help you deliver a better training program. But to achieve this quality, preparing and using effective and attractive presentational aids often take considerable time. If your presentation aids require technology, you're at the mercy of the technology working and working well. Rather than using presentation aids just for the sake of using them, it's best to have a clear purpose in mind for using any presentation aid. An important question to ask is: How will presentational aids enhance your training program? Here are a few reasons why we have found them to be useful.

Promote Interest

Presentational aids promote interest, and interest captures attention. How long is your attention span? Does another person easily distract you in your training room? Are you distracted by what the trainer is wearing, by the graffiti that appears on your desktop, or by the humming exit sign? Our attention spans are minimal, and effective trainers understand that they are constantly competing for their trainees' attention. One way to compete in a world with limited attention spans is to use presentational aids.

Illustrate and Clarify

Use of a presentational aid can help explain complex concepts to trainees. Sometimes trainees need to be able to see or hear an example of something to fully understand it. Telling front-line managers about a model of conflict management can be enhanced by using a presentational aid that visually depicts the model that the managers are about to learn. Or, if your goal is to train managers in how to use nonverbal behavior to decrease defensiveness in their employees, it might be useful to have a video aid that compares and contrasts the effective and ineffective nonverbal behaviors that managers use when addressing performance deficiencies in their employees.

Demonstrate a Principle or Action

One way to help trainees understand a skill or a behavior is to demonstrate it. In a **demonstration,** the trainer or a model performs or enacts the desired behavior. If you will recall from Chapter 4, we discussed a model for training others in how to perform a skill by telling, showing, inviting, encouraging, and correcting. The showing step of this training model includes a demonstration aid. Demonstrations are particularly useful in communication training programs. Unlike a hard skill, where there is usually a right and a wrong way, communication is a soft skill, with right and wrong ways that are less rigid and more flexible. Using a demonstration as a presentational aid allows trainees not only to see the communication skill in action but also to see the various ways communication can be enacted to achieve similar results.

Enhance Retention

As noted in Chapters 2 and 4, trainees have a tendency to remember training content based on their level of involvement. **Retention** is simply the amount of material that a trainee can remember when the training session is over. Presentational aids that integrate both visual and auditory stimulation are engaging because they require us to use multiple senses to process information. Some of us have visual "snapshots" of events that have happened in our lives that we will never forget. Few of us will ever forget the horrifying images we saw on television on September 11, 2001. We will retain these visual images for a lifetime; these images are seared into our brains the way you burn music to record a compact disk. There are also selected sounds that we have heard, some positive and some that we would just as soon forget, that are also etched permanently into our mind. We learn to see, hear, and feel long before we learn to use language.[1] The memories stimulated by our five senses start sooner, go deeper, and last longer than those we gain simply from language. With this in mind, then, it only makes sense that a trainer would need to use presentational aids to make concepts last in trainees' minds. Seeing, hearing, and doing are more likely to create a vivid experiential memory for trainees, which in turn tends to promote the memory of training content.

Motivate Trainees

Motivating trainees to use new skills and behaviors is a typical goal of any professional trainer. If you recall from Chapter 4, trainers are encouraged to use a set induction when introducing a training program module or skill. A set induction hooks the trainees to buy into the training program. It gets them ready to learn. One of your authors uses a series of overheads that contain startling statistics about divorce and relational violence before training others in communication behaviors that have been shown to reduce conflict in intimate relationships. He begins the training program by asking trainees to consider the following statistics and then slowly presents the information using overhead transparencies, allowing ample time for trainees to read and digest the information. The trainees are riveted to attention; they are ready to learn. Using presentational aids well can be a powerful strategy to help motivate trainees to change their ineffective behaviors.

Provide a Context

Another challenge for trainers is to get trainees to use the behaviors and their new skills on the job. It's one thing to read and discuss material from a training manual in a training session, and it is quite another to be able to apply and enact the material in a particular job context. Trainers should help trainees transfer what they're learning to their jobs. Presentational aids may help in this transfer process. Technology and media allow trainers to turn sterile training classrooms into simulated work environments that more closely resemble what trainees encounter on a daily basis while on the job. For example, some training programs contain CD-ROMs, or a set of CDs, that simulate workplace situations asking trainees to play certain characters in role-play simulations. Trainees can actually try out communication strategies with an angry customer in the "safe zone" of what in essence is nothing other than a simulated computer game. Once trainees have seen conflict in motion, they can then be more prepared and skilled when encountering the real thing.

RECAP

Purposes for Using Presentational Aids in Training

Purpose	Description
Promote interest	Stimulates attention and involvement with your training content Draws your trainees to want to know more about the training concept Motivates trainees to attend to, look at, and involve themselves in training concepts
Illustrate and clarify	Provides a visual or auditory example of how the training concept works Shows a model of how something works conceptually Makes important explanations about the training content
Demonstrate a principle or action	Shows how a training concept can be or should be used (for example, how to handle a hostile customer) Takes the concept and puts it into an observable and concrete form for the trainees
Enhance retention	Complements training material in such a way that trainees can remember it longer Makes information stick in their minds to recall at a later time.
Motivate	Causes trainees to want to use training concepts and recommended behaviors; generally, seeing how training concepts work successfully makes trainees more apt to desire or to enact training concepts.
Provide a context	Shows how the training concept fits in the world of the trainee Shows a setting where a specific concept or approach could actually be used.

Strategies for Using Presentational Aids

From our experiences, trainers have a difficult time using presentational aids well. The purpose of this section is to help you use them well by reviewing some of the fundamental principles that apply to all presentational aids. Later on this chapter, we offer specific advice when using particular types of presentational aids.

Keep Presentational Aids Simple

There is a temptation to put too much material on a presentational aid. This results in information overload and confusion. Trainees don't know where to direct their attention. Here are a few ways to keep your presentational aids simple:

- *Decide the purpose of the aid:* Each presentational aid should serve a single purpose that is related to a training objective that ultimately meets the needs of your trainees. If it's not related to a training objective, then it's probably not needed.
- *Use key words or short phrases:* Rather than placing long sentences or portions of text on an aid, use **bullet points,** which are short phrases, key words, or short quotes.
- *Use appropriate fonts:* A **font** is a full set of printing type that is of the same design and size. You're probably familiar with the font styles on your computer. Which one should you use when preparing presentational aids? When using printed materials, the following fonts are recommended: Times New Roman, Book Antiqua, Bookman Old Style, Calisto, and Garamond. When using electronic materials, the following fonts are recommended: Arial, Century Gothic, Eras, Franklin Gothic, Helvetica, Lucida Sans, Tahoma, and Verdana.[2]

Talk with Trainees and Not to Your Presentational Aids

Many trainers have a bad habit of talking to their flip charts, white boards, and overhead projectors rather than to their trainees when presenting information. Looking at your presentation aid instead of your trainees reduces your eye contact with the trainees. Here are a few of our recommendations:

- *Make sure the presentational aids are arranged in the appropriate order:* It's very easy for presentational aids to get out of order. This can be very embarrassing, because you will take valuable training time to rearrange your aids. When this happens, you lose your trainees' attention. Make sure all of your aids are in the appropriate place and order so that when it's time to use them, you don't even have to break eye contact with your trainees. From our experience, this is a sign of a true professional.
- *Make sure the equipment is fully functioning and focused:* Your presentational aids may be in order; but if the equipment, which is needed to use the aids, is not fully functioning or focused, then you again lose eye contact with your trainees. You begin talking to the equipment using words that your trainees should probably not hear. Spend time testing your equipment before the training module begins.
- *Establish rapport with your trainees before using presentational aids:* When using extensive multimedia presentational aids, it's recommended that you first make personal contact and establish rapport with your trainees before launching into your multimedia presentation.[3] If you fail to make contact first, trainees may perceive the training to be a bit impersonal.

Make Presentational Aids Large Enough to Be Seen Easily

Many trainers, unfortunately, fail to use presentational aids effectively because their aids remain too small for all trainees to see clearly. So how large is large enough? The general rule of thumb is to make presentational aids large enough so trainees in the last row can see them. Another rule of thumb that we follow is that when in doubt, make it larger. Here are a few additional suggestions that might prevent you from making this classic presentational aid mistake:

- *Confirm how many trainees you're going to have in the training classroom:* Attendance at training programs has a tendency to fluctuate. From our experiences, you never seem to have what you were expecting. Either you have too many or too few, but it's seldom the number you were expecting. A day or two prior to the training program, we recommend you confirm your attendance. This number will enable you to gauge how large your presentational aid needs to be. The presentational aid you use for a group of 100 should not be the same size as the one you use for a group of 25.
- *Find out the size of your training classroom:* It's also recommended that you preview the training classroom to see its shape. Is the room long and narrow, or is it short and wide? The shape of the room will influence the size of your presentational aid. The presentational aid you use for a long and narrow training classroom should not be the same size as the one you use for a short and wide training classroom.
- *Have handouts available and ready to distribute if needed:* Regardless of the number of trainees you have or the shape of the training classroom, it's always recommended that you have handouts of your presentational aids available for those who are positioned behind pillars or for those who are in the back of the room and cannot hear or see as a result of faulty equipment.

Be Ready to Present without Presentational Aids

Murphy's Law, the notion that what can go wrong will go wrong, is often in full force when using presentational aids, especially when using technology. In short, expect the worst when it comes to using your presentational aids. From our experience, it's not uncommon for presentational aids to be lost or damaged while being shipped to a training location. It's not uncommon for the technology you requested, confirmed, and verified on a daily basis for the past 30 days preceding your training program to be inoperable or unavailable at the last minute. It's also not uncommon for computer systems to be incompatible in terms of converting computer-generated presentational software programs from one computer's operating system to another computer's operating system, even if Bill Gates and Steve Jobs themselves told you that this conversion process would not be a problem.

Here are a few suggestions that will help you beat Murphy's Law:

- *Don't make your training program dependent on presentational aids:* Presentational aids should not *be* the training message, they should only *enhance* the training message.
- *Carry one copy of the original presentational aid on your person:* Even if your presentational aids fail to make it to the training location, you will have an original copy

with you that you can have reproduced easily at any office supply store, professional printing company, or professional business center. Many of the businesses that support professional trainers operate 24/7 and can make hundreds of bound copies in seconds with professional quality.

- *Anticipate that the technology you need will fail you:* When your computer crashes and tells you that you have a "corrupted file," or when the computer you're using to run the presentation decides to give you the infamous "cannot read file" error message, it's important that you have a stack of handouts that you can quickly distribute to your trainees without missing a beat.

Practice Using Presentational Aids

The difference between poor, fair, and excellent training presentations often shows up in the actual delivery of the material. Knowing your material inside and out and hav-

RECAP

Presentational Aid Strategies and Recommended Prescriptions

Presentational Aid Strategies	Recommended Prescriptions
Keep presentational aids simple.	Don't use ornate fonts or formats. Make points short and concise. Use bullets to itemize lists. Keep the focus on the main ideas rather than on the "decorations."
Talk with trainees and not presentational aids.	Interact with people, not inanimate presentational aids. Establish and maintain eye contact with the trainees.
Make presentational aids large enough.	Don't copy text directly out of a training manual; make a transparency so it can be enlarged and projected on a screen. Presentational aids must be large enough to see, or you are wasting your time and frustrating your trainees.
Be ready to present without presentational aids.	Don't totally rely on your presentational aids. If something goes wrong with the presentational aids, keep moving forward; or, if needed, take a short break to fix the problem. The goal is to ensure that problems with presentational aids do not cause you to cancel presentation.
Practice using presentational aids.	Make sure you have actually used the presentational aids. Rehearse beforehand how you will actually use them in your presentation.

ing excellent presentational aids prepared does not necessarily mean that the delivery will go well. To use your presentational aids with ease and comfort, we recommend the following:

- *Practice to get a feel for the training classroom:* This may not always be possible; but, if it is possible, it's a good thing to get familiar using your presentational aids in the actual training classroom. With practice, you will locate electrical plugs, light switches, window blinds, breaker switches, and heating and air conditioning controls.
- *Practice to ensure ease of using equipment:* One of the authors of this text saw a business presentation where the speaker had not considered what to do with the presentation posters once they were used. As the first poster was removed from the tripod, the expression of panic on the face of the presenter showed that he had no idea what to do with the used poster. On the spur of the moment, a desperate decision was made and each poster, as it was used, was tossed sloppily in a distracting pile of posters on the floor. This is obviously unprofessional. Other problems can occur when you have not rehearsed with your equipment. With practice you will figure out where to stand when using an overhead projector, how to advance or backtrack slides, and how to distribute handouts quickly and efficiently.
- *Practice to ensure smooth transitions:* Spend time developing and working through your transitions so that you can transition to and from presentational aids in a smooth and meaningful manner. You want the training presentation to appear seamless.

Types of Presentational Aids

There are a number of presentational aids available to help trainers enhance the meaning of their training messages. We're going to discuss how to use some of the more popular aids such as handouts, posters and flipcharts, dry-erase boards, overhead projectors, and video. Following this review, we will examine two additional presentational aids rather extensively: using computer-generated slide presentations and the Internet.

Handouts

We begin with the most basic of presentational aids, known as handouts. **Handouts** are documents that you design, copy, and distribute to your trainees. In many training sessions, trainers prepare a booklet or three-ring binder, sometimes called a participant's manual, which contains all training handouts; the manual is typically distributed to trainees at the beginning of the training session. These documents usually contain a summary of the training content as well as models, graphs, drawings, statistics, photographs, maps, or charts. We're certain you're familiar with the phrase, "a picture is worth a thousand words." Rather than spending your time using a thousand words, you're encouraged to use a handout that accomplishes the same effect with better results. When time is limited, and it usually is, handouts save you time. Here are a few of our suggestions for how to use handouts well in your training classroom:

- *Make sure handouts are error free:* You would be surprised at the number of handouts we have received over the years that contain typographical or statistical errors. Proof your work and make sure your handouts are error free. They're a reflection of you and your work. Sometimes it is hard to proofread your own material. If you know you're not an expert proofreader, ask someone else to read your materials before you present your training workshop.
- *Do not distribute handouts while you are speaking:* This can be incredibly distracting to both you and your trainees. When you're passing out handouts during the presentation, no one is listening to you. They're either too busy distributing the handouts to each other or reading them rather than listening to you. You're encouraged to distribute the handouts before you begin speaking and ask all trainees to leave the handouts face down on the table in front of them until you instruct them to view them. Another strategy is to take a break in your training presentation to distribute the handouts. Once all trainees have a copy, you can resume your training presentation. Or, you could distribute a training manual and carefully control the attention of the trainees by indicating which page of the training manual the trainees should have in front of them.
- *Instruct trainees when to view handouts:* When appropriate, ask trainees to view their handouts. Take time to review the documents with them and be prepared to answer their questions. When you're finished, ask trainees to place the handout face down on the table and then resume your training presentation. These strategies allow you to manage your trainees' attention patterns.
- *Consider advantages and disadvantages:* In addition to the advantages already listed, handouts are inexpensive, efficient in that they can convey a lot of information in a short amount of time, easy to transport, and dependable in that they don't require technology for viewing. Most of the disadvantages are not the result of the handouts, but how the handouts are used. You want to make sure that you manage your handouts rather than letting your handouts manage you. To avoid this problem, you're encouraged to follow the suggestions listed above.

Posters and Flipcharts

Posters and flipcharts are some of the more basic, reliable, and inexpensive types of presentational aids. You're probably familiar with posters and perhaps less familiar with flipcharts. A **flipchart** is a large pad of paper that is usually mounted on a **tripod,** which is a three-legged stand. Here are a few of our suggestions for how to use posters and flipcharts well in your training classroom:

- *Use with small groups and in small rooms:* Posters and flipcharts are ideal when working with training groups from 15 to 20 people and in a relatively small training classroom. With a larger group, it's wiser to use an overhead transparency that can be enlarged for a larger group to see more clearly.

- *Write large enough for all to see:* When writing on a poster or flipchart, make sure you're writing large enough so the trainee in the back row can read your writing.
- *Use display-and-hide techniques:* It is recommended that trainers use a blank poster in front to hide other posters until they're ready to use their presentational aids. Without the blank poster, trainees are distracted by reading and viewing your presentational aid rather than listening to your message. When it's time to use the posters or flipcharts, simply remove the blank poster.
- *Place the tripod and poster or flipchart in a front corner of the training classroom:* This allows the trainer to use the entire space in front of the trainees rather than tripping over the tripod while moving from side to side.
- *Use quality materials:* Regular posters have a tendency to curl on the top and bottom edges, especially with frequent use and when used in humid environments. This type of curling can and will cause the poster to slide off the tripod during the presentation. Many trainers prefer using foam board posters that remain stiff to deal with this problem. Foam board posters are a bit easier to manipulate during presentations as well.
- *Practice using your posters and flipchart:* At times, posters and flipcharts can be awkward to use. A little practice will allow you to use the aid with ease and comfort. If you have a series of posters, consider a place to put them when you're finished with them. Rather than tossing them on the floor, place them in back of each other.
- *Consider advantages and disadvantages of using posters and flipcharts before you decide to use them:* Posters are great with small groups of people and can be used to record group ideas for immediate display. Computer programs allow trainers to create professional-looking slides that can be easily attached to posters. There are some drawbacks, however, in using posters. Though the tripod can be compact and easily transported, a poster portfolio is bulky and hard to carry, especially when traveling from place to place. Windy days, airport baggage handling procedures, and rental cars are not your friends when using posters. Also, as the posters are used, they begin to show wear and tear. Edges fray, glue and tape begin to weaken, and colors fade after repeated and extended use.

Dry-Erase Boards

Dry-erase boards are a modern version of the old chalkboard and are a little less messy and easier to use. **Dry-erase boards,** also known as white boards, consist of white, laminated panels that allow trainers to use markers rather than chalk, and they erase with ease. They can be an immediate presentational aid and, with various markers, can be quite colorful. If the training room does not have one mounted on the wall, dry-erase boards can be quickly set up on tripods and used quite effectively. Here are a few of our suggestions for how to use dry-erase boards well in your training classroom:

- *Use appropriate markers and erasers:* For those who have never used a dry-erase board before, regular markers and chalkboard erasers will not work with this type of presentational aid. Your markers and erasers are your tools. Make sure your training tools are dry-erase appropriate.

- *Bring your own dry-erase markers:* Don't depend on the training facility to provide you with dry-erase markers. If they're available, chances are they're out of ink and the color options are limited. You'll want to use fresh markers with enough ink to get you through the day and with an assortment of color options for highlighting training content.
- *Bring your own dry-erasers:* Like dry-erase markers, you will want your own erasers. When erasers are available, chances are they have seen better days. They have erased one too many dry-erase boards. Bringing your own will ensure that you can erase quickly and easily. Fresh erasers will come in handy, especially for dry-erase boards that are used heavily. At times, dry-erase markers have a tendency to stain if they're not erased promptly. Fresh erasers will ease this potential problem.
- *Use dry-erase markers correctly:* One should remember that most markers must be held at a down angle when writing on the board, or the ink flow will begin to fade quickly and the marker will stop working right in the middle of your training presentation.
- *Consider advantages and disadvantages of using dry-erase boards:* Advantages of this type of presentational aid include ease of use, immediate display of trainee comments, no chalk dust on hands or clothes, and dynamic picture or graphic possibilities. Dry-erase boards can be used as screens for projected pictures as well. Disadvantages with this presentational aid include difficulty of transport (if it is portable) and limited ability to prepare graphics beforehand (you have just one "screen") or during the presentation (unless you are a great spontaneous artist). Whether an advantage or a disadvantage, one must also consider the handwriting quality of the trainer when using this presentational aid.

Overhead Projectors

The overhead projector is another presentational aid that trainers can use to enhance their training messages. **Overhead projectors** contain a flat transparent top on which a sheetlike transparency is placed that allows trainers to project enlarged images onto a screen. Overheads are ideal for projecting text, graphics, and pictures and can even be used for live listing of trainees' comments or ideas. Here are a few of our suggestions for how to use overhead projectors well in your training classroom:

- *Place the projector in the appropriate place:* With practice, you will find the appropriate place. If the projector is not appropriately placed, the projected image will be too small, the machine itself will block the views of some of your trainees who are sitting closer to the front of the training classroom, or you will be tripping over the machine and its electrical cord while using the overhead projector. As with all presentational aids, you must take time to practice using the equipment.
- *Turn the projector off when not in use:* The trainer should take care to turn off the lamp or to cover the screen when there is not an image being shown. The "white dwarf star" or "supernova" effect happens when the trainer removes a trans-

parency but forgets to turn the overhead projector off. The large, intensely bright-lighted square on the screen is distracting and blinding to the audience. In addition to covering the screen when lit but not in use, the trainer can also strategically cover parts of the transparency and move the cover down as he or she covers new points. This technique of "cover and reveal" works quite well.

- *Take spare overhead projector lamp bulbs with you to the training classroom:* The last thing you need is for a bulb to burn out on you during your presentation. Most projectors take standard halogen lamp bulbs that are easy to remove and install. It's worth your time to practice replacing a lamp bulb. When a bulb does blow during your presentation—and it's only a matter of time before this happens— you can easily and quickly replace the bulb and continue your training presentation without missing a beat. It's also an easy way to impress trainees.
- *Bring an extension cord:* Electrical outlets are never where you want or need them. To eliminate this problem, pack some heavy-duty extension cords with you.
- *Use color transparencies, if possible:* A basic principle of presentation aids is: Black and white will do, but color is better. With computers, color copiers, and color inkjet or laser printers, it's easy for trainers to use color transparencies. Additionally, pictures can easily be transferred onto overhead transparencies. When using colors, make sure they are dark enough to be seen easily at the back of the room. Light yellows, pinks, and blues, for example, may look brilliant on your small computer screen but may look washed out when projected on a larger screen.
- *Consider advantages and disadvantages of using overhead projectors:* There are many advantages to using an overhead projector in the training classroom. Though many of the older models were bulky, new business models are compact, easily transportable, and easy to set up. Advanced technology has allowed these projectors to produce bright images that can be seen even in well-lit training rooms. Controlling the lighting is no longer a problem.

Video

Videotape and DVD (digital video disks) are two additional presentational aids that trainers can use with a degree of ease and effectiveness in the training classroom. Again, both of these video formats require the appropriate equipment and require trainers to either transport their own or arrive early enough to the training classroom to verify that the equipment works properly. Assuming you have the necessary equipment and it works well, here are a few of our suggestions for how to use video in your training classroom:

- *Use brief clips and excerpts:* Rather than using an entire video, it's best to use brief clips or excerpts from the video or DVD. Because video can be seductive, many trainees get caught up in the video and forget to view the video critically for its training content. To minimize video seduction, show a five- to ten-minute clip rather than the entire 60-minute video program.
- *Provide guiding questions:* To inoculate against the seduction effect, provide trainees with guiding questions that you would like them to answer while viewing the

RECAP

Advantages and Disadvantages to Using Various Presentational Aids

Presentational Aid	Advantages	Disadvantages
Handouts	Relatively inexpensive Provide much information Provide trainees something to take back to the office with them Do not require technology to use Easy to transport	Hard to control trainee attention once they are distributed May compete with trainee attention on presenter
Posters and flipcharts	Best with small groups of people Can be used spontaneously for good effect	Bulky and difficult to transport Must have a tripod or some place to display them If spontaneously created, writing may not be as legible or professional looking
Dry-erase boards	No chalk dust Can double as a projection screen Easy to use	Hard to transport; needs to be already in the room Must make sure you have your own markers Must know how to use markers properly Does not compensate for bad trainer handwriting
Overhead projectors	Easy to use Versatile Can be used spontaneously or with prepared slides	Bulbs can burn out at inopportune times Old models can be dim and problematic
Video	Attention-catching visual possibilities, static or moving Captures the audience attention Gives great mental images of concepts in action	Equipment failure always a possibility May compete with trainer for attention May take over center stage or emphasis unless the trainer uses it carefully Audio capabilities sometimes a problem, especially in large rooms

video excerpt. These questions will help trainees focus on the training content and less on the entertainment value of the video. You can unpack or process the questions following the video.

■ *Cue up your clip:* Take time to cue up your video or DVD. Before you begin your training program, review the video and know where you're going to begin and end. It's a waste of time to fast-forward through video during a training program looking for the appropriate place. If you do this, you'll lose your training momentum. You want the video presentation to be an extension of your oral presentation. It needs to appear seamless to the trainee.

■ *Provide an introduction or context:* Rather than starting the cued video cold, take a few moments and introduce the video. Warm your trainees up to the video. Who are the characters? Where are they? What has been happening? This will help trainees interpret the video and extract the appropriate meaning for your training objective.

■ *Consider advantages and disadvantages of using videos and DVDs:* The advantages are obvious. We love video. Videos and DVDs provide rich images and appeal to our various senses. Videos capture our attention unlike any other presentational aid. As discussed, the disadvantages occur when video is not used well in the training classroom. Trainees begin viewing the video for entertainment purposes rather than for training purposes. You're encouraged to use the preceding suggestions to avoid the video seduction effect.

Computer-Generated Visual Presentations

Today, trainers have access to a few software packages that enable them to develop and present training programs using computer-generated images. The images can be projected directly from a computer to a projector or be reproduced as overhead transparencies. Presentation software programs allow trainers, with some computer experience, to design color slides using a variety of audio and visual options including text, bulleted points, pictures, graphs, sounds, and even video clips. Next, we review several suggestions for designing and delivering computer-generated presentations.

Designing Your Computer-Generated Visual Presentation

Here are a few basic design principles we encourage you to consider using when designing your slide presentation using presentation software:

■ *Don't clutter images:* Images cluttered with varying fonts, multiple distracting animations, crowded pictures, and miniature video clips will detract from the message. Pick one or two design features and stick to it. With visual design, less is more.

■ *Balance images:* Make sure your images have symmetry and balance. You don't want all of the text at the top or off to one side of the slide. Graphic experts Joyce

Kupsch and Pat Graves encourage slide designers to strive for balance, symmetry, and placement on each slide to avoid slides that are lopsided.[4]

- *Use minimal animation:* Animations related to the main point are good but should be kept to a tasteful minimum throughout the presentation. Comments from business professionals trend toward the following: "I'd abolish 99 percent of all transition and animation effects. There is almost nothing as annoying as sitting through 23 text slides with *every bullet* flying in one at a time."[5] If you want to use these, you should do so strategically and unobnoxiously.

- *Use sound effects strategically:* Slide sounds (e.g., car crash, breaking glass, etc.) are novel but can get old and irritating very quickly. These sound effects should be kept to a minimum and, again, should be used for punctuation or emphasis.

- *Use preprogrammed color schemes and formats:* For the most part, these default templates have been tested for visibility and symmetry and are generally quite good.

- *Avoid design shock:* Shocking your audience with your own garish colors, poor contrast, or limited visibility will detract from the content of the slide. Cool colors like blues, greens, and purples are best suited for backgrounds, whereas hot colors such as reds, oranges, yellows draw attention and thus are best suited for foreground items.[6] Interestingly, the color blue is the "background color of choice in over 90 percent of business presentations."[7]

- *Strive for uniformity and consistency:* Carry your design theme throughout the entire presentation. Your design theme will not only provide a common thread throughout the presentation but will provide your trainees with a pattern that will make it easier for them to digest the information.

- *Regulate and coordinate the number of visuals:* Trainers should match the number of images with the amount of time allotted for the presentation. Making 50 images meaningful to your trainees in a 15-minute presentation may be a bit unrealistic. One or two slides per minute is a good rule of thumb.[8]

Finally, Jennifer Rotondo and Mike Rotondo offer the following checklist of items that you might find helpful when designing your slides:

- Use only one point or major concept per visual.
- Leave out information that the presenter can say.
- Use phrases, not sentences.
- Use parallel structure (all phrases start with verb or noun and in the same form).
- Use 24-point font size.
- Avoid cartoon clip art.
- Spell check!
- Use 8 × 8 rule: No more than eight words per line and eight lines per slide.
- Put in a graphic or chart every three to five slides.[9]

To provide a frame of reference for these presentation aid principles, please notice the examples in Figures 7.1 through 7.4. Notice the contrast between the examples of poor sides and examples of better slides.

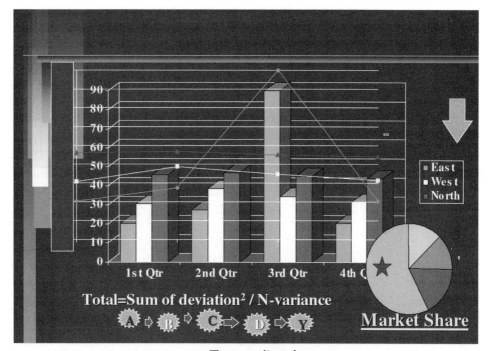

a. Too complicated

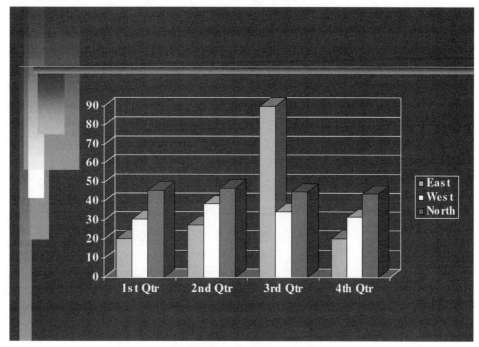

b. Simple and easier to read

FIGURE 7.1   Complicated versus Simple

a. Too complicated

b. Simple and better

FIGURE 7.2   Complicated versus Simple

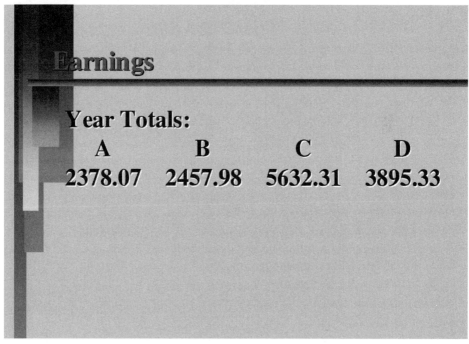

a. Too small

b. Easy to read

FIGURE 7.3 Appropriate Size: Too Small versus Large Enough to Be Seen Clearly

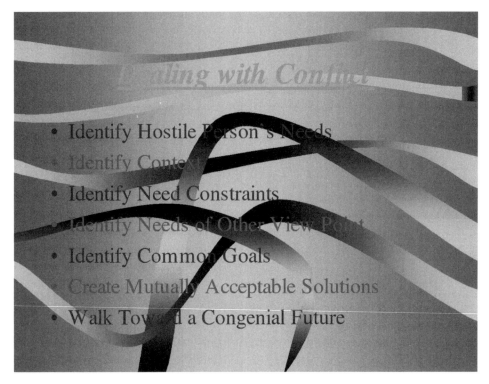

FIGURE 7.4   Too Complex and Detailed; Inappropriate Contrasts

Delivering Your Computer-Generated Presentation

After you've designed your images, it's time to deliver your training presentation. You'll use the same presentational software program you used to design your visuals to display them in your presentation. Note the following suggestions that can help you polish your presentation:

- *Plan set up and test the presentation:* Trainers should arrive early to the training classroom and locate all necessary electrical outlets, hook up and boot up all necessary equipment, check out sight lines, and do a test run through the presentation. Any equipment or compatibility problems should be quickly identified and addressed. All of this should be done and in place before the trainees begin to arrive for the training program.
- *Control the lighting in the training classroom:* Even though projector bulbs are getting brighter, some manipulation of room or background lighting is often necessary, especially with older projectors. With older projectors, the room lights must be dimmed sufficiently for the projection image to be seen clearly. Too much ambient room or window light will cause eyestrain and frustration for you and your trainees. Many corporate conference rooms are built with these issues

RECAP

Design Principles and Prescriptions for Computer-Generated Presentations

Design Principle	Design Prescription
Don't clutter images.	Keep fonts consistent. Concentrate on including only the main ideas or images. Leave off the details. Don't crowd your pictures. Less is more.
Balance visuals.	Make sure there is symmetry to your visuals. Place text in logical places in symmetrical formats. Balance your pictures. Pay close attention to constructing a professional-looking layout.
Use minimal animation.	Use sparingly. Remember that too many animations, especially little extra moving cartoons, are distracting. Use only animations that are central to your main ideas. Text constantly zipping in to the sound of breaking glass or car crashes becomes irritatingly obnoxious to trainees.
Use sound effects strategically.	Use only when needed. Avoid constantly using Powerpoint sounds. Use sounds primarily with audio or video clips.
Use preprogrammed color schemes and formats.	Computer programs have been carefully programmed with balanced formats and coordinated colors. Default templates generally have visually appealing symmetry and visibility. Standard schemes and formats are the safest route.
Avoid design shock.	Use caution when changing standard color schemes. Be cautious of using colors that clash, irritate the trainees, or are hard to see.
Strive for conformity and consistency.	Avoid having new colors or designs for each slide. Stick with a standard template and use for all slides. Use the same fonts and fonts sizes throughout the presentation.
Regulate and coordinate the number of images.	Though a picture speaks a thousand words, one can have too many pictures or slides. You don't need pictures for every slide. Limit your number of slides in terms of your allotted presentation time.

in mind and may have separate lighting controls for the lights nearest the projection screen. Such a training facility allows trainers to dim or turn off the lights that are nearest the screen while leaving enough lighting so that trainees can take appropriate notes.

- *Turn off the screen saver:* Incidentally, but importantly, trainers should remember to turn the screen saver off on the presentation computer. Neglecting to do so could interrupt the slide presentation. If, for instance, the trainer pauses a bit too long in the presentation for a necessary comment or to follow up on a trainee's question or comment, the computer screen saver might kick in, blank out the slide, and thus interrupt the intensity or focus of the moment. Additionally, on some computers, going back from the screen saver to the slide presentation might take some time or might even require rebooting the program (or even the computer). This is an interruption and distraction that is not needed and can be prevented with just a bit of forethought and planning.

- *Prepare handouts:* Many presentational software programs allow trainers several handout options when printing from the toolbar of the software program. The **toolbar** is a row of icons on the computer screen that are used to perform certain frequently used functions, such as printing. One of the advantages of preparing handouts of your training presentation would be in the event that there is a technological problem and you're unable to use the computer to present the slide program. Another advantage to handouts is that they help trainees take notes. It gives them a **schema,** which you will recall from Chapter 2 is a way to organize and classify information. Rather than jotting down all of the information that is in front of them, they can focus on taking notes that will help them understand and remember the training content. One disadvantage to using handouts is that they can be distracting at times. Rather than focusing on the trainer's message, some trainees get caught up in the note taking process.

- *Develop a contingency plan:* Especially with multiple and linked electronic devices, you simply must have **contingency plan,** which is backup in the event that you're unable to use the computer to present your training program. Power surges, electromagnetic pulses, viruses, and hard-drive crashes are unpredictable and hard to prevent or control. Many trainers will prepare transparency backup slides of their presentation to use in the event of a crash. In the event of a power loss, however, the overhead projector will not work either. In situations such as this, the trainer needs to be mentally ready to do something else—for instance, making use of the dry-erase board, which will mean coming prepared with dry-erase markers. Experienced and prepared trainers have contingency plans that allow them to effectively facilitate the content without any presentational aids if necessary.

- *Prepare a closing to the training presentation:* Closing out the slide presentation gracefully is a must. Placing a blank slide or title slide at the end of your presentation is a nice touch. This will keep the last content slide from being followed by a thumbnail projection of your entire listing of slides. You should be ready to make closing comments that lead toward the next session, application of the material, or the like. Restoring room lighting quickly will also be important at this point.

RECAP

Delivery Principles and Prescriptions for Computer-Generated Slide Presentations

Delivery Principle	Delivery Prescription
Plan set up and test slide presentation.	Set up the room early. Set up your presentation aids strategically. Make sure your slides are working and are in the proper order. Make sure that all trainees will be able to see the screen. Check to ensure all equipment cords and links are working. Check for boot-up time.
Control lighting in the training classroom.	Check to ensure that the your projected images can be seen and are not faded by the room lighting (overhead or window light). Determine whether you must dim or turn out room lights for trainees to be able to see your projected images. If the room does not have ambient light, for safety's sake bring a small flashlight just in case so you can see when the lights are out.
Turn off the screen saver.	Having the screen save cut in during one of your slides is distracting.
Prepare handouts.	Make sure the handouts are grammatical, neat, and purposeful. If trainees are inappropriately looking at your handouts and not at you, redirect their attention where you want it to be.
Develop a contingency plan.	In case problems occur, have a plan B. Sooner or later a bulb will go out, the electricity will go off, the computer will crash, your handouts will be lost in your luggage at the airport. If one thing breaks, plan how to use the rest of the equipment that still works.
Prepare a closing to the training presentation.	Have a blank or concluding slide prepared, so that your ending image will not be the construction view of all of your PowerPoint slides. Close out your images so that the trainee focus is directed where you want it to be directed. Make sure room lighting is brought back to normal levels during or quickly after your conclusion.

The Internet as a Presentational Aid

Increasingly, corporate training rooms are being wired with Internet hookups. Using the Internet can open up numerous possibilities for trainers. One such possibility is for the trainer to use the Internet as a visual aid in the training presentation. There are many informational Web sites that could be explored and projected on the screen for the entire training group. Trainees can be "transported" as a group to different countries, corporations, and meetings around the world. The live, real-time nature of the information may be advantageous to your trainees. Obviously, if you want to use this as a trainer, you need to visit the site beforehand, take time before the session to setup your laptop with the Internet hookup, carefully consider the speed of your connection, consider the possibility of high Internet traffic that might slow your progress during the training session, and be ready to do without any of this if the system breaks down. There is a very real possibility that, even with careful preparation and testing of connections, the **server,** which is a computer in a network that stores application programs and data files that are accessed by other computers in the system, might be down or go down during your presentation. Many times, for the sake of time, it might be more advantageous to make a CD-ROM version of your visit to the site. Though this would limit the "liveness" and interactive nature of the joint Web experience, it would also make the transitions between screens much faster and would sidestep problems of heavy Internet traffic.

In addition or as an alternative to using the Internet as a presentational aid in the training presentation, the trainer might choose to have trainees engage in hands-on computer visits to preselected Web sites relevant to the content of the session. This could be done as a group in a training room equipped with multiple computers or could be accomplished by having trainees return to their office computers for a prescribed amount of time with a Web assignment. The trainer could personally prepare Web-based activities, assessments, or simulations that could be accessed from training sessions all over the world. Trainees for example might visit a site where they could complete a self-assessment of their own management communication skills and then receive an instantaneous score. These scores, in turn, could be used in training session discussions on management communication skills and the enhancement thereof.

Another possibility is to use the Internet to engage trainees in joint interactive training activities that require them to work together. A variety of simulations, threaded discussions, or group interactions could be used to provide trainees hands-on experience using the content derived in the training sessions. Obviously, this type of Internet use in training would require a great deal of preparation time, equipment linking, and software capabilities, but if administered carefully, it could be quite rewarding and successful in meeting training objectives.

Summary

How a training program is presented and packaged is important. Although the training content is of primary importance, how this material is presented and displayed can make a significant difference in how it is received and remembered. The communication channel is not the message, but the message is indeed influenced by the communication channel. Presentational aids, then, are of critical importance to trainee learning and trainer credibility.

Before using presentational aids, the trainer should have a good understanding of the basic purposes for using presentational aids. The trainer must not only be aware of all of the different types of presentational aids, but he or she must also be very familiar with basic strategies for constructing and using them effectively. New technologies, like computer-generated and assisted presentational aids, allow useful opportunities for trainers to enhance training sessions. The Internet provides even more opportunities for trainers in this regard. The key is for trainers to remember the basic purposes of presentational aids, then to use them wisely and effectively.

QUESTIONS FOR DISCUSSION AND REVIEW

1. Explain how and why presentational aids enhance trainee retention of the material presented.

2. Discuss what will happen if you are not prepared to give your training session without your presentational aids. Why is this important? What are the implications of this?

3. Why is it so easy to get caught up in talking to your presentation aids rather then keeping your focus and face on the trainees? Why is talking to the presentational aids a problem?

4. What types of things could happen if you fail to practice with your presentational aids?

5. Compare the advantages of using overhead slides to using computer-delivered Power-point slides.

QUESTIONS FOR APPLICATION AND ANALYSIS

1. Dominique is an incredibly effective speaker and motivator. He has constructed attractive training material for middle management on how to control and cut operating production costs. The problem is that he is a bit apprehensive about computers, so he tends to write most of his statistical data on the dry-erase board as he trains. He has bad board handwriting, so his drawings generally look sloppy and are hard to read. What are some suggestions that you could make to Dominique on how to improve his training presentation?

2. What are advantages and disadvantages of distributing copies of computer-generated images so trainees can follow along as you train? Should you give your presentation content and then pass them out so your trainees can have a printed version of the material to take back to the office with them?

3. What significant issues and challenges in developing and using presentational aids do trainers face when using distance delivery systems such as the Internet for training? How are these issues different or similar to questions trainers face when presenting material in the training room? How should trainers adjust their choice and use of presentational aids to achieve maximum results when using a distance delivery system?

8 Developing Training Plans

The Purpose of Training Plans
  Connecting Trainee Needs with Objectives
  Connecting Trainee Objectives with
    Methods
Preparing to Write a Training Plan
  Conducting Research
  Developing Training Content
  Determining Training Time Frames
  Determining Training Methods
  Selecting Training Materials
Training Plan Formats
  Descriptive Format
  Outline Format
  Multicolumn Format
Preparing the Participant's Guide

Practical Training Planning Tips
  Draft the Participant's Guide First
  Remember the 20-Minute Rule
  Build in the Skill Training Sequence
  Plan for Contingencies
  Revise, Revamp, Reconstruct
Testing the Training Plan
  Conduct a Focus Group
  Conduct a Pilot Test
  Invite an Expert to Review the Training
    Materials
Summary
Questions for Discussion and Review
Questions for Application and Analysis

CHAPTER OBJECTIVES

After studying this chapter, you should be able to:

1. Describe the key purposes of a training plan.
2. Identify and perform the key steps in writing a training plan.
3. Develop and use three different types of training plan formats.
4. Write a training plan using four practical training planning tips.
5. Identify, describe, and implement three methods of testing the quality of a training plan.

Training plans are to training what a symphonic musical score is to a conductor; a training plan is like musical notation that can become glorious musical sound in the hands of a skilled maestro. In many respects, being a trainer is like being a conductor. The conductor does not make the music; rather he or she facilitates it into being. Similarly, the trainer does not make learning happen but is a resource to assist the learner to learn. And just as musicians learn how to transcribe music into musical notes that can be reproduced by others, so a trainer should develop the skill of preparing a training plan.

This chapter discusses how to prepare the training plan. A **training plan** is a written description of a training session, which contains: (1) the objectives, (2) a summary of the training content, (3) a description of the training methods, and (4) a detailed description of all presentation aids and resources (e.g. handouts) that are needed to transform the plan into a training session. Training plans can range from a simple narrative description that a trainer will develop and personally use to a detailed minute-by-minute plan that is written to be used by other trainers.

Why is it necessary to learn how to prepare a training plan? Can't a trainer just make a few notes or jot down a few ideas? No, it's vital to learn how to assemble a training plan in order to ensure that each of the elements that make training instruction effective have been incorporated. Just having a general idea in your head of what you'll do during a training session, even a short training session, is not adequate. A professional trainer prepares a written plan to capture all of the necessary information that should be incorporated into a comprehensive training plan. And as noted previously, some trainers are employed to prepare training plans for others. Designing curriculum for another trainer is sometimes important training function that may be a job in and of itself. One bit of encouragement we offer is that as you gain experience and additional knowledge about both your subject matter and how to prepare training plans, the task will get easier.[1]

In the previous chapters of this book, we've discussed various pieces of a training plan: objectives, methods, audiovisual resources. We've also discussed strategies for sequencing instruction (tell, show, invite, encourage, and correct). In this chapter we describe how to put these pieces together in a written format that describes how to bring the training to life.

The Purpose of Training Plans

Although you may have a general idea of what training plans are, we identify two specific purposes. First, training plans connect what the trainee needs to learn (needs assessment) with training objectives. Second, a training plan also connects the training objectives with the methods the trainer uses to help trainees master the objectives. If the training objectives aren't clearly linked to what trainees need to do in order to successfully perform their job, the training will have little value. The training plan describes the step-by-step behaviors that the trainer performs in presenting the training; the plan provides the sequence and detailed overview of what you will present.

Without reviewing the trainee needs, objectives, and methods, the training plan sequence may not achieve your intended results.

Connecting Training Needs with Objectives

As we have emphasized throughout our description of how to design and deliver communication training, the process of planning a training session begins with a focus on what a trainer needs to learn. As shown in Figure 8.1, the development of the training plan occurs after the trainer has made several decisions about key elements of training

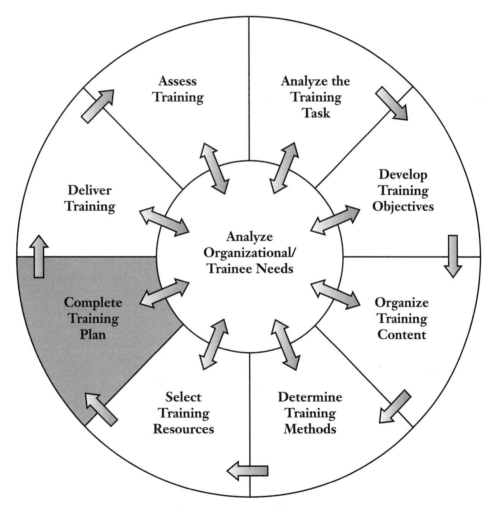

FIGURE 8.1 Needs-Centered Training Model The trainer is ready to develop and complete the training plan after decisions have been made about training content, methods, and resources.

design. Driving the entire process is an ever-present focus on the needs of the trainee. We will discuss several types of training plan designs in this chapter. Regardless of the specific training plan format you select, each training session should be focused on a clearly worded training objective, which is based on what the trainee needs to learn. If a training plan fails to make the link between needs and objectives, the training plan will be ineffectual.

How do you ensure that a training plan is built on the strong foundation of addressing trainee needs? As you begin to assemble the pieces of the training plan (e.g. lecture content, activities, presentation aids) to organize into a coherent whole, review the results of the trainee needs assessment that you've conducted. If you or the organization for which you're preparing the training session has not conducted a formal needs assessment, you should nonetheless marshal what information you do have about your trainees. What skills do they need? What is your best guess as to their current levels of competency? At a minimum, talk with supervisors or human resource personnel to ensure that your objectives appropriately address trainee needs. In essence, we suggest that you reflect upon the alignment between the perceived trainee deficiencies and the training objectives.

Connecting Trainee Objectives with Methods

Once you are reasonably certain that the training objectives are appropriate, the next critical function of a training plan is to align the training methods you've selected with the training objectives. How do you do this? In Chapter 6, we reviewed classic training methods and described their primary functions. Before developing your training plan, reflect upon the primary methods you've selected to confirm that what you *do* during the training is the best strategy for accomplishing what you want trainees to be able to perform. If, for example, the objectives call for the development of specific communication or leadership skills and you are primarily lecturing to the trainees, there is a disconnect between what you're trying to accomplish (skill development) with the method of achieving your objective (in this case, lecturing). Skill development occurs when trainees have ample opportunity to practice the skill you are teaching. Training plan objectives that contain verbs such as *demonstrate, perform,* and *present* should include training methods that give trainees an opportunity to enact the skill being taught.

The primary functions of a training plan are to document that the planned training meets trainee needs and that what occurs during the training (training methods) will appropriately address the planned objectives. Building in success starts by ensuring that the critical training functions are aligned; the trainee needs, training objectives, and training methods should be clearly and logically connected. Without an alignment of these critical functions, the training plan will be flawed.

Preparing to Write a Training Plan

While you may have an understanding of the elements of a training plan, you may still wonder, "How do I actually write a training plan? What do I do first?" If you've been following the action steps described in the needs-centered training model, you've got most of the information you need to start drafting your plan. After developing your objectives, you assemble the information and methods you need to accomplish your goal. The typical action steps include: (1) conducting research, (2) developing training content, (3) determining training time frames, (4) selecting training methods, and (5) selecting training materials. Let's review each critical step.

Conducting Research

You're a human resource trainer because you undoubtedly already know something about communication, leadership, managing change, organizational development, or other human resources skills. But whether you have a Ph.D. in communication or have only a limited academic background in "people skills," you will not be able to draft training plan content off the top of your head. You will need to read, review, and research to find the most up-to-date information for your training presentation. Consider reviewing such sources as the World Wide Web and library sources, as well as interviews. Review our strategies for conducting research, presented in Chapter 5.

Developing Training Content

Training content is the information, definitions, descriptions, concepts and skills that you present to trainees. The information could be spoken or written. The training content is the heart of the training session. How do you transform your research efforts into material that you can use in a training session? The short answer is: Focus on trainee needs. It is possible to feel overwhelmed with the avalanche of information that you could present in a training session. One of the reasons that a trainer may spend too much training time lecturing and not enough time developing skills is because the trainer has been a good editor. Just because you have information to present does not mean the information is useful. Edit, sift, evaluate, and cut training content that does note relate to your training objectives. Review Chapter 5 for some specific tips on developing training content.

One strategy to developing training content is to identify key action steps or skills that trainees need to master; consult your task analysis. As you are surfing the Internet and reading books and journals, keep your training objectives handy. Consider organizing your notes so that you have each training objective on a separate sheet of paper or in a separate computer file. As you find information that relates to an objective, summarize the information using the objective as the heading. Using your training objectives will help you focus your research and develop training content that is aligned with trainee needs. In the early stages of drafting training content, don't worry about capturing all of the details of a training resource that you uncover. Make your notes brief and consider jotting down references to page numbers where you can go back and find more detailed content if you need the information. When sketching out the training content, many trainers like to begin with a general outline of key points rather than developing a detailed script of the training content. (In fact, we don't recommend that you develop a word-for-word transcript of your training presentation.)

Focus first on general ideas and skills and come back later and fill in the details as needed. Using the music analogy that began this chapter, first develop the general melody before working out the details of the harmony, rhythm, or instrumentation.

Each trainer may use a slightly different method of drafting training content. Some trainers grab a pad of paper and find a place where they won't be disturbed and begin jotting down ideas. Do you think better at a keyboard? If so, you may want to reflect on your research and the notes you've taken as you've read and begin tapping out your ideas into your computer. At this point in drafting training content, the goal is to generate more ideas than you'll use. The brainstorming technique involves generating as many ideas as you can without evaluating them. Once you've assembled a draft of your ideas, then go back and edit and revise. Many people can be more creative if they give themselves permission to capture all ideas before self-censoring them. Once you have a list of key topics, you can begin to whittle on the list. One of the key criteria for determining what eventually will remain in your training session is the amount of time you have to present your training.

Determining Training Time Frames

As you begin making decisions about training content, you should simultaneously being making preliminary decisions about time constraints. One of the primary limitations of a trainer is time. In the corporate world, the cliché "time is money" remains true. Managers and supervisors want training to be presented in as short an amount of time as possible so as to minimize trainees' time off from their jobs. As we've noted, one of the reasons training is expensive is not only the cost of designing and delivering the training but also the lost work time invested when trainees are in a training session rather than performing their duties. Multiply the hourly wage of a worker (plus benefits) times the number of trainees in the training session, and you can quickly identify the true cost of training. Thus, there is pressure to make training as efficient as possible while also being effective.

Although training could be presented in any number of time blocks, standard time formats for a training period are typically two-hour sessions, half-day sessions, six-hour sessions, or a full eight-hour day of training. A skill such as listening could be introduced in a two-hour training session, but it may take a full day or longer to incorporate ample practice to master the skill. There is often tension between the need for additional time to adequately present training skills and the drive for trainees to "get in and get out" of the training session. The complexity and importance of the skill coupled, with the training budget, are factors that determine the amount of time devoted to a particular training session.

A training session longer than one or two hours is constructed around a sequence of training modules. A **training module** is a specific block of training that is focused on a particular skill or concept without a break. Most training modules run from a minimum of 30 minutes to no longer than two hours. It would be ideal if each training module could focus on one or more training objectives that are focused on a cogent, discrete skill or set of skills. Sometimes, however, breaks may need to be scheduled before the conclusion of a module to accommodate the needs of the trainees.

Determining Training Methods

With a knowledge of the essential training content as well as a general understanding of the time constraints, the trainer can make more informed choices as to what precise methods will be used to deliver the training. Until you have an idea of the general time parameters, you will have difficulty selecting appropriate methods that can be implemented in given time frame. If time is short, you'll need to select a method that is efficient as well as effective. As discussed in Chapter 6, the lecture method is often the most efficient way to present training content, but it's typically not the most effective. In Chapter 2 we noted how adult learners prefer to be actively involved in solving problems that affect them rather than passively listening to someone present information to them. Work sheets, structured discussions, videos, or reading material offer an alternative strategy to lectures when you need to present information in a short period of time.

In addition to time constraints, another factor that will influence your choice of training methods is the size of the audience you're training. It's easier to make a training session interactive if your training group is small (20 people or fewer); inviting trainees to practice listening and feedback skills and to participate in role plays are examples of interactive experiential methods. With a very large group of people, it is more difficult to monitor the trainees' behavior and gauge whether they are appropriately performing the skill or activity. There are, nonetheless, ways of maintaining the attention and active involvement of trainees, even in a large group. Using structured worksheets and dyadic activities that can be performed while people are seated are two strategies that can be used to make even a large group session interactive.

As you're making decisions about which training method to use, you may need to revise your decisions as you look at such factors as time constraints and the size of the audience. When developing your training plan, remain flexible as you consider a number of training method alternatives. When you write a research paper you rarely use your first draft; so it is when you prepare a draft of your training plan.

Selecting Training Materials

Although our needs-centered training model in Figure 8.1 presents the elements of training in a seemingly step-by-step sequence, the truth is you are making several decisions about training design simultaneously. As you are making decisions about training methods, you are also making decisions about the materials that you will need to implement your training. Some decisions will be easy. If, for example, you plan to show a video, you will obviously need the appropriate equipment. If you plan to use a case study, then you will need a printed copy of the case for participants to read. Other decisions are less obvious. When, for example, you are presenting lecture material, you'll need to decide whether you'll want to display some of the information you share on overhead transparencies or use a PowerPoint display.

Your training plan should include a reference to all materials that you will need to conduct the training. Audiovisual equipment, transparencies, PowerPoint slides, activities, case studies, and role play instructions should all be clearly described in your

RECAP

Steps in Preparing a Training Plan

What to Do	How to Do It
Develop training content.	Identify key training topics. Be guided by training objectives. Brainstorm training content based upon research.
Determine training time frames.	Determine or conform to training time limits. Make decisions about the length of each training module.
Determine training methods.	Use a variety of training methods to achieve the training objective. Use active rather than passive training methods.
Select training materials.	Develop the participant's guide. Identify and describe all training tools, such as PowerPoint visuals, flip charts, and markers, that you need.

plan. To make it simple, you may want to reference the page number in the training plan from the participant's guide so that you can quickly direct trainees' attention to the information or case study when needed. The **participant's guide** is the workbook that each trainee will have in front of him or her during the training that contains all handouts and any other information needed during the training. The participant's guide is analogous to the textbook you have for a class; it includes essential training content that you'd like the trainee to remember. In most cases, it should eliminate the need to pass out separate sheets of paper during your training session. We'll offer some tips on preparing the participant's guide later in the chapter.

Training Plan Formats

Once you've researched your topic and decided on the essential content of your training, as well as made decisions about the time frame, methods, and materials, you're ready to draft the training plan. But precisely what does a training plan look like? If you are working as a trainer in a large organization, the department in which you work may provide a specific format for you. Regardless of the way the training plan looks, five elements should be included in any written plan:

1. *Objectives:* A complete statement of all training objectives.
2. *Training content:* A summary of the information you will present either in lecture, lecture/discussion, video, or key information from the participant's guide.
3. *Time:* An estimate of the amount of time needed for each lecture, activity, video, or other component of the training.

4. *Method:* A clear description of the methods that will be used.
5. *Materials:* A brief description of all materials that will be used in the training session.

If you have the option of developing your own approach, we offer three formats for including these five elements. The format you select is based on your own preferences or the preferences of the client if you're preparing a training plan that others will use. First, we'll discuss the **descriptive format;** it is the least structured approach. It consists of a narrative, using subheadings and paragraphs to describe each training element. The second format it the **outline format.** As the name implies, the essential elements are organized much as you would a typical outline. Finally, the **multicolumn format** organizes the information in four columns that support each training objective. What's the best training plan format? It depends. If you need considerable detailed instruction for presenting a training plan, the descriptive format may be best. The outline format proves additional structure so that you can easily find information and lecture notes. The multicolumn format is preferred by many trainers because of the ease of finding information and noting time cues for each activity or change of activity.

Descriptive Format

The descriptive format presents the five essential elements of a training plan in much the same way as you would write a paper. Using subheadings, this format presents the information in an expository style. Figure 8.2 on page 172 illustrates a training plan using a descriptive format.

Outline Format

The outline training plan format provides more structure than a narrative format. As with other training plan formats, the same five elements of objectives, time, methods, content, and materials should be included in the plan. The difference is that, as you might suspect, the outline format presents the training content using an annotated outline. The training content is organized using a traditional outline style (roman numerals, capital letters, Arabic numbers, lower-case letters). Annotations of the lecture contact can be written as bracketed notes to indicate how long each part of the training should last. Methods are labeled, and enough information is presented so the trainer can follow the outline and annotations to present the training. Many trainers like the structure of the outline format because it makes it easier to find information at a glance. Figure 8.3 on page 174 presents an example of the outline training plan format.

Multicolumn Format

The most structured training plan format presents the essential training plan elements in four columns of information that support one or more training objectives. The specific training objective should be written at the top of the page; the information in the four columns (time, content, method, materials) supports the objective or objectives. Some trainers write the training objective at the top of the long side of the page so there is more room for information in the four columns.

FIGURE 8.2   Descriptive Training Plan Format

Session I: Introduction to Listening

Objective: At the end of this session, the participants should be able to describe three reasons why listening skills are important to their job.

Time: 9:00 AM–9:30 AM

Materials needed: Flip chart and markers
                    Participant's Guide, page 1
                    Overhead Transparency # 1

Training Content and Methods

Introduction:

Introduce yourself and describe the logistics for the workshop (e.g. where the refreshments are located, ground rules for attendance, restroom location). Establish set induction with the following question: Do you know a good listener? [Ask for a show of hands.] Ask: Do you know a bad listener? [Ask for a show of hands.] Ask participants to write brief responses to the following questions, which are listed on page 1 of the participant's guide:

1. Describe the characteristics of a good listener.
2. Describe the characteristics of a bad listener.
3. What would you like to learn about listening skills today?
4. Why are listening skills important?

[Give the participants five minutes to write responses to these four questions. After they have made written responses, place them in groups of four or five people and ask them to share their responses. After about seven minutes of discussion, debrief the activity by asking participants how they responded to the first question. Record their responses on a flip chart. Ask them how they responded to the second question. Record their responses on a flip chart.] Tell them that they have just given themselves the short version of the seminar: Do what they said good listeners do and don't do what they indicated bad listeners do. Then ask them: If you already know this information why should we have this seminar? Summarize their responses orally. They will probably talk about how it is one thing to know what to do and another skill to put what they know into practice.

Ask them what they would like to learn. [Record their answers on the flip chart or on a pad of paper that you can use to guide you through the activities. In essence, you are conducting a brief needs assessment to check your understanding of what skills they need.]

Importance of Listening Skills Lecture/Discussion

Ask them to share their responses to the fourth question. [Invite them to tell you why today's workshop is useful (e.g. get the message out of them rather than putting a message in them)] After they have shared their reasons, present a short lecture in which you describe why listening skills are important. Include the following information:

(continues)

FIGURE 8.2   Descriptive Training Plan Format (*Continued*)

1. Some research suggests that listening comprehension of a message drops 50 percent 24 hours after it was heard.
2. Additional research indicates that listening comprehension is reduced to 25 percent comprehension 48 hours after the message was heard.
3. Younger children are attentive listeners, but their attention span is short: 90 percent of first graders could repeat what the teacher was saying in the class; 80 percent of second graders could repeat what a teacher had just said; 44 percent of junior high students could repeat the teacher's message; and 28 percent of high school students could repeat their teacher's lecture content. There is evidence that as we get older we become less attentive.
4. We spend more of our communication time listening than any other activity, but we spend relatively little time receiving listening skill training.

Conclude this section of the training providing a preview of what will be presented in the seminar.

Each of the four columns describes crucial information the trainer needs in order to present the training session. The first column includes the time frame for each training event or activity. The next column describes the key training content. The information in this column may include some of the same information from the participant's guide, which summarizes essential training content. Although you don't need to provide a complete transcript of your lecture content, you should provide enough detail so that the information makes sense to you. The third column provides a description of the training methods used. It is helpful if each method is clearly labeled (e.g. lecture, case study, role play) so that the trainer can easily identify the training method being used. Again, provide enough detail so that the description of the method is clear to you or whomever will use the training plan. The final column describes any materials that are needed to present the training. Figure 8.4 (pages 175–185) presents a sample half-day training program using the multicolumn format. One disadvantage of the multicolumn format is that is may be more challenging to draft because of the constraints of organizing material in each column. Consider using the table function on your word processing program to create the columns. A key advantage of the multicolumn format is the ease with which a trainer can identify what should be taking place at any given moment in the training.

Preparing the Participant's Guide

At the beginning of most training sessions, each participant is given a participant's guide—a collection of handouts or a workbook that contains the core information, worksheets, and activity instructions that will be presented in the workshop. Adult learners like to have a comprehensive summary of all information that will be shared during the workshop. Many participant's guides are assembled in three-ring binders; some are simply stapled together. In seminars that will be presented to a large number of people, the participant's guide may be professionally published. Appearance counts.

FIGURE 8.3 Outline Training Plan Format

Module 3: How to Prepare a Meeting Agenda

Objectives: At the end of this session, training should be able to write an agenda for a team meeting using the four principles of an effective meeting agenda.

Lecture/Discussion [15 minutes]

I. Determine meeting goals [Overhead # 1]
   A. Information items include what the team needs to know.
   B. Discussion items give the team an opportunity to share information.
   C. Action items are those are those in which the team needs to make a decision or do something.

II. Identify agenda items that need to be included on the agenda [Overhead # 2]
   A. Brainstorm for meeting agenda items.
   B. Eliminate agenda items that do not relate to meeting goals.

III. Organize the agenda items to achieve the meeting goals [Overhead # 3]
   A. The first item on the agenda should be to ask for other agenda items.
   B. Consider high-priority items early in the meeting.
   C. Place items early where you think there may be consensus.
   D. If the information is not needed in the meeting, place information items last.

IV. Test and evaluate the agenda before the meeting [Overhead # 4]
   A. Before the meeting, ask for feedback about the agenda.
   B. At the beginning of the meeting, ask if everyone can agree on a meeting ending time.
   C. List major topics for discussion using a flipchart, overhead projector, or PowerPoint slide.
   D. At the end of the meeting, evaluate the effectiveness of the meeting and meeting agenda.

Demonstration [2 minutes]: Show participants examples of well-constructed meeting agendas.

Individual Activity [10 minutes]: Ask participants to individually draft a meeting agenda for their next meeting using the principles and strategies for drafting an agenda.

Group Activity [15 minutes]: Place participants in groups of four or five people to share their agendas and ask group members for feedback about their agendas.

Instructor Feedback [10 minutes]: Following the group activity, the instructor can point out examples of effective agenda design and offer any suggestions for improving participant's agendas.

FIGURE 8.4 Multicolumn Training Plan Format[2]

Training Topic: Welcome & Overview

Behavioral objectives: *At the end of this section, trainees will be able to:*

1. Identify at least three things that can be accomplished through interviewing.
2. Recognize the three general elements of interviewing that will be discussed.

Time	Content	Methods	Resources
8:00 AM		Introduce self	Overhead #1 (Welcome; overhead projector and screen)
8:05 AM		**SET INDUCTION:** What's this all about? As managers, you're required to conduct one-on-ones each quarter. How many of like to do them? Would you you like to know some ways to make them a little easier? This seminar is designed to present you with some tools that will help you be more comfortable with conducting one-on-ones.	
8:10 AM		**GROUP DISCUSSION:** Why do you conduct one-on-one interviews?	Overhead #2 (write answers on the overhead)
8:15 AM	I. Why one-on-one interviews can accomplish all of these purposes: A. Individualized B. Specific to the employee C. Other responses from the group	**LECTURE/DISCUSSION** *Discussion Question:* What are some strengths and weaknesses of one-on-ones?	Overhead #3 (strengths & weaknesses; write responses on the overhead)

(continues)

175

FIGURE 8.4 Multicolumn Training Plan Format[2] (*Continued*)

Time	Content	Methods	Resources

8:20 AM	II. Preview of the seminar
	   A. Preparation
	   B. Conducting the one-on-one
	     1. Opening the one-on-one
	     2. Leading the main
	       discussion
	     3. Closing the one-on-one
	   C. Evaluating effectiveness
	III. Emphasis is on communicating
	     the appraisal
		LECTURE/DISCUSSION	Overhead #4
			(Preview)

8:25 AM		**PRETEST ACTIVITY** Please take a few minutes to complete the questionnaire. Survey the results by raise of hands.	Overhead #6 (Pre-test) Participant's Guide page 6.

Training Plans/Module 2

Training Topic: Planning the One-on-One Interview

Behavioral objectives: *At the end of this section, trainees will be able to:*

1. List five elements of interview preparation.

2. Complete an interview plan in preparation for a one-on-one interview.

Time	Content	Methods	Resources
8:30 AM		**SET INDUCTION:** Were any of you involved in sports? How much time did you spend preparing for the game? I was an equipment manager. We spent 2–3 hours gathering everything together. Your job is to gather	

Time	Content	Materials
	pieces together. Would you like to know how to gather pieces more easily?	

8:35 AM	**LECTURE/DISCUSSION**
	
	I. Guiding principle: One-on-one = investment (Quote)
	II. Identify who
	III. Identify purpose
	  A. What do you want to do?
	  B. What do you want employee to do as a result?
	IV. Plan discussion topics (Evaluation)
		Overhead #7 (Guiding principle II)
		
		Overhead #8 (Preparing the one-on-one)
		
		Overhead #9 (Identify purpose)

8:40 AM	**DYADIC ACTIVITY:** Place trainees in dyads to discuss this question: What are some of the factors you take into account when preparing an evaluation?	Overhead #10 (Preparing the evaluation activity) Participant's Guide page 10
8:43 AM	**CIRCLE RESPONSE:** The group reassembles and forms a circle. Each group member shares best answer.	Overhead (write answers)
8:45 AM	**LECTURE/DISCUSSION** A. Identify gap between desired and actual performance B. Determine business reasons for change C. Determine consequences if no changed D. Determine appropriate action to facilitate change	Overhead #11 (Preparing the evaluation) Overhead #12 Participant's Guide page 12 (Different perceptions)

(continues)

FIGURE 8.4 Multicolumn Training Plan Format² (*Continued*)

Time	Content	Methods	Resources

	V. Arrange the Meeting
	  A. Time
	    1. Convenient
	    2. No conflict
	    3. Ample time for both of you
	  B. Place/Environment
	    1. Accessible
	    2. Comfortable
	    3. Free from distractions
	    4. Free from clutter
	VI. Inform the Employee
	  A. How communicated?
	    1. In person
	    2. Telephone
	    3. E-mail
	  B. When
	  C. Reminders
	    1. How early?
	    2. How often?
		Discussion questions:
		From your experiences, are some times better than others?
		What logistics do you think about when setting up a one-on-one?
		
		Discussion questions:
		What are some different places where you have conducted your one-on-ones?
		Did certain places work better than others?
		
		Discussion question:
		What are some ways that you have informed employees of pending interviews?
			Overhead #13
			(Reveal "Time")
			Flipchart: Write responses
			
			Overhead #13
			(Reveal "Place")
			
			Overhead #14
			(Inform the employee)

9:00 AM		**CLOSURE** Quote: "You may look at an interview as merely an administrative chore; for the subordinate, it is very serious business." Match their seriousness?	Overhead #15 (Just another one-on-one?)
9:07 AM		**INDIVIDUAL ACTIVITY:** Follow the steps just discussed. Identify an employee with whom you need to conduct a one-on-one interview. Determine the purpose(s) of the meeting, the discussion topic(s), where and when the meeting will be held and how you'll tell him.	Overhead #16 Participant Guide page 16 (Practice preparation)

five-minute break until 9:20 AM

Training Topic: Conducting the One-on-One

Behavioral objectives: *At the end of this section, trainees will be able to:*

1. Give one original example of a behavioral description.
2. List the four components of training a skill.
3. Set SMART goals with your employees.
4. List four ways to encourage employee participation.

Time	Content	Methods	Resources
9:20 AM		**SET INDUCTION:** Remember that game you prepared so long for? The key to winning was implementing all the individual skills you had learned. All the dribbling and shooting practice, etc., had to be in sync all at once. Next, we'll talk about all the individual pieces of conducting the one-on-one.	
9:25 AM	I. Opening the one-on-one interview A. Greet B. Visit informally to establish climate C. Ask open-ended questions to encourage talk	**LECTURE/DISCUSSION**	Overhead #17 (3 part of the one-on-one) Overhead #18 (Opening the one-on-one) Reveal one part at a time
9:30 AM		**INDIVIDUAL ACTIVITY** Write an original question for an interview.	Overhead #19 (The opening question) Participant's guide page 19
9:32 AM		**BUZZ GROUP** Share the question with a neighbor.	
9:34 AM		**GROUP DISCUSSION** What are some questions?	

(continues)

179

FIGURE 8.4 Multicolumn Training Plan Format[2] (*Continued*)

Time	Content	Methods	Resources
9:35 AM	D. Preview interview 1. Why the employee is here 2. Preview topics 3. Intended length (45 min to 1 hr)	**LECTURE/DISCUSSION**	Overhead #20 (3 parts of the main discussion)
9:37 AM	II. Lead main discussion A. Follow-up on previous goals 1. Review previous meeting 2. Evaluate success of goals		
9:40 AM		**SET INDUCTION** Bubba—"You're a different person"	
9:42 AM		**GROUP DISCUSSION** Discussion prompt: "What's wrong?"	
9:45 AM	B. Present evaluation 1. Behavioral description a. Objective b. Specific c. Tell what was good d. Ask what could be better	**LECTURE/DISCUSSION**	Overhead 321 (Behavioral descriptions)
9:55 AM		**SMALL GROUP ACTIVITY:** In groups of three, modify the sample evaluations I provided for you.	Overhead #22 Participant's guide page 22 (Sample evaluations)
10:00 AM		**INDIVIDUAL ACTIVITY:** Write an original behavioral description for the previous employee. Share it with your neighbor.	Overhead #23 Participant's guide page 23 (Behavioral descriptions)

Time	Activity	Content	Media
10:02 AM	**SET INDUCTION:** How could you use a one-on-one as a time for training? What kind of skills could you train?		Flipchart: Write answers
10:05 AM	**ROLE PLAY ACTIVITY:** In pairs, one of you teach the other how to complete the special order form (see page 24 for more instructions).		Overhead #24 Participant's Guide page 24
10:10 AM	**LECTURE/DISCUSSION**	C. Training 1. Explain 2. Demonstrate 3. Practice 4. Evaluate	Overhead #25 (Quote) Overhead #26 (Training new skills)
10:15 AM	**DYADIC ACTIVITY:** Teach the same skill using four steps.		Overhead #27 Participant's Guide page 27
10:20 AM	**GROUP DISCUSSION:** How did it improve with four steps?		
10:25 AM	**LECTURE/DISCUSSION** *Discussion question:* Why do we set goals? What are examples of success?	D. Setting Goals that are SMART: 1. Specific 2. Measurable 3. Achievable 4. Realistic 5. Time sensitive	Overhead #28 (Setting goals)
10:35 AM	**SMALL GROUP ACTIVITY** Evaluate sample goals.		Overhead #29 Participant's Guide page 29
10:40 AM	**GROUP DISCUSSION** Review group's evaluations. Tip: Use five-point scale		Overhead #29

(*continues*)

181

FIGURE 8.4 Multicolumn Training Plan Format[2] (*Continued*)

Time	Content	Methods	Resources
10:45 AM		**INDIVIDUAL ACTIVITY** Write an original SMART goal for the previous employee. Then share with neighbor. Rewrite, if needed, for five points.	Overhead #30
10:50 AM		**CLOSURE:** Goals make the world go 'round. An effective goal will force the employee to stretch him- or herself. Even if the goal is not completely met, progress will have been made. You need only be sure to make him or her aware of it.	
five-minute break			
11:00 AM		**SET INDUCTION** Have you ever conducted a one-on-one where the employee said very little if anything at all? You felt like you were talking to the wall. Would you like to know how to get the employee to talk a little more?	
11:03 AM	E. Encouraging participation 1. Ask questions a. Leading questions b. Closed questions c. Open questions d. Probing questions 2. Paraphrase a. Ideas b. Feelings c. Expectations	**LECTURE/DISCUSSION** Brief overview/suggestions to encourage participation	Overhead #31 Overhead #32 Overhead #33

Time	Content	Media

	3. Listen
	  a. Look
	  b. Nod
	  c. Sigh
	  d. Pause
	4. Nonverbal
	  a. Appearance
	  b. Gestures
	  c. Posture
	  d. Eye contact
	  e. Facial expressions
	  f. Voice
		Overhead #34
		
		Overhead #35

11:15 AM	F. Closing the one-on-one
	  1. Review topics
	  2. Make goals (SMART)
	  3. Arrange for follow-up
	  4. Give sincere praise
	
	LECTURE/DISCUSSION
		Overhead #36

11:25 AM	**CLOSURE:** It seems like a lot of pieces. Once your skills are polished, the pieces fit together easily. Remember the circle? The one-on-one will progress naturally around it as you guide the employee through the interview.	Overhead #20

(continues)

FIGURE 8.4 **Multicolumn Training Plan Format[2]** (*Continued*)

Training Topic: Evaluating the One-on-One

Behavioral objectives: *At the end of this section, trainees will be able to:*

1. Evaluate the one-on-one using the criteria presented
2. Create interview evaluation instruments

Time	Content	Methods	Resources
11:30 AM		**SET INDUCTION:** Remember that game? Did you ever watch game films? Evaluating the one-on-one is just like watching those game films. There are some tools that you need to know how to use.	

11:33 AM	I. Evaluating the one-on-one
	  A. Self
	    1. Review purposes/goals
	    2. Assess if met
	  B. Employee
	    1. Feedback form
	    2. Follow-up meeting
	II. Record results
		LECTURE/DISCUSSION	Overhead #37
			(Evaluating the one-on-one interview)
			
			Overhead #38
			Participant's Guide page 38
			
			Overhead #39
			Participant's Guide page 39
			(sample forms)

11:40 AM		**CLOSURE:** Why should you take time to evaluate the one-on-one? . . . As we said earlier, the one-on-one is an investment of your time and energy. Evaluating it helps that investment mature. You are able to improve your own performance and your ability to influence that of your employee.	

Training Topic: Evaluating the One-on-One

Behavioral objectives: *At the end of this section, trainees will be able to:*

1. List a few tips to increase interview effectiveness.

Time	Content	Methods	Resources
11:50 AM		**GROUP DISCUSSION** At scout camp my favorite activity was archery. We shot for the bull's eye. Today I hope I hit your bull's eye. What are some of the things that will stick with you? (write answers on overhead)	Overhead #40 (Bull's eye)

12:00 AM	I. Too often appraisals lead to apathy
	  A. These skills prevent that
	  B. Feedback must be given often
	  C. One-on-one must be consistent with day-to-day feedback
		LECTURE/DISCUSSION	Overhead #41
			(Appraisals & apathy)
			
			Overhead #42
			(A final note)

12:10 AM	II. Thanks III. Seminar evaluation forms	**SEMINAR ASSESSMENT**	
12:15 AM		**CLOSURE:** Appraisal interviews are essential to the continual development of your employees. It just can't be a bunch of words though. You need to back up everything you say with the things you do. Poem: "A sample, not a sermon"	Participant's Guide page 43 (poem) Overhead #43 (Thank you)

Source: Training plan prepared by Nathan Faylor, Southwest Texas State University. Used by permission.

Your credibility as a trainer is often first made based upon the quality and appearance of the participant's guide.

Some participant's guides consist of nothing more than all of the PowerPoint visuals that are presented during the workshop. One visual may be printed per page, or perhaps three slides are presented on the left-hand side of the page with room for participants to make notes on the right-hand side. Although the duplicate PowerPoint approach will work, it's not very creative. Also, the PowerPoint slides may not contain all of the information and experiential activities presented in the workshop. With the advent of computers with desktop publishing software, most participants will expect an attractive and polished set of materials.

A useful way of preparing the participant's guide is to use your learning objectives as the overall outline of the seminar. Draft training content that relates to each learning objective. You don't necessarily have to include the learning objectives in the participant's guide (some trainers do and many trainers don't), but the learning objectives can help you frame the content you're including in the workshop.

In addition to the key content, the participant's guide should contain directions for participating in the activities and exercises you're presenting in the workshop. During a training session, it's helpful if *every* activity, even very simple ones, has written directions that can be read in the participant's guide. There will always be some participants who won't be listening and will need the redundancy of having directions they can see as well as hear.

Organize the participant's guide just as you organize the workshop. Each training module could be given a title to help the participants understand the overall structure of the training. A table of contents at the beginning of the participant's guide will help the participants quickly locate information.

Some trainers like to put only a few words or phrases on each page of the participant's manual. This helps you control the attention of the participants. If, for example, a page has a list of only four or five principles, you can keep the participants focused on only the page with those principles rather than having them read information that is not supporting your spoken comments. Other trainers like to economize and make the participant's guide as brief as possible, which means that each page of the participant's guide is packed with considerable information. We suggest, however, that the participant's guide have information organized in such a way that you control the focus of your trainees' attention. We think less is more. A brief list of information or skill steps is preferred in that your participants aren't tempted to read detailed descriptions of information you're presenting while you're presenting it. If you want to provide extensive information on a topic, more than you'll be discussing in the workshop, consider putting that information in an appendix at the back of the participant's guide. The participants will have the information but not be distracted by it while you're talking.

Be sure to clearly number each page of the participant's guide. You'll want to be able to tell participants how to quickly and easily find the information in the guide. You will also reference the page numbers in your training plan.

If the material that you are presenting is not original material, you should provide a reference to the source of the information in the participant's guide. At the bottom of the page you could provide the full bibliographic citation. Or you can provide a brief citation with the complete bibliography listed at the end of the participant's guide. If you're adapting material, you'll need to also indicate which material is adapted. As we indicated in Chapter 5, you will need to ask for permission to include more than 250 words of material from a source if the material is to be published. *Always* document your sources and, when in doubt, write for copyright permission if you are using extensive material that has been published.

Rather than using one of the training plan formats that we presented in this chapter, some trainers simply annotate their participant's guide including notes, examples, and other material that they plan to present during the workshop. An experienced trainer may find this training plan format the most useful. For beginning trainers, developing a comprehensive training plan helps the trainer think through the entire presentation.

Practical Training Planning Tips

Most experienced trainers have learned some useful tips that serve them well when constructing training plans. The following suggestions may help you coordinate the complex task of planning a training workshop.

Draft the Participant's Guide First

Because the key information that you want trainees to learn is contained in the participant's guide, consider drafting the participant's guide first. Once you have assembled the handouts and lecture summary and thought about when you may need activities, simulations, case studies, or other more interactive methods, you're really preparing the training plan itself. Even if you don't incorporate all of the activities and other variety of methods that you'll use in the workshop, preparing the participant's guide may help you distill the key content you're presenting to the trainees. Such a fine-tuned focus on the content can help you also fine-tune the decisions you'll make in constructing the overall structure of the trainings you present.

Remember the 20-Minute Rule

Every 20 minutes, you should strive for a change in method or activity. The exception to this rule is that, if the activity involves considerable interaction on the part of the trainee, then the activity can be sustained for longer than 20 minutes. After you've drafted your training plan, review the length of each separate activity. If you planned on lecturing for more than 20 minutes, consider an interactive training strategy that can be more engaging (andragogical) than passively sitting and listening to you talk. You can do the math. If you have a one-hour training session, you should have at least three different types of training activities or methods within that hour. If it's a 90-minute block of time, then you'll need from four to five different types of activity. Although you could have two 20-minute blocks of lecture, because there is a change in training method, it's best to sprinkle lecture or lecture/discussion sessions evenly throughout the day rather than having a heavy dose of lecture concentrated in one segment of the training session. Once you've drafted your training plan, it should be easy to see if you've violated the 20-minute rule; if you have, develop creative options to keep the training interesting and trainees involved (stimulus variation).

Build in the Skill Training Sequence

One way to ensure that you have a variety of training methods is to review your training plan to determine if you have used the five-step sequence for teaching a skill we introduced in Chapter 4: Tell, Show, Invite, Encourage, Correct. Incorporating the "tell" step is usually the easiest but least novel method to incorporate in training; the challenge will be to ensure that you're not overdoing the "tell" step. After you present a lecture about your training topic, do you have a "show" step? Have you demonstrated either in person, with a simulation, or using a video example, how the skill you are teaching should be incorporated? Check to make sure that you appropriately demonstrate how to perform the skill you're teaching. If you're truly teaching a skill, the next activity should invite participants to perform the skill. If you're not teaching a skill, this step will be hard to incorporate. Invite the participants to practice the skill you've taught. After performing the skill, find ways to provide feedback to the trainees so that they are given positive messages to encourage their accurate performance. But also make sure you've provided appropriate correction. If trainees perform a skill but are not given corrective feedback to improve their performance, they may leave the session thinking they have mastered the skill when, in actuality, they haven't.[3]

Plan for Contingencies

Although we've stressed the importance of careful training planning in this chapter, realize that rarely does a trainer follow the exact time frame that has been planned. Why? Things happen. For example, if your session starts a few minutes late, you'll have to shorten a lecture or an activity. If participants take longer than expected with a group activity or need more time to complete an assessment inventory or to respond to an activity in which they write their responses, you'll need to find ways to save time. In some instances you zip through material more quickly than you've planned. If your trainees can master the objectives in less time than needed, there is no need to prolong a session unless, for some reason, they can't return to work or you cannot dismiss them early.

One technique to speeding up or slowing down a session is to alter the size of groups for group activities. The larger the group, the longer it usually takes for discussion; the smaller the group, the less time it takes for the conversation to occur. Putting people in a dyad rather than a five-person group can significantly reduce the time of the activity. If you really need to cut time, you could eliminate the group activity completely. But without the interactive component, you may reduce the effectiveness of the session.

Another time-consuming part of many training sessions occurs when each small group that has been discussing a question or brainstorming solutions reports back to the larger group. One way to speed up the process is to have each group record their key ideas on a flip chart and then post their ideas for others to observe. Rather than having oral reports, have each participant take a few moments to walk around the room and observe the posted summaries. All ideas are presented, yet precious training time is not spent in oral presentations. Another approach is to have each small group present their one or two best ideas rather than a summary of the entire conversation. After the entire group has heard the top two ideas, invite groups to share other ideas. We're not suggesting that small group reports should always be eliminated, but when you need to speed up the training process, these short cuts can help keep you on schedule while still capturing the most important ideas shared in small groups.

Revise, Revamp, Reconstruct

Before the age of word processing, it was more difficult to revise and edit a training plan that the trainer may have thought was complete. Today, however, words are malleable. There's really no excuse not to revise training plans before the training is presented. If at all possible, complete a draft of the training plan far in advance of the training date so you will have time to let your ideas incubate.

Testing the Training Plan

The plan is prepared, and you're ready to put the plan into action—or at least almost ready. If you have the luxury of time consider several strategies to help you test the effectiveness of your plan. Here are several strategies that can help you avoid training problems with new training plan.

Conduct a Focus Group

A **focus group** is a small group of people selected to discuss a particular topic so that others can better gauge how people will respond to a product, topic, or corporation. Advertisers often use a focus group for market research. The objective of most focus groups is to analyze or evaluate information, ideas, or products. A focus group could be asked to review a draft of a training plan and then asked for feedback about the objectives, content, methods, and materials that are proposed. Or, the group could respond to an oral description of the training program. The focus group leader will then ask questions and probe for a detailed response to the planned training. The reactions of focus group members can be used to improve the training session.

Conduct a Pilot Test

To **pilot test** something means that a test or trial run is performed before being officially released for wider presentation; the goal is to determine how effective the program is or identify what needs to be changed. Instead of having a focus group read about the training or react to verbal descriptions of a training session, the training could be presented for a small group of people and then, following the training session, they could be asked several questions to enhance the training as well as express the virtues of the training. A pilot test is especially useful if the training is going to be presented to many groups of people. The pilot test can be used to make changes and adjustments to the training as well as the participant's guide before the training is rolled out for its final presentation. A pilot test is to training what a beta test is to assessing new software. The bugs can be identified and fixed before the product is made available to the entire population.

Invite an Expert to Review the Training Materials

Besides focus groups or a pilot test, the training could be given to experts in the subject matter area for review and refinement. If, for example, you have designed a training program that focuses on cultural diversity, it would be wise to have one or more experts review the training design and the training content to ensure the training information is accurate. Before printing dozens, hundreds, or even thousands of participant's guides, an expert may be able to spot errors in the applications of research conclusions. It's also useful to have another set of eyes review the training material to proofread the grammar, spelling, and punctuation of the text. After working with a manuscript or training material for some time you may become oblivious to errors that are readily apparent to someone else. Most publishing houses have expert copyeditors and proofreaders to review final manuscripts before a book is published. You may not be able to secure the services of a professional, but it is a good idea to have someone other than the author of the words to read through all material before presenting it to others.

Summary

The practical process of developing training plans has been the focus of this chapter. First we discussed the purpose of training plans—to provide a written description of the content, methods, materials, and time sequence of a training session. Specifically, we discussed how training plans should connect trainee needs with the training objectives. They should also provide a connection between the objectives and training methods. A well-written training plan has training objectives and methods that are aligned with the trainee needs.

The steps of preparing a training plan include first conducting research to gather accurate material for the training. The content for the training is developed from the reading and research; training content forms the essence of what is presented in lectures and other training methods. The trainer should also be mindful of the time constraints of a training session during the training planning process. The amount of time for the training will dictate the amount of information that can be presented and also has obvious implications for the methods that may be used. The shorter the time frame, the more efficient the training methods should be, while also providing opportunities for the trainees to be actively involved in the learning. Final decisions about the training method are determined after the content has been determined. The audiovisual materials and other tangible materials are also selected and described on the training plan.

We discussed three types of training plans. The descriptive plan presents the information in a narrative format while also including information about the content, methods, time, and materials. The training objective is also identified. The outline format offers more structure than the descriptive format in that an outline pattern is used to organize the training content. The multicolumn format is often the most preferred format because of its ease of use; trainers can easily identify the content, methods, and materials at given time periods throughout the training session.

Practical training planning tips include: Draft the participant's guide first; remember the 20-minute rule; build in the tell, show, invite, encourage, and correct training sequence; plan for contingencies; and constantly revise and edit the training plan.

We concluded the chapter by offering three strategies for testing a training plan before the training is presented to a larger population of trainees. A focus group may be used to ask for feedback about the training based upon a written or verbal description of the training. Conducting a pilot test (trial run) of the training for a small group and then asking for feedback is especially effective in determining if there are any problems with the training content or training sequence. Or ask an expert to review the training plan to evaluate both the content of the training and the strategies for presenting the training.

QUESTIONS FOR DISCUSSION AND REVIEW

1. What are the primary purposes of developing training plans?

2. What steps are involved in preparing a training plan?

3. What are the three formats for developing a training plan? Describe the advantages and disadvantages of each format.

4. What are five practical tips for developing training plans?

5. How can you test a training plan to ensure that it will achieve your training goals?

QUESTIONS FOR APPLICATION AND ANALYSIS

1. Tiffiny is having a hard time getting started in developing a training plan on the topic of how to give an effective performance appraisal interview. She's having difficulty because she's not sure how to go about presenting an effective performance appraisal interview. What advice would you give her to help her get started with her task?

2. Travis has completed his training plan, but he'd feel more comfortable if someone else reviewed it before he presents his training session. He's asked you to do this. What criteria could you use to evaluate his training plan?

3. Mandee is not sure which training plan format to use—descriptive, outline, or multicolumn. She is presenting a half-day workshop on the topic of how to be interviewed by a member of the media. She's not very knowledgeable about this topic and will need to be able to present her training session without appearing to spend considerable time reading from her training plan. Which training plan format would you recommend that she use? Explain your choice.

Ask the trainees:
- can you see yourself doing
this? → relevance!!

CHAPTER

9 Delivering the Training Session

time
eye contact
delivery/facial expressions
vocal cues - prosody

CHAPTER OBJECTIVES

After studying this chapter, you should be able to:

1. Deliver a training session that considers the physical and psychological needs of the trainees.
2. Identify, analyze, and appropriately use environmental factors to enhance the training session.
3. Describe four characteristics of seating arrangement as they relate to training delivery and response.
4. Describe and use nonverbal techniques that promote nonverbal immediacy during a training session.
5. Describe and make language choices that promote verbal immediacy during a training session.

Imagine that a CEO has commissioned that a new symphony be composed for a special benefit concert for the local hospital; the performance is one month away. The composer, working frantically, has written the music in less than 25 days. The composer then selected the orchestra performers from the best orchestras available. But although the music is written and the orchestra members are skilled professionals, the orchestra has not had time to rehearse. Having the completed musical score on the music stand ready to perform does not mean the orchestra is ready for a performance. Similarly, having well-prepared training plans neatly placed on the lectern does not mean that you're ready to deliver your training session. This chapter explores delivery from a practical, how-to perspective. Specifically, we explore how to plan and deliver a training presentation in a way that enhances trainer credibility and facilitates learning. We'll discuss ideas to help you plan your delivery and then offer strategies to help you deliver a well-polished presentation. We conclude the chapter by offering some suggestions to help you develop a personal improvement plan to enhance your training delivery skills.

Planning Your Delivery

"Just do it" may be a good slogan for selling tennis shoes, but it's *not* a good motto when it comes to delivering a training session. Successful delivery happens by careful planning, not by accident. But even with your best planning effort, things can go wrong or just not work out well when delivering your training presentation. In general, however, success favors the prepared trainer. Spontaneity is good, but "planned spontaneity" is better.

Planning your delivery means giving careful consideration to and detailed integration with training methods, content, and objectives. Planning delivery without considering these factors is incomplete and is likely to lead to problems. Specifically, when preparing to deliver your training session, it's important to consider two primary elements: (1) your audience (the trainees) and (2) the training environment. We'll offer strategies help you answer audience and training environment considerations.

Consider Your Trainees

True to our emphasis on need-centered training, among the first considerations when preparing your training delivery are the needs of your trainees. With trainee needs in mind, it is critical to ponder such basic issues as: What are the physical needs of the trainees? How long can trainees be attentive to a training presentation? What delivery method will best reach this group of trainees? No matter how mesmerizing a trainer's delivery, listeners need periodic breaks in the training. Over a half century ago, psychologist Abraham Maslow suggested that people have five basic need categories that are arranged in a specific order (i.e., a **hierarchy of needs.**) If you've had a course in psychology you probably remember that the first and most fundamental of these categories is **physiological needs.**[1] Trainees will need access to water and food, particularly during a daylong training session. Classic training advice suggests, "Don't keep adults sitting for more than two hours at a time." You'll find that as you approach 90 minutes of talk and activity, most trainees are ready for a break; at the absolute maximum, two hours is the limit. To refine this principle further, as we've noted in Chapter 8, trainers should talk no more than 20 minutes at a time without switching to another training method. Though you are energized and ready to plow through your training material, it's important to plan for stretch breaks during the training sessions.

Some trainees may have medical conditions that require them to take medications at certain intervals. Requiring adults to sit and focus for long periods of time is likely to foster drowsiness, lack of attention, or even agitation. If your training plans don't call for a break but you see trainee attentions wandering during the training, you need to be flexible enough to provide a short spontaneous stretch break, even if trainees just stand for a couple of minutes to stretch a bit.

In addition to physical needs, another aspect of audience consideration is **attention span**—the amount of time people can focus on a given event or activity. Some speculate that adolescents have attention span limits of about eight minutes, corresponding roughly to television programming time sequences between commercial breaks. Adults, too, have attention span limits. Lengthy, drawn-out training sessions that drone on and on are likely to lose trainee attention, even if the information and delivery are great. Even a motivated, interested audience can stay focused on any one task for only a certain amount of time (roughly only 20 minutes or so). Effective trainers keep the pace of the sessions moving and use various engagement strategies to deliver the material. When planning the delivery of your training material, segment and sequence your material in to manageable "bite sizes." **Apportioning** (how a trainer segments material into separate units) is a key to successful training.

In addition to being mindful of the length of training sessions and using a variety of methods, consider the overall tone you wish to establish. You need to develop a training style that connects to people rather than one that just flings information out into space. Presenting information is not the same thing as communicating with others. Communication occurs when listeners understand and respond to the content presented. Successful presentations are dialogues between trainer and trainee even when the trainer is the only one talking.

The best way to create a sense of dialogue during lecture portion of the training—to create a human-to-human connection—is to adopt a **conversational delivery style.** As we've emphasized throughout the book, training material should not primarily be presented via the lecture method. But when a brief lecture is warranted, trainers who are perceived as pompous or who speak over the heads of the trainees will not be successful. In addition, trainers who use an extended vocabulary, exaggerated verbal cleverness, and sentences that are at least a page long will not be warmly received. The best approach is to be authentic, sincere, and natural. Talk to the trainees conversationally just like you would talk to a colleague or friend in a professional setting.

Public speakers are taught that there are four methods of delivering a speech: (1) manuscript, (2) memorized, (3) impromptu, and (3) extemporaneous. A conversational delivery style uses an **extemporaneous** approach. You may use notes or an outline when you speak, but you're not reading from a manuscript, and you haven't memorized your talk, nor are you speaking "off the cuff" in an impromptu style. When you speak extemporaneously, you plan your message; your exact words are not written down; and you have the flexibility to adapt and respond to your trainee comments and reactions to your presentation. If you need to, you can stop, ask questions, and discuss what you've been discussing. If you've mechanically memorized your message or are reading from a script, you won't have the flexibility to make your session a dialogue.

As part of your planning when preparing to deliver a training session there are many things you need to keep in mind. Remember not to talk too long; training is not public speaking. You need to vary your training methods so that the focus is on trainee needs. This focus is important. As we learned in Chapter 2, good training uses andragogical methods rather than a pedagogical approach. Pedagogy is teacher-directed learning; andragogy is student-centered learning. In addition to your approach, you also need to consider how you will talk. You need to speak conversationally; don't plan to writing your material out to read or have memorized. Speak extemporaneously.

Consider Your Training Environment

A second major consideration for a trainer in planning delivery is the training environment. There are at least two relevant environments to consider: the **physical** and the **psychological environments.** On a physical level, questions to consider include: Where will the training take place? What is the building like where I'll be training? Will the concrete demolition project outside the room noticeably detract from the activities of the training sessions? Where do the trainees need to park, and what special parking rules will they need to observe? Are there special zones where smoking is permitted or not permitted? It is important for a trainer to find out about any special building constraints and policies before the training sessions start. Where are the vending machines? The restrooms? Is there phone and Internet access? What other activities or conferences are also being held in the building at the same time as the training sessions? Knowing and sharing these details with the trainees is an important part of the general delivery of the sessions. Being mindful of Maslow's observation that each person has physiological as well as safety needs can help you maintain the comfort and security of your trainees.

Physical Environment.   In the training room, many other environmental issues arise that can potentially influence the delivery of the training material. Where is the thermostat, and who has control over the settings? Many times it is actually an advantage if the trainer has no or limited control over the temperature of the training room. Trainee preferences are extremely varied on this issue, and trying to accommodate all requests on this is absolutely impossible. Still, a training context that is too cold or too hot will detract from the delivery of the material and the overall success of the session. Other room environment issues including lighting, audio and visual controls, and where you will stand while presenting your training session.

An especially important environmental factor is that of seating arrangement. The seating arrangement often determines the amount and type of interaction you'll receive during the training session. If you want to lecture in your training session, the traditional row and column arrangement of chairs is generally best (see Figure 9.1). If you want to promote interaction and discussion among trainees, the horseshoe or circle arrangement is best. If you want to foster team brainstorming activities, the modular arrangement will work best.

In addition to considering how you want the trainees to be positioned in seating patterns, you will also need to consider your own location as a presenter and the posi-

Traditional Seating	**Horseshoe Seating**	**Modular Seating**
		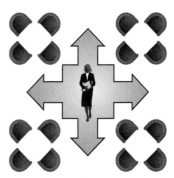

Delivery goal:
  Lecture
Purpose:
  Information dispensing

Delivery goal:
  Facilitated discussion
Purpose:
  Application, participation

Delivery goal:
  Facilitated small group
Interaction purpose:
  Brainstorming, group
  discussion, teamwork

FIGURE 9.1   Seating Arrangements by Trainer Goals

tioning of your presentational aids. It is easy to fall into the trap of inadvertently standing in front of your presentation screen or of placing your presentational aid in a place that is not easy for the trainees to see. Be mindful of where you are in relationship to your PowerPoint screen, flip chart, or other visual aid.

Another issue to consider regarding the physical environment is potential sources of **distractions**—both visual and auditory. Potentials for distractions could come from simple things like unfamiliar parking rules or procedures, building policies regarding smoking zones, or unfamiliarity with restricted access zones in the building. Sometimes it is permissible to bring beverages and food into the training rooms; sometimes it is not. Sometimes there are other activities going on in the building that will disrupt training sessions. Anticipate and identify activities or events that might halt, hamper, or hassle the delivery and momentum of the training sessions.

One technological advancement in particular that has great potential to interrupt, distract, and annoy trainees is the cellular phone. Imagine the irritation of hearing someone's cell phone go off, playing an electronic version of "Happy Birthday," while you are in a movie theater or at the symphony. In libraries, courtrooms, airplanes, and university classrooms, there are firm restrictions regarding cell phone use, and people are directed to turn their cell phones off. Judges often levy stiff fines for people in the courtroom whose cell phones ring during the trial. Cell phones ringing (or playing a tune) during a training session are a distraction. The wise trainer should politely ask that cell phones be turned off at the beginning of the day.

Other potentials for distractions would include hall traffic, clanging construction noise, music wafting down the hall, surprise fire drills, and sputtering intercom systems.

A simple visit to the training site the day before can allow time for the trainer to manage or alleviate potential environmental distractions that could interfere with training sessions. Find out what other corporate activities are scheduled next to your training room. Determine where trainees can and cannot smoke, find snacks (if refreshments are not served during the training), make phone calls, park, and take breaks. In short, make your training session as free as possible from distractions.

Psychological Environment. There are additional characteristics of an environment that are psychological in nature that may have an effect upon your message delivery. One psychological consideration is to assess the organizational culture of the organization. **Organizational culture** refers to the norms, rules, policies, customs, practices, values, history, and characteristics of an organization. To assess the organizational culture you need to consider such questions as: Are innovativeness and diligence perceived as valued and rewarded in this organization? Who are the organizational "heroes" and "villains"? Is the supervisor who arranged your training session seen by the trainees as a villain—someone who is not held in high esteem? What are the organizational myths and legends? Is this training intended to really help trainees and make a difference or is it just management's way of doing lip service to federal requirements? What are the informal norms and formal rules? In addition to the culture, part of the relevant psychological environment will include recent world, state, community, and organizational events. Has there been a recent plant accident where workers were injured? Lastly, the trainer should also consider the mindset and attitude of the trainees.

RECAP
Planning Your Delivery

What to Do	How to Do It
Consider your trainees.	Meet the needs of your listeners. Arrange for breaks. Pace your delivery. Be interesting. Be relevant.
Consider the training environment.	Make sure that environmental conditions are favorable—not distracting— for training delivery. Identify potential visual, auditory, thermal, and psychological disruptions and work beforehand to alleviate or dampen their effects. Ask that cell phones be turned off. Consider where you will stand during the training. Plan for the specific trainee seating arrangement that will suit your training purposes best.

Are they forced to be at this training? Is the training topic controversial? Do they view this training as valuable, a necessary evil, or a waste of time? Though trainee mindset is arguably an audience factor, individually and collectively it shapes and frames the training landscape, and thus must be considered in the environment category as well. The better you can answer questions about the organizational culture and the trainee mind set, the better you'll be able to customize your delivery and address issues of interest to the trainees.

A sensitive trainer is aware of the environmental factors surrounding the training session, both physical and psychological factors. Awareness is just the first step, however. With an awareness of environmental factors, the trainer must plan and shape delivery to maximize results. Different environments will call for different delivery formats, sequences, and styles. Different trainee and organizational cultures call for different types of delivery. The trainer should adapt delivery in view of trainee needs and environmental constraints.

Delivering the Training Session: Establishing Nonverbal Immediacy

After the trainer has spent considerable time planning the session, including planning those training elements that have an impact on presenting the material, the moment finally arrives to deliver the material. But you may wonder, "What constitutes effective training delivery?" At its essence, training delivery is effective if it facilitates learning. Conversely, poor training delivery is any delivery that hampers or detracts from achieving the training objectives. Effective delivery should not call attention to itself; it should enhance the achievement of the training objectives without trainees thinking or saying "What effective gestures" or, "What excellent vocal cues."

Trainers should deliver a session that ultimately enhances trainee desire to approach the material—not avoid it. Audience approach–avoidance feelings are highly influenced by trainee delivery. Effective delivery helps trainees to listen and pay attention; ineffective delivery triggers inattentiveness. Psychologist Albert Mehrabian coined a concept known as **immediacy,** which is defined as "the degree of physical or psychological closeness between people."[2] **Immediacy behaviors** are those behaviors that communicate liking and engender feelings of pleasure. Immediacy behaviors develop a positive relationship between the trainer and the trainees. An immediate or close relationship is fostered largely by communication behaviors. Certain verbal and nonverbal behaviors are perceived as immediate or as nonimmediate and thus foster a general level of immediacy (liking) between trainer and trainees. A trainer fosters immediacy if he or she establishes eye contact with the trainees, avoids distracting movement and gestures, has a pleasant and varied voice, and conveys interest and enthusiasm.

Communication research about immediacy clearly suggests that when instructors are perceived as immediate teachers, student learning,[3] motivation,[4] and ratings of instructional quality are enhanced.[5] Each of these variables is vital in the training context as well. Being an immediate trainer will positively influence the learning and motivation of your trainees. It will also affect their perceptions of your skills as a trainer. In view of the research, when you deliver your training content, it is important to be perceived as immediate.

Precisely what should trainers do to be perceived as immediate? To answer this question in detail, we will consider two types of immediacy: nonverbal and verbal immediacy. **Nonverbal immediacy** focuses on the unspoken aspects of how you present yourself, such as eye contact, posture, and movement, which influences how you are perceived by others. **Verbal immediacy** includes the way you use words and language to convey a sense of interest and involvement with others.

Nonverbal immediacy (feelings of pleasure and liking) is communicated by unspoken, nonverbal behaviors. **Nonverbal communication** is behavior other than written or spoken language that creates meaning for someone. Typically, **nonverbal channels** include things such as vocals, eye contract, gestures, space, and touch. A trainer, for example, does not have to hear a trainee say "I am bored with this session" to know the trainee is bored. The trainer can *see* trainees' bored facial expressions, drumming fingers, wiggling legs, or slouching posture without hearing any words. A trainer might also *hear* the exasperation in a trainee's voice when responding to questions.

Nonverbal communication tends to be more influential and believable than is verbal communication.[6] Nonverbal communication transmits, shares, and connotes meanings that are more fundamental, more relationship oriented, and more loaded with emotions or attitude than those fostered by verbal communication. If there is a discrepancy between what a trainer is saying verbally and what is expressed nonverbally, the trainees will almost always believe the nonverbal message.[7] If, for example, a trainer begins a training session by stating how happy he is to be here today but has a monotone voice with a frowning facial expression and no eye contact, the trainees are not likely to believe the verbal statement. Nonverbal communication is also the primary way people communicate emotions and attitudes. Because of the importance of nonverbal messages in communicating feelings and emotions, a trainer's delivery style plays an important role in how trainees evaluate the entire training experience. Many post-training evaluations tap trainees' affective response to the training (e.g., did they like the trainer and the training?). Because affective responses are often related to how a message is delivered, it is important for a trainer to wisely focus on a training style that communicates immediacy; the evaluations of the trainer's work are highly correlated with the quality of training delivery.

A key focus of this chapter is to identify how to communicate to trainees by being immediate and delivering a message that enhances rather than detracts from a trainer's credibility. Understanding the role and importance of various nonverbal sources of information can provide a framework for enhancing nonverbal immediacy. Typical sources of nonverbal information include appearance, facial expressions, eye contact, movement, use of space, and vocal cues. Through these sources of information, nonverbal messages convey interest, openness, friendliness, helpfulness, relationship, willingness to communicate, and emotional mood. Each of these message outcomes, either positive or negative, has a significant influence on perceptions of immediacy; thus, it is important for a trainer to be aware of effective nonverbal communication and behaviors in each nonverbal channel. In the next sections, we will examine nonverbal channels of appearance, facial and eye behaviors, kinesics, proxemics, and vocal cues, and will look specifically at how to promote immediacy through each channel.

Appearance

Appearance is generally the first set of potential nonverbal messages we receive from another person. Powerful messages, intentional or unintentional or even fallacious, are perceived through this channel. Based on both research and experience, public speaking educators note that "there is considerable evidence that your personal appearance affects how your audience will respond to you and your message."[8]

If you're training in a large corporate environment, a "business look" is often expected in a training setting. One rule of thumb for trainers is to dress slightly better than the trainees. As one personal appearance expert stated, "People who look successful and well educated receive preferential treatment in almost all of their social or business encounters."[9] Trainers need to carefully observe appearance trends and norms in business and adjust their appearance accordingly, paying special attention so that clothing, grooming, artifacts, and formality match that of the trainees.

An important appearance category is that of clothing. In a college classroom, research suggests that student perceptions of instructor dress (formal and professional) are significantly associated with learning and ratings of instruction.[10] Similarly, research indicates that "formally-dressed instructors are perceived as more credible than casually-dressed instructors."[11] In a junior high and high school study, students "liked and could relate to informally dressed teachers" but in fact "they produced more work, and better-quality work, for conservatively dressed faculty members"[12] Other studies have shown that, whereas more casually dressed female instructors were seen as more approachable and flexible, they also were given ratings of least respect.[13] Based on these studies in educational classroom settings, it is reasonable to conclude that in the corporate classroom, trainers should look their best to achieve a positive image.

Precisely what should trainers wear? The short answer: It depends on the expectations (and needs) of your trainees. Over 15 years ago a popular "dress for success" expert, John T. Molloy, suggested, "Traditional, conservative attire works best in at least eighty-five percent of American corporations and in almost all foreign companies."[14] The expert also suggested that for men working in the corporate arena, silk ties, shined shoes, clean-shaven face (no beard), and white or blue shirts work best.[15] For women, suits are the key for success in business.[16] The expert prescribed that closed-toe pumps, neutral-colored hosiery, and matched pantsuits or skirts with a jacket are important to create that business image for women.[17] For men and women, dark grays, charcoals, and navy blues are best. Although these prescriptions may have been good in the late 1980s and 1990s and may still have merit in large traditional corporations, these directives may be of less prescriptive value for trainers today. With more corporations encouraging casual attire, a trainer who presents a too formal appearance may lower rather than increase credibility if he or she overdresses for success. We can't tell you precisely what you should wear; we do suggest that you should dress a bit better than your trainees. If you are in doubt about the expected dress code, either observe what others are wearing (if you are an external consultant, you could

TABLE 9.1   Guidelines for Trainer Appearance

1. Strive for a professional but approachable look.
2. Keep jewelry to a minimum—small not large, tasteful not gaudy; view jewelry as an accessory rather than being the focal point of your appearance.
3. Dress at the same level or slightly more formally than your trainees.
4. Your grooming should be crisp and clean.
5. Your attire should be clean, crisp, pressed, and professional.
6. The attire differential should not be too large between you and the trainees.

visit the organization before training day to assess personal appearance norms) or ask for specific advice. Bottom line: It's usually better to dress more conservatively and formally than attempting to adopt the most recent trendy "look" presented in *Glamour* magazine or *Gentleman's Quarterly*.

In general, it is important to strive for balance and flexibility in terms of how appearance influences immediacy. If, for instance, the trainer is very formally dressed and all of the trainees are oil rig workers in oil-soaked jumpsuits with steel-toed workboots, perceptions of immediacy and connection are likely to be lower between trainer and trainees. In this context, the trainer would obviously want to dress down just a bit to reduce the differential between attire levels and to foster greater immediacy. On the other hand, if the trainer is in an expensive business suit and all of the trainees are middle management in expensive business suits as well, the similarity of attire is likely to produce higher perceptions of connection and immediacy.

Facial Expressions

The face is the primary source of emotional expression.[18] We naturally and spontaneously look to the face of someone to determine his or her mood, intentions, and connotative meanings for what is said. When a training session starts, it is a new and uncertain journey for the trainees. Many times they don't know what to expect and look to the trainer for preview, assurance, and motivation. The trainer may have many of the same uncertainties and reservations, but the trainer really bears the responsibility for setting the stage, establishing interpersonal bridges to the trainees, initiating relationships, and building trust.

It is important that the trainer have a positive, professional, and friendly face. A simple, genuine smile from the trainer at the beginning of the training session has a tendency to relax the audience and open lines of communication. Remember the general facial principle for training situations: Positive, concerned, and sincere facial expressions generally produce better results than do exasperated, sarcastic, and faked facial expressions. Positive facials tend to foster immediacy; neutral, negative, or no facials tend to be perceived as nonimmediate.

It is also important for trainers to have a good "response face" and a good "listen face" when trainees are making comments or are asking questions. Part of this entails making sure to look at the faces of trainees when they are talking; but, even more than this, you must be nonverbally responsive while listening. Smiles, facial reactions, head nods, or even grimaces would all serve to let the trainee know that she or he was being heard. You don't get credit for being a listener unless you look like you're listening.

Eye Contact

The eyes have been poetically referred to as the "windows of the soul."[19] Much information can be sent and gathered via eye behaviors. In North America, direct eye contact is expected, especially in a business context, as a sign of respect, openness, and that you are listening to the other person.[20] One of your authors found that in public speaking situations, increased speaker eye contact enhances speaker credibility.[21] Functionally, trainer eye contact does much to influence how trainees will respond to the training. Even in a large group, each trainee needs to feel that the trainer is making specific and personal eye contact with him or her frequently during the session. This is called **eye depth**—how deeply or personally you see your audience.

The scope of trainer eye contact is also important. **Eye scope** is the range of available eye contact—making sure that all trainees receive eye contact from the trainer during the sessions. Even the best of trainers will gradually tend to look most frequently in certain sections of the room. Sometimes "look" zones are predominately focused in the V pattern (see Figure 9.2). When this happens, trainees sitting outside the V are not visually engaged by the trainer. The "overlook" happens when the trainer misses the first few rows of people and looks primarily at those in the middle and back of the room. The "no look" happens when the trainer looks above the heads of the trainees and never gets "radar lock" with their faces. Sometimes, as noted in Chapter 7, trainers commit the sin of no or little eye contact with the audience because they are spending too much time looking at their elaborate presentation aids. Trainers should always remember that the dialogue is between the trainer and the trainees—not between the trainer and the PowerPoint slides.

There are several methods to use in achieving good eye contact, and thus immediacy, with a training audience.[22] First, the trainer can use a **scan**. An eye scan generally starts at one side of the room and sweeps inclusively and systematically to the other side of the room. If done carefully and naturally, this technique will ensure trainer eye contact with all trainees on a continuous basis. A **spot grid** is a second technique, where the trainer systematically looks at specific zones in the room. If the spots are

The V　　　　　　**The Overlook**　　　　　　**No Look**

FIGURE 9.2　Poor Trainer Eye Contact: Avoid looking only at the center of the room, looking over trainees' heads, or avoiding eye contact with trainees.

strategically spread across the room, the trainer will be able to visually contact clusters of people continuously. In both of these eye contact techniques, the trainer needs to remember to garner **depth** of eye contact. There is a difference between making eye contact with a trainee and simply glazing in the general direction of his or her face. You must have a personal visual contact with the trainee. It is especially important for trainers to maintain good eye contact with trainees when they ask questions. This lets the trainees know that the trainer is giving them careful and personal attention, and that the trainer values and respects the comments being made. The trainer must discipline him- or herself to do this, because it is sometimes easy to shuffle papers, check notes, start looking at notes for the answer, check the time, or look at presentational aids during trainee questions.

In most training contexts, trainer eye contact will typically track closely with trainee perceptions of trainer immediacy. The more eye contact a trainer has and the deeper the eye contact is, the more he or she will be perceived as immediate.[23] Conversely, less trainer eye contact will be associated with less immediacy. This basic pattern holds true for the most part in mainstream North American culture, but not necessarily in all cultural settings. A trainer must be cognizant of various cultural norms for eye contact and must flex accordingly to promote the most optimum levels of immediacy.

Movement

Kinesics is the study of human movement and gestures. People have a tendency to notice and pay attention to things that move—living things. Trainees will tend to pay more attention to trainers who use appropriate gestures in their presentation. In contrast, it is very difficult to look at a trainer who is stiff and still for long periods of time. Gestures should be natural (like those used in informal conversations) and should serve to illustrate and emphasize the material. Interestingly, one cannot assume that more is necessarily better with gestures. There is a range of acceptability. If, for instance, a trainer parks her or his hands on the lectern or in her or his pockets for the entire presentation, immediacy will be diminished for North American listeners. If the trainer's hand and arm motions are wild, exaggerated, and overdone with every word spoken, these overdone gestures will be distracting and will diminish immediacy as well. A normal, conversational balance is needed for optimum effectiveness.

Trainers who typically do not use gestures but would like to incorporate them to enhance their delivery quality are often uncertain as to when or how to incorporate gestures into their presentation. Note the following ways in which gestures can add support to what you have to say: (1) repeating, (2) contradicting, (3) substituting, (4) complementing, (5) emphasizing, and (6) regulating.

- *Repeating:* Gestures can simply repeat what you've spoken to a training group. For example, you can say, "I have four major points to talk about today," and then hold up four fingers.
- *Contradicting:* Because more trainees will believe what you communicate nonverbally than verbally, monitor your gestures to ensure that you are not contradicting what you say. Saying, "Have a nice day," with a frown on your face would be contradictory.

- *Substituting:* Without saying a word you can hold up the palm of your hand to calm a noisy class or put your index finger to your lips to signal that you would like the class to be quiet.
- *Complementing:* Gestures can also add further meaning to your verbal messages by underscoring the importance of a point with a sweeping motion of your hand. Gestures can be used to flesh out—develop more fully—what you are saying verbally.
- *Emphasizing:* By shaking a fist, making a slicing gesture, or pounding your fist on the lectern you can emphasize or underscore a point. Be cautious, however, of overusing gestures for emphasis.
- *Regulating:* Gestures can also regulate the interaction between you and your trainees. If you want your class to respond to a question, you can extend both palms to invite a response. During a question-and-answer session, your gestures can indicate when you want to talk and when you want to invite others to talk.

Should you walk around the room during your training presentation, or should you stay in one place? The answer to this question is: It depends. You may want to move purposefully about while you're presenting information, but take care that your movement does not distract from your key points. If the listeners focus on your movement rather than on what you are saying, it is better to stand still. No movement at all is better than distracting movement. Your movement should be consistent with the verbal content of your message. It should make sense rather than appear as wandering.

A specific time to incorporate movement in your message is to signal the beginning of a new idea or major point. As you move into a transition statement or change from one point to the next, you can signal a change by moving from one point in the room to another.

Posture is another consideration for trainers. Whereas your face and voice play the major role in communicating a specific emotion, your posture communicates the intensity of that emotion. If, for example, you are happy, your face and voice reflect your happiness; your posture communicates the intensity of your joy. A trainer who slouches over the lectern does not send a message of credibility and professional confidence to the trainee audience. Or a trainer who stands at the front of the room with one hip out and all his or her weight on one foot presents a tired, off-stage picture for trainees. Obviously such poses impact the perception of trainer competence, positiveness, and professionalism.

What's the best posture? A century ago elocution teachers prescribed various postures for maximum effectiveness. Today we simply suggest that, for most of your training session, you should stand evenly on both feet with shoulders back and head up; this provides a picture of poise, confidence, and professionalism. Vary your posture to be consistent with what you are saying and to support the emotional content of your message.

Another aspect of movement that requires careful trainer consideration is that of adaptive behaviors. **Adaptors** are nonverbal behaviors that satisfy some physical or psychological need. A wise trainer will watch to see when audience fidget behaviors indicate that they need a stretch break. Trainees also have psychological needs that may show up in adaptive behaviors. Trainees who are nervous or bored will often reveal their true emotional state by consciously or unconsciously enacting a variety of adaptors such as bouncing a leg, drumming fingers, fidgeting, twirling hair, twitching a pencil, looking furtively around the room, or doodling on note paper.

Trainees are not the only ones who will enact adaptive behaviors. Trainers also may enact adaptors, consciously or unconsciously, that may have a negative influence on the training sessions. Trainers who are nervous will often have idiosyncratic behaviors that accomplish no apparent function, such as twitching, rubbing their nose repetitively, head scratching, twirling hair with their fingers, cracking their knuckles over and over, pacing, or jingling the keys in their pockets. Make sure you're not saying one thing ("I'm enjoying being a trainer") but sending another message nonverbally ("I'm bored").

Interestingly, most of the time people who engage in adaptive behaviors do not realize they are doing it. A trainer's adaptive behaviors typically have a tendency to reduce perceptions of his or her immediacy. Trainer adaptive behaviors may also damage trainee perceptions of the trainer's credibility or simply may call attention to themselves and thus serve as a distraction in the session. It is wise, consequently, for trainers to be aware of and to control and eliminate as many of their own adaptive behaviors as possible.

Space

Proxemics is the study of space and how the use of space communicates. Every individual has an invisible bubble of space that surrounds him or her. There are specific needs for specific distances in front of you, in back of you, and to the sides of you. This is true of the physical distance between a trainer and the trainees. To a point, the further you are away from people, the less immediate they perceive you. If you violate someone's space by getting too close to him or her, perceptions of immediacy will go down as well.

Anthropologist Edward Hall presents a classification system of interaction proxemics and the types of behaviors that typically occur in each classification zone.[24] The *intimate zone* has the proxemic characteristics of touching to 18 inches. Typically this zone is reserved for intimate or very close friends. Generally, trainers would want to stay out of this zone with their trainees. The *personal zone* is generally 18 inches to about 4 feet. This zone is reserved for family and close friends. Again, trainers would probably not want to enter this zone with their trainees for the most part. The *social zone* measures 4 to 12 feet and is populated by casual friends and acquaintances. This also the zone in which most business encounters occur. This is the optimum proxemic zone for a trainer. Most training sessions and even break time visits with trainees will and should occur in this zone. The *public zone* measures 12 feet and up and is generally the zone used for public speaking and presentations. Obviously, a trainer presenting a PowerPoint presentation at the front of the training room is likely to be operating in this zone. A training session in a small conference room would probably function in the socio-consultive zone instead.

A trainer who stays too far away from the trainees or hides behind podiums will not be perceived as immediate. In fact, trainees may perceive her or him as cold and distant. Conversely, a trainer who consistently violates personal space norms by getting

RECAP

Classification of Spatial Zones

Zone	Distance	Activity
Intimate space	0 to 18 inches	Communicating personal information
Personal space	18 inches to 4 feet	Personal conversation with friends
Social space	4 feet to 12 feet	Working in teams and small groups
Public zone	12 feet and beyond	Public lectures and presentations

in the personal or intimate zones of trainees will be perceived negatively as well. There is a time and place for different proxemic behaviors. Before sessions, at break time, and after sessions, it is appropriate for the trainer to interact with trainees in social zone and perhaps in a very limited way on the outer fringes of the personal zone. During training sessions, it is most appropriate for trainers to use the social and public zones, proxemically. Careful balance and attention to proxemic norms and expectations will promote good levels of trainer immediacy with the trainees.

Vocal Cues

It's been said that it's not what you say, but how you say it that really makes the difference in how a message is interpreted. This principle aptly describes the role of vocal cues in training sessions. The term **vocal cues** refers to the volume, articulation, dialects, pitch, inflection, rate, and use of pauses as you speak. In keeping with the principles that nonverbal messages are more believable than verbal messages, if vocal cues conflict with verbal messages, the audience will typically put more weight on the vocal messages. Vocal messages provide much information about the speaker's emotions and interest in a topic. Given the power of vocal messages to communicate enthusiasm and interest, one of the worst errors a trainer can make is to speak with a monotone voice.[25] A **monotone** delivery is one with a droning, one-pitch vocal tone. A monotone delivery is boring, and listeners typically tune out the message.

Predictably, if a trainer is monotoned, the trainees will perceive him or her as being low in immediacy.[26] Trainees are likely to conclude that the trainer is bored with the material and with them and think that he or she really does not want to be there. Admittedly, there may be some trainers who really are excited about the material but simply have monotoned voices. Most people are not monotoned when they are in a dyadic conversation with a friend. Therefore, most people expect and prefer a natural, varied speaking voice rather than droning monotone. Even a trainer who has presented the same material dozens of times needs to have the same vocal excitement and energy and emotion that was characteristic of the first few times through the material.

Other specific vocalic characteristics that need careful attention include volume and projection. Speak with appropriate intensity—the combination of volume and

RECAP
Guidelines for Nonverbal Immediacy

1. *Appearance:* Take your cue from the appearance of your trainees; dress better than trainees, but don't over do it.
2. *Facial expressions:* Trainers should openly express interest and positive feeling through their face and eyes for optimum immediacy. Sincerely smile and appear genuinely friendly.
3. *Eye contact:* Eye contact—have it in abundance! Remember scope and depth.
4. *Movement:* Involve your body with the message. Appropriately move with the material.
5. *Space:* Vary the space between yourself and your trainees depending upon the training activity. When lecturing you can be further away (12 feet or more) than when working with trainees in small groups or teams.
6. *Vocal cues:* If you are bored with the material, trainees will hear it in your voice. Speak so your audience can always hear you clearly and distinctly.

appropriate pitch variation. Trainers need to vary the loudness and softness of their voices to match the meaning of the content and momentum of the delivery. When speaking softly, trainers need to ensure they are still projecting enough to be clearly heard. In addition, trainers should avoid talking to training audiovisuals rather than to the audience; a corresponding reduction of volume, projection, and clarity (as well as eye contact) results from talking away from the audience.

In large training sessions, carefully consider how you use the microphone and electronic public address system. Most microphones, including hand-held or clip-on models, are unidirectional (they pick up sound from only one direction). If you're using a unidirectional microphone, remember to talk into the top end of the microphone rather than into the side of the microphone. In addition, spare the audience the piercing feedback scream that results when the microphone is positioned in front of the speakers. And even though you may assume there will be a working amplification system, be prepared to deliver the training sessions without a microphone if necessary.

Delivering the Training Session: Establishing Verbal Immediacy

In addition to nonverbal immediacy, a trainer needs to be aware of verbal immediacy as well. Verbal immediacy is the psychological closeness that is promoted by words and word choice. The specific language or wording you use as a trainer promotes or discourages immediacy. A verbally immediate message communicates liking and inclusion.

One of the best ways to be verbally immediate is to use personal pronouns and other words in your talk that reference you and the trainee as a team. Words such as *we*, *us*, and *our* communicate that you and the trainees are joint participants working on the same side for common goals. Trainer talk should build bridges of relationship or "we-ness" between the trainer and the trainee. Such work choices help connect you and your trainees. Using the word *we* implies that we are a team and are going to do something together. It shows that trainees can approach you as the trainer with questions, comments, and ideas.

Nonimmediate verbal messages are talk that divides, puts the trainer on one side and the trainees on the other side, and frames the trainer as an impartial observer. The key is to use phrases and words that align you as the trainer with your trainees. Examples of inclusive immediate and noninclusive, nonimmediate statements can be seen in the following statements:

Verbally Immediate Statements	*Verbally Nonimmediate Statements*
As *we* consider this problem *together*, *we* need to generate a plan that is better than that of *our* competition. When we go on break, we need to not smoke inside the building.	*Your* goal is to formulate a better plan than that of *your* competition. You can't smoke in the building. It violates company policy.
So how are *we* going to address this *problem?* What causes *us* difficulty in listening to opposing viewpoints in a conflict? *Our* goal is to work together better in teams.	So what are *you* going to do about this *mess* you've caused? Why won't *you* employees listen when *your* manager is telling *you* about necessary cost reductions? *Your* supervisor says *you* don't work well in teams. This has to stop.

In addition to using inclusive language, verbally immediate trainers attempt to actively involve trainees in discussion rather than treating trainees as passive listeners. Interacting with trainees before and after the formal training session also increases verbal immediacy—it suggests you're not just interested in trainees as people in your training class, but that you have a genuine interest in them. Additional verbal immediacy behaviors include:

- Using personal examples or talking about your personal experiences outside of class.
- Asking questions to encourage trainees to talk.
- Addressing trainees by their first names.
- Providing feedback on individual trainee work by offering specific, relevant comments.
- Asking trainees how they feel about requests and assignments given by the trainer.

Being verbally immediate requires you as the trainer to "think immediately"—to be immediate by including your trainees in your conversation. Don't talk at them; talk with them. We don't encourage you to try to write specific verbal immediacy phrases down that you can then periodically insert in your conversation. Scripted verbal immediacy is likely to be ineffective; most listeners can spot a phony. Work to develop inclusive, immediate ways of talking with your trainees by encouraging interaction and dialogue. If you condition yourself to "think immediate" with your trainees, being verbally immediate will come more naturally.

Strategies for Evaluating and Improving
Your Training Delivery

Every trainer has unique personality and communication characteristics that will influence the delivery of the training material. As you prepare to conduct the training sessions, consider your strengths and weaknesses in terms of delivery. It may be helpful to reflect on these questions: Do you manage time well, or do you always find yourself running overtime? Do you have a tendency to hurry through your material and get done very early? Do you find yourself dominating all of the talk time in the session, even during discussions, or are you good at drawing participation from the trainees? Do you tend to stand in front of the screen, blocking the view of one side of the room? Are you good at planning or spontaneously using humor in your presentations, or does your humor typically fall flat or cause problems in your sessions? Do you appear credible and organized to your audience, or is there something about your delivery that typically undermines audience confidence in you and your material? Do you have a tendency to get enamored with the concept (or even the "PowerPoint" animations) so much so that you forget to spend sufficient time in the application thereof? Do you have a tendency to become exasperated by "stupid" questions? All trainers have delivery techniques that are really strong and work very well. All trainers have delivery characteristics that tend to detract from the message and make the sessions less effective. Being aware of how to improve your training delivery is the first step in improving your delivery style.

There are several ways to identify and address your delivery weaknesses as a trainer. From time to time you may want to videotape your training sessions so you can view the tape and analyze your delivery strengths and weaknesses. Watch the videotape imagining that you are a trainee listening and watching the presentation. Observing yourself train on videotape is especially helpful when evaluating your nonverbal behavior.

Another effective way to examine your delivery is to pay careful attention to trainee comments on the training session evaluation forms. It is likely that you will get random negative comments from time to time, but if you notice clusters and trends of comments that address certain aspects of your delivery, you might want to take notice and adjust accordingly. Asking a fellow trainer to attend one of your sessions and to critique your delivery would be a third way to develop your delivery. Colleagues who do training as well will be especially tuned to how you are doing what you are doing in a training session and thus will be valuable sources of insight and development. No training presentation is ever perfect, and no trainer reaches a point in which training delivery is flawless.

Professional trainers constantly assess and adjust their delivery for maximum effectiveness. The checklist in Table 9.2 is designed to be used by trainees in reference to the session, you referencing your own delivery as the trainer, or a colleague rating your delivery.

In addition to your specific delivery strengths and weaknesses, when evaluating your delivery you should consider whether you are perceived as credible. **Credibility** is the trainee perception of your character, competence, and dynamism. Credibility is not something you have; it is given to you by the audience. It is a trainee perception about you. There are things about you, your communication style, what you do, how

TABLE 9.2   Trainer Delivery Evaluation: Please rate your trainer's delivery skills, using the following items and scale.

	Poor	Fair	Average	Good	Excellent
1. Vocal projection	1	2	3	4	5
2. Eye contact	1	2	3	4	5
3. Credibility	1	2	3	4	5
4. Use of natural gestures	1	2	3	4	5
5. Conversational style	1	2	3	4	5
6. Connection with audience	1	2	3	4	5
7. Confidence	1	2	3	4	5
8. Responsiveness to audience	1	2	3	4	5
9. Facial expression	1	2	3	4	5
10. Vocal variety	1	2	3	4	5
11. Time use	1	2	3	4	5
12. Pacing of presentation and material	1	2	3	4	5
13. Use of presentation aids	1	2	3	4	5
14. Ability to hold audience attention and interest	1	2	3	4	5

you act, your delivery traits, that trigger audience perceptions of whether or not (or perhaps, to what degree) you are credible as a trainer. You might be perceived as a trainer who is a pleasant person but one who doesn't always have a deep understanding of the material or how it applies realistically in a corporate setting. You might be perceived as a person who is a jerk but who knows what he or she is talking about and has great experience in that area. The ideal is to be perceived as a sincere, authentic person who is both knowledgeable of and successful in applying the training concepts being presented. You want to be perceived as an expert who can be trusted.

Being perceived as credible has important benefits. If you have high credibility, the trainees may forgive some of the delivery errors you commit. If you are not perceived as credible, the audience is more likely to focus on each delivery mistake you make and see it as proof of your incompetence and insincerity. Ways to increase perceptions of your credibility include the following top 10 Be's:

1. *Be confident:* Act as if you know what you are doing. Look with friendly face and eyes directly at the trainees. Stand up straight. Be poised.
2. *Be well marinated in your material:* Know your material backward and forward. Know material that surrounds your actual session material. Make sure your material is current. Soak in your material.
3. *Be authentic:* Adopt a conversational, natural, and personal style. Don't be too slick or impersonal. Use verbally immediate language. Treat and interact with trainees in the way you want to be treated.

4. *Be responsive to trainee comments and needs:* Listen. Don't interrupt. Don't be so focused on your training agenda that you sideline or ignore trainee comments. Address trainee comments verbally. Look at trainees while they are speaking. Be nonverbally immediate when responding to questions.

5. *Be polished in your delivery:* Maintain personal eye contact with the entire audience. Move smoothly yet appropriately around the room. Enact natural gestures and movements—gestures that fit your style of communicating with others. Pay attention to even small delivery details, such as what you are doing with your hands as you speak.

6. *Be open to new perspectives:* A contradiction is an opportunity to have a dialogue. Be willing to question your prepared material aloud. Use trainee comments to complement training materials.

7. *Be professional:* Respond to trainees in a friendly and diplomatic way. Handle conflict calmly. Refuse to argue but be open to discuss new ideas.

8. *Be prepared:* Test your microphone settings before anyone arrives for the training session. Make sure your slides are sequenced and your computer is booted and ready to go. Make sure all copies are made in sufficient number for your trainees. Make sure you have contingency plans.

9. *Be on time:* Show up to your training session site significantly early. Start punctually. Stop for a break on time. Dismiss for lunch punctually. Expect timeliness from trainees. Move through training materials in a balanced and flowing manner.

10. *Be relevant:* Make sure that your training materials address trainee needs. Relate training content to the trainee in-baskets—their everyday lives and jobs. Relate materials to the organizational functions and activities. Relate materials to current events.

Summary

Effective delivery starts in the planning stage. When planning your delivery, consider both the needs of your trainee and the physical and psychological training environment. When considering your trainees' needs, remember not to talk too long without varied methods or without taking a break. Be guided by the organizational culture to help you fine-tune your delivery approach, content, and style.

As you deliver your training material, monitor your appearance, facial expressions, eye contact, movement, space use, and vocal cues in such a way that the trainees are drawn to you and to your material. Establish nonverbal immediacy between you and the trainees. Immediacy cues communicate liking and closeness between you and others. Immediacy cues include having an appropriately professional appearance, eye contact with your trainees, and appropriately reinforcing movement and gestures to support your verbal message. In addition, use space appropriately and speak with interest, appropriate volume, and enthusiasm. Finally, establish rapport with your trainees by using verbally immediate statements that include rather than exclude trainees from your conversation. Speak *with* rather than *at* trainees.

Improving your delivery skills is an ongoing process. After you present a training presentation, watch videotapes of your training to assess your nonverbal behavior. Make a special note of comments from trainees on evaluation forms that address delivery issues. Then, adjust!

QUESTIONS FOR DISCUSSION AND REVIEW

1. Explain how poor delivery of training content can severely limit the effectiveness of training outcomes.

2. Why is it important to plan for effective delivery? What are the prime considerations when planning to deliver a training session?

3. What is effective training delivery?

4. What is the difference between verbal and nonverbal immediacy? How do each of these influence your training delivery?

5. What principles should guide a trainer's selection of clothing and appearance?

6. What are the four space zones, and what kinds of communication activities occur in each zone?

QUESTIONS FOR APPLICATION AND ANALYSIS

1. Alan's cultural background and personality predispose him to stand quite close to people when he is delivering a training session or just talking with trainees at break time (sometimes as close as 12 to 24 inches). This has made several trainees uncomfortable. Alan is not aware that he violates other people's space. He believes that he is being appropriately immediate. Explain how Alan is violating Edward Hall's interaction zones.

2. Savannah wants to facilitate small group interaction during her training session. List and discuss three seating arrangements that she might use in her training, with the relative advantages and disadvantages of each for promoting interaction. Which seating arrangement would maximize interaction?

3. Tynisha has been receiving poor training evaluations following her training session presentations. Several of the trainees in Tynisha's sessions have made general comments about her overall ineffective delivery and her low level of enthusiasm exhibited during the training, but they have not offered specific comments to help her improve her training. What should Tynisha do to develop a plan to improve her training delivery? What kinds of delivery cues would increase Tynisha's perception as an immediate trainer? How can she increase her credibility?

CHAPTER OBJECTIVES

After studying this chapter, you should be able to:

1. Identify strategies to manage quiet, talkative, "bigheaded," negative and aggressive trainees.
2. Describe three conflict management styles and how to select an appropriate style for managing conflict during training sessions.
3. Use conflict management skills appropriately and effectively during a training session.
4. Reduce conflict during a training session by using appropriate affinity-seeking, nonverbal and verbal immediacy, and prosocial behavior alteration techniques.
5. Manage and eliminate trainer misbehaviors.

Although the majority of trainees whom you will be working with during your career as a trainer will be pleasant and cooperative, you will also be confronted with problem trainees. Talk to any experienced trainer, and you will hear him or her saying that "there's one in every group." Many trainers call it the "dark side" of the training business, because you never know what to expect when you enter the training room. Sometimes it is hard to predict how your trainees are going to react to you or your training material. Some trainers ignore the problem trainee, thinking that the problem will go away. Other trainers approach the problem trainee assertively and directly to find out that they only made the problem trainee more irritable and disruptive. Although conflict during a training session can be useful in that it may signal that trainees' needs are not being met, conflict can also be a major source of disruption to your training plans. Conflict can resemble a malignant tumor in that it rarely goes away on its own. Unmanaged conflict spreads and infects other trainees. As a trainer, your job is to see that the conflict is managed constructively.

This chapter is divided into four sections. First, we discuss how to anticipate and then minimize unproductive conflict during training. The second section examines conflict management styles. Third, we identify conflict management skills. Finally, we discuss ways that you can reduce conflict in the training classroom; we provide an assortment of strategies that might help you prevent or reduce conflict from occurring in your training classrooms.

Precisely what is conflict? **Conflict** is typically defined as the disharmony between individuals as a result of differing goals, objectives, values, beliefs, and attitudes. The type of conflict that we're discussing in this chapter is referred to as **interpersonal conflict,** or conflict that occurs between two people and is the result of one person blocking the achievement of the goals of at least one other person. In the training classroom, if you have a trainee who is dominating the discussion and not allowing other trainees to participate, your goal of engaging all trainees in the discussion is blocked. If this problem goes unmanaged, the problem increases. From our experiences, trainees who observe the domineering colleague have little patience for trainers who fail to reduce or manage such a distraction. If the talkative or dominant trainee is not controlled, then other trainees will become resentful of your inability to control the training classroom. Now you have another problem on your hands—resentful trainees. As you can see, one simple problem can be contagious; and, before you know it, you have an epidemic on your hands. Consider this chapter a minicourse in trainer first aid. It's not going to prevent conflict, but it will stop the bleeding.

Anticipating Problem Trainees

Many problem trainees are somewhat predictable; after you gain experience you begin to see the same training problems occur. Before delving into each of the problem trainee types, we'll discuss some of the more common causes of trainee misbehaviors. If you understand the cause, you might be able to treat the symptoms or classroom behaviors that are problematic more effectively. To focus on causes rather than symptoms, consider identifying the underlying trainee needs. According to communication researcher Will Shutz, all humans have three interpersonal needs: *control, inclusion,* and *affection.*[1] We each have a need to control others and to be controlled by others. We also each have a need to be included in others' lives or to include others in our lives. Finally, we each have a need for affection or being liked by others and the need to express our liking for others.

One way to help develop a strategy to approach disruptive trainees is to consider their underlying interpersonal needs. Is their disruptive behavior the result of an unmet interpersonal need for control, inclusion, or affection? What is it that they need more or less of that might alter their behavior? For example, with a trainee who is being overly dramatic and off task, the disrupting behavior may occur because he or she has either no control over the particular task at hand or too much control. If it's not enough control, then build control into the task. Allow trainees some room to make decisions and deviate from your instructions if needed. If the offending trainee has too much control, then rein in some of the control. Put some parameters and guidelines on the training task. If you have a trainee who is trying too hard to be everyone's friend and is driving everyone crazy in the process, try including the overly affectionate trainee in a group so that inclusion needs are met. Similarly, if you have a trainee who is dominating the discussion, this person might have a high need to be liked. Find a way to provide her more attention and to express your appreciation for the trainee's contributions. In short, hypothesize what the problem trainee needs and, if possible, meet those needs.

Here are a few of the problem trainee types that you can anticipate working with in your training classrooms and some specific suggestions for how you might want to manage them.

Quiet Trainees

Quiet trainees are those who rarely talk and are oftentimes misperceived as lacking interest, being slow learners, being aloof, and being apathetic. Some quiet trainees deserve one if not all of these labels. Other trainees, however, are mislabeled or misdiagnosed. Many trainees, because of their personalities or temperaments, prefer not to talk or are apprehensive and fearful about communication in the training classroom.[2] It's not that they are apathetic or lack interest in the training program, it's just that they don't feel comfortable participating in the training classroom. This is problematic, especially in America, where talk gets rewarded. Quiet people are often ignored or overlooked entirely.

Here are a few suggestions for how you might want to work with quiet trainees.[3] Some of these ideas echo those discussed in Chapter 6, which focused on how to use training methods.

- *Avoid consistently calling on quiet trainees:* If you've made an attempt or two to bring the quiet trainees into the discussion without success, wait for them to indicate that they would like to say something. If you continue to call on apprehensive trainees, you will only make them more fearful and more quiet.

- *Avoid assigned seating:* Apprehensive students do not want to sit in what is referred to as the "training zone," or the area immediately in front of the trainer. Communication-apprehensive or quiet students prefer sitting on the perimeter of a training classroom where they are less conspicuous. Let quiet trainees find their comfort zone.

- *Avoid evaluating trainees based on how much they have participated in the training classroom:* Participation is not always an accurate predictor of whether or not learning has occurred. Instead, have quiet trainees complete an exam or have them perform the skill in an environment that remains authentic to their own workplace environment. A silent trainee may have mastered the material; don't always assume that a trainee who doesn't participate is not mentally involved in your material. Some people are just quiet.

- *Make communication a rewarding experience:* Praise trainees for talking, especially quiet ones. Avoid saying "wrong answer." Instead, find a way to encourage the quiet person for contributions; but also find a way to clarify his or her response. You don't want to spread misinformation. Finally, try not to enforce quietness as a punishment.

- *Avoid ambiguity, novelty, and evaluation:* Make all training activities and assignments clear. Make sure your activities and assignments include well-written training objectives and evaluation criteria. Your objective should be to remove any surprises.

- *Increase trainees' control over their success:* Provide trainees with options. Increase their control by allowing them multiple ways to demonstrate their knowledge and skill proficiency.

- *Use the think, pair, share technique:* If you ask a question and get no response, ask trainees to answer the question individually. Then pair the trainees together and have them share their ideas with their partners or in small groups. This gives trainees the opportunity to try out their ideas in a safe environment. They can refine their thinking based on the feedback they get from their peers. Now they're ready to talk to the class as a whole. At this time, pull out answers to your questions by asking the pair rather than the individual trainee. This takes the burden of the individual trainee and makes it safer to talk in the training classroom.

Talkative Trainees

Talkative trainees are compulsive communicators who like to hear themselves talk and who like to dominate the training classroom discussion. Some compulsive communicators are unaware of how they dominate a discussion. Other talkative trainees communicate in order to control the discussion. Again, many trainees find these individuals annoying; and, if they go unmanaged, they will eventually shut down.

Here are a few ways to phrase responses to curb the talkative trainee:

- "I would like to thank you for your contributions, they have added much to our understanding, but I would like to hear from some of the others."
- "Hold that idea for now. Is there anyone else who would like to make a contribution?"

- "I know you know the answer, but I would like to see if someone else might have an answer or an idea."
- "I have only been hearing from a few of you. How about the rest of you? What do you think?"
- "Before I let Carol Ann respond to the question, I would like to hear what the rest of you think."

Usually, these kinds of regulatory statements will work. If not, then it's recommended that you discuss the trainee's dominant communication style using the conflict management skills we present later in the chapter.

Bigheaded Trainees

Bigheaded trainees or know-it-alls are self-proclaimed experts who have done and seen it all. In fact, if they had their way, they would be the trainer rather than the trainee. I'm sure you know the type that we're describing. At times, they're intolerable. Again, if they're not managed well, they have a tendency to hijack the training by shutting everyone else down.

Here are a few suggestions for how you might want to work with bigheads:

- *Meet their control, inclusion, and affection interpersonal needs:* Sometimes these individuals mean well; however, they're unaware of how annoying and disruptive their behaviors are to others. They're also unaware of what is motivating them to communicate in a bigheaded way. Give them more opportunities to be in control. Include them in a group. Express your affection and appreciation for them.
- *Reduce your communication with them:* Rather than agreeing or disagreeing with bigheaded trainees, which they may want you to do, redirect your communication to other members of the training class.
- *Move away from them physically:* Distance has a way of shutting down some of the problematic behaviors. Position yourself next to trainees who are behaving appropriately. When the bighead's behavior improves, reposition yourself closer to the know-it-all trainee whose behavior has improved. This type of reinforcement shapes trainees' behaviors by subtly rewarding appropriate behaviors and punishing inappropriate behaviors by not giving bigheaded trainees the attention they crave.
- *Use their expertise, but channel it so it's not disruptive:* A person who really does have much to contribute can be a training asset, not a problem, if the trainee's comments are structured or if the trainee is given a specific task to perform. Give the knowledgeable trainee a three- or five-minute opportunity to share information and expertise; but carefully reinforce the time limits you impose. Another approach is to give the talkative trainee a specific job to do, such as write information offered by others on a flip chart or white board. The assigned task may meet the trainee's need for attention and minimize the disruption. If all else fails, you may need to politely yet assertively ask the ototototerverbalizing trainee to limit his or her contributions so that others can contribute to the conversation.

Negative Trainees

Negative trainees find the fault in everything you and others do. Rather than seeing the glass as being half full, they see the glass as empty. These employees are pessimistic and are oftentimes defensive. Their negative communication can also shut down others' communication in the training classroom.

Here are a couple of suggestions you might find helpful for how we've worked with them in our training classrooms:

- *Make the training relevant:* Some trainees remain negative because they perceive your training program to be irrelevant to their needs. Once they get into your training program and find out that it's relevant to their needs, then there's a good chance that their negative communication will become less problematic. We doubt that they will become positive trainees, but they will probably become less negative.
- *Give trainees some options:* Negative trainees often feel as though they are out of control when training is mandated from their superiors. No one likes being told what to do. Allow trainees options and choices. Rather than making trainees take a standard training program, allow them to choose from an assortment of training modules, if appropriate. One of your authors remembers conducting a training program where a negative trainee was problematic and infectious from the very beginning of the day. He realized that this trainee was going to be a problem, so he took a chance and invited the trainee to leave the training program without penalty. After break the trainee returned to the training program and was on task for the duration of the day. By being offered an out, without penalty, he was allowed to feel as though he were in control and made the right decision to return to the training classroom.

Another problem that trainers have to manage is when negative trainees share their negative experiences with other trainees. You don't want to prevent them from speaking their mind, because some of their negative experiences can add a level of authenticity or "real-worldness" to the training program, but you also don't want their negative experiences to become defeating to the other trainees who are trying to better themselves. Here are a few suggestions for how to manage negative trainees' troublesome experiences. These strategies echo suggestions discussed in Chapter 6:

- *Acknowledge negative trainees' less-than-positive experiences and empathize with them, but don't dwell on their negative experiences:* Acknowledge their unfortunate experiences and quickly move on. Your job is not to relive the negative experiences but to empower trainees with new skills.
- *Acknowledge the fact that negative experiences are inevitable and that the job of training is to reduce the number of negative experiences:* Use negative trainees' unfortunate experiences as an argument for your training program. It's an automatic way to make your training relevant.
- *Ask negative trainees how new training content might address some of their negative experiences:* Get negative trainees involved by asking them to apply the new training content.

■ *Place negative trainees' unfortunate experiences in a context:* Ask them enough questions so that the other trainees get a fuller picture of the conflict situation. If other trainees begin to understand why the negative trainee has such a negative attitude, it may at least help minimize the distraction of the barrage of negative comments; if possible, attempt to reframe the negative trainees' examples and comments so that they become instructive rather than disruptive.

Aggressive Trainees

Aggressive trainees lack social skills and, rather than arguing constructively or being appropriately assertive, they go on the attack. They attack your character and verbally hit below the belt. This type of trainee behavior is not only considered problematic but is also inappropriate and not tolerated in most training classrooms. Aggressive trainees need to be managed well using a more formalized process of conflict management, which will be introduced in the next section.

Many of the preceding problem trainees can be managed well by using some of the strategies listed above. When these strategies fail, then it's time to approach the

RECAP

Identifying Problem Trainees and Communication Strategies for How to Manage Them

Source of Conflict	Communication Strategies
Quiet trainees	Avoid calling on them to speak. Avoid assigning seats to them. Don't evaluate them or assess them based on how much they talk. Make discussions "safe" for them to express their feelings and opinions. Remove all surprises from session activities. Try to ensure communicative success for them.
Talkative trainees	Find positive ways to curb their domination of the talk time. Find ways to allow other trainees to have input.
Bigheaded trainees	Don't encourage them to keep talking. Acknowledge their contributions graciously and note that there may be differing and equally valid perceptions from others. Make sure other trainees also get the floor to share their views.
Negative trainees	Make sure what you have to say is relevant and practical to them. Try to give them some control and choice in the training process. Empathize and then redirect to the positive. Show how your training is purposed to make things better.
Aggressive trainees	Try to establish rapport. Let them know that you do not condone nor will you allow them to be verbally aggressive to others in the training session.

conflict using some of the conflict management skills listed below. Before delving into the skills, however, it's important to understand that there are three major approaches to managing conflict. We refer to these approaches as conflict management styles.

Understanding Conflict Management Styles

Individuals have different conflict management styles or various ways of dealing with conflict situations. What's your approach to dealing with conflict? Do you run from it? Do you view it as a game where there is a winner and a loser? Or do you view it as problem that can be solved together? In the **nonconfrontational** conflict management style, one fails to manage the conflict by avoiding it or by giving in to the other person's requests. A **confrontational** conflict management style is a win–lose approach, where one wins at the expense of others. The **cooperative** conflict management style, which is the style this book advocates, is one in which you view the conflict as a set of problems to be solved rather than a competition where one person wins and the other person loses.

If you understand the other person's conflict management style, you can then adapt your communication accordingly. For example, if you have a conflict with an aggressive trainee and you know this trainee's conflict management style is more confrontational than cooperative, you can anticipate the trainee's behaviors. This particular trainee will probably attack you verbally. Because you anticipated this type of communication behavior from the trainee, you also make sure that you don't become defensive and return similar attack behaviors. Rather, you keep your emotions in check and process the conflict using many of the conflict management skills listed below.

If, on the other hand, you have to address a conflict with a quiet trainee whose conflict management style is more nonconfrontational than cooperative, then you can anticipate how uncomfortable this trainee is going to be working through the conflict situation with you. It might be most appropriate to manage this type of conflict using e-mail. Regardless of the conflict management style, if you understand the trainee's style, you're more likely to manage the conflict situation well.

Using Conflict Management Skills

This section of the chapter introduces you to conflict management skills to consider using the next time you have to manage conflict with a problem trainee. These communication skills will allow you to remain professional in your communication with a problem trainee. It's important to remember that if the trainee is a problem for you, then the trainee is also a problem for the others in the training classroom. From our training experiences, the other trainees who are performing well want you to address the problem trainee's behaviors. If you avoid the conflict, they become resentful of you and not the problem trainee. If you manage the problem trainee well, you automatically enhance your professionalism with the other trainees, which ultimately allows you to be more influential as a trainer.

Manage the Emotions

Many conflict encounters are emotionally charged situations. If you're not aware of your own emotions, they can sometimes get in the way and exacerbate the conflict. In short, they can add fuel to the fire. In conflict situations, emotions need to be managed. It's not that you're going to ignore them completely, but you don't want them getting out of control. Here are a few pointers to help you manage emotions:

- *Take time to cool off:* Rather than jumping head first into a conflict situation with a problem trainee, take a few minutes to calm down and to collect your thoughts. You might need to take a break and leave the training classroom to give yourself some space. Take a few slow deep breaths. Time and space allow you to take perspective and to analyze the situation. It's also important to monitor the problem trainee's emotions. If the trainee gets emotional, offer a time out so that all of you can collect your thoughts.

- *Select an appropriate time and place to address the conflict:* Another way to manage emotions is not to address the problem in front of other trainees. If you address the conflict in front of others, the problem trainee is going to feel humiliated and resentful. Similarly, the other trainees will be uncomfortable and will find your approach to managing conflict inappropriate. Although this approach may be cathartic for you in the short term, your long-term relationship with this problem trainee will be jeopardized. Finding privacy in many training situations is next to impossible, but do your best to find a more private area such as an empty office, hallway, break room, or even a restroom. If the problem trainee's behaviors are severe enough, the problem needs to be addressed immediately. Give the class a break and ask the problem trainee to remain behind. Once all trainees leave, close the door and begin your discussion.

- *Remain nonverbally responsive:* One way to prevent defensive behaviors in others is to remain nonverbally responsive, interested, and open to them and their communication. In conflict situations, our natural tendency is to close up nonverbally. We fold our arms, we decrease eye contact, we lean backward, and we distance ourselves from others. These nonverbal messages make us unapproachable to others.[4] Our suggestion is to resist this natural tendency to back away. Instead, use forward body leans and head nods and make eye contact. These nonverbal messages make us approachable and help reduce defensiveness.[5]

- *Plan the conversation:* Another luxury that is not always afforded trainers is taking the time to plan that conversation you will have with the problem trainee. Unlike many superior–subordinate relationships, where the two see each other on a daily basis, the trainer–trainee relationship is more temporary. If time permits, write out your goal for the conversation. Outline how you see the discussion unfolding. Describe the behaviors you consider problematic. When addressing the conflict with the problem trainee, stick to your plan.

Describe Behaviors Rather Than Evaluate the Person

With your emotions in check, you're ready to address the conflict with the problem trainee. We recommend a two-step process. The first step is to describe the behaviors you consider problematic rather than evaluating the person. The second step is to self-disclose how you feel in the situation. It's important to separate, if possible, the behaviors from the person. It's not the trainee that you consider problematic, it's the trainee's behaviors. Here are two suggestions:

- *Identify and describe the problematic behaviors:* Take a few seconds and identify the behaviors that you consider to be the problem. Many times, it will be the trainee's communication style. What exactly is bothering you about the trainee's communication style? What do these problematic communication behaviors look and sound like? Be prepared to describe the problem trainee's behaviors. For example, the trainee interrupts others when they are talking. The trainee always has a response to every question. The trainee dominates the discussion by not letting others talk and by controlling the conversation with nonverbal behaviors. The trainee personally attacks other trainees by name-calling. The trainee uses profanity.
- *Use "I" messages rather than "you" messages:* One strategy that can help you describe the problematic behaviors rather than evaluate the trainee is to use an "I" message rather than a "you" message. Statements that begin with the word "you" often have an edge or bite to them. "You have an attitude problem," "you're a know-it-all," "you're rude." These "you" messages are likely to create emotional backlash and, instead of helping to describe the problem at hand, they may result in an escalation of anger and frustration.

A better approach is to use an "I" message: Make the first word of your sentence "I" rather than "you." This takes a hard edge off the statement by making your message more a description of what the other person is doing that is causing the conflict and a description of how you feel rather than an accusatory, attacking message. Some "I" message examples follow.

Rather than saying "You have an attitude problem," consider saying, "I see you rolling your eyes, crossing your arms, and sighing. I feel frustrated when I see these behaviors."

Rather than saying "You're a know-it-all," say "I see and hear you responding to every question I ask. I see you dominating the discussion not only with your talk, but also with your nonverbal hand gestures where you shut others down. I feel annoyed when I see you doing this."

Rather than saying "You're rude," say "I see and hear you attacking others by calling them names rather than addressing the training-related issues. I see and hear you interrupting others while they are talking. I see and hear you using unnecessary profanity. I feel angry when I see and hear you treating others in this manner."

Paraphrase Content and Emotions

To ensure accurate understanding of each other's messages, it's always important to paraphrase. **Paraphrasing** is the process of restating in your own words what you heard the other person saying. Paraphrasing is not the same as parroting. In **parroting,** someone repeats back to you what she or he heard you saying exactly using your words and not her or his own. After you describe the problem trainee's behaviors and self-disclose your feelings, it's a good thing to ask the trainee to paraphrase back to you what it is he or she heard you saying. At times, you'll be amazed at what you hear. The message the problem trainee received is not the message you sent. This process allows you to clarify misunderstandings.

Here are a few suggestions that may enhance how well your problem trainee understands you:

- *Ask the problem trainee to paraphrase the content of the conflict conversation:* You can do this by asking the problem trainee to complete one of the following statements:

  "So, here is what seemed to happen . . ."
  "Here's what I hear you saying the problem is . . ."
  "This is what I hear you telling me . . ."
  "You seem to be saying . . ."
  "Are you saying . . ."

- *Ask the problem trainee to paraphrase the emotional content of the conflict conversation:* You can do this by asking the problem trainee to complete one of the following statements:

  "So you feel . . ."
  "Emotionally, you are feeling . . ."

Adapt Communication Accordingly

Another important conflict management skill is in your ability to adapt your communication to ensure that the problem trainee understands you. Paraphrasing is only one way to enhance understanding; adapting is another communication strategy that ensures understanding. Too many times, a trainer will describe the problem trainee's behaviors and automatically assume that the problem trainee understands the problem. Assuming that the trainee is on board and fully understands the problem, you and the trainee generate possible solutions to the problem. A solution is agreed upon; however, the problem trainee never implements the solution. You come to realize that the problem trainee was only going through the motions to please and accommodate the trainer. Research suggests that problem trainees or employees are less likely to implement solutions to performance problems if they don't fully understand and take ownership of the problem.[6]

In order to adapt your communication, you need to ask a few questions. How the trainee responds to these questions determines how you adapt your communication. For example, if you ask, "Do you agree that there's a problem?" and she answers "Yes, I understand why my behavior is problematic," then ask for a paraphrase to ensure understanding. If you're satisfied with her level of understanding, then the two of you can work on a solution to solve the problem. Chances are the problem trainee will implement the solution and change the problematic behavior.

If you ask, "Do you agree that there's a problem?" and he answers, "No, I don't know what the big deal is," then rather than generating possible solutions to the problem, return to the beginning and start redescribing the behaviors that you considered

RECAP

Conflict Management Skills and Communication Strategies

Conflict Management Skills	Conflict Communication Strategies
Manage the emotions.	Calm down before speaking or acting. Choose the most appropriate time and place to address the conflict. Be appropriately responsive to the other person. Breathe calmly and slowly.
Describe the behaviors rather than evaluate the person.	Focus on behaviors and not on the person. Identify the problem behaviors; use "I" messages; maintain objectivity and personal self control. Focus on the issue and on solving the problem.
Paraphrase content and emotions.	Communicate that you understand what the trainee is saying by saying it back to him or her in your own words. Express the emotions that the other person may be feeling.
Adapt your communication accordingly.	Be audience focused when you are working through a conflict. Understand what the trainee needs. Use language that identifies with the communication being used by the trainee.

to be problematic. It's premature to move into a solution stage if the problem trainee is not on board in terms of the problem. Rather than using the same "I" statements, you will need to be even more descriptive than you were before. Before you said, "I see and hear you attacking others by calling them names rather than addressing training-related issues." Now, you will need to say, "I heard you calling Connie names (and bad ones at that) rather than focusing on the supervisory issue where the two of you disagreed. Do you understand why making this personal is disruptive and unprofessional?" The general rule of thumb is that the more descriptive and specific you are with your communication, the greater the chances that the problem trainee will come to understand his or her classroom behaviors as being inappropriate.

Reducing Conflict

Some communication researchers say that the best way to manage conflict is to prevent it from occurring in the first place. Others argue that this position is a bit naïve and believe that conflict is inescapable. During the past two decades, researchers who examine communication in instructional settings have identified communication behaviors and strategies that have been shown to reduce conflict and enhance the overall learning climate in the classroom.[7] Your using these strategies will allow you to create a training environment that will let you meet your learning objectives.

Before we get to the communication strategies, it's important to understand just a brief overview of the theory and research that undergirds these strategies. Much of this theory and research comes from the work of communication researchers James McCroskey and Virginia Richmond and their colleagues at West Virginia University. Their research examines how teachers (or trainers) can use communication in the classroom to reach learning objectives by viewing teaching and learning as a relational process. They argue that, in order for instructors to be influential in the classroom, they need to use communication carefully so that students (or trainees) perceive their instructors to be approachable, which is also referred to as immediacy, which we discussed in Chapter 9. **Immediacy** is the degree of physical or psychological closeness between two individuals.

When students perceive their instructors to be approachable or immediate, they also tend to like them more; and it is this liking that students have for their instructors that gives instructors power in the classroom. Rather than possessing power because of their "instructor" title, teachers and trainers need relational power. **Relational power** is not something that an instructor possesses. Instead, it is power that is granted to him or her by the students because the students like and respect the instructor. With relational power, students grant instructors special permission that is not granted to unliked teachers or trainers—to influence them in the classroom. This type of instructional influence reduces trainees' resistance and increases trainees' compliance with the trainer's requests.

In other words, if your trainees like and respect you, they're more willing to follow your requests. Often they will remain on-task and will require little direction or motivation because they have become self-motivated. They don't want to let you down. They don't want to disappoint you. If they dislike you or do not respect you, then they're more willing to resist your training attempts and act out.

To reduce conflict, it's important that you develop professional and constructive relationships with your trainees. Again, you want your trainees to perceive you as being approachable. You want them to like you. Relational communication strategies can help you achieve influence in the training classroom while at the same time reducing conflict.

Use Affinity-Seeking Strategies

Have you ever wondered why you go out of your way to help some people, even if it's a big inconvenience for you? The answer usually comes down to liking, or affinity. **Affinity** is a positive attitude that one person has for another, and **affinity-seeking** is the process by which individuals attempt to get others to like and feel positive about them.[8]

We are more willing to do what others ask us to do and less willing to resist others if we like them.[9] Think about an instructor you recently had that you liked and another one that you disliked. Assume they both gave you very demanding assignments that were going to require extensive research in the library. Research suggests that many of you would consider the liked instructor's request to be reasonable and appropriate, and you would probably work hard to please this instructor.[10] You wouldn't want to let this instructor down.

Research also suggests that your level of cooperation with the disliked instructor would be quite different. First, you would consider the assignment unreasonable; and, second, you would probably resist completing the assignment in a meaningful manner. If you decided to complete the unreasonable assignment, you would probably resent the instructor and complete the assignment just to obtain the reward or to avoid the punishment.[11]

Some of you have no problem getting other people to like you. Others find it a bit more difficult. In 1984, two communication researchers focused on the communication strategies people use to get others to like them.[12] Their researched yielded a list of 25 affinity-seeking strategies. Seven of the more powerful or effective strategies, along with communication examples, are listed in Figure 10.1.[13] You're encouraged to give these seven affinity-seeking strategies a try. We believe you will see a difference in how your trainees behave toward you.

Use Nonverbal Immediacy Behaviors

Another set of behaviors that have been shown to reduce or manage conflict is the same set of behaviors we discussed in Chapter 9 when we discussed training delivery: Use immediacy behaviors or behaviors that stimulate perceptions of physical or psychological closeness between two individuals. As we also discussed in Chapter 9, there are two sets of immediacy behaviors—nonverbal and verbal. In this section, we'll review nonverbal immediacy behaviors.

One of the reasons why nonverbal immediacy behaviors are effective in managing conflict and tension is that they promote liking; we are more willing to do what others want us to do and less willing to resist those we like. In other words, we are attracted to and like those who are nonverbally expressive and responsive to us, and we have a tendency to dislike and avoid those who are nonverbal unexpressive and unresponsive to us.

To assess how nonverbally immediate you are in the training classroom, copy and distribute the nonverbal immediacy behaviors instrument, which is represented on page 230 in Figure 10.2.[14] This assessment instrument contains eight nonverbal behaviors that have been shown to enhance perceptions of closeness. Because 20 is the midpoint on this instrument, one way to interpret the results would be that scores 20 and higher indicate high trainee perceptions of trainer nonverbal immediacy, and scores 20 and lower indicate low trainer perceptions of trainer nonverbal immediacy.

Use Verbal Immediacy Behaviors

Verbal immediacy behaviors, like their nonverbal counterpart, are also effective in terms of enhancing the trainer–trainee relationship. To assess how verbally immediate your trainees perceive you to be in the training classroom, copy and distribute the verbal immediacy behaviors instrument, which is presented in Figure 10.3 on page 231.[15] This assessment instrument contains 16 verbal behaviors that have been shown to enhance perceptions of closeness. Because 32 is the midpoint on this instrument, one

FIGURE 10.1 Affinity-Seeking Strategies and Example Behaviors

Assume equality: The trainer attempting to get a trainee to like him or her presents him- or herself as an equal of the other person. For example, he or she avoids appearing superior or snobbish and does not play one-upmanship games.

Comfortable self: The trainer attempting to get a trainee to like him or her acts comfortable in the setting the two find themselves, comfortable with him- or herself, and comfortable with the trainee. He or she is relaxed, at ease, casual, and content. Distractions and disturbances in the environment are ignored. The trainer tries to look as if he or she is having a good time, even if he or she is not. The trainer gives the impression that nothing bothers him or her.

Conversational rule-keeping: The trainer attempting to get a trainee to like him or her follows closely the culture's rules for how people socialize with others by demonstrating cooperation, friendliness, and politeness. The trainer works hard at giving relevant answers to questions, saying the right thing, acting interested and involved in conversation, and adapting his or her messages to the particular trainee or situation. He or she avoids changing the topic too soon, interrupting the trainee, dominating classroom discussions, and making excessive self-references. The trainer using this strategy tries to avoid topics that are not of interest to his or her trainees.

Dynamism: The trainer attempting to get a trainee to like him or her presents him- or herself as a dynamic, active, and enthusiastic person. For example, he or she acts physically animated and very lively while talking with the trainee, varies intonation and other vocal characteristics, and is outgoing and extroverted with the trainees.

Elicit other's disclosure: The trainer attempting to get a trainee to like him or her encourages the trainee to talk by asking questions and reinforcing the trainee for talking. For example, the trainer inquires about the trainee's interests, feelings, opinion, views, and so on. He or she responds as if these are important and interesting and continues to ask more questions of the trainee.

Facilitate enjoyment: The trainer attempting to get a trainee to like him or her seeks to make the situations in which the two are involved very enjoyable experiences. The trainer does things the trainees will enjoy, is entertaining, tells jokes and interesting stories, talks about interesting topics, says funny things, and tries to make the classroom conducive to enjoyment. The trainer attempting to get a trainee to like him or her includes the trainee in his or her social activities and groups of friends. He or she introduces the trainee to his or her friends and makes the trainee feel like one of the group.

Optimism: The trainer attempting to get a trainee to like her or him presents her- or himself as a positive person—an optimist—so that he or she will appear to be a person who is pleasant to be around. He or she acts in a happy-go-lucky manner, is cheerful, and looks on the positive side of things. He or she avoids complaining about things, talking about depressing topics, and being critical of him- or herself and others.

way to interpret the results would be that scores 32 and higher indicate high verbal immediacy, and scores 32 and lower indicate low verbal immediacy. If you want to increase your chances of reducing or preventing conflict, you are encouraged to give these verbal behaviors a try.

FIGURE 10.2 Nonverbal Immediacy Behaviors Instrument

Instructions: Below is a series of descriptions of things some trainers have been observed doing in some classes. Please respond to the items *in terms of the class you are taking now.* For each item, please indicate on a scale of 0–4 how often your trainer in that class engages in those behaviors.

Use this scale: never = 0, rarely = 1, occasionally = 2, often = 3, and very often = 4.

_____ **1.** Gestures while talking to the class.

_____ **2.** Looks at the class while talking.

_____ **3.** Smiles at the class while talking.

_____ **4.** Touches trainees in the class.

_____ **5.** Moves around the classroom while teaching.

_____ **6.** Has a very relaxed body position while talking to the class.

_____ **7.** Smiles at individual trainees in the class.

_____ **8.** Uses a variety of vocal expressions when talking to the class.

Use Prosocial Behavior Alteration Techniques

Yet another set of strategies that may prevent conflict from occurring in the first place involves compliance-gaining strategies, or what some classroom researchers refer to as behavior alteration techniques.[16] **Behavior alteration techniques** are communication strategies that are intended to control and direct student behavior. These are the ways you get other people to do what you want them to do. There are basically two types of behavior alteration techniques—prosocial and antisocial. **Prosocial techniques** are those strategies that are positive and grounded in constructive trainer–trainee relationships. For example, "From my experience and from what I have learned, it's a good idea. I encourage you to do it." The prosocial power trainers possess comes from the quality relationships they have with their trainees. **Antisocial techniques** are those strategies that are negative and grounded in destructive trainer–trainee relationships. For example, "I'm the trainer, do it or else." The antisocial power trainers possess comes from their "trainer" titles and from their ability to punish and reward trainees.

It's also important to understand that the techniques you use as a trainer ultimately influence relational development. If you use prosocial behavioral alteration techniques, you will be more successful in establishing, developing, and nurturing constructive trainer–trainee relationships, which in turn will reduce trainee conflict in the classroom and increase trainees' willingness to do what you need them to do in order to reach your training objectives. Conversely, if you use antisocial behavioral alteration techniques, you will be less successful in developing relationships. Your trainees will resent you and ultimately resist your training attempts. You will encounter conflict more often. One thing we know for sure is that when you are managing conflict, you're not moving toward reaching your learning objectives, which is ultimately what you're getting paid to do.

FIGURE 10.3 Verbal Immediacy Behaviors Instrument

Instructions: Below are a series of descriptions of things some trainers have been observed saying in some classes. Please respond to the items *in terms of the class you are taking now.* For each item, indicate how often your trainer responds this way when teaching.

Use this scale: never = 0, rarely = 1, occasionally = 2, often = 3, and very often = 4.

_____ 1. Uses personal examples or talks about experiences she or he has had outside of class.

_____ 2. Asks questions or encourages trainees to talk.

_____ 3. Gets into discussions based on something a trainee brings up even when this doesn't seem to be part of his or her lecture plan.

_____ 4. Uses humor in class.

_____ 5. Addresses trainees by name.

_____ 6. Addresses me by name.

_____ 7. Gets into conversations with individual trainees before or after class.

_____ 8. Has initiated conversations with me before, after, or outside of class.

_____ 9. Refers to class as "our" class or what "we" are doing.

_____ 10. Provides feedback on my individual work through comments on papers, oral discussions, and the like.

_____ 11. Asks how trainees feel about an assignment, due date, or discussion topic.

_____ 12. Invites trainees to telephone or meet with him or her outside of class if they have questions or want to discuss something.

_____ 13. Asks questions that solicit viewpoints or opinions.

_____ 14. Praises trainees' work, actions, or comments.

_____ 15. Will have discussion about things unrelated to class with individual trainees or with the class as a whole.

_____ 16. Is addressed by his or her first name by the trainees.

Figures 10.4 and 10.5 represent prosocial and antisocial behavioral alteration techniques. Specific examples of **behavior alteration messages** (BAMs) are included by each technique. We encourage you to review this list of communication strategies for at least two reasons. First, you can reduce conflict if you use the prosocial instead of the antisocial behavioral alteration techniques. And second, when conflict does occur, we encourage you to diagnose your communication in the training classroom to determine your possible role in creating the conflict. Were you getting your trainees to do what you wanted them to do by pushing your weight around, pulling power plays on them, or threatening them? If so, you may be partially responsible for creating and possibly exacerbating the conflict. Stepping back and realizing this will save you a lot of trouble in the future. Rather than using antisocial approaches to power, we encourage you to focus on using prosocial approaches to power, which are listed in Figure 10.4.

FIGURE 10.4   Prosocial Behavioral Alteration Techniques and Sample Messages

Immediate reward from behavior: You will enjoy it. It will make you happy. Because it is fun. You will find it rewarding or interesting. It is a good experience.

Deferred reward from behavior: It will help you later on in life. It will prepare you for getting a job.

Reward from others: Others will respect you if you do. Others will be proud of you. Your friends will like you. Your supervisor will be pleased.

Self-esteem: You will feel good about yourself if you do. You are the best person to do it. You are good at it. You always do such a good job. Because you're capable!

Responsibility to others: Your group needs it done. The group depends on you. All your friends are counting on you. Don't let your group down. You'll ruin it for the rest of the group.

Normative rules: The majority rules. All of your friends are doing it. Everyone else has to do it. The rest of the class is doing it. It's part of growing up.

Altruism: If you do this, it will help others. Others will benefit if you do. It will make others happy. I'm not asking you to do it for yourself; do it for the good of the group.

Peer modeling: Your friends do it. Peers you respect do it. The friends you admire do it. Other trainees you like do it. All your friends are doing it.

Positive trainer–trainee relationship: I will like you better if you do it. I will respect you. I will think more highly of you. I will appreciate you more if you do. I will be proud of you and supportive of you.

Trainer modeling: This is the way I always do it. When I was your age, I did it. People who are like me do it. I had to do this when I was in business. Trainers you respect do it.

Expert trainer: From my experience, it is a good idea. From what I have learned, it is what you should do. This has always worked for me. Trust me—I know what I'm doing. I had to do this before I became a trainer.

Trainer feedback: Because I need to know how well you understand this. To see how well I've trained you. To see how well you can do it. It will help me know your problem areas.

Eliminate Trainer Misbehaviors

Yes, it's true, college teachers have been shown to misbehave in the classroom, and we suspect trainers as well.[17] A **"misbehavior"** is a behavior from the instructor (or student) that is unacceptable and that detracts from the learning environment. One way to prevent or reduce conflict from occurring in the classroom is to make sure *you're* not the source of the conflict. In some ways, it's quite unfortunate that we even have to be addressing our own behaviors as teachers or trainers, but the research is convincing. In a study focusing on students' perceptions of college teachers' misbehaviors, 28 misbehaviors were identified. Table 10.1 on page 234 reflects all of the cited misbehaviors, ranked by frequency, along with strategies for how to avoid the misbehavior from occurring in the classroom.[18]

FIGURE 10.5   Antisocial Behavior Alteration Techniques and Sample Messages

Punishment from trainer: I will punish you if you don't. I will make it miserable for you.

Punishment from others: No one will like you. Your friends will make fun of you. Your supervisors will punish you if you don't. Your peers will reject you.

Guilt: If you don't, others will be hurt. You'll make others unhappy. Others will be punished if you don't.

Negative trainer–trainee relationship: I will dislike you if you don't. I will lose respect for you. I will think less of you if you don't. I won't be proud of you. I'll be disappointed in you.

Legitimate higher authority: Do it, I'm just telling you what I was told. It is a rule; I have to do it, and so do you. It's policy.

Legitimate trainer authority: Because I told you to. You don't have a choice. You're here to work! I'm the trainer; you're the trainee. I'm in charge, not you. Don't ask, just do it.

Debt: You owe me one. Pay your debt. You promised to do it. I did it the last time. You said you'd try this time.

What we do know from this line of research is that most students and trainees pay attention to what we do in the classroom. In fact, many of them don't miss a beat. They're aware of our unprofessional behavior if it occurs. If conflict is occurring in your training classroom, we encourage you to examine your own behavior first and then your trainees' behaviors. Are you the source of the conflict? If so, identify the behavior that your trainees perceive to be a misbehavior, and then seek to make necessary adjustments. For example, if trainees aren't paying attention because your lectures are boring, we encourage you to revisit Chapter 6, on Training Methods.

Summary

The purpose of this chapter was to review some of the conflicts that trainers encounter in the training classroom and then to offer suggestions and recommendations for how to manage and possibly reduce conflict. Reducing conflict will enhance the learning climate. First, we discussed some of the problem trainee types that trainers need to anticipate encountering, such as quiet, talkative, bigheaded, negative, and aggressive. We also examined communication strategies that trainers can use to work with each of these types of problem trainees.

Second, before delving into how trainers can use communication skills to manage conflict, we reviewed three types of conflict management styles, including nonconfrontational, confrontational, and cooperative. Understanding a trainee's conflict management style or his or her approach to conflict is information that a trainer can use to better manage the conflict situation. Next, we reviewed four communication strategies that trainers can use to manage conflict in the training classroom, including how to manage emotions, how to describe problem behaviors rather than evaluate the

TABLE 10.1   Ranked Instructor Misbehaviors by Frequency and How to Avoid

Instructor Misbehavior	How to Avoid
1. Boring lectures	1. Make sure materials are audience centered.
2. Straying from subject	2. Keep close to your planned agenda.
3. Unfair testing	3. Make sure testing addresses desired objectives.
4. Confusing or unclear lectures	4. Follow sequential outlines and delivery.
5. Late returning work	5. Set and keep due dates for returning grades.
6. Information overload	6. Consider audience when apportioning material.
7. Deviating from syllabus	7. Treat the syllabus as a contract.
8. Tardiness	8. Treat time from a displaced point perspective.
9. Keeping students overtime	9. Keep to your schedule and be considerate.
10. Early dismissal	10. Make sure you have twice the material needed.
11. Unfair grading	11. Grade by objective and be equitable to all.
12. Negative personality	12. Monitor how others are perceiving you.
13. Foreign or regional accents	13. Bolster interpersonal relationships with students.
14. Information underload	14. Prepare plenty of material and emphasize application.
15. Sarcasm and putdowns	15. Correct without comment.
16. Bad grammar or spelling	16. Prepare visual material in advance.
17. Absent	17. This is your job! Be professional!
18. Apathy toward students	18. Good teaching involves developing a relationship.
19. Inappropriate volume	19. View a videotape of yourself. Ask students.
20. Shows favoritism or prejudice	20. Be professional and equitable.
21. Unreasonable or arbitrary rules	21. Have specific and obvious objectives for rules.
22. Unresponsive to student questions	22. Practice active listening.
23. Negative physical appearance	23. You are a professional. Dress like one!
24. Inaccessible to students	24. Keep your office hours religiously.
25. Unprepared or disorganized	25. Marinate in the class schedule before you teach.
26. Verbally abusive	26. Be assertive and don't denigrate the person.
27. Does not know subject matter	27. Marinate in the content. Practice and absorb.
28. Sexual harassment	28. Students are people—not objects. Behave!

problem trainee, how to paraphrase content and emotions, and finally how to adapt communication to achieve some type of resolution to the conflict.

Finally, we discussed strategies that trainers might consider using that have been shown to reduce or even prevent conflict from occurring in the first place. Communication strategies and behaviors such as affinity-seeking strategies, nonverbal and verbal immediacy behaviors, prosocial behavior alteration techniques, and the elimination of instructor misbehaviors have all been shown to enhance instructor–student relationships in instructional settings and have been shown to increase student compliance with instructors' requests and decrease student resistance.

QUESTIONS FOR DISCUSSION AND REVIEW

1. List various types of problem trainees you will likely encounter in a training situation. Explain the situational constraints, organizational history, or just basic human nature that lead to these behaviors. As a trainer, outline the strategies you would use to deal with these trainees that would have the most positive, prosocial, and effective outcomes.

2. Explain the difference between nonconfrontational and confrontational conflict management styles. What are the advantages and disadvantages of each?

3. List the types of trainer "misbehaviors" that you have experienced. Describe your reactions to these misbehaviors. Describe resulting trainee attitudes and subsequent behaviors. What potential dangers for trainer misbehaviors do you see in yourself? How are you addressing and eliminating these?

4. What are some strategies to manage your emotions when emotions become aroused? Is it possible to manage the emotions of others?

5. Describe a situation where the nonconfrontational conflict style might be most appropriate. Does such a situation exist? Discuss.

QUESTIONS FOR APPLICATION AND ANALYSIS

1. Patrick has a small group of individuals in his training sessions who are consistently late in coming back from break or from lunch. These individuals make a loud entrance, disrupt training activities that are in progress, and generally must ask that the directions be repeated. Analyze this situation. How could Patrick use a nonconfrontational, a confrontational, and a cooperative approach to managing this conflict? Which of these responses would be best? Explain why.

2. Bethany notices that the supervisor who has requested her training services is a domineering authoritarian personality. Bethany notices that the supervisor constantly uses negative, antisocial behavior alteration strategies and that the employees do not respond favorably to this. Bethany has been called in to promote teamwork and to build employee satisfaction in the company. She knows, however, that the supervisor's negative communication and compliance-gaining style will completely undo what she is trying to accomplish. In fact, it is the very reason employee morale is so low. What can Bethany do to diplomatically bring the supervisor into the training process and to correct some of the problems that the supervisor is fostering in the corporation? What can Bethany do to introduce the concept of effective affinity-seeking to this supervisor?

3. As a trainer, Martha has some interesting group members in her training session. There is at least one bigheaded trainee who is teamed up with an aggressive trainee, and none of the rest of the trainees (who happen to be quiet trainees) will go up against these first two, much less participate in discussions. What can Martha do to cope with the inappropriate and dominating behaviors of the first two trainees, so that the rest of the group will join in and participate? Discuss the conflict management style and techniques that are most appropriate in this situation.

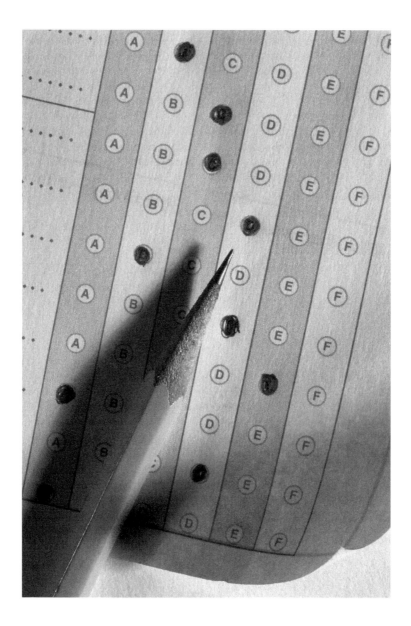

11 Assessing Learning Outcomes

CHAPTER OBJECTIVES

After studying this chapter, you should be able to:

1. List and explain two reasons that assessment is important.

2. Develop a series of Likert-type and semantic differential scale items that assess trainees' affect or liking for their trainer, training content, and trained behaviors.

3. Develop multiple-choice, matching, and essay exam items to assess cognitive learning outcomes.

4. Differentiate among atomistic, analytic, and holistic or general impression levels of behavioral assessment.

5. Develop a behavioral assessment instrument for a communication behavior that includes behavioral items, skill ratings, and skill criteria.

6. Explain the importance of inter-rater reliability.

7. Differentiate between pre/post-test, pre/post-test with control group, post-test only with control group, and repeated measure designs.

8. Explain the advantages and disadvantages to the pre/post-test, pre/post-test with control group, post-test only with control group, and repeated measure designs.

9. Explain the importance of triangulation.

10. Complete a cost/benefit ratio to document the value of a training program.

There is always a sense of accomplishment and relief for the trainer at the end of a long day of training or at the end of an extensive training program. Many trainers call it a day by packing their bags and moving on to the next training assignment. But for others, the process remains incomplete until the training program has been fully assessed to determine its overall effectiveness. These trainers want to know if they're getting a return on their investment. They invest considerable resources, such as time, money, and energy, planning and developing their programs. These training professionals meticulously walk through the training strategies outlined in Chapters 3 through 10 of this textbook. They want to know if their training is making a difference.

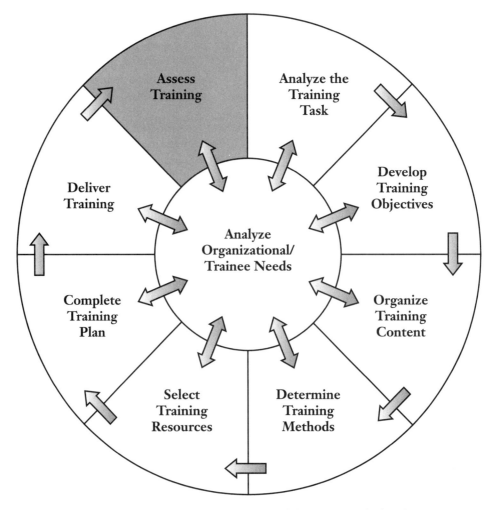

FIGURE 11.1   The Needs-Centered Training Model Assessing whether the training program addressed the needs of the trainees is the last step in the needs-centered training model.

One way to see if your hard work is making a difference is to assess your training program, which is the final step of the needs-centered training model illustrated in Figure 11.1. **Training assessment** is a systematic process of evaluating training programs to ensure that they meet the needs of the trainees and organization. In Chapter 3, you were introduced to the needs assessment, which occurs at the front end of the training model in the "analyze the training task" step. If you will recall, a needs assessment is the process of identifying what learners do not yet know or the skills and behaviors they cannot yet perform. Now we're ready to conduct another assessment, but this time at the end of the training model. We want to know if the trainees learned anything from the training program. These two assessment processes are like bookends. The needs assessment identifies what trainees *need to learn* and the final assessment identifies *if trainees learned* what they were supposed to learn.

Before we review how to assess learning outcomes, we introduce a model in Figure 11.2 that focuses on assessment as a systematic process that ultimately recycles itself. Our assessment model includes three stages. In the first stage, you develop learning objectives as discussed in Chapter 4. Assessing learning outcomes is not possible without learning objectives. Learning objectives describe the outcomes trainers are looking for at the end of the training program, such as trainees being able to recall specific pieces of information, express certain attitudes, or perform a set of skills. In the second stage, learning outcomes are measured by collecting data from trainees using many of the same methods reviewed in Chapter 3, such as surveys and interviews. In the third stage, the assessment data are interpreted. Once your trainees complete the surveys and other assessment measures, you make sense of the information you

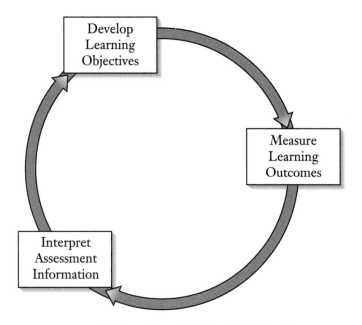

FIGURE 11.2 A Three-Stage Model of Training Assessment

collected. What does the information mean? What do you do with the information? This assessment model ultimately recycles itself. After interpreting the information, it's important to use the information obtained through the assessment process to improve your training program. Before beginning the next training program, it might be necessary to modify the learning objectives, to refine the training curriculum, or to use different methods to more accurately measure the learning outcomes. Information collected from the assessment process is invaluable feedback that can be used to improve your training effectiveness.

There are four sections to this chapter. First, we focus on why the assessment process is important. Second, we discuss how to measure affective, cognitive, and behavioral learning outcomes. Third, we present various assessment designs; and, finally, we discuss how to interpret assessment information.

The Importance of Assessment

Assessment remains important to trainers for at least two reasons. Assessment ensures survival of the fittest, especially in an organizational climate of downsizing or doing more with less. Assessment also ensures quality, which remains consistent with contemporary management philosophies where work processes must be constantly reexamined to ensure efficiency and effectiveness.

Assessment Ensures Survival of the Fittest

Assessing training effectiveness has become a priority in many training organizations throughout the country. As the marketplace becomes more competitive, organizations are constantly looking for ways to trim operating costs in order to increase profit margins for investors. Many organizations accomplish this by downsizing, by reducing the number of employees, or by eliminating departments that do not contribute directly to the organization's bottom line.

Until recently, trainers have never had to document their value to an organization with such precision. It was typically assumed that they were invaluable. This assumption is no longer to be taken for granted. In today's marketplace, trainers who cannot show their value to the organization don't last long in an organization. Trainers who survive downsizing are those who are able to demonstrate that they make a difference to organizations in terms of increasing income and reducing expenses.

Executives make decisions based on what is referred to as a return on investment (ROI) ratio.[1] **Return on investment** is a phrase that suggests that an investment should yield or produce a return that is greater than its initial investment. For example, an advertising department that invests huge sums of money in developing ineffective advertising is cut from the food chain. It doesn't survive. Conversely, a department of training and development that invests thousands of dollars in communication training for front-line managers that reduces employee grievances and sick-time usage and increases employee morale, motivation, productivity, and commitment to the organization survives and flourishes.

Assessment Ensures Quality Training

Assessing learning outcomes also remains consistent with many organizational cultures that subscribe to total quality management (TQM). **Total quality management** is a management philosophy that advocates that doing a job right is more important than doing a job quickly. W. Edwards Deming, the person primarily responsible for this shift in management philosophy, believed that in order to improve quality with fewer resources and fewer employees, organizations must remove all barriers that prevent employees from doing their best work.[2] According to Deming, employees should be trained in how to do their jobs right the first time and not the second or third time.

Total quality management is partially responsible for the assessment culture that exists in many of today's organizations. Training from a total quality management perspective means that you get and use feedback from your trainees to ensure that you're meeting the learning objectives that undergird the training program.

Although assessment may seem incredibly intuitive and useful, trainees have only been systematically assessing learning outcomes in the training classroom for the past 25 to 30 years. Today, if we learn that our trainees are not learning, we make immediate changes to the training program to ensure that it remains needs-centered and effective. If we find that our trainees are learning, then we continue to refine the training program, making it even better and of a higher quality.

Measuring Learning Outcomes

The three domains of learning introduced in Chapter 3 are cognitive, affective, and psychomotor or behavioral. Donald Kirkpatrick's "Four Levels of Training Evaluation," which remains popular with many training and development practitioners, parallels the three domains of learning nicely.[3] Kirkpatrick's first level assesses trainees' cognitive learning. What principles, facts, and techniques were used? The second level assesses trainees' reactions to the training program or their affective learning. How well did they like the training program? The third level assesses trainees' behavioral learning. What changes in job behavior resulted from the training program? The fourth and final level answers such practical questions as: What were the tangible results of the program in terms of reduced costs, improved quality, and improved quantity? Very simply, your mission is to see if the trainees learned it (cognitive), liked it (affective), and can do it (psychomotor).[4] Once these questions are answered, you should then be able to measure the tangible and practical benefits of the training program. We will address the practical benefits of a training program in the final section of this chapter, when we discuss how to interpret or make sense of the assessment information. To begin assessing learning outcomes, a trainer needs three sets of measuring instruments, one for each domain of learning.

Assessing Cognitive Learning: Did They Learn It?

Cognitive learning focuses on whether or not your trainees learned the training content. Kirkpatrick referred to this level of assessment as learning.[5] Did the trainees understand the material? If you will recall from Chapter 3, the cognitive domain of learning emphasized your ability to understand knowledge and facts. When we conducted our needs assessment at the front end of the training program, we were interested in understanding how much our trainees knew about the ideas and behaviors we were considering including in our training program. We wanted to make sure that our training was adapted appropriately to meet the needs of the trainees.

When assessing cognitive learning at the back end of the training program, you will use many of the same assessment methods discussed in Chapter 3. We begin by constructing a survey or an exam. An **exam** is a specially designed survey or pencil and paper test that assesses whether or not trainees learned the training content. Exams contain a variety of items or questions. The most popular items are multiple choice, matching, and essay or fill in the blank.[6]

Multiple-choice exam items.   **Multiple-choice** is a type of exam item that challenges trainees to decipher between three to five possible answers to a particular question. See Figure 11.3 for an example of a multiple-choice item. This type of an exam item contains two parts, including the stem and a set of foils, which were introduced in Chapter 3. As a review, a **stem** is the question or incomplete statement that you want your trainees to answer or complete. In Figure 11.3, the stem is the following question: "Which of the following reflects the appropriate order of the listening process?" For each stem, there is a set of foils. **Foils** are the alternative choices that follow the stem and ultimately answer or complete the stem. In Figure 11.3, the foils are the four lists of verbs following the question. The foil that contains the correct answer is considered the **keyed response.** The other foils are incorrect and are considered **distractors.**

There are advantages to using multiple-choice exams as post-training assessment measures. Here are a few of them for you to consider:

- They're inexpensive compared to other assessment instruments.
- They require minimal time to administer and score.
- They're flexible. They can be easily adapted and revised to assess specific cognitive learning outcomes.

There are also disadvantages to using multiple-choice exams that are poorly written:

FIGURE 11.3   Multiple-Choice Exam Item

Which of the following reflects the appropriate order of the listening process?

A.   attending, selecting, responding, understanding, retaining

B.   selecting, attending, understanding, remembering, responding

C.   selecting, attending, understanding, remembering, retaining

D.   responding, selecting, attending, understanding, retaining

- Trainees can decipher the correct answer through a process of elimination.
- The exam may assess trainees' test-taking abilities rather than cognitive learning outcomes.
- The exam may require trainees to use only rote memorization to correctly answer the item rather than having them apply the training content to various situations and contexts.

To avoid some of these pitfalls when writing and using multiple-choice exam items, consider some of the following suggestions:

- Avoid making the correct answer too obvious. Distractor foils or incorrect responses should be plausible. Administer the items to a colleague and have him or her check for item difficulty.
- Avoid making the correct and incorrect responses appear different in their appearance. All foils should appear similar in length, parallel in construction, and equally precise in expression. Notice in Figure 11.3 that all foils contain five words and are the same length.
- Avoid making the "C" foil the correct response too often. Keyed responses should be evenly distributed among the letters and throughout the test items.
- Avoid negatively worded or double-negative stems and/or foils. This becomes an assessment in logic rather than training content. An example of this would be, "Which of the following responses is *not* an *in*effective sequence of how the discussion should unfold with the customer?"
- Avoid grammatical cues that give the correct answer away (i.e., a, an). The following multiple-choice test item contains this error: "When listening to a customer on the telephone, make sure you use a _____. (a) affect displays, (b) back channel cue, (c) adaptors, (d) emotional cues." The keyed response, which is (b), is obvious for two reasons. The foil is written in such a way that only the singular noun would be appropriate, and when the article *a* is used, it is followed by a noun that begins with a consonant.
- Avoid using "all" or "none of the above" foils. This is usually the sign of a lazy and/or uncreative exam writer. Develop four to five complete foils for each stem.

Matching exam items.   A **matching** exam item asks trainees to connect or attach two words and/or phrases together. These exam items contain a set of stimuli and another set of possible responses. See Figure 11.4 on page 244 for an example of a matching exam item. Stimuli are usually presented as a set of terms, statements, phrases, definitions, or incomplete statements. With most exams, the set of stimuli is presented on the left side of the exam with a list of possible responses appearing on the right side. Responses are possible answers that can be matched to stimuli on a *specified* basis.

Matching exam items are useful especially when there is a lot of content to assess, and they require minimal space on the exam. Similar to the disadvantages of the multiple-choice exam items, matching items, if written poorly, can allow students to decipher correct answers through a process of elimination. Additionally, matching

FIGURE 11.4   Matching Exam Item

Please match the definitions on the right with the terms on the left.

Set of Stimuli	Set of Possible Responses
1. ____ Selecting	**A.** Focusing on a particular sound.
2. ____ Attending	**B.** Physiological process of decoding sounds.
3. ____ Understanding	**C.** Arousal of the senses.
4. ____ Remembering	**D.** Information that interferes with reception.
	E. Confirming your understanding of a message.
	F. Recalling information.
	G. Sorting through competing sounds.
	H. Assigning meaning to messages.

items do not always allow a trainer to assess higher forms of cognitive learning, such as how trainees might apply or evaluate training content. Using an essay exam item, which will be discussed in the next section, may more appropriately assess higher forms of learning.

To avoid some of the pitfalls when writing and using matching exam items, consider some of the following suggestions:

- Make sure that the two sets (stimuli and responses) remain similar in terms of the content. If you're assessing the five listening activities (selecting, attending, understanding, remembering, and responding), make sure all of the items in your two sets are related to the listening process. It would not be appropriate to include items related to the process of resolving conflict.
- The list of stimuli should be no longer than eight items, and the list of responses should be 50 percent longer than the list of stimuli to prevent trainees from selecting the correct response using process of elimination.
- The list of possible responses should contain plausible answers. As in multiple-choice items, incorrect responses should include common misinformation. For example, if you were assessing listening, you would want to include responses that assessed hearing, because listening and hearing are often confused.

Essay exam items.   With **essay** items (and also fill-in-the-blank items), trainees are not given a list of possible responses but are asked to generate the correct response. They must recall, explain, and organize information in a manner that addresses the particular exam item. Similar to the other two types of exam items (multiple-choice and matching exam items), there are advantages and disadvantages to essay exam items. Two advantages to consider when using essays include:

- Essay items eliminate the possibility of guessing and focusing only on rote memorization. Trainees have the ability to discuss, in their own words, what they have learned and what the concepts mean to them.
- Essay items allow trainees to apply information they're learning directly to their personal and professional lives.

Two disadvantages to consider when using essay exam items include:

- Essay items require more time to read and evaluate. They're not as efficient as multiple-choice or matching exam items. A trainer must carefully read each essay, looking for a discussion and application of key concepts and ideas.
- The quality of a trainee's answer is often only as good as the quality of the trainer's question. If you develop an ambiguously and poorly focused essay question, you will get an ambiguously and poorly focused answer.

To avoid some of the pitfalls when writing and using essay exam items, consider some of the following suggestions:

- *Define the task presented in the essay question:* The trainer's intent must be obvious to the trainee taking the exam. For example, if you want the trainee to compare and contrast the informative and persuasive speech making processes, make sure your essay question includes the terms "compare and contrast."
- *Focus the essay question:* If essay questions are not properly defined and limited, trainees will experience frustration in deciding how much to write, how many aspects of the problem to address, and where to put the emphasis. Essay questions are developed to assess trainees' cognitive learning, not their ability to assess the trainer's intent. Here's an example of how you might focus an essay question using the example from above. "In a 250-word essay, compare and contrast the informative and persuasive speech making processes, paying particular attention to audience analysis and adaptation."
- *Write clear and specific directions:* Directions should be thorough and specific. Trainees need to be informed of how much time they have to take the exam, how important each essay question is in relation to the whole exam, and what factors will affect the grading of the essay exam items.
- *Allow ample time for trainees to answer all essay questions:* Essay exam items require more time for a trainee to complete, therefore it's important to develop an exam with the appropriate number of essays in relation to the amount of time allotted for completing the exam.

Regardless of the types of questions you include in your exam, we recommend you consider the following guidelines when writing and administering exams:

- Write exams that cover each aspect of the training program, making sure the exam items are proportional to the amount of time invested with each of the training concepts. For example, if the training program covered content from Chapters 1 through 5, although Chapter 5 was only briefly discussed, then the bulk of the exam items should reflect content from Chapters 1 through 4.

- Write exams making sure that items are grouped by chapters or units. Most trainees study for an exam by chapter or units, and therefore they should be tested in a similar manner.

- Write exams that include a variety of items, including multiple choice, matching, essay, and so on. This will help you assess all levels of cognitive learning.

- Write exam items in a way that remains consistent with how the content was presented to trainees. The research suggests that you test it the way you taught it.[7] For example, assume your training a group of executives on how to avoid groupthink. Groupthink is when group members fail to challenge each other's ideas for fear that it may cause group conflict. There are certain communication behaviors that group members can use in order to avoid groupthink. You walk your trainees through a list of behaviors you would like them to be able to list and recall. To assess their cognitive learning appropriately, you might ask them to list and explain each of these behaviors in a short essay. It would be incorrect for you to ask them to analyze the groupthink processes that may have caused the space shuttle Columbia to explode, because this was not the focus of your training program.

- Pilot the exam by asking your colleagues to take the exam before you administer it to your trainees. You want to make sure that your exam is free of the errors discussed in this chapter before you invest time copying and collating all of the required copies.

- Administer the exam in the same instructional environment where students learned the content. The research suggests that you test them where you trained them.[8] It would not be advisable to conduct a training program with only 15 trainees in a small and intimate training room, but then test them with 2000 other, unfamiliar trainees in a large and impersonal lecture hall. Similarly, if you train them with classical music playing in the background, you need to test them with classical music playing in the background.

Assessing Affective Learning: Did They Like It?

Affective learning focuses on whether or not your trainees liked the training program and found it valuable. Kirkpatrick referred to this level of assessment as reaction.[9] **Affect** is the degree of liking, appreciation, respect, or value that one has for something. In the training context, affect would be the amount of liking trainees have for their trainers in addition to how valuable they considered their training. At the back end of assessing the training program, we're interested in knowing if there was a change in trainees' attitudes and motivation levels.

You want your trainees not only to like you but to like and respect your training content. Training is more than just conveying content and developing skills. It's also teaching trainees how to value and respect what it is you're training them to do. Research suggests that if trainees like or have affect for you and your training content, then they're more motivated to learn the training content and use their new skills on the job.[10]

The most common method of assessing affective learning is to develop a survey or questionnaire. Your survey or questionnaire should include items that measure at least four clusters of attitudes:

1. Did the trainees like, value, respect the training content?
2. Did the trainees like, value, respect the behaviors that they were trained to do?
3. Did the trainees like, value, and respect you?
4. How likely is it that your trainees will use the training content and skills they learned in your training program?

Two scales that can help you measure trainees' affect for you and the training content following a training program are the Likert scale (introduced in Chapter 3) and the semantic differential scale. With a Likert-type scale item, trainees are usually presented with a statement in the questionnaire that asks them to indicate whether they "strongly agree," "agree," "disagree," "strongly disagree," or "are undecided" about the content of the statement. The survey illustrated in Figure 11.5 contains a variety of Likert-type scale items that measure trainees' affect for a training program just completed.

The **semantic differential** scale measures attitudes by asking people to choose between two opposite positions, for example, good and bad or liked and disliked. Again, you would need a stem or an incomplete statement followed by a series of two

---

FIGURE 11.5 Measuring Affective Learning Using Likert-Type Scale Items

Directions: For each item, circle the number that reflects your level of agreement.

I considered the content of this training program to be valuable.

Strongly Disagree	Disagree	Undecided	Agree	Strongly Agree
1	2	3	4	5

The skills we developed in this training program are important to me.

Strongly Disagree	Disagree	Undecided	Agree	Strongly Agree
1	2	3	4	5

The trainer was effective in helping me develop the skills I need to do my job well.

Strongly Disagree	Disagree	Undecided	Agree	Strongly Agree
1	2	3	4	5

I will use what I learned in this training program.

Strongly Disagree	Disagree	Undecided	Agree	Strongly Agree
1	2	3	4	5

opposite or bipolar terms. The bipolar terms would then be separated by a series of numbers, and trainees would be asked to circle the number that most accurately reflected the degree or strength of their attitude (belief, value, or feeling) for each pair of bipolar words.

The survey illustrated in Figure 11.6 is an affective learning measure developed by communication researcher James C. McCroskey and his colleagues (primarily Jan

---

FIGURE 11.6   Measuring Affective Learning Using Semantic Differential Scale Items

Instructions: Using the following scales (there are four scales for each item), evaluate the training class you just completed. Circle the number for *each scale* that best represents your feelings.

The behaviors recommended in this training program were:

Bad	1	2	3	4	5	6	7	Good
Worthless	1	2	3	4	5	6	7	Valuable
Unfair	1	2	3	4	5	6	7	Fair
Negative	1	2	3	4	5	6	7	Positive

The content or subject matter of this training program was:

Bad	1	2	3	4	5	6	7	Good
Worthless	1	2	3	4	5	6	7	Valuable
Unfair	1	2	3	4	5	6	7	Fair
Negative	1	2	3	4	5	6	7	Positive

The trainer was:

Bad	1	2	3	4	5	6	7	Good
Worthless	1	2	3	4	5	6	7	Valuable
Unfair	1	2	3	4	5	6	7	Fair
Negative	1	2	3	4	5	6	7	Positive

In real-life situations and on the job, your likelihood of actually attempting to use the behaviors developed in this training program is:

Unlikely	1	2	3	4	5	6	7	Likely
Impossible	1	2	3	4	5	6	7	Possible
Improbable	1	2	3	4	5	6	7	Probable
Would Not	1	2	3	4	5	6	7	Would

Your likelihood of wanting to take another training program related to this topic is:

Unlikely	1	2	3	4	5	6	7	Likely
Impossible	1	2	3	4	5	6	7	Possible
Improbable	1	2	3	4	5	6	7	Probable
Would Not	1	2	3	4	5	6	7	Would

Andersen) at West Virginia University.[11] This affective learning measure assesses trainees' attitudes toward the content and behaviors taught in the training course, trainees' attitudes toward their trainer, and their anticipated behavioral choices. Remember, if a training program increases trainees' affect, then they're more likely to engage in the behaviors recommended in the training program, which is ultimately your learning outcome.[12]

You might also want to complement your assessment of affective learning outcomes with a more traditional evaluation form, such as the one illustrated in Figure 11.7.[13]

FIGURE 11.7 Training Program Evaluation Form

Directions: For each item, circle the number that reflects your level of agreement.

Training Content

Learning objectives were clear.

Strongly Disagree	Disagree	Undecided	Agree	Strongly Agree
1	2	3	4	5

Training content was interesting.

Strongly Disagree	Disagree	Undecided	Agree	Strongly Agree
1	2	3	4	5

Training content was relevant to my job.

Strongly Disagree	Disagree	Undecided	Agree	Strongly Agree
1	2	3	4	5

Training Resources and Methods

Participant guide was organized well.

Strongly Disagree	Disagree	Undecided	Agree	Strongly Agree
1	2	3	4	5

Experiential learning activities were appropriate.

Strongly Disagree	Disagree	Undecided	Agree	Strongly Agree
1	2	3	4	5

There was adequate balance among lecture, experiential activities, and group discussion.

Strongly Disagree	Disagree	Undecided	Agree	Strongly Agree
1	2	3	4	5

(continues)

FIGURE 11.7   **Continued**

Trainer's Presentational Skills

Trainer was organized.

Strongly Disagree	Disagree	Undecided	Agree	Strongly Agree
1	2	3	4	5

Trainer was clear and articulate.

Strongly Disagree	Disagree	Undecided	Agree	Strongly Agree
1	2	3	4	5

Trainer was expressive and energetic.

Strongly Disagree	Disagree	Undecided	Agree	Strongly Agree
1	2	3	4	5

Trainer answered our questions satisfactorily.

Strongly Disagree	Disagree	Undecided	Agree	Strongly Agree
1	2	3	4	5

Trainer integrated our life experiences into training program.

Strongly Disagree	Disagree	Undecided	Agree	Strongly Agree
1	2	3	4	5

Overall Assessment

I would recommend this training program to my colleagues.

Strongly Disagree	Disagree	Undecided	Agree	Strongly Agree
1	2	3	4	5

I would recommend this trainer to my colleagues.

Strongly Disagree	Disagree	Undecided	Agree	Strongly Agree
1	2	3	4	5

Assessing Behavioral Learning: Can They Do It?

Behavioral learning focuses on whether or not your trainees can do what they have been trained to do. Kirkpatrick referred to this level of assessment as behavior.[14] In addition to assessing whether or not your trainees *can do it*, it's also important to assess *if they do it*. How many times have you been trained in how to do something, yet, when you're on the job, you rarely use the skills you've been taught. It happens all the time. Just because we're trained in how to perform a behavior doesn't mean we always perform the behavior. In order to assess whether trainees can actively perform the skills you've taught, you will need to design yet another evaluation instrument. Before developing this instrument, consider these two questions:

1. On what level will you be assessing the trained behaviors?
2. Who will be conducting the behavioral assessment?

To answer the first question, note that behaviors can be assessed on three different levels.[15] The lowest level of behavioral assessment is referred to as **atomistic assessment** or the identification of small, observable behaviors. When you assess on this level, you're only interested in determining if the behaviors were performed or not. For example, imagine that you're assessing a sales presentation. Did the sales presentation include an introduction? At the atomistic level, you're not interested in how well the introduction was performed, just that the sales presentation included an introduction. This level of assessment may also include some form of quantification. How many times was the trained behavior performed or not performed? For example, a part of your training included eye contact. At the atomistic level, an assessor might count the number of times the speaker delivering the sales presentation looked at his or her audience.

In many management training programs, managers are trained in how to communicate performance deficiencies with employees. These dialogues are referred to as coachings. In order for a coaching dialogue to be constructive and effective, it's important that managers successfully walk through a series of steps and in the appropriate order. If you were to assess at the atomistic level, you would be assessing whether or not the behaviors occurred, and, if they occurred, were they performed in the appropriate sequence.

The midlevel of behavioral assessment is referred to as **analytic assessment** or assessing how *well* each of the individual behaviors was performed. In order for a coaching dialogue to be constructive and effective, it's important not only that managers walk through the steps and in the appropriate order but that each step is performed well. If one of the steps is performed poorly, employees are more likely to perceive the coaching dialogue as punitive. For example, the manager may have opened the coaching dialogue with the employee successfully; but, when describing the employee's performance deficiency, she was accusatory, which caused defensiveness in the employee. Again, at the analytic level, an assessor observes to see not only that the behavior was performed but also how *well* was it performed.

The highest level of behavioral assessment is referred to as **holistic** or **general impression assessment,** which is where the assessor determines the overall quality of the employee's behavioral performance. Assessors are not so much interested in the process as they are in the product. The process consists of the individual behaviors that are performed well and in the appropriate sequence. The product is the overall outcome of the individual's ability to perform the individual behaviors well and in the appropriate sequence. If you were assessing the manager's ability to conduct an employee coaching, the assessor would be looking for the following: Did the employee leave the dialogue realizing that there was a performance deficiency? Did the employee know how to modify his or her behavior to remedy the problem? And did the employee leave the coaching session perceiving it as constructive or destructive and punitive?

The second question that needs to be answered prior to developing an instrument that assesses behavioral learning is: Who will be completing the behavioral assessment? Today, many companies use the 360-survey method assessment, which was discussed in Chapter 3. In this form of assessment, an individual's behavior is assessed and evaluated not only by people trained in behavioral assessment but also by the individual's subordinates, peers, and superiors. In the customer service industry, many corporations take it a step further and have customers evaluate employee behavior as well. Some corporations hire "phantom" customers to assess employee front-line behavior. These assessors pose as customers and challenge customer service employees by asking difficult questions and by being demanding and hard to please.

Behavioral assessment instruments need to be designed to assess at the appropriate level (i.e., atomistic, analytic, general impression) and tailored to the individuals conducting the assessment whether they be trained assessors or superiors, peers, subordinates, and/or some other types of "phantom" or customer assessor.

Although all behavioral assessment instruments vary, many of them share three components: behavioral items, skill ratings, and skill criteria. The obvious components are the **behavioral items,** or the behaviors that were developed in the training program. Figure 11.8 is an example of a behavioral assessment instrument that contains behavioral items developed as part of the communication training program.

If you were assessing behavioral learning at the atomistic level with this instrument, assessors would check whether or not the behavior occurred and in the appropriate sequence. If the assessment is to occur at the analytic level, then assessors will need skill ratings. **Skill ratings** are a series of numbers or a scale that indicates the level or quality of performance. Many behavioral instruments include five skill ratings where $1 = $ very poor, $2 = $ poor, $3 = $ fair, $4 = $ good, and $5 = $ very good.

Figure 11.9 contains a behavioral instrument that assesses an informative speech presentation.[16] This assessment instrument contains clusters of behavioral items along with skill ratings. Like many assessment instruments, this one assesses informative speech making skills at both the atomistic and analytic levels. The instrument asks you to check off those behaviors you observed, which is the atomistic level of assessment, and also asks you to place a skill rating next to the behavioral skill cluster (i.e., Introduction, Content, Organization, Language, Delivery, Conclusion), which is the analytic level of assessment.

FIGURE 11.8   Coaching Behavioral Items

____ Manager greeted employee.

____ Manager described employee's inappropriate behaviors by using "I" statements.

____ Manager was able to get employee to agree that a problem exists by paraphrasing.

____ Manager and employee discussed and analyzed solutions to performance problem.

____ Manager and employee agreed upon a solution.

____ Manager received verbal commitment from employee on agreed-upon solution.

____ Manager reviewed with employee consequences for not meeting commitment.

____ Manager offered encouragement and support.

____ Manager thanked employee for his or her time.

FIGURE 11.9 Informative Speech Assessment Instrument

Instructions: Place a check mark next to each behavior that you see and then rate the skill cluster with an overall skill rating.

Skill Ratings: 1 = Very Poor, 2 = Poor, 3 = Fair, 4 = Good, 5 = Very Good

____ Introduction (1 = Very Poor, 2 = Poor, 3 = Fair, 4 = Good, 5 = Very Good)
 ____ Introduction gained attention.
 ____ Introduction was effective in establishing credibility of speaker.
 ____ Introduction included thesis.

____ Content (1 = Very Poor, 2 = Poor, 3 = Fair, 4 = Good, 5 = Very Good)
 ____ Speaker maintained audience interest.
 ____ Speaker showed relevance of information.
 ____ Speaker used information that was intellectually stimulating.
 ____ Speaker explained information appropriately.
 ____ Speaker used the following to aid audience understanding and retention:
  ____ Repetition ____ Humor ____ Associations
  ____ Transitions ____ Visual aids

____ Organization (1 = Very Poor, 2 = Poor, 3 = Fair, 4 = Good, 5 = Very Good)
 ____ Speech contained three to four clear main points.
 ____ Speech followed a:
  ____ Time order.
  ____ Space order.
  ____ Topic order.
  ____ Causal order.
 ____ Speech organization was appropriate for topic.
 ____ Speech contained appropriate summaries and previews.

____ Language (1 = Very Poor, 2 = Poor, 3 = Fair, 4 = Good, 5 = Very Good)
 ____ Language was clear.
 ____ Language was vivid.
 ____ Language was expressive.
 ____ Language was appropriate.

____ Delivery (1 = Very Poor, 2 = Poor, 3 = Fair, 4 = Good, 5 = Very Good)
 ____ Speech was delivered enthusiastically.
 ____ Speech was delivered with appropriate eye contact.
 ____ Speech was delivered spontaneously.
 ____ Speech was delivered using appropriate vocal variety and emphasis.
 ____ Speech was delivered using appropriate pronunciation and articulation.
 ____ Speech was delivered using appropriate bodily action.

____ Conclusion (1 = Very Poor, 2 = Poor, 3 = Fair, 4 = Good, 5 = Very Good)
 ____ Conclusion tied speech together.
 ____ Conclusion brought closure to speech.

In addition to skill ratings, assessors need **skill criteria.** Skill rating criteria describe, in behavioral terms, what each skill rating reflects. What does a skill rating of 1 look and sound like? How does a skill rating of a 1 differ from a skill rating of 2? Before assessors can begin the behavioral learning assessment process, they must be clear in terms of the behavior(s) that must be demonstrated in order to receive a particular skill rating. At the analytical level of assessment, assessors discriminate between varying levels of performance. The descriptive statements listed in Figure 11.10 reflect a set of skill criteria for the coaching behavioral items listed in Figure 11.8. Notice how all of the evaluative terms in the criteria are described in behavioral terms.

Each skill rating contains criteria that allow trainers to assess their trainees' behaviors. Another reason why skill criteria remain important is that they allow a team of assessors to have **interrater reliability,** which occurs when all assessors, using the same instrument, assess trainees' behaviors the same way. Interrater reliability is needed in order for your instrument to be considered useful. If one assessor rates a trainee's behavioral performance as very poor and another assessor rates the same performance as good, then interrater reliability would be low, and the assessment remains questionable.

Two factors that contribute to interrater reliability problems are unclear skill rating criteria and poor training. One example of an unclear skill criterion remains in the example in Figure 11.10. The skill criteria for rating 5 indicate that proficiency is

---

FIGURE 11.10   Skill Criteria for Behavioral Items

1 = *Very Poor:* Manager failed to demonstrate behaviors, and/or behaviors were demonstrated without proficiency. Without proficiency = language does not have clarity, language remains evaluative rather than descriptive, nonverbal messages remain incongruent with verbal messages, nonverbal cues are not appropriately expressive for coaching conversation.

2 = *Poor:* Manager demonstrated few behaviors, and most of them were demonstrated without proficiency. Without proficiency = language does not have clarity, language remains evaluative rather than descriptive, nonverbal messages remain incongruent with verbal messages, nonverbal cues are not appropriately expressive for coaching conversation.

3 = *Adequate:* Manager demonstrated some behaviors, and all demonstrated behaviors were moderately proficient. Moderately proficient = not all language has clarity, not all language remains descriptive, not all nonverbal messages remain congruent with verbal messages, not all nonverbal cues are appropriately expressive for coaching conversation.

4 = *Good:* Manager demonstrated all behaviors, but not all behaviors were proficient. Proficiency = language has clarity, language remains descriptive, nonverbal cues remain congruent with verbal messages, nonverbal cues are appropriately expressive for coaching conversation.

5 = *Very Good:* Manager demonstrated all behaviors, and all behaviors were demonstrated with proficiency. Proficiency = language has clarity, language remains descriptive, nonverbal cues remain congruent with verbal messages, nonverbal cues are appropriately expressive for coaching conversation.

reached when nonverbal cues are appropriately expressive for coaching conversation. What does "appropriately expressive for the coaching conversation" mean? To enhance interrater reliability, assessors would want to make sure that evaluative terms such as "appropriately expressive" are defined better, such as: "The nonverbal cues, such as facial expressions, tone of voice, vocal inflections, and gestures are expressed in a manner that remains congruent with the seriousness of the performance deficiency."

Realizing that not all criteria can be explicitly explained and defined, appropriate training remains another remedy for increasing interrater reliability. If not all skill criteria are clearly defined, then members of an assessment team need to decide for themselves what evaluative criteria such as "appropriate" or "effective" mean to them as a team. During their training, they also need to see examples of communication behaviors that would be considered appropriate or inappropriate and effective or ineffective.

Assessment Designs

Having reviewed assessment instruments and how to develop them, it's time to decide how and when to administer them in order to assess the overall effectiveness of your training program. Kirkpatrick referred to this level of assessment as results.[17] It's important to know up front that isolating the effects of training remains very challenging to the trainer. Kirkpatrick referred to it as the "separation of variables," or, how much of the improvement in trainees' performance is due to the training program and how much is due to other factors unrelated to the training program?[18] Assessment designs allow you to answer this question and to examine the effects of your training program. There are four basic designs for measuring training objectives: pre/post-test, pre/post-test with control group, post-test only with control group, and repeated measures design. In order to discuss each of these designs, you will need to understand the following symbols: G = Group, O = Test or Observation, X = Training Program/ Intervention. This section of the chapter concludes with a brief discussion of qualitative assessment methods that allow assessors to get a more complete picture of the learning outcomes by augmenting their quantitative assessment data with descriptive data.

Pre/Post-Test Design

With the **pre/post-test design,** you administer your assessment instruments to the trainees before the training takes place to find out what they know (cognitive), feel (affective), and can do (behavioral) prior to being exposed to the training program. You administer the same assessment instruments again immediately following the training program to see if there was a change in knowledge, attitudes, and/or behaviors. This type of measuring design is depicted in the following manner:

$$G1 \quad O1 \quad X \quad O2$$

G = Group	O = Test	X = Training Program

G1 represents a group of your trainees. O1 represents your pre-test. X represents the training program. And O2 represents your post-test. You would hope that the O2 scores were statistically different from the O1 scores.

The one major limitation of this measuring design is that if there is a difference in the post-test (O2) scores, trainers really don't know for sure whether the training program caused the difference. Other factors could have influenced the post-test scores such as maturation or testing effects. People change every day. We are not the same people today that we were yesterday simply because of the experiences we have had throughout the past 24 hours. So, was it our maturing and growing one day older that caused the change, or was it the training program? Another problem or threat to the validity of the measuring design may be that the pre-test sensitized trainees while taking the post-test. Depending on the amount of lapsed time, many trainees remember completing the same tests just a few days earlier. One way to avoid some of these limitations is to add a control group to the measuring design.

Pre/Post-Test with Control Group Design

This design remains identical to the pre/post-test design with the exception that a control group has been added. A **control group** is a group of similar individuals who will not be exposed to the treatment, or in this case will not receive the training program. This type of measuring design is depicted in the following manner:

$$
\begin{array}{llll}
G1 & O1 & X & O2 \\
G2 & O1 & & O2 \\
\end{array}
$$

G = Group	O = Test	X = Training Program

G2 represents your control group. To determine if your training had an effect on the trainees, you would compare the post-test scores (O2) for G1 with the post-test scores (O2) for G2.

This measuring design has two major strengths. Adding a control group helps to eliminate the maturation threat, and the pre-test allows trainers to ensure that the two groups (G1 and G2, the control group) are starting off on equal footing. Are the pre-test scores on the assessment instruments similar between G1 and G2? If not, then one would question whether or not the groups are similar. Remember, the control group is simply another group of similar individuals who will not be receiving the training program. If the groups remain similar in nature, then their pre-test scores should also be similar. Adding a control group allows you with more confidence to conclude that it was the training program that caused the change in post-test scores and not maturation.

Although the pre-post test with control group is a more robust measuring design, both groups still receive the pre-test and may be equally sensitized to the pre-test effect. To eliminate this threat while retaining the control group, you might want to consider assessing your training objectives using the post-test only with control group design.

Post-Test Only with Control Group Design

With this measuring design, you control for both the maturation and testing effects by only administering a post-test to the members of the training group as well as the members of the control group who did not receive the training. The post-test only with control group design is depicted in the following manner:

G1	X	O1
G2		O1

G = Group	O = Test	X = Training Program

Here as you can see, only one test is administered, and that test is given following the training program. Similar to the designs above, the control group (G2) receives the same test during the same time frame as G1. This measuring design allows the trainer to control for both the maturation and pre-test effects. The one limitation with this design is that there is no way to determine if the two groups were equal to begin with. Post-test score differences may be the result of the two groups not being similar.

Repeated Measures Design

The fourth and final measuring design integrates many of the design features listed above; however, this design allows trainers to identify where in a training program changes in knowledge, attitudes, and behavior occur. This measuring design is referred to as the repeated measures design and is depicted in the following manner:

G1	O1	X	O2	X	O3
G2	O1		O2		O3

G = Group	O = Test	X = Training Program

With this design, assessors not only administer a pre and post-test, but they also administer tests at various intervals throughout the training program. There are two major reasons why an assessor might want to use this particular measuring design. First, as previously stated, it allows a trainer to identify where in a training program changes in knowledge, attitudes, and behaviors occur. Assume you were administering a costly four-week training program, and your superiors wanted you to cut your training time in half. Where would you make the cuts? How would you make the decisions? Prior assessments suggest that significant changes in learning occurred in the O1 to O2 time interval with no changes occurring between the O2 and O3 time intervals. With this type of assessment data, training managers can make informed programmatic decisions that don't negatively influence learning outcomes.

The second reason for using a repeated measures design would be to determine the long-term effects of a training program. In the literature, this is referred to as a longitudinal assessment. Many training and human resource managers are interested in determining whether or not training has long-term effects. The repeated measures design would allow managers to answer this type of question by repeating the testing six months following the training period while again using a control group with no exposure to the training intervention.

Qualitative Assessment Designs

One way to get a more complete picture of learning outcomes is to augment quantitative assessment data with qualitative or descriptive data. Trainers who use **quantitative assessment** measure learning outcomes using numbers and statistics. Trainers who use **qualitative assessment** are more interested in describing learning outcomes rather than measuring them. Rather than using numbers and statistics, a trainer would interview trainees and ask them to describe how they have changed, if at all, as a result of training.

Two popular qualitative assessment methods include focus groups and interviews. If you were to augment your measuring design with a **focus group,** you would invite a group of trainees to an informal but focused discussion following the training program. During the focus group, you and possibly other trainers would ask a series of open-ended questions, or questions that cannot be answered with a simple "yes" or "no" answer, that would tap into the training program's learning objectives. Conducting a focus group is very similar to facilitating a group discussion, which was discussed in Chapter 6. After obtaining permission from the participants, you would record and/or videotape the discussion. Following the group discussion, you and your colleagues would transcribe and analyze the recordings looking for patterns of responses or themes in the discussion that reflect learning outcomes.[19]

If you were to augment your measuring design with **interviews,** you would conduct a series of open-ended, one-on-one interviews with randomly selected individuals who have completed the training program. Prior to conducting the interview, the assessor would develop an interview guidebook that contains open-ended questions that would allow the assessor to determine whether or not the learning objectives were met. The guidebook would ensure that all interviewees receive the same set of questions. If an assessor is to draw conclusions from the qualitative data, the interviews need to be standardized. Similar to the focus group method, the assessor would record the interviews, transcribe the notes, and analyze the data looking for patterns of responses or themes in the answers that reflect learning outcomes.

In the assessment literature, assessing learning outcomes by using both quantitative measuring designs (i.e., pre/post-tests) and qualitative descriptive methods (focus groups or interviews) is referred to as **triangulation.** Assessing with both methods allows training managers to assess more fully the effects of the training program.

Interpreting Assessment Information

Figure 11.2, which introduced this chapter, depicted the assessment cycle. If you'll recall, the first stage in the assessment process focused on developing learning objectives. This was the focus of Chapter 4. The second stage examined how to measure learning outcomes, which is the focus of this chapter. Now, we're ready for the third and final stage of the assessment process, which is interpreting or making sense of the assessment information. Kirkpatrick referred to this level of assessment as results.[20] What do you do with the data once you have them? In this section of the chapter, we will review how to analyze and interpret assessment data, how to use assessment data as feedback, and how to report assessment data.

Analyzing Assessment Data

To begin analyzing the assessment data, it will be necessary to use the learning objectives developed in the first stage of the assessment process as benchmarks or starting points. Assume that the following behavioral learning objective was developed after an extensive needs assessment:

> *Behavioral learning objective:* At the end of the training session, front-line customer service employees will be able to reduce customer complaints by 25 percent over a six-month period.

This objective, which is observable, measurable, attainable, and specific, serves as a benchmark to determine if the training program was effective. Without a training objective, there is no way to assess training effectiveness. One way to analyze this objective would be to use the post-test only measuring design with a control group. We would analyze the post-test data between the training group and the control group (or the group that was not trained) to determine if there was a 25 percent reduction in customer complaints within a six-month period following the training program. To determine training effectiveness, the training group would have to show a 25 percent decrease in customer complaints while the control group would have to show little to no change in their number of customer complaints.

Using Assessment Data

After analyzing the assessment data, you should be able to determine which learning objectives were met and unmet. It is important that you act on this information. Unfortunately for many assessment experts, the assessment process ends here because of a lack of time and resources. This remains important, especially because assessment data are important feedback that can be used to make poor training programs better and good training programs excellent. Similar to feedback in the communication process, feedback from trainees allow trainers to refine their training messages.

If you met your learning objectives, then you'll want to refine the training program with the assessment data you've collected and administer the program again. This time, however, you'll want to see even more improvement in cognitive, affective, and behavioral learning objectives. Never settle for the same level of learning outcomes. Continue to raise the benchmark on your training effectiveness. Make yourself and your training team indispensable to the organization.

If your data analysis reflects that you did not meet your learning objectives, then you'll need to return to the training curriculum and/or instruction and diagnose the problem(s). Where is the training deficiency? Is it with the cognitive, affective, and/or behavioral learning objectives? Having three sets of objectives and assessment instruments allow trainers and assessors to more accurately diagnose the weaknesses and limitations of a training program.

If you augmented your quantitative assessment data with qualitative data, you'll also want to look for themes in the qualitative assessment data. What are your trainees trying to tell you? These data remain incredibly important because they capture and describe nuances that quantitative data sometimes fail to detect.

Reporting Assessment Data

At this point, we've reviewed how to analyze the assessment data to determine if learning objectives were met. We have also stressed the importance of using feedback data to improve training program quality. Now, it's time to return to an idea that we used to introduce this chapter. One of the main reasons assessment is conducted today is to show decision makers and senior executives that training makes a difference in the organization. In a corporate culture of downsizing, if training and development departments cannot show their effectiveness, they will be vulnerable to being downsized if not eliminated entirely. Departments that remain immune from personnel cuts and funding are usually those that remain profit centers for the organization or can show their effectiveness in terms of improving the organization's bottom-line performance and profitability.

Ultimately, executives are looking for a return on their training investment. When organizational dollars are invested, most executives are looking for some type of return that shows that their investment was a wise one. One way to show this is by preparing a report that documents the cost/benefit ratio (CBR).[21] The **cost/benefit ratio,** which is depicted in Figure 11.11, examines the training program's benefits to the organization in relation to how much the training program cost. If there are more benefits than costs, then decision makers are probably more likely to reinvest in the training department's efforts. However, if the program's costs are greater than the program's benefits, decision makers are less likely to reinvest in additional training programs.

When reporting assessment results, we encourage you to find ways of showing the benefits of your training to the organization's bottom line. Using the behavioral learning objective from above, where front-line customer service employees will be able to reduce customer complaints by 25 percent over a six-month period, is a place to start. Assume we met this objective, how much does a 25 percent reduction in customer complaints save or benefit the organization?

$$CBR = \frac{Program\ Benefits}{Program\ Costs}$$

FIGURE 11.11   Cost/Benefit Ratio to Determine Return on Investment

$$CBR = \frac{\$17,500}{\$6000}$$

FIGURE 11.12   Return on Investment

Although benefits are sometimes difficult to compute, we believe most organizations can probably estimate how much a single customer complaint costs the organization. If not, you need to find out. Here are a couple of places to start in order to get a conservative estimate. Start by determining how much it costs the organization to process the complaint. How long does it take a customer service employee to resolve the complaint? How much do these employees get paid? Most complainants are also requesting some type of financial compensation for their inconvenience. Let's assume that it takes $25 of an employee's time, on average, to process a customer complaint and it takes $150 compensation, on average, to make the customer happy. Therefore it cost the organization $175, on average, to process a single customer service complaint.

Using the same scenario, we believe that our communication training has reduced customer complaints by 25 percent, and let's just assume that this equals 100 fewer complaints. In order to calculate the benefit, we take the average costs per complaint, which is $175, times 100 fewer complaints, which equals $17,500. The benefit to the organization is that it is spending 17,500 fewer dollars over a six-month period than it has in the past. We now know the benefit to the organization.

In order to calculate you how much the training program cost the organization, you would need to review the training budget. The budget is an important part of your training proposal, which will be reviewed extensively in the next chapter. Let's assume that the communication training program, which was used to train employees on how to resolve customer complaints, cost the organization $6000. To calculate the CBR or the organization's return on investment, you would simple divide the benefits by the costs, which is reflected in Figure 11.12.

Although the training professional cannot say with certainty that it was his or her training program that reduced the number of customer complaints by 25 percent, it's safe to assume that the training program did play a role in saving the organization $17,500 with an initial investment of only $6000. This type of reporting will resonate with organizational decision makers and will ensure that trainers continue to thrive in an era of downsizing.

Summary

The assessment process contains three stages, including developing learning objectives, measuring learning objectives, and finally interpreting or making sense out of the measurement data. The first stage was the focus of Chapter 4, and the remaining two stages were the focus of this chapter.

Before delving into how training practitioners measure learning outcomes, we reviewed two reasons why the assessment process remains critical to trainers. First, in a corporate culture of downsizing, trainers must be able to show that they positively influence the organization's bottom line. Trainers who cannot show their value to the organization remain vulnerable to downsizing or to being eliminated all together. Assessment is no longer an option for trainers.

Second, in a corporate culture of efficiency and quality management, assessing learning outcomes allows training practitioners to constantly improve the quality of their training. Assessment data allow practitioners to identify weaknesses and strengths. If the data are used appropriately, ineffective training programs are transformed into effective programs. Similarly, effective training programs are refined further, creating "optimal" effectiveness in terms of learning outcomes.

The next section of the chapter discussed how to measure cognitive, affective, and behavioral learning outcomes. To assess whether or not trainees learned the training content, you were instructed on how to develop an exam using multiple-choice, matching, and essay exam items. In order to assess whether or not trainees liked the trainer and the training program content, we discussed on how to develop a questionnaire using Likert-type and semantic differential scale items. Finally, to assess whether or not trainees' can perform the behaviors, you were instructed on how to develop an assessment instrument that contains behavioral items, skill ratings, and skill criteria.

Measuring designs was the focus of the next section of the chapter. In this section, we reviewed not only the measuring designs, including pre/post-test, pre/post-test with control group, post-test only with control group, and repeated measures, but also the strengths and weaknesses of each of the measuring designs.

The final section of the chapter, which focused on how to make sense of the assessment data, provided practical suggestions for how to analyze, use, and report assessment data. Training practitioners must make sense of their assessment data and then use the data to improve their training practices. This section of the chapter examined how practitioners use learning objectives as benchmarks to determine training effectiveness. Learning outcomes must be translated in ways that make sense to key decision makers. One way to do this is by computing a cost/benefit ratio by which decision makers can see how their organization benefited from the training program and that the benefits outweigh their initial investment in the training program.

QUESTIONS FOR DISCUSSION AND REVIEW

1. List and explain two reasons why assessment remains important.

2. Develop a series of Likert-type and semantic differential scale items that assess trainees' affect or liking for their trainer, training content, and trained behaviors.

3. Develop multiple-choice, matching, and essay exam items to assess cognitive learning outcomes.

4. Differentiate between atomistic, analytic, and holistic or general impression levels of behavioral assessment.

5. Develop a behavioral assessment instrument for a communication behavior that includes behavioral items, skill ratings, and skill criteria.

6. Explain the significance of interrater reliability.

7. Differentiate between pre/post-test, pre/post-test with control group, post-test only with control group, and repeated measure designs.

8. Explain the advantages and disadvantages to the pre/post-test, pre/post-test with control group, post-test only with control group, and repeated measure designs.

9. Explain the significance of triangulation.

10. Complete a cost/benefit ratio to document the value of a training program.

QUESTIONS FOR APPLICATION AND ANALYSIS

1. Devin is a manager of a local restaurant. He just completed a two-hour customer service training program with his wait staff. Now he would like to see if his training made a difference in how his servers perform their jobs. He has never had any type of training and development course and doesn't know anything about assessment. He would like you to develop a *behavioral* assessment instrument. Before you can develop this instrument, you have a series of questions that you will need to ask Devin. For example: What was your behavioral learning objective? What level of behavioral assessment would you like me to assess—atomistic, analytic, or holistic? What are the other questions you would need answered before you can develop this behavioral instrument? Why are these questions important to your being able to assess Devin's training?

2. Jodi trains sales representatives for a national pharmaceutical company. She trains representatives in all five regions of the country including the Northeast, Midwest, Northwest, Southwest, and Southeast. She just completed a new training program with her reps in the Southwest. She wants to know if her training is making a difference. She wants a rigorous assessment design. Which assessment design would you recommend she use and why?

3. Clay just completed a four-hour training program with 150 student leaders at his college. This training program focused on issues related to college life including date rape, diversity issues, sexual harassment, and binge drinking. How would you advise Clay to calculate his cost/benefits ratio? What would be some of his costs? How could he go about assessing the benefits of the training program? How would you advise him to report his findings to the Dean of Student Life at his college?

12 Trends and Career Opportunities in Training and Development

CHAPTER OBJECTIVES

After studying this chapter, you should be able to:

1. Describe the three trends in training and development and the implications for the training and development practitioner.
2. Differentiate teletraining from computer-mediated training by explaining the advantages and disadvantages of both.
3. List and describe the different types of training jobs.
4. Differentiate training generalists from training specialists.
5. Differentiate the needs-assessment proposal from the training proposal.
6. Write and present a needs-assessment proposal, making sure that it includes all of the necessary sections: briefing of problem, needs-assessment procedures, results, and conclusions.

7. Write and present a training proposal, making sure that it contains all of the necessary sections: introduction of trainer and credentials, title and description of training program, target audience, details of training program, assessment of learning objectives, training budget, and return on investment report.

What is the future of training and development? And, more specifically, what is your future in communication training and development? This chapter focuses on three topics that will address and, we hope, answer these important questions. First, we focus on three trends that are currently influencing those who work in training and development. Second, we discuss career opportunities. We'll recommend ways you can get into the training business and introduce you to the various types of training jobs. We also include a special focus on Web-based training specialists, who are currently in demand throughout the country. Finally, we discuss how to write and present training proposals, which could be your "foot in the door" or your introduction to the communication training and development business. Although this section on training proposals may seem out of place, we consider it to be just in time. Before you can propose a training program, it's important to understand the needs-centered training and development model and how training programs are developed. After reading Chapters 1 through 11, you're now ready to learn about how to write training proposals.

Trends in Training and Development

Technology and the advent of the Internet continue to transform home and work life throughout the world. They have changed the way we communicate in terms of whom we communicate with and the way we communicate with them. To get an idea of how e-mail has altered our communication, consider some of the turn-of-the-century findings from a study conducted by Forrester Research and John Carroll University in 2001:[1]

- We send 1.1 trillion e-mail messages worldwide annually.
- We send 3 billion e-mail messages worldwide daily.
- There are 150 million users who send e-mail messages daily.
- We spend, on average, 50 minutes reading e-mail everyday.
- We spend, on average, 60 minutes responding to e-mail messages everyday.

These numbers are predicted to increase. According to Andy Marken, president of Marken Communications, who cites a recent issue of *Business Week*, 10,000 new Web sites are added to the Internet daily. Technology and the Internet have "forced management, as well as marketing and support people, to broaden their knowledge areas. In has forced people to deal in a rapidly changing environment of uncertainty."[2]

These changes and trends, which will continue to evolve and transform how we communicate and live, provide a number of new opportunities for communication training and development practitioners. Three trends we consider noteworthy are our changing economy, technology, and training delivery systems.

Changes in the Economy: From Industrial Society to Information Society

To understand how the skills needed today vastly differ from those needed during the industrial revolution, it's important to chart the changes in the American economic system. This change transformed the training and development profession.

In the late 1800s, the United States was an agrarian society. The bulk of the U.S. economy was based on the production and selling of food, such as meats, vegetables, and fruits. Americans worked on farms and ranches across the country. As the country moved out of the 19th century and into the 20th century, the country was in the midst of the industrial revolution. Our economy was slowly moving away from the production and selling of food to the production and selling of hard goods such as the automobile and later the jet airliner. Americans were slowly moving off the farms and away from rural areas and moving into more urban centers, where they were working in factories.

Following World War II, the United States was in the process of making yet another transition. Americans were introduced to automation and, in the 1980s, the computer. Factory work was becoming automated and specialized. Many factory workers were displaced as a result of automation and were retrained for what would become the new information and service economy. With the invention of the personal computer, the American economy focused on the collection, processing, and distribution of information. The new information/service economy was based less on industry or the production of cars and jet airliners and more on information work and the providing of services.

According to Peter Drucker, management expert and author, two-thirds of U.S. employees collect, process, produce, and sell information products and services.[3] We use information products and services everyday. Many of these products and services have become commonplace. We don't know for sure where they come from, like milk in the grocery store, but we sure do like them and depend on them. Some of the information products include calling cards, call waiting, caller ID, instant messaging, frequent flyer programs, credit cards, electronic banking services, software programs, and Web pages that allow us to shop, pay bills, go to school, and communicate with friends, family members, and colleagues all over the world.

This shift from an industrial society to an information society has had a significant impact on training and development. Specifically, there is a growing need for communication skill development. Where trainers were once primarily helping trainees develop "hard skills," or mechanical and manufacturing skills that were required for assembly-line work, today's trainers are increasingly helping trainees develop "soft skills," or communication and relational skills that are needed to support the information and service economy.

Many of the information products we've mentioned are supported by 24/7 customer service hotlines. Customer service employees must be able to communicate effectively with people from all over the world using mediated forms of communication such as the telephone and the computer. From our experience, it seems that face-to-face customer service is becoming a thing of the past. Customer service representatives must be able to collect accurate information in order to place orders. They must be able to listen empathically and ask appropriate questions in order to help troubleshoot the problems customers have with products such as computers and software programs and with services such as long distance telephone plans and Internet service providers. Without seeing the customer, reps must be able to diffuse anger and resolve customer complaints by generating appropriate solutions and by giving customers options.

Changes in Technology: From Typewriter to Personal Computer

The personal computer and the Internet have revolutionized how we work. If you're like most people, you are always feeling a little behind and inadequate when it comes to technology. For example, the computer you're using now, even though it may be new this year, is already outdated. The software program you've just mastered after many long hours of trial and error is now being replaced by a newer version. Additionally, the vocabulary that was once used on the job is no longer meaningful in today's workplace. Today, it's not uncommon to hear, "Hey, when you get a second populate your roster and don't forget to forward an e-copy of the document you want me to distill. I will return the pdf along with the .jpg you requested." Just when you think you're current and up-to-date with technology, you're not.

Not remaining current with technology can quickly leave you, as a trainer, behind. It's disabling and hazardous to your occupational health. To keep employees current, marketable, and competitive in an age of the Internet and personal computers, there is a growing need for departments of training and development to focus on three areas of employee training and development. The first is in information technology, the second is mediated communication, and the third is change management.

In terms of information technology, it's important for trainers to help employees understand fully how to maximize their hardware and software. Most employees continue to underutilize what their personal computers are capable of doing. Employees must also become more proficient in how they network and share their files with others in their work groups and teams. Most personal computers have file-sharing software that allows you to share not only your work with multiple work partners but also to work from more than one computer, keeping all files and hard drives current and synchronized. Trainers and developers must help employees maximize their computing and networking potential and effectiveness.

Another area where employees will need assistance is in learning how to communicate in mediated environments. Electronic mail, voice mail, and teleconferencing have the ability to alter how we interact with others. **Teleconferencing** consists of two-way audio and video technology that allows people to participate in meetings even though they're not in the same physical location. Here are just a few of the questions communication researchers have been examining in their research that focus on mediated communication:

- How do synchronous (talking on the phone or instant messaging in real time) and asynchronous (leaving voice mails or e-mailing friends) forms of communication affect the accuracy of how information is transmitted?
- How do synchronous and asynchronous forms of communication affect how we feel about the other person?
- How does the absence of nonverbal cues influence how we perceive and interact with those around us?
- Can we achieve the psychological closeness needed to close a sales call when communicating via phone, fax, or e-mail?

Communication and leadership training and development practitioners must not only keep abreast of the research examining mediated communication but also find ways of translating the research findings, making them applicable to the workplace and making them useful to the men and women who use the technology to relate to others. These applications and skills are becoming the communication training content of the 21st century.

The third issue related to the technology trend has to do with helping others adopt new technology and helping trainees adapt to new ways of working using technology. Helping trainees change how they work might be one of your greatest challenges as a training and development practitioner. As you know from your own personal experiences, most people resist change. Even though employees have undergone enormous change during the past 25 years, they resist it. They often don't like it.

Many of today's departments of training and development include men and women who work in a specialty area referred to as "change management."[4] As a change agent specialist, your job is to manage change by helping others adapt to change. Training others in how to use new technology and software programs, in addition to how to communicate and conduct business using new communication technologies, is only one aspect of the training curriculum. The other part of the training curriculum, which is by far more challenging, focuses on training others *how* to change. There are a number of different models that change agent specialists can use to help others through the change process.[5] It's important that training and development practitioners remain abreast of this change research literature and, again, find ways of making it useful for trainees.

Changes in How Training Is Delivered: From Face-to-Face to Mediated

Another changing trend in the training business is in how training is delivered. Traditionally, trainers worked with trainees in real time and space, meaning that the trainer was face-to-face with trainees in the classroom. Today, there is a growing shift away from the traditional face-to-face training format and toward mediated forms of training that are channeled to trainees using a variety of telecommunication technologies.

In fact, one expert claims that training delivery shifted from 25 percent technology based and 75 percent face-to-face instructor based to a 50/50 ratio in 2002.[6] Other researchers believe these claims are exaggerated. The American Society for Training and Development reports that on-line training or e-training accounts for 10.5 percent of all training.[7] Regardless, face-to-face training tends to be decreasing. Whether face-to-face or mediate, the principles of the needs-centered training model apply to all methods of delivery.

Similar to teleconferencing, **teletraining** is training that is broadcasted from a studio to others in remote or distant training locations using two-way audio and video interactive television technology. Trainers and trainees are separated in space, meaning that they're not in the same physical location. With teletraining, you might have a trainer working from a studio classroom in Des Moines with the training broadcasted to trainees located in numerous training classrooms throughout the United States. Trainers use interactive television to transmit their training. With interactive television technology, trainers can see and hear their trainees in remote training classrooms, and trainees in these remote classrooms can also see and hear their trainers in the studio classroom. Trainers will often see their trainees by using multiple video monitors, one for each of their remote training locations.

There are advantages and disadvantages to teletraining and using interactive television to broadcast training to numerous locations throughout the United States and the world. First, let's discuss the advantages. Teletraining remains economical. One trainer can reach a number of trainees via the television. Organizations don't need multiple trainers in multiple cities. This also helps reduce the costs associated with business travel. The other advantage is that trainees in remote locations may have access to training that was not available to them before.

There are a number of disadvantages as well. Although with today's technology the disadvantages may outweigh the advantages, it's important that training and development practitioners find ways of overcoming these disadvantages if they're to remain successful in the interactive television training classroom. Here are a few of the disadvantages:

- *Teletraining favors cognitive rather than behavioral or affective learning objectives:* It's difficult to train a skill or behavior when you're not in front of trainees to see whether or not they're performing the skill(s) in the appropriate manner. If you will recall from Chapter 4, teaching skills or behaviors effectively requires trainers to tell, show, invite, encourage, and correct. This training process is challenging enough even when your trainees are with you in a traditional face-to-face classroom. It becomes much more challenging when teletraining is involved. Because of this challenge, trainers will oftentimes focus more on cognitive learning objectives, such as making sure trainees understand the theory behind conflict resolution rather than actually developing and practicing conflict resolution behaviors.

- *Teletraining favors a trainer-centered rather than a trainee-centered approach to training:* It's more difficult to engage trainees in remote training classrooms using interactive television; and, because of this, many trainers rely too much on the lecture training method rather than on other methods that are more trainee focused. If you will recall from Chapter 2, adult learners prefer to be actively engaged in their learning. Most adult learners know what they need to learn and bring their experiences to the classroom. They learn not only by listening to their trainer, but by listening to the experiences of their fellow trainees as well. With teletraining, it's difficult for a trainer to facilitate a discussion among trainees, especially when multiple sites are taking part in the teletraining program. Other technical problems that favor a more trainer-centered approach include getting the audio and video channels to sync. Depending on the technology, sometimes there is a time delay in the audio/video transmission, which makes synchronous conversation difficult. If you've ever watched a movie where the audio and video tracks are not synched, you know how frustrating this can be.

■ *Teletraining requires a different curriculum from that used in the traditional face-to-face training classroom:* Many trainers believe they can take what they do in the face-to-face training classroom and do the same in the interactive television classroom. Those who attempt this soon learn that it doesn't work. Teletraining promotes passivity in trainees. If you want trainees to engage in the training content, you must plan for interaction. It doesn't just happen. For example, it's much harder to facilitate a discussion or to conduct an experiential activity in the interactive television classroom. These methods can be used, but considerable preparation must be made if they're to work well. For example, instructors have to plan ahead and train facilitators who will be placed in remote locations to manage group discussion. Training packets need to be prepared ahead of time and mailed to all trainees. These packets contain experiential activities that can be completed easily by trainees, with minimal direction, along with probing questions that trainees can answer and that are later discussed by the trainer in the studio classroom.

■ *Teletraining doesn't easily allow trainers to get trainees' feedback:* Research suggests that distance educators who use interactive television perceive fewer nonverbal feedback cues from their students.[8] Unfortunately, technology has a way of blurring or filtering out important nonverbal cues that we depend on when we communicate with others. Head nods, forward body leans, vocal interrupters or starters that suggest that students want to say something, and vocal assurances that signal student understanding are important sources of information for most instructors. When these cues are filtered out or blurred, teachers perceive their students as being less intelligent, and they perceive their own training as being less satisfying and less effective.[9] We usually don't appreciate these important nonverbal feedback cues until we don't have them. Then we miss them.

All of these disadvantages provide opportunities for the communication training and development practitioner. Future practitioners must understand how they can use various communication theories and the skills and behaviors yielded from these theories to improve training effectiveness in the teletraining or mediated training classroom. Communication trainers must be able to help their fellow trainers use instructional forms of communication in the teletraining classroom. Numerous research articles address these concerns and offer recommendations to the educator/trainer who works with the interactive television medium.[10]

Computer-mediated training is training that is delivered using the personal computer and the Internet. This type of training has also been referred to as e-training, computer-assisted instruction (CAI), computer-based instruction (CBI), computer-based training (CBT), and computer-mediated learning (CML). Web-based instruction (WBI), or what is also becoming known as on-line video on-demand courses, is also expected to grow rapidly over the next two years as more and more corporations continue to invest in the development of their human resources.[11] On-line video on-demand courses are training programs that are videotaped and then placed on the Internet for trainees to access at their convenience. Using the computer to deliver the training allows trainers and trainees to be separated in both space and time, meaning that they're not together in the same physical location nor or they necessarily working together at the same time.

There are a number of advantages and disadvantages to using computer-mediated training, and many of these are similar to those for teletraining. The first advantage is that it remains economical for organizations to use computers to deliver training. Rather than paying for a number of stand-up trainers and their travel expenses, a computer programmer can write a training program, and trainees can access the training via their personal computer using a **CD-ROM** or accessing it on-line using their organization's intranet (an internal communication server) or the Internet.

Another advantage is that employees and trainees can access computer-mediated training that accommodates their schedules. This eliminates the challenge that many trainers face when it comes to the scheduling and rescheduling of training programs. Additionally, trainees can self-pace their computer-mediated instruction. If you will recall from Chapter 2 on how adults learn, we all have learning time preferences. Some of us are reflective learners, and others are impulsive learners. Computer-mediated instruction accommodates these learning differences, which should maximize learning outcomes.

Computer-mediated training also has disadvantages. Like teletraining, it tends to favor cognitive rather than behavioral learning objectives. This may be changing, however, as software programming becomes more sophisticated. For example, airline pilots must complete numerous hours of flight simulation training before they're allowed into an actual cockpit of an airplane. The flight simulator is a virtual cockpit that allows pilots to maneuver airplanes in a variety of flight conditions. Future software programs may become available for soft skills or communication training where trainees are placed in difficult situations and are asked to use certain communication skills to process the situation such as a disgruntled customer.

Another disadvantage is that not all trainees are self-motivated to complete a training program. It's not that they're necessarily lazy or being rebellious, it's just that they have interpersonal needs that a computer doesn't meet. Face-to-face communication has a way of motivating people in ways that computers can't. If you've enrolled in a correspondence course, you know what we're talking about. In a correspondence course, you complete a number of units using study guides and self-paced quizzes and then submit your completed work to an instructor at some other location using e-mail or the postal service. Computer-mediated training is very similar to completing a correspondence course.

Teletraining using interactive television and computer-mediated training using personal computers and the Internet are on the increase and are slowly replacing the traditional stand-up trainer. Future training and development practitioners must be receptive and skilled in how to develop and use these new delivery systems if they're to remain marketable in the 21st century. Similar to teletraining, there are a number of resources available to training and development practitioners who want to learn more about how to develop computer-mediated training.[12]

Career Opportunities in Training and Development

Having reviewed some of the changing trends influencing the training business, we now focus on how you can get a job as a communication training and development practitioner.

Getting a Training Job

There are a number of ways for you to gain entry into the communication training and development profession. Here are some of our recommendations:

- *Obtain a college education:* Most training positions will require that you have a college degree. While just getting the college degree is sometimes more important than the type of major one gets, we recommend you take courses that focus on training. Many of these courses will be offered in departments of communication and business. Look for courses titled Training and Development, Human Resource Development, Employee Relations, Instructional Communication, Communication Assessment, Organizational Communication, and Small Group Communication, to name just a few. It's also recommended that you take courses in research methods and social science statistics. These two courses will be particularly useful when conducting needs assessments and when assessing overall learning outcomes.
- *Complete an internship in a training department:* **Internships** are opportunities for students to obtain college credit toward their degrees by working in a supervised work environment. It's an opportunity for students to apply what they're learning in the classroom to the workplace. Most colleges and universities have career centers where students can obtain information about internship programs. Many internships are available during summer vacations or throughout the school year. Completing an internship not only gives you professional work experience that you can place on your resume but also allows you to begin networking with other

training professionals. One of the authors of this textbook completed summer internships while in college at a Six Flags theme park. For four summers he developed and presented weekly training orientations to new park employees and also developed and presented annual supervisory training programs to new shift supervisors. This internship led to a management position within a training department for an international airline following college graduation.

- *Join a professional training organization:* One of the most prestigious and respected training organizations is the American Society for Training and Development or ASTD.[13] This professional training organization currently serves 70,000 members in 100 countries with 15,000 local chapters. As a member of a professional training organization, you receive professional journals, admission to professional seminars and workshops, and a comprehensive directory of members. Local chapters conduct monthly meetings, which allow for networking and professional development. Local chapters also encourage students to get involved in ASTD by offering their services at a reduced cost. Again, belonging to ASTD allows you the opportunity to network with professionals in the training field, which may ultimately lead to your finding mentors, internships, and job opportunities.

- *Focus less on getting your first job in a training department and more on getting a job in an industry, corporation, or organization that excites you:* Sometimes it's more important just to get your foot in the door of an exciting industry than it is to wait for the perfect training position. You don't want a training job in an organization that doesn't excite you. Once you get into an industry or organization that is a fit with your interests, you often have the opportunity to transfer into the training department, which is usually located in the department of human resources. For example, at the Walt Disney corporation it's rare for an outsider, or someone without any Disney work experience, to be hired to work in the training department or what they refer to as "Central Casting." Disney hires from within the organization for many of their management positions. You must first pay your dues by working on the front line or as what is referred to as a "cast member." After working successfully as a cast member, you then put in for a transfer to the training department or human resources when a position becomes available.

- *Develop relationships with continuing education programs:*[14] Community education is growing in popularity, and there is a need for instructors. Volunteer to conduct a training program for your school, religious organization, or community and civic groups. If you have advanced training or are certified in a particular area of study, such as conflict negotiation or leadership, you might want to consider teaching a course in one of the many community education programs that are sprouting up throughout the country. Most of these programs are offered through local colleges, universities, community colleges, and county extension offices. Teaching in a community education program can benefit you in a couple of ways. First, these programs offer an excellent way to meet people who may later hire you. Second, these programs give you an opportunity to try out new training material and content in a venue that may resemble what you would find in more formal training environments.

Types of Training Jobs

Once you get your foot into a training position, you might be asked to do a variety of jobs, depending on the type of organization you have joined. There is a training job for almost every step of the "Needs-Centered Training Model," which was introduced in Figure 1.5 in Chapter 1. Here are nine jobs, tasks, or roles you might be asked to complete or fill:[15]

1. The **needs analyst** is responsible for conducting the needs assessment, which was reviewed in Chapter 3. Again, the needs analyst identifies what learners do not yet know or the important or necessary skills that they can't yet perform.

2. The **task analyst,** like the needs analyst, was reviewed in Chapter 3. As a task analyst, your primary job is to take the important skills identified by the needs analyst and break them down into a step-by-step outline. Trainers will use this step-by-step outline to teach others in how to perform the skill.

3. The **program designer** translates needs into learning objectives (Chapter 4), develops training curricula (Chapter 5), selects appropriate training methods (Chapter 6), and develops lesson plans (Chapter 8).

4. The **media specialist** works closely with the program designer in selecting and/or designing audio and visual media to complement and support the training program. Some of these ideas were discussed in Chapter 7. Today's media specialists are also advising and coaching teletrainers, who use interactive television to broadcast their training in addition to developing and designing sophisticated multimedia software programs that allow trainees to complete their training programs at their leisure and at their own pace using their own personal computer.

5. The **presenter** or trainer delivers the training program, which was the focus of Chapter 9. Presenters work closely with program designers and media specialists to make sure that training programs are delivered in an effective manner. They present information and direct structured learning activities so that trainees ultimately learn.

6. The **assessment specialist** is responsible for measuring the outcomes of the training program, which was the focus of Chapter 11. Was the training program effective? Did the trainees reach the intended learning objectives? Did the training fill the need that was identified by the needs analyst?

7. The **training and development manager** is responsible for planning, organizing, staffing, controlling training and development operations, and bridging the operations of the department with other units within an organization to ensure that the organization's training and development needs are met.

8. The **training and development administrator** works closely with the manager and ensures that the facilities, equipment, materials, participants, and other components of a learning event are present and that training programs run smoothly.

9. The ninth and final job that we would like to spend some time discussing is the **Web-based training specialist.** In the coming years, more and more training is going to be designed, developed, and delivered using the personal computer and

the Internet. One of the reviewers for this textbook, who is a training practitioner, recently attended a national training conference in Atlanta where over 75 percent of the panels at the conference focused on Web-based training and technology's impact on the training industry. Knowing this, we encourage new trainers to remain abreast of various multimedia technologies and Web-authoring tools that are used to create Web pages and Web-based training programs. Although we don't have room in this chapter to explore this topic in great length, we do want to give you a sampling of what Web-based training specialists know and do. We have also provided you with some resources at the end of this chapter that you might find beneficial.

Web-Based Training Design

Web-based training specialists know the differences between information and knowledge and how to convert information into knowledge. So what's the difference? **Information** is an assortment of facts and data that have limited meaning for the trainee until they are organized. If you will recall from Chapter 2, a schema is a way to organize and classify information. **Knowledge** is organized information. Once the assorted facts and data (information) are organized in a manner that fits the schema that trainees already possess, or a new schema given for how to organize the information, then information becomes knowledge. When surfing the Web, you expect Web sites to look a certain way. This expectation is your schema. There is usually some type of a "Welcome Page" along with a navigation or menu bar that previews the Web site. By using your schema, Web designers turn information into knowledge. They help you organize the information you are about to view. Without the navigation bars and various menu options, you would quickly become lost and overloaded with information rather than knowledge.

Now that you understand the differences between information and knowledge, how does a Web-based training specialist design a training curriculum for the Web, or how does a specialist convert an existing training curriculum written for the traditional face-to-face training classroom and make it suitable for Web-based training? A trainer cannot just simply transfer training curricula designed for the face-to-face classroom to the Web. Rather than transferring curricula, a Web-based training specialist converts the curriculum using two sets of principles: Web-based organizing principles and Web-based design principles.

The first set of principles focus on how to organize training content for the Web, including organizing by topic, procedure, or process:[16]

- *Organize training content by topic:* When you organize training content by topic, you organize information into categories based on "kinds of things." For example, your Web site might include information on leadership styles, coaching models, and types of oral presentations. Each category is unique and unlike the others. If trainees needed to learn about the different types of leadership, they would click on "Leadership Styles." From this Web page, they might be able to read about the various leadership styles and be directed to additional Web pages that would allow them to view short video segments demonstrating these various styles of leadership.

- *Organize training content by procedures:* When you organize training content by procedure, you organize information based on how to perform a specific set of skills. For example, your Web site might include procedures for how to conduct an audience analysis or how to adapt a message to a particular audience. Trainees needing to learn how to develop a sales presentation would click on the "How to Conduct an Audience Analysis" button to learn the steps involved in analyzing an audience. Once this procedure was finished, trainees would then click on "How to Adapt a Message to a Particular Audience" to learn how to adapt a sales message to a hostile or friendly audience.

- *Organize training content by process:* When you organize training content by process, you organize information based on "if this happens, then you can expect this to occur." For example, your Web site might demonstrate how to process conflict with employees. You showcase what new supervisors can expect when they process conflict. For example, as a new supervisor, if you discuss employee behavior in evaluative rather than descriptive terms, then you can expect to get the following reaction from your subordinate. Another way to think about this system of organization is to think of it as a trouble-shooting guide. If you do this, then you can probably expect this to occur. Organizing by process lays out all of the possible contingencies.

The second set of principles focus less on how to organize the on-line training Web site and more on how to design the Web site. Here are six basic design principles from the experts:[17]

1. *Use a coherent and consistent layout style:* Make sure that the site has a table of contents or a navigation menu that shows trainees all the major sections of the training Web site. This orients the trainee to the Web site. Make sure to carry your layout style and navigation menu throughout the Web site. It is also recommended that you provide trainees with a rationale for how the training Web site is organized.
2. *Use consistent and clear language:* Make sure your labels, names, tags, and titles remain consistent throughout the Web site. It is also suggested that you limit your use of jargon or "shop talk" as much as possible.
3. *Use emphasis techniques sparingly:* Avoid the overuse of large text, major heading tags, bold style, all caps, and colored text. Again, if you use emphasis, make sure you remain consistent throughout the Web site.
4. *Use hyperlinks sparingly:* Links are attached to a few key words, rather than to sentences or paragraphs. Your training Web site should contain a glossary, and all unfamiliar words should be highlighted and linked to the glossary. It is also suggested that you provide backward links so that trainees can easily return to their starting point.

5. *Use white space judiciously:* Rather than filling each page full of text, make sure to leave enough white or blank spaces so that you don't overload trainees with dense information. Open space helps set up text and images and makes it easier for trainees to focus. You are also encouraged to use the whole width of the Web page.

6. *Use action statements throughout the Web site:* Your objective is to get trainees involved in their learning. Each page of your Web site should state what trainees should do (i.e., read, write, discuss with a colleague, join the chat room, post an announcement to the list serve). Web site navigation must tell trainees what they are to do on each page and where to go or what to do next. Trainees should never be asking: "What do I do next?"

Training Generalist versus Training Specialist

If you belong to a small organization, chances are you'll be considered a training generalist. If you belong to a large organization, you'll probably work as a training specialist. **Training generalists** are practitioners who perform all of the jobs and tasks listed above that are related to training and development. They conduct the needs assessment, write learning objectives, develop training curricula, present training content, and assess training effectiveness. Rather than specializing in any one area, they do it all and remain a training generalist.

The advantages to being a training generalist are that it offers variety and it allows you to grow professionally. Rather than specializing in only one area, such as curriculum development, you become knowledgeable and skilled in all training tasks. This also makes you highly marketable if you decide to look for another training position elsewhere. The one main disadvantage is that your job may seem a bit fractured, meaning that one day you're presenting a training program and the next day you're conducting a needs assessment in order to develop the curriculum for yet another training program.

Training specialists are practitioners who specialize in only one area of the training and development profession. Some of the titles associated with training specialists include curriculum developers, program designers, trainers, and assessment specialists. Rather than becoming a jack-of-all-trades, specialists master one particular facet of the training and development process.

Many large training departments are housed in departments of human resources or what were once referred to as personnel departments. Training and development is just one of the subdivisions within a department of human resources, as illustrated in Figure 12.1. Other divisions might include staffing and benefits, to name just a couple. Members of the training and development subdivision then are arranged in teams by specialty. All needs and task analysts, in addition to curriculum developers, are part of the program design team. Presenters, software designers, and media specialists might be a part of the training team. All individuals who focus on training program effectiveness might be part of the assessment team.

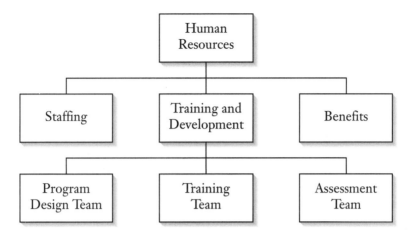

FIGURE 12.1   Human Resource Organizational Chart

Writing and Presenting Proposals

Regardless of your specific training position, one task that all training practitioners should learn is that of writing and presenting training proposals. A **proposal** is a formal document that sells the training program to the key decision makers in an organization. Key decision makers are usually men and women in upper management who make budgeting decisions. They decide how the organization's money will be invested. They ultimately decide what gets funded and what doesn't. A proposal includes the who, what, where, when, how, and why of a potential training program. In order for most training programs to get off the ground, executive management must endorse and financially support the program. A training proposal is your way of showing the executive management team why a training program is necessary, how training will be conducted, who will be involved, where and when the program will be conducted, and the payoffs or the return on the investment that training will bring to the organization. Sometimes, the executive management team will come to you with a problem and ask the training department or outside consultants for their assistance in addressing the problem. External trainers, or trainers who work for themselves, also typically develop a training proposal before being hired to present a training program.

There are essentially two types of proposals. The first is a needs-assessment proposal, and the second is the actual training proposal, which will be discussed later in this chapter. The **needs-assessment proposal** explains to the organization's key decision makers why their organization or some aspect of their organization deserves to be examined more closely. Your job is to convince the management team that there may be a deficiency of some type within the organization and that training may be the solution to the problem. For example, assume that you manage a telemarketing group and a trainer comes to you to suggest that your telemarketers may be losing too many telephone sales as a result of poor persuasive communication skills. The needs-assessment proposal would confirm the problem by identifying, describing, and explaining this particular problem.

Writing the Needs-Assessment Proposal

The needs-assessment proposal remains brief and succinct. Key decision makers tend to overlook lengthy documents. Include only essential information. You can always elaborate on the proposal later when you present your findings to key decision makers. Figure 12.2 shows an outline of what we recommend you include in your needs-assessment proposal, along with approximate page lengths for each section.

The first section of a needs assessment, the introduction, gives you the opportunity to introduce yourself to the organization's key decision makers. In addition to introducing yourself, you will also want to review your credentials, which give you **credibility,** a perception of your believability. Are you competent, and can they trust you to go snooping around their organization? You get credibility by reporting your **credentials,** which include your prior training experiences, your education, your research, and other forms of recognition you've received for your professional work experience. Your credentials help shape how others perceive you in terms of your competence and character. If you're already a member of the organization's training and development team, decision makers may not need an introduction. We recommend you have one available just in case they ask.

The second section, briefing of the problem, is where you describe the problem and explain why the potential problem remains significant to the organization. Just describing a problem is not always sufficient. To document the significance of the problem, show decision makers how the problem affects the bottom line of the organization. For example, you learn by reading the *Journal of Applied Communication*[18] that telemarketers lose sales as a result of their poor phone and persuasive communication skills. You also learn how sales have been shown to improve with appropriate training. Your job is to remain current with communication research and to inform key decision makers of critical research findings that affect their bottom-line profits.[19]

FIGURE 12.2   Needs-Assessment Proposal Outline

Introduction of Trainer and Credentials (2 pages)
Briefing of Problem (4 pages)
Needs Assessment Procedures (2 pages)

     Sampling

     Methodology

     Data Analysis

The third section of the proposal, the needs-assessment procedures, includes a brief discussion of the sample, methodology, and data analysis. In the sampling section, you will want to inform decision makers of whom within the organization you're going to include in your needs-assessment study. Using the example above, our sample would include all telemarketers. In the methodology section, you will discuss the methods by which you would conduct your needs assessment. This was discussed in great detail in Chapter 3. The final part of the procedures section will include a brief discussion of how you will analyze the data. It's not necessary to get into a lengthy statistical discussion here, but assume that some of your key decision makers will have backgrounds in statistics. Not discussing your data analysis could damage your credibility.

Presenting the Needs-Assessment Results

Assuming that key decision makers give you permission to conduct the needs assessment, you will need to present your results to them once the assessment is completed. We recommend you prepare both a written report and an oral presentation showcasing the results of your assessment.

To prepare the written report of your results, you can simply add to your needs-assessment proposal, which is outlined in Figure 12.2. Thus far you have an introduction, a briefing of the problem, and a discussion of the procedures you used to conduct your needs assessment. Now, you will need to add two additional sections, results and discussion. Again, a well-written brief and succinct report is more likely to be read than a long, detailed report that lacks clarity. Refer to Figure 12.3 for an outline of what we recommend you include in your needs-assessment results written report along with approximate page lengths for each section.

In the results section, present your findings in a clear and concise manner.[20] Give your key decision makers a snapshot of what you found in your needs assessment. One

---

FIGURE 12.3   Needs-Assessment Results Written Report Outline

Briefing of Problem (2–4 pages)

Needs Assessment Procedures (2 pages)

    Sampling

    Methodology

    Data Analysis

Results (2–4 pages)

Conclusions (2–4 pages)

    Problem Confirmed/Disconfirmed

    Possible Causes

    Possible Solutions

of the easier ways to do this is by reporting your results organized around the questions you asked in your needs assessment survey. As shown in Figure 12.4, the results for each survey item are organized using the questionnaire format. This figure illustrates how a training and development practitioner in a telemarketing organization presented her results to key decision makers. One part of her needs-assessment survey focused on how effective telemarketers perceived themselves to be on the job.

When presenting the results, simply compute the percentages for each of the response categories. By looking at this snapshot of the data, decision makers begin to see that there may be a problem among the telemarketers in the organization. From this snapshot, it appears that telemarketers consider themselves to be most ineffective when it comes to getting customers to talk to them on the phone and in getting customers to commit to purchasing the product. As a result of these two problem areas, which remain critical to a successful sales call, telemarketers in this organization don't consider themselves to be effective, with 75 percent of them considering themselves to be average to very ineffective in terms of their telemarketing effectiveness.

FIGURE 12.4 Reporting of Survey Results Using Questionnaire Format

How effective are you in getting customers to talk to you?

Very Ineffective	Somewhat Ineffective	Average	Somewhat Effective	Very Effective
30%	35%	20%	10%	5%

How effective are you in discussing the advantages of the product?

Very Ineffective	Somewhat Ineffective	Average	Somewhat Effective	Very Effective
2%	2%	19%	47%	30%

How effective are you in answering customers' questions about the product?

Very Ineffective	Somewhat Ineffective	Average	Somewhat Effective	Very Effective
12%	15%	47%	18%	14%

How effective are you in getting a commitment from the customer?

Very Ineffective	Somewhat Ineffective	Average	Somewhat Effective	Very Effective
12%	26%	34%	18%	10%

How effective are you as a telemarketer?

Very Ineffective	Somewhat Ineffective	Average	Somewhat Effective	Very Effective
15%	30%	30%	18%	7%

The final section of the written report, conclusions, confirms or disconfirms that there is a problem in addition to discussing possible causes and possible solutions to the problem. If a problem exists, this is where you suggest or hint at a training intervention. You don't sell the training program in this report, you simply offer training as a possible suggestion. The second type of proposal that we're going to discuss, which is referred to as the training proposal, is where you actually sell the training program.

To prepare your oral presentation of the needs-assessment results, we recommend the following:

- *Invite key decision makers and opinion leaders to attend your presentation:* Don't waste your time with those who don't have the power to decide if you're hired for the job. Invite key decision makers or individuals who make budgetary decisions. Ultimately, your training program is going to cost money. Ideally, invite other key opinion leaders in the organization. An **opinion leader** is an informal role within an organization that people look to in order to understand how they should interpret certain information. People learn from opinion leaders how they should respond to particular issues. Opinion leaders are usually respected individuals who have, on average, more education than others in their peer group, are well read and informed, and remain articulate.[21] Using the example from above, it would be wise to invite key opinion leaders from the telemarketing group to your presentation. You will want and need this group on board with you when and if you get the training contract.

- *Be brief:* Don't waste people's time. Present short briefing summaries for each section of the presentation. A **briefing summary** is a succinct statement that includes the who, what, where, when, how, and why of your needs assessment. Provide handouts that include additional information for those who might need it in order to make a training decision. They can refer to this document when time permits.

- *Use visual aids:* Use appropriate visual aids, such as a PowerPoint presentation that includes brief summary statements, to help your audience interpret more accurately the assessment results. One example of an appropriate visual aid may be the questionnaire items that were used above along with percentages for each response category. A visual representation of the results will not only help audience members interpret and retain the results more accurately but will also help you present and discuss the findings of the needs assessment in a more concise manner.

- *Be prepared to answer questions during your presentation:* Your presentation should be interactive. Encourage questions throughout the presentation and anticipate questions. Be prepared to answer, "How do you know this?" Be prepared to defend your needs assessment.

- *Ask for approval in developing a training proposal:* Once you've presented your results and discussed your conclusions, ask key decision makers for their approval to develop a training proposal, which will highlight how you anticipate addressing the problems or the identified needs of the organization.

Writing Training Proposals

After presenting the results of the needs assessment and assuming that the key decision makers are interested in what you can do to help them solve their problem, you prepare a training proposal. The **training proposal** is a formal document (see Figure 12.5) that outlines the training program in detail, including the length of the program, the training content, strategies, materials, an assessment plan, and finally a training budget.

As represented in Figure 12.5, most training proposals include eight sections:

1. *Introduction of trainer and credentials:* This section remains the same as the one you prepared for the needs-assessment proposal. Remind key decision makers of who you are by reviewing your credentials.
2. *Title and description of the training program:* Provide key decision makers with the information they will need to sell and market the training program to the respective members of the target audience. Title your training program and write a brief promotional summary describing the training program and the benefits one will receive for attending the training.
3. *Target audience:* This section also remains the same as the one you prepared for the needs-assessment proposal. Summarize for key decision makers the audience to whom the training is targeted.
4. *Learning objectives:* This section includes the learning objectives that undergird the training program and that address the needs identified in the needs assessment. Review Chapter 4 for the different types of learning objectives and how to write them. If your training program includes a variety of smaller training ses-

FIGURE 12.5   **Training Proposal Outline**

Introduction of Trainer and Credentials (1 page)

Title and Description of Training Program (1 page)

Target Audience (1 page)

Learning Objectives (1 page)

Details of Training Program (5 pages)

       Length of Program

       Training Curriculum

       Training Methods

       Training Facility

       Training Equipment

Assessment of Learning Objectives (1 page)

Training Budget (1 page)

Return on Investment Report (1 page)

sions or **training modules,** which were described in Chapter 8, you might want to include learning objectives for not only the entire training program, but also for each of the smaller training modules. For example, you might be doing an entire training session for the telemarketing group on how to increase phone sales; however, the trainees will complete a series of training modules including phone skills, influence and persuasion strategies, and how to close a sale. It is preferred that you write objectives for the entire training program and specific objectives for each of the smaller training modules.

5. *Details of the training program:* In this section, review not only how long the entire training program will last but also how long each training module will take trainees to complete. Time is money, so you'll want a pretty good estimate of how long you believe the training program will take. Be liberal with your estimates. From our experience, it always takes longer than what one expects.

   Give decision makers an idea of the training curriculum, the training methods you will use, the number of rooms or space you will need to conduct the training, and the equipment your training will require. If the organization doesn't have the necessary equipment such as computers, visual presenters, and overhead projectors, you'll need to budget accordingly.

6. *Assessment of learning objectives:* This section reviews how you will assess the effectiveness of your training program. Include some of the instruments for assessing cognitive, behavioral, and affective learning objectives in this section of the training proposal.

7. *Training budget:* Training proposals must include your **training budget,** which is a document that outlines all of the anticipated costs needed to develop, present, and assess a training program. How much money do you need in order to conduct the training program you're proposing? One way to develop a training budget is by using contact hours. A **contact hour** is the time you spend in the training classroom working with trainees. However, you're paid for more than just the time you spend working with trainees in the training classroom. Factored into each contact hour are the numerous hours you've invested in conducting the needs assessment, writing and presenting training proposals, writing learning objectives, developing the training curriculum, and assessing learning objectives. Additional costs, such as rental fees associated with equipment and facilities and travel costs (including hotel, food, and transportation) are either factored into the contact hour pay rate or billed individually to the organization.[22]

   Another way to write a training budget other than using contact hours is by developing three separate budgets. The first is a preparation budget. This budget includes all costs associated with the needs assessment, the development of the training curriculum, and all costs related to assessing learning outcomes. The second budget is a presentation budget, which includes all costs associated with presenting the training program, including your training fees and rental fees for audiovisual equipment and training rooms.[23]

   The third budget is for a separate "Train the Trainer" program. These programs are useful when there are hundreds or even thousands of employees who need to be trained. Because it's impossible for a single trainer or even a team of trainers to instruct hundreds or thousands of employees, some organizations select key individuals from the front line or rank and file to serve as trainers. Your job is to train the trainers who will eventually train the employees.

8. *Return on investment (ROI) report:* This concept was reviewed in Chapter 11. Key decision makers are more willing to invest in your training program if they believe they will get a return on their investment. In this section of the training proposal, you're encouraged to prepare a brief report that examines the cost/benefit ratio or the CBR. The ratio is illustrated in Figure 12.6.

The **cost/benefit ratio** examines the training programs' benefits to the organization in relation to how much the training program will cost. If there are more benefits than costs, then decision makers are probably more likely to accept your training proposal. However, if the program's costs are greater than the proposed program's benefits, decision makers are probably less likely to accept your training proposal.

Using the same example from above, assume that you will need $4000 from the organization in order to conduct the training program you're proposing. Let's also assume that you have calculated an estimate that suggests that the organization is losing approximately $15,000 per year in sales as a result of their telemarketers' deficient telephone and persuasive communication skills. If the key decision makers accept your training proposal, and they should with this projected cost/benefit ratio, you will save them approximately $15,000 per year with a one-time cost of only $4000.[24] This type of CBR will be persuasive to many of the key decision makers who will be reviewing your training proposal.

Although we've described eight sections of a typical training proposal, each proposal may not include all eight sections. To make sure that you are meeting the needs of the person or persons who will decide whether the proposal is accepted, ask questions to ensure that your training proposal includes the information the key decision makers need to approve your training proposal.

Presenting Training Proposals

As with the presentation you made for the needs-assessment proposal, you will also want to present your training proposal to key decision makers and opinion leaders. Use your training proposal document as a guide for your presentation. Consider presenting a **job talk,** which is a brief demonstration of one of the shorter training modules. A job talk will give decision makers and opinion leaders an idea of your training style

$$CBR = \frac{Program\ Benefits}{Program\ Costs}$$

FIGURE 12.6   Cost/Benefit Ratio

and a preview of the training curriculum you will use in the proposed training program. Remember, keep your presentation brief, be prepared to answer questions during your presentation, prepare handouts, use appropriate visual aids, and don't forget to ask for the training job.

One of the more important aspects of the training proposal presentation is to ask for the training job. You won't get the job unless you ask for it. After reviewing the training budget and the return on investment report, ask the client or organization for the job. Also be prepared to negotiate some of the budgetary concerns that key decision makers might have. Key decision makers may ask for a reduction in some of your budget items. Know in advance where the wiggle room is in your budget. In other words, know which items are negotiable and which items are nonnegotiable.

Learning how to write and present training proposals remains incredibly important for new training practitioners. It's your foot in the door or introduction to most organizations. This introduction must be impressive. Proposals must be well written and succinct. They must also be presented well and to the right audience of men and women who have the power to make budgetary decisions.

Summary

The focus of this chapter has been on trends that are currently influencing training and development and career opportunities. First we discussed three trends influencing the training and development industry. The first trend examined the changing economic system in the United States. Our shift from an industrial to an information and service economy has provided new opportunities for training and development practitioners, especially in the area of soft skills or communication training. The second trend focused on the influence of technology in our society. To remain current in today's workplace, employees must be willing to adopt and remain abreast of new workplace technologies. Again, this provides new opportunities for training and development practitioners. The third and final trend focused on new delivery systems, such as teletraining and computer-mediated instruction that many departments of training and development are using instead of the traditional stand-up trainer or the face-to-face trainer. Training practitioners must remain abreast of how these new delivery systems will ultimately change the focus of their work.

The second section of this chapter focused on career opportunities in the training field. We offered some practical advice on how to get a training job. Take a variety of courses in training and development and in business and communication studies. Other suggestions included obtaining an internship; joining a professional organization such as the American Society for Training and Development (ASTD); getting a job in an industry that excites you even if you're not in a training job, knowing that you can later transfer when positions do become available; and finally teaching in a community education program. We then discussed the different types of training jobs, paying particular attention to the Web-based training specialist and the difference between a training generalist and training specialist.

The third and final section of the chapter focused on how to write and present needs-assessment and training proposals. A training proposal is usually your first foot in the door, or your introduction to a possible training job either within a department of training and development or working as a communication training and development consultant. This section introduced you to the various parts of a needs-assessment and training proposal and offered practical advice on how to present your proposals to key decision makers in the organization.

Resources for the Training Practitioner

The following resources are just a sampling of what's out there in terms of helpful guides for the new training practitioner.

Training Guides

Caffarella, R. S., & Knowles, M. S. (2001). *Planning programs for adult learners: A practical guide for educators, trainers, and staff developers.* San Francisco: Jossey-Bass Publishers.

Craig, R. L. (Ed.) (1996). *The ASTD training and development handbook: A guide to human resource development.* New York: McGraw-Hill Professional Publishing.

Lawson, K. (1998). *The trainer's handbook.* San Francisco: Jossey-Bass/Pfeiffer.

Pfeiffer. J. W. (Ed.) (1972–1998). *The Annual* series. San Francisco: Jossey-Bass/Pfeiffer.

Piskurich, G. M., Beckschi, P., & Hall, B. (Eds.) (1999). *The ASTD handbook of training design and delivery.* New York: McGraw-Hill Professional Publishing.

Silberman, M. (1994). *Twenty active training programs: Vol. II.* San Francisco: Jossey-Bass/Pfeiffer.

Silberman, M., & Lawson, K. (1995). *101 ways to make training active.* San Francisco: Jossey-Bass/Pfeiffer.

Web-Based Training Guides

Beer, V. (2000). *Web learning fieldbook: Using the World Wide Web to build workplace learning environments.* San Francisco: Jossey-Bass/Pfeiffer.

Hall, B. (1997). *Web-based training cookbook.* New York: John Wiley & Sons.

Hanna, D. E., Glowacki-Dudka, M., & Conceicao-Runlee, S. (2000). *147 Practical tips for teaching on-line groups: Essentials of Web-based education.* Madison, WI: Atwood Publishing.

Horton, W. K. (2000). *Designing Web-based training: How to teach anyone anything anywhere, anytime.* New York: John Wiley & Sons.

Rosenberg, M. J. (2000). *E-learning: Strategies for delivering knowledge in the digital age.* New York: McGraw-Hill.

Wilson, S. (1995). *World Wide Web design guide.* New York: Hayden Books.

Professional Associations

American Society for Training and Development
1640 King Street, Box 1443
Alexandria, VA 22313-2043

On the Web at www.astd.org. To locate the chapter closest to you, click on www.astd.org and select the "Find a Chapter" menus option.
1-800-628-2783 or 703-683-8100

National Communication Association
1765 N Street, N.W.
Washington, DC 20036
202-464-4622

On the Web at www.natcom.org.

QUESTIONS FOR DISCUSSION AND REVIEW

1. Describe the three trends in training and development and the implications for the training and development practitioner.

2. Differentiate teletraining from computer-mediated training by explaining the advantages and disadvantages of both.

3. List and describe the different types of training jobs.

4. Differentiate training generalists from training specialists.

5. Differentiate the needs-assessment proposal from the training proposal.

6. List and describe the sections included in a needs-assessment proposal: briefing of problem, needs-assessment procedures, results, and conclusions.

7. List and describe the sections included in a training proposal: introduction of trainer and credentials, title and description of training program, target audience, details of training program, assessment of learning objectives, training budget, and return on investment report.

QUESTIONS FOR APPLICATION AND ANALYSIS

1. The company you work for is interested in teletraining and computer-mediated or Web-based training. You're being asked to serve on an advisory board, which will guide this process. What are the issues related to your company moving into mediated forms of training? What questions should the decision makers in your organization be considering? Why are these questions important?

2. Develop an action plan for how you're going to get your first training job. To develop this action plan, answer the following questions: What strategies will you use to get a training job? What type of a training job would you like to obtain and why? Knowing that a lot of future training will be delivered over the Internet, what can you do now to enhance your technology skills? Would you prefer being a training generalist or specialist? Why?

3. Your instructor would like you to develop a return on investment report for the training class you currently taking. How would you go about doing this? What types of information would you need? How would you go about computing your cost/benefit ratio?

NOTES

Chapter 1

1. See J. L. Winsor, D. B. Curtis, & R. D. Stephens (Sept. 1997). "National Preferences in Business and Communication Education: A Survey Update," *Journal of the Association for Communication Administration, 3,* 174; *The Wall Street Journal* (2002) September 9: 1A.
2. E. E. Scannell & L. Donaldson (2000). *Human Resource Development: The New Trainer's Guide.* Cambridge, MA: Perseus, p. 1.
3. Scannel & Donaldson, *Human Resource Development,* 1.
4. Winsor, Curtis, & Stephens, "National Preferences in Business and Communication Education."
5. J. A. Kline (April 1983). *Spectra: Newsletter of the Speech Communication Association.*
6. Kline, *Spectra.*
7. E. Schein (1987). *Process Consultation. Volume II: Lessons for Managers and Consultants.* Reading, MA: Addison-Wesley. For applications to communication consultation see E. E. Rudolph & B. R. Johnson (1983). *Communication Consulting: Another Teaching Option.* Urbana, IL: ERIC Clearinghouse on Reading and Communication Skills.
8. F. E. X. Dance & C. Larson (1972). *Speech Communication: Concepts and Behavior.* New York: Holt, Rinehart and Winston.
9. Dance & Larson, *Speech Communication.*
10. J. T. Masterson, S. A. Beebe, & N. H. Watson (1989). *Invitation to Effective Speech Communication.* Glenview, IL: Scott, Foresman and Company.
11. E. T. Klemmer & F. W. Snyder (June 1972). "Measurement of Time Spent Communicating," *Journal of Communication, 20:* 142.
12. B. Pike (1994). *Creative Training Techniques Handbook.* Minneapolis, MN: Lakewood.

Chapter 2

1. Adapted from W. H. Burton (1963). Basic principles in good teaching–learning situations. In L. D. Crow and A. Crow (Eds.), *Readings in human learning* (pp. 7–19). New York: McKay.
2. W. F. Hill (1990). *Learning: A survey of psychological interpretations.* New York: Harper & Row Publishers. For additional applications to the training context, refer to E. E. Scannell & L. Donaldson (2000). *Human resource development: The new trainer's guide.* Cambridge, MA: Perseus Publishing.
3. V. P. Richmond (1996). *Nonverbal communication in the classroom.* Edina, MN: Burgess Publishing. K. Kougl (1997). *Communicating in the classroom.* Prospect Heights, IL: Waveland Press.
4. Hill, *Learning.* For additional applications to the training context, refer to Scannell & Donaldson, *Human resource development.*
5. W. F. Hill, *Learning.* For additional applications to the training context, refer to Scannell & Donaldson, *Human resource development.*
6. M. Knowles (1990). *The adult learner: A neglected species.* Houston, TX: Gulf Publishing Company. Also refer to the following resources for andragogical training applications: M. S. Knowles, E. F. Holton & R. A. Swanson (2001). *The adult learner: The definitive classic in adult education and human resource development.* Woburn, MA: Butterworth-Heinemann. M. Silberman (1990). *Active training: A handbook of techniques, designs, case studies, and tips.* San Francisco: Jossey-Bass Publishers. R. J. Wlodkowski (1999). *Enhancing adult motivation to learn: A comprehensive guide for teaching all adults.* San Francisco: Jossey-Bass Publishers.
7. P. Hersey & K. Blanchard (1992). *Management of organizational behavior: Utilizing human resources* (6th ed.). Englewood Cliffs, NJ: Prentice-Hall.
8. R. Zemke & S. Zemke (1984). Thirty things we know for sure about adult learning. *Innovation Abstracts, 6* (8). Downloadable at: http://www.hcc .hawaii.edu/intranet/committees/FacDevCom/ guidebk/teachtip/adults-3.htm.
9. Zemke & Zemke. Thirty things we know for sure about adult learning.
10. Zemke & Zemke. Thirty things we know for sure about adult learning.
11. H. Gardner (1983). *Frames of mind: The theory of multiple intelligences.* New York: Basic Books.
12. V. P. Richmond, & J. Gorham (1998). *Communication, learning, and affect in instruction.* Acton, MA: Tapestry Press.
13. D. H. Schunk (2000). *Learning theories: An educational perspective.* Upper Saddle River, NJ: Prentice Hall.
14. Zemke & Zemke. Thirty things we know for sure about adult learning.

15. L. B. Resnick (1985). Cognition and instruction: Recent theories of human competence. In B. L. Hammonds (Ed.), *Psychology and learning: The master lecture series*, vol. 4, pp. 127–186. Washington, DC: American Psychological Association.
16. D. K. Kolb (1999). *Learning Style Inventory, Version 3*. Boston, MA: Experience Based Learning Systems.
17. Richmond & Gorham. *Communication, learning, and affect in instruction.*
18. B. McCarthy (1981). *The 4Mat system: Teaching to learning styles with right/left mode techniques*. Oakbrook, IL: EXCEL.

Chapter 3

1. M. Silberman (1998). *Active Training*. San Francisco: Jossey-Bass/Pfeiffer.
2. B. S. Bloom, M. B. Englehart, E. J. Furst, W. H. Hill, & O. R. Krathwohl, (1956). *Taxonomy of educational objectives: The classification of educational goals. Handbook I: The cognitive domain*. New York: Longman.
3. Silberman, *Active Training*, p. 35.
4. K. Lawson (1998). *The Trainer's Handbook*. San Francisco: Jossey-Bass/Pfeiffer, p. 17.

Chapter 4

1. For a discussion of differences between goals and learning objectives see: J. E. Brooks-Harris & S. R. Stock-Ward (1999). *Workshops: Designing and Facilitating Experiential Learning*. Thousand Oaks, CA: Sage.
2. R. F. Mager (1975). *Preparing Instructional Objectives* (2nd ed.). Belmont, CA: Fearon.
3. A brief but clear discussion of training objectives may be found in: E. E. Scannel & L. Donaldson (2000). *Human Resource Development: The New Trainer's Guide*. Cambridge, MA: Perseus Publishing.
4. Michael Argyle was the first social psychologist to suggest a model of social skills training. Our skill development model is based on work by: M. Argyle (1994). *The Psychology of Interpersonal Behaviour*. London: Penguin Books; D. A. Romig & L. J. Romig (1985). *Communication and Problem Solving Skills: Trainer Guide*. Austin, TX: Performance Resources; D. A. Romig (2001). *Side by Side Leadership: Achieving Outstanding Results Together*. Austin, TX: Bard Press, p. 146; and

R. R. Carkhuff & R. M. Pierce. (1975). *The Art of Helping: An Introduction to Life Skills: Teacher Guide*. Amherst, MA: Human Resource Development Press.
5. E. T. Emmer & G. B. Millett (1970). *Improving Teaching through Experimentation*. Englewood Cliffs, NJ: Prentice-Hall.
6. S. A. Beebe & S. J. Beebe (2003). *Public Speaking: An Audience-Centered Approach*. Boston: Allyn & Bacon.
7. D. H. Schunk (1987). Peer models and children's behavioral change. *Review of Educational Research*, 57, 149–174; B. Sulzer-Azaroff & G. Mayer (1986). *Achieving educational excellence using behavioral strategies*. New York: Holt, Rinehart & Winston.

Chapter 5

1. V. Montecino (July, 2002). "Criteria to Evaluate the Credibility of WWW Resources." http://mason.gmu.edu/~montecin/web-eval-sites.htm. Fairfax County, VA: George Mason University.
2. V. P. Richmond & J. C. McCroskey (1998). *Communication apprehension, avoidance, and effectiveness* (5th ed.). Boston: Allyn and Bacon.
3. S. A. Beebe & S. J. Beebe (2003). *Public speaking: An audience-centered approach* (5th ed.). Boston: Allyn & Bacon.

Chapter 6

1. M. Knowles (1990). *The adult learner: A neglected species*. Houston, TX: Gulf Publishing Company.
2. Refer to E. Dal & D. R. Woods (1989). Developing student's problem-solving skills, *Journal of College Science Teaching*, 13.
3. Reported in W. E. Arnold & L. McClure (1993). *Communication training and development*, p. 36. Prospect, IL: Waveland Press.
4. D. H. Schunk (2000). *Learning theories: An educational perspective*. Upper Saddle River, NJ: Prentice Hall.
5. For additional tips on how to make the lecture training method more active, refer to M. Silberman (1990). *Active training: A handbook of techniques, designs, case examples, and tips*. San Francisco: Jossey-Bass Publishers.
6. A. Mehrabian (1971). *Silent messages*. Belmont, CA: Wadsworth. Also refer to V. P. Richmond & J. C. McCroskey (Eds.) (1992). *Power in the class-*

room: Communication, control, and concern. Hillsdale, NJ: Lawrence Erlbaum Associates.

7. G. A. Sorensen (1989). The relationships among teachers' self-disclosive statements, students' perceptions, and affective learning. *Communication Education, 38,* 257–276.

8. J. Gorham & D. M. Christophel (1990). The relationship of teachers' use of humor in the classroom to immediacy and student learning. *Communication Education, 39,* 46–62.

9. G. L. Peterson (2000). *Communicating in organizations* (2nd ed.). Boston: Allyn & Bacon. Other case study resources include B. D. Sypher (Ed.) (1997). *Case studies in organizational communication: Perspectives on contemporary work life.* New York: Guilford Press, and J. Keyton & P. Shockley-Zalabak (Eds.) (in press). *Case Studies for Organizational Communication: Understanding Communication Processes.* Los Angeles, CA: Roxbury.

10. Arnold & McClures. *Communication training and development.*

11. Refer to the following resources for assistance in preparing experiential activities: J. W. Pfeiffer (Ed.) (1972–1998). The *Annual* series. San Francisco: Jossey-Bass/Pfeiffer; E. E. Scannell & J. W. Newstrom (1991). *Still more games trainers play.* New York: McGraw-Hill; M. Silberman & K. Lawson (1995). *101 ways to make training active.* San Francisco: Jossey-Bass/Pfeiffer.

12. Adapted from G. E. Myers & M. T. Myers (1976). *Instructor's manual to accompany the dynamics of human communication.* New York: McGraw-Hill.

13. K. Kougl (1997). *Communicating in the classroom.* Prospect Heights, IL: Waveland Press.

14. B. S. Bloom (1956). *Taxonomy of educational objectives: Handbook I: Cognitive domain.* New York: McKay.

15. Adapted from R. R. Allen & T. Rueter (1990). *Teaching assistant strategies: An introduction to college teaching.* Dubuque, IA: Kendall/Hunt Publishing Company; W. J. McKeachie (1999). *Teaching tips: Strategies, research, and theory for college and university teachers.* Boston: Houghton Mifflin Company.

16. Refer to D. E. Hanna, M. Glowacki-Dudka, & S. Conceicao-Runlee (2000). *147 Practical tips for teaching on-line groups: Essentials of Web-based education.* Madison, WI: Atwood Publishing. Also refer to T. P. Mottet & S. L. Stewart (2002). Teacher communication in the distance education context. In J. L. Chesebro & J. C. McCroskey (Eds.), *Communication for teachers,* pp. 157–171. Boston: Allyn and Bacon.

Chapter 7

1. M. L. Hickson & D. W. Stacks (1993). *Nonverbal communication: Studies and applications* (3rd ed.). Dubuque, IA: WCB Brown & Benchmark Publishers.

2. J. Rotondo & M. Rotondo, Jr. (2002). *Presentation skills for managers.* New York: McGraw-Hill.

3. J. Kupsch & P. R. Graves (1993). *Create high impact business presentations.* Chicago: NTC Learning Works.

4. Kupsch & Graves (1993). *Create high impact business presentations.*

5. C. Wilder & J. Rotondo (2002). *Point, click & wow: A quick guide to brilliant laptop presentations* (2nd ed.). San Francisco: Jossey-Bass/Pfeiffer.

6. Rotondo & Rotondo. *Presentation skills for managers.*

7. Rotondo & Rotondo. *Presentation skills for managers.*

8. Rotondo & Rotondo. *Presentation skills for managers.*

9. Rotondo & Rotondo. *Presentation skills for managers.*

Chapter 8

1. D. C. Berliner (1991). Educational psychology and pedagogical expertise: New finds and new opportunities for thinking about training. *Educational Psychologist, 26*(2), 145–155.

2. These lesson plans were developed by Nathan Faylor, Southwest Texas State University. Used with permission.

3. For an excellent review of literature about principles and strategies for informing others see: K. E. Rowan (2003). "Informing and explaining skills: Theory and research on informative communication," In J. O. Greene and B. R. Burleson, *Handbook of communication and social interaction skills,* pp. 403–438. Mahwah, NJ: Lawrence Erlbaum Associates, Publishers.

Chapter 9

1. A. Maslow (1954). *Motivation and personality.* New York: Harper & Row.

2. A. Mehrabian (1971). *Silent messages.* Belmont, CA: Wadsworth.

3. V. P. Richmond, J. Gorham & J. C. McCroskey (1987). The relationship between selected immediacy behaviors and cognitive learning. In M. McLaughlin (Ed.), *Communication Yearbook 10* (pp. 574–590). Beverly Hills, CA: Sage; J. Gorham (1988). The relationship between verbal teacher immediacy behaviors and student learning. *Communication Education, 37,* 40–53.

4. D. M. Christophel (1990). The relationship among teacher immediacy behaviors, student motivation, and learning. *Communication Education, 39,* 323–340; V. P. Richmond (1990). Communication in the classroom: Power and motivation. *Communication Education, 39,* 181–195.

5. J. C. McCroskey, V. P. Richmond, A. Sallinen, J. M. Fayer & R. A. Barraclough (1995). A cross-cultural and multi-behavioral analysis of the relationship between nonverbal immediacy and teacher evaluation. *Communication Education, 44,* 281–291.

6. V. P. Richmond & J. C. McCroskey (1999). *Nonverbal behavior in interpersonal relations* (4th ed.). Boston: Allyn & Bacon.

7. Richmond & McCroskey (1999). *Nonverbal behavior in interpersonal relations.*

8. S. A. Beebe & S. J. Beebe (2003). *Public Speaking: An audience-centered approach* (5th ed.). Boston: Allyn & Bacon.

9. J. T. Molloy (1988). *New dress for success.* New York: Warner Books.

10. K. D. Roach (1997). Effects of graduate teaching assistant attire on student learning, misbehaviors, and ratings of instruction. *Communication Quarterly, 45,* 125–141.

11. S. A. Westmyer & L. M. Flaherty (1996, November). *Student perceptions of instructors based upon clothing, credibility, and context.* Paper presented at the Speech Communication Association Convention, San Diego, CA.

12. J. T. Molloy (1996). *New women's dress for success,* p. 2. New York: Warner Books.

13. J. Lukavsky, S. Butler & A. J. Harden (1995). Perceptions of an instructor: Dress and students' characteristics. *Perceptual and Motor Skills, 81,* 231–240.

14. Molloy. *New dress for success,* p. 154.

15. Molloy. *New dress for success.*

16. Molloy. *New women's dress for success.*

17. S. Bixler & N. Nix-Rice (1997). *The new professional image: From business casual to the ultimate power look.* Holbrook, MA: Adams Media Corporation.

18. M. L. Knapp & J. A. Hall (1997). *Nonverbal communication in human interaction* (4th ed.). Orlando, FL: Harcourt Brace & Company.

19. D. L. Leathers (1997). *Successful nonverbal communication: Principles and applications* (3rd ed.). Boston: Allyn & Bacon.

20. S. Bixler & L. S. Dugan (2001). *5 steps to professional presence: How to project confidence, competence, and credibility at work.* Holbrook, MA: Adams Media Corporation.

21. S. A. Beebe (1974). Eye contact: A nonverbal determinant of speaker credibility. *Speech Teacher, 23,* 21–25.

22. V. P. Richmond (2002). Teacher nonverbal immediacy: Use and outcomes. In J. Chesebro and J. C. McCroskey (Eds.), *Communication for teachers,* pp. 65–82. Boston: Allyn & Bacon.

23. V. P. Richmond (2002). Teacher nonverbal immediacy, pp. 65–82.

24. E. T. Hall (1966). *The hidden dimension.* Garden City, NJ: Doubleday.

25. D. O'Hair & R. A. Stewart (1999). *Public speaking: Challenges and choices.* Boston: Bedford/St. Martin's.

26. Richmond. Teacher nonverbal immediacy. Adapted from S. A. Beebe & S. J. Beebe (2003). *Public speaking: An audience-centered approach* (5th ed.) Boston: Allyn & Bacon.

Chapter 10

1. W. C. Schutz (1958). *FIRO: A three-dimensional theory of interpersonal behavior.* New York: Holt, Rinehart, & Winston.

2. V. P. Richmond & J. C. McCroskey (1998). *Communication apprehension, avoidance, and effectiveness* (5th ed.). Boston: Allyn & Bacon.

3. J. C. McCroskey (1998). *An introduction to communication in the classroom.* Acton, MA: Tapestry Press.

4. Mehrabian. *Silent messages.* Belmont, CA: Wadsworth.

5. Mehrabian. *Silent messages.*

6. Adapted from F. F. Fournies (1987). *Coaching for improved work performance.* Blue Ridge Summit, PA: Liberty House Publishers.

7. See: V. P. Richmond & J. C. McCroskey (1992). *Power in the classroom: Communication, control, and concern.* Hillsdale, NJ: Lawrence Erlbaum Associates.

8. J. C. McCroskey & L. R. Wheeless (1976). *An introduction to human communication.* Boston: Allyn and Bacon.

9. J. C. McCroskey & V. P. Richmond (1992). Increasing teacher influence through immediacy. In J. C. Mcroskey and V. P. Richmond (Eds.), *Power in the classroom: Communication, control, and*

concern, pp. 101–119. Hillsdale, NJ: Lawrence Erlbaum Associates.

10. T. G. Plax & P. Kearney (1992). Teacher power in the classroom: Defining and advancing a program of research. In J. C. McCroskey and V. P. Richmond (Eds.), *Power in the classroom: Communication, control, and concern*, pp. 67–84. Hillsdale, NJ: Lawrence Erlbaum Associates.

11. P. Kearney & T. G. Plax (1992). Student resistance to control. In J. C. McCroskey and V. P. Richmond (Eds.), *Power in the classroom: Communication, control, and concern*, pp. 85–100. Hillsdale, NJ: Lawrence Erlbaum Associates.

12. Refer to R. A. Bell & J. A. Daly (1984). The affinity-seeking function of communication. *Communication Monographs, 51*, 91–115. J. C. McCroskey & L. L. McCroskey (1986). The affinity-seeking of classroom teachers. *Communication Research Reports, 3*, 158–167.

13. See: A. B. Frymier (1994). The use of affinity-seeking in producing liking and learning in the classroom. *Applied Communication Research, 22*, 87–105.

14. See: V. P. Richmond, J. S. Gorham & J. C. McCroskey (1987). The relationship between selected immediacy behaviors and cognitive learning. In M. L. McLaughlin (Ed.) *Communication Yearbook, 10*, 574–590. Beverly Hills, CA: Sage.

15. J. Gorham (1988). The relationship between verbal teacher immediacy behaviors and student learning. *Communication Education, 37*, 40–53.

16. See: P. Kearney, T. G. Plax, V. P. Richmond & J. C. McCroskey (1984). Power in the classroom IV: Alternatives to discipline. In R. Bostrom (Ed.), *Communication yearbook, 8*, 724–746. Beverly Hills, CA: Sage.

17. See: P. Kearney, T. G. Plax & T. H. Allen (2002). Understanding student reactions to teachers who misbehave. In J. L. Chesebro and J. C. McCroskey (Eds.), *Communication for Teachers*, pp. 127–140. Boston: Allyn & Bacon.

18. P. Kearney, T. G. Plax, E. R. Hays & M. J. Ivey (1991). College teacher misbehaviors: What students don't like about what teachers say and do. *Communication Quarterly, 39*, 309–324.

Chapter 11

1. For more information on return on investment, refer to J. J. Phillips (1997). *Handbook of training evaluation and measurement methods* (3rd ed.). Houston, TX: Gulf Publishing Company.

2. For more on Deming's total quality management philosophy, refer to R. Aguayo (1990). *Dr. Deming: The American who taught the Japanese about quality*. New York: Fireside.

3. Refer to D. L. Kirkpatrick (1994). *Evaluating training programs: The four levels*. San Francisco: Berrett-Koehler Publishers. Also refer to D. L. Kirkpatrick (1996). Evaluation. In R. L. Craig (Ed.), *The ASTD training and development handbook: A guide to human resource development* (4th ed.), pp. 294–312. New York: McGraw-Hill.

4. This three-question approach to assessment was discussed by J. D. Bell & D. Kerr (1987). Measuring training results: Key to managerial commitment. *Training and Development Journal, 41*, 70–73.

5. Refer to Kirkpatrick. Evaluation.

6. For a complete review of how to construct these exam items, please reference D. P. Scannell & D. B. Tracy (1975). *Testing and measurement in the classroom*. Boston: Houghton Mifflin Company.

7. Reference encoding specificity in J. R. Anderson (1995). *Cognitive psychology and its implications*. New York: W. H. Freeman and Company.

8. Reference context effects in Anderson (1995). *Cognitive psychology and its implications*.

9. Refer to Kirkpatrick (1996). Evaluation.

10. For a review of this research, reference V. P. Richmond & J. C. McCroskey (1992). *Power in the classroom: Communication, control, and concern*. Hillsdale, NJ: Lawrence Erlbaum Associates.

11. For a review of this measure, reference T. P. Mottet & V. P. Richmond (1998). New is not necessarily better: A reexamination of affective learning measurement. *Communication Research Reports, 15*, 370–378. Also refer to R. B. Rubin, P. Palmgreen & H. E. Sypher (Eds.). (1994). *Communication research measures: A sourcebook*. New York: The Guilford Press.

12. See Richmond & McCroskey. *Power in the classroom*.

13. Partially adapted from Nathan Faylor's final class project, submitted on September 15, 1998, in partial fulfillment for Communication Training and Development (COMM 3318D) at Southwest Texas State University.

14. Refer to Kirkpatrick. Evaluation.

15. Refer to N. R. Goulden (1992). Theory and vocabulary for communication assessments. *Communication Education, 41*, 258–269.

16. For additional communication assessment instruments, reference S. Morreale and P. Backlund (1996). *Large scale assessment of oral communication: K–12 and higher education* (2nd ed.). Annandale,

VA: Speech Communication Association. This resource contains valid and reliable instruments that are adapted to educational environments. With minimal revision, many of these instruments remain appropriate for professional education in the organizational setting. This resource is available by contacting the National Communication Association at www.natcom.org. Also reference W. G. Christ (Ed.) (1994). *Assessing communication education: A handbook for media, speech, and theatre educators.* Hillsdale, NJ: Lawrence Erlbaum Associates, Publishers.

17. Refer to Kirkpatrick. Evaluation.
18. Refer to pages 309–310 of Kirkpatrick. Evaluation.
19. For a review of how to process qualitative data, please refer to J. Lofland & L. H. Lofland (1995). *Analyzing social settings: A guide to qualitative observation and analysis.* Belmont, CA: Wadsworth Publishing Company.
20. Refer to Kirkpatrick. Evaluation.
21. For a review of the cost/benefit ratio, reference Phillips. *Handbook of training evaluation and measurement methods* (3ʳᵈ ed.).

Chapter 12

1. A. Marken (2001). Skills training is becoming a never ending process. *Office World News*, June, 1, 2001. Available on-line: http://www.winstonbrill .com/bril001/html/article_index/articles/ 451-500/article468_body.html.
2. Reference Marken. Skills training is becoming a never ending process.
3. Reference Marken. Skills training is becoming a never ending process.
4. The Motorola Corporation in Austin, Texas is one organization that has an extensive department within human resources devoted to change. They hire men and women who have a background in communication training and development as "change agent specialists" who are responsible for managing change within the organization.
5. See E. M. Rogers (1995). *Diffusion of innovation* (4ᵗʰ ed.). New York: Free Press; S. DeWine (2001). *The consultant's craft: Improving organizational change* (2ⁿᵈ ed.). Boston: Bedford/St. Martin's; and P. G. Clampitt, L. Berk, & M. L. Williams (2002). Leaders as strategic communicators. *IVEY Business Journal, 66,* 50–55.
6. Reference Marken. Skills training is becoming a never ending process.
7. C. Thompson, E. Koon, W. H. Woodwell, Jr., & J. Beauvais (2002). *Training for the next economy:*

An ASTD state of the industry report on trends in employer-provided training in the United States. Available at www.astd.org.

8. See T. P. Mottet (2000). Interactive television instructors' perceptions of students' nonverbal responsiveness and their influence on distance teaching. *Communication Education, 49,* 146–164.
9. See Mottet. Interactive television instructors' perceptions of students nonverbal responsiveness and their influence on distance teaching.
10. See P. Comeaux (1995). The impact of interactive distance learning network on classroom communication. *Communication Education, 44,* 353–361; L. McHenry & M. Bozik (1995). Communicating at a distance: A study of interaction in a distance education classroom. *Communication Education, 44,* 362–371; T. P. Mottet & S. L. Stewart (2002). Teacher communication in the distance education context. In J. L. Chesebro & J. C. McCroskey (Eds.), *Communication for teachers,* pp. 157–171. Boston: Allyn & Bacon.
11. Reference Marken. Skills training is becoming a never ending process.
12. See Mottet & Stewart (2002). Teacher communication in the distance education context; D. E. Hanna, M. Glowacki-Dudka & S. Conceicao-Runlee (2000). *147 Practical tips for teaching on-line groups: Essentials of Web-based education.* Madison, WI: Atwood Publishing; and E. E. Scannell & L. Donaldson (2000). *Human resource development: The new trainer's guide* (3ʳᵈ ed.). Cambridge, MA: Perseus Publishing.
13. To obtain additional information on ASTD, call 1-800-628-2783 or 703-683-8100; write American Society for Training and Development, 1640 King Street, Box 1443, Alexandria, VA 22313-2043; or locate them on the web at www.astd.org. To locate the chapter closest to you, click on www.astd.org and select the "Find a Chapter" menu option.
14. This idea was discussed in J. A. Daly (1999). Consulting. In A. L. Vangelisti, J. A. Daly, & G. W. Friedrich (Eds.), *Teaching communication,* pp. 507–516. Mahwah, NJ: Lawrence Erlbaum Associates; and in M. D. Merrill and D. G. Twitchell (Eds.), *Instructional design theory,* pp. 79–91. Englewood Cliffs, NJ: Educational Technology Publications.
15. For a review of training positions, please refer to: P. McLayan (1982). The ASTD training and development competency study: A model building challenge. *Training and Development Journal, May,* 18–24; W. E. Arnold & L. McClure (1993). *Communication training and development.* Prospect

Heights, IL: Waveland Press; and Scannell & Donaldson. *Human resource development.*

16. Adapted from C. M. Reigeluth, M. D. Merrill, B. G. Wilson & R. T. Spillers (1994). The elaboration theory of instruction: A model for sequencing and synthesizing instruction. In M. D. Merrill and D. G. Twitchell (Eds.), *Instructional design theory*, pp. 79–91. Englewood Cliffs, NJ: Educational Technology Publications.

17. Adapted from the following sources: V. Beer (2000). *Web learning fieldbook: Using the World Wide Web to build workplace learning environments.* San Francisco, Jossey-Bass/Pfeiffer; B. Hall (1997). *Web-based training cookbook.* New York: Wiley; and S. Wilson (1995). *World Wide Web design guide.* New York: Hayden Books.

18. The National Communication Association publishes the *Journal of Applied Communication.* The journal examines communication problems and solutions in applied or workplace settings. To learn more about this publication, log on to the NCA Web site at www.natcom.org and select the "Publications" menu option.

19. Other communication and management journals available in most college and university libraries that may be beneficial to training and development professionals and communication consultants include *Communication Education, Human Communication Research, Communication Monographs, Communication Research Reports, Communication Quarterly, Management Communication Quarterly, Training and Development Journal, International Journal of Training and Development, Academy of Management Review,* and *Academy of Management Journal.*

20. Consult the *Publication Manual* of the American Psychological Association for a complete review of how to present your assessment results. You can order the manual from APA Order Department, P.O. Box 92984, Washington, D.C. 20090-2984. You can also get frequently asked questions answered by logging on to their Web site at www.apa.org/journals/faq.html.

21. Refer to J. C. McCroskey & V. P. Richmond (2000). *Organizational communication for survival: Making work, work* (2nd ed.). Boston: Allyn & Bacon.

22. For additional information on how to prepare training budgets, it is recommended that you consult professionals in your local chapter of ASTD, because rates vary by location. To locate the chapter nearest you, click on www.astd.org and then select the "Find a Chapter" menu option.

23. Another resource for learning how to market and budget your services is by consulting with Elsom Eldridge, Jr., at Enterprise Development, which is a consulting firm for consultants. You can reach Enterprise Development by calling 612-387-8521, by emailing shaas@cus4results.com, or by logging on to www.cus4results.com.

24. For additional information on how to compute the CBR, please reference J. J. Phillips (1997). *Handbook of training evaluation and measurement methods* (3rd ed.). Houston, TX: Gulf Publishing Company.

GLOSSARY

Accommodators: Trainees who learn primarily from hands-on field experience and by trial and error. They enjoy carrying out plans and involving themselves in challenging experiences.

Adaptors: Nonverbal behaviors or movements that are enacted to satisfy some physical (e.g., scratching an itch) or psychological need (e.g., drumming fingers when nervous).

Affect: The degree of liking, appreciation, respect, and/or value that one has for something.

Affective domain: The domain of learning that focuses on changing or reinforcing attitudes, feelings, and motivation.

Affinity: The degree to which you like or favor something.

Affinity-seeking: Things that you do to try to get other people to like you.

Aggressive trainees: Trainees with poor social skills who are vigorously interested in getting their way.

Analytic assessment: The midlevel of behavioral assessment. Trainers evaluate how well certain behaviors or clusters of behaviors were performed.

Andragogy: The science and art of teaching adults. An andragogical approach to teaching and learning is self-directed rather than teacher-directed.

Antisocial BATs: compliance-gaining strategies that are negative and coercive in nature.

Apportioning: How the trainer divides or segments training material into discreet and separate units.

Assessment center: A room or suite of rooms where employees are given performance tests to identify strengths and weaknesses in their jobs.

Assessment specialist: The training job responsible for measuring the learning outcomes of the training program.

Assimilators: Trainees who value sequential thinking and trust expert opinion. They enjoy collecting data and then organizing it or assimilating it into a concise, logical form. Assimilators remain less interested in learning from others' concrete experiences and are more interested in learning from experts.

Atomistic assessment: The lowest level of behavioral assessment. Trainers identify and observe discrete behaviors to determine if they were or were not performed. This form of behavioral assessment does not include evaluation, just description.

Attention span: Duration of time that trainees can focus cognitively on a given training activity.

Attitudes: Learned predispositions to respond favorably or unfavorably toward something.

Aural learners: Those who learn through hearing and speaking. Auditory-oriented learners need opportunities to not only hear what they are to learn but also to articulate what it is they're learning.

Behavior alteration message (BAM): The actual message used to enact a compliance-gaining strategy.

Behavior alteration technique (BAT): A strategy for gaining compliance.

Behavioral items: The individual behaviors that are to be assessed in a trainee's behavioral performance.

Bigheaded trainees: Trainees who are know-it-alls and have a tendency to share all they know.

Brainstorming: A free flowing of ideas or solutions to problems offered in an evaluation-free environment. This technique encourages creativity among group members.

Bridging: An approach to training where trainers instruct trainees using their own training style, but are however willing and able to adapt to a trainee's learning style if there is a learning problem.

Briefing summary: A succinct statement that includes the who, what, where, when, how, and why that is included in a needs-assessment proposal or a training proposal.

Bullet points: Content concepts, generally one word or short phrases, that are printed with little "bullets" or dots or marks out to the left side. This type of format allows the reader to get a quick listing of the concepts.

Buzz group: A small group, usually consisting of five to ten people who discuss a chosen or selected topic.

Case study: An experiential activity that includes a narrative or short story about some organizational issue where a problem, the history of the problem, and the characters involved with the problem are described in detail

CD-ROM: A compact disk containing data that can be read by a computer.

Chronological order: Organization of information in a time sequence.

Closed questions: Questions that require the recall of specific information. There is a right and wrong answer to the question.

Closure: To provide a conclusion to one element of a training lesson and point the learner to the next learning task.

Cognitive domain: The domain of learning that focuses on the acquisition of facts, information, theories, principles, and knowledge.

Communication: The process of acting on information.

Computer-mediated communication: Using the computer terminal to channel or facilitate a group discussion rather than using face-to-face communication.

Computer-mediated training: Training that is delivered using the personal computer.

Conflict: The disagreement and/or disharmony between individuals as a result of differing goals, objectives, values, beliefs, and attitudes.

Confrontational conflict management style: Managing conflict by winning at the expense of others—a win–lose approach.

Contact hour: A method for calculating the cost of a training program. Factored into each contact hour are the numerous hours invested in conducting needs assessments, writing and presenting training proposals, writing learning objectives, developing training curricula, presenting training programs, and assessing learning objectives.

Contingency plan: What the trainer will do (a plan B) if presentational aids do not work as planned. A backup plan to use if something goes wrong with the original plan of action.

Control group: A group of trainees who do not receive training. This group is then compared to a group of trainees who have received training to determine training effectiveness in terms of learning outcomes.

Convergers: Trainees who prefer looking for the utility in ideas and theories. They prefer analyzing problems and testing theories in order to find solutions to problems.

Conversational delivery style: The style of presenting that is informal, spontaneous, natural, and similar to a conversation.

Cooperative conflict management style: Managing conflict by approaching it as a mutual problem that needs to be solved mutually in a win–win approach.

Correct: Providing feedback that identifies errors in the performance of a skill and presents strategies for improving the performance.

Cost/benefit ratio: A ratio that examines the training program's benefits to the organization in relation to how much the training program costs the organization.

Credentials: An individual's prior training experience, education, research, and other forms of recognition that make one credible or believable to others.

Credibility: A perception of believability that is based on perceptions of another's competence or knowledge and character or trustworthiness.

Criteria: Standards for an acceptable outcome or decision.

Curriculum: The training content organized to achieve the training objectives.

Demonstration: An experiential activity where the trainer, a trainee, or pairs of trainees show others how a certain process or set of behaviors is to be used and applied.

Descriptive training format: A narrative that includes subheadings and paragraphs, which describes each element in a training session.

Development: Any behavior, strategy, design, restructuring, skill or skill set, strategic plan, or motivational effort that is designed to produce growth or positive change in an individual or organization.

Distractions: Physical or psychological factors that would take trainee attention away from the training content and activities.

Distractor foils: A set of foils that incorrectly answer the stem of a multiple-choice exam item.

Divergers: Learners who prefer observing a situation rather than taking action. Divergers tend to be innovative, imaginative, and concerned with personal relevance. They have a need to know how new information relates to prior experiences before they're receptive to learning new information.

Doctor–patient consulting model: Model in which a consultant is hired to both diagnose a problem and recommend an intervention strategy to solve or manage it.

Dry-erase board: A flat white surface mounted on a board that can be written on with special markers. It works similarly to a chalkboard but is much less messy.

E*D*I*T: An acronym that represents a method for processing or unpacking experiential activities; E is engaging in an experiential activity: D is describing the experience; I is making inferences or generalizations beyond the experience; and T is transferring the experience from the training context to other contexts such as the workplace, school, or home.

Education: The process of imparting knowledge or information.

Emotions: Feeling states that often, but not always, result in behavior change.

Encourage: A step in teaching a skill in which positive, reinforcing comments are made about the trainees' performance.

Engagement strategy: A message that encourages trainees to reflect on or to interact with the information they are receiving.

Essay: A type of exam item that challenges trainees to generate the correct answer. Rather than being given a list of possible responses, trainees are challenged to answer the essay question in paragraph form, meaning that the question cannot be answered adequately using a simple response.

Exam: A questionnaire that is specially designed to measure cognitive learning outcomes.

Experiential activity: Any training activity that requires trainees to involve themselves physically and/or psychologically in the training content.

Extemporaneous presentation: The delivery approach where the speaker uses outline notes rather than reading from a manuscript.

External source: Ideas and information gathered from sources other than yourself.

Eye depth: The personal-ness or realness of trainer eye contact with the trainee.

Eye scope: The range and breadth of a trainer's eye contact with the group of trainees.

Facilitated group discussion: Training method that includes three to ten trainees who interact with the assistance of a facilitator who manages the interaction and guides the discussion toward specific learning objectives.

Feedforward message: A message that informs others of how to process information.

Flipchart: A large pad of paper with pages that you can lift and drape over the back of the pad. Generally this is placed on a tripod or chalkboard tray.

Focus group: A small group of people selected to discuss a particular topic so that others can better gauge how people will respond to a product, topics, or program. May be used to pretest the utility of a training program.

Foils: The alternative choices that follow a stem and ultimately answer or complete the stem. There are usually three to five foils per multiple-choice item.

Font: A certain style of lettering. Some are simple in form; others are more ornate.

Handouts: Papers or pictures, having to do with your training session, that you pass around to each trainee. A document that they can hold and take back to the office with them.

Hierarchy of needs: A model proposed by Abraham Maslow that suggests that all people have certain common needs and these needs are in a hierarchy such that you must have one need satisfied before you are interested in the next need.

Holistic or general impression assessment: The highest level of behavioral assessment. Rather than assessing discrete or clusters of behaviors, trainers assess the overall quality of the behavioral performance. This form of behavioral assessment focuses on the product rather than the process.

Human communication: The process of making sense out of the world and sharing that sense with others and creating meaning through the use of verbal and nonverbal messages.

Immediacy: A perception of physical or psychological closeness that is stimulated in others by using inclusive verbal messages and expressive nonverbal messages.

Immediacy behaviors: Behaviors that indicate and even foster the degree of physical or psychological closeness between two individuals. These behaviors can be enacted verbally or nonverbally.

Impulsive learners: Learners who work quickly and with less determination. Impulsive learners are less concerned about producing a perfect learning product.

Information: An assortment of facts and data that have limited meaning for the trainee until they are organized. Once information and data are organized for the trainee, they become knowledge.

Internal review/preview: A message that informs trainees of where they have been and where they are going in a lecture or presentation.

Internal source: Your own personal knowledge and experiences.

Internships: Opportunities for students to obtain college credit toward their degrees for working in a supervised work environment.

Interpersonal conflict: Conflict that occurs between individuals.

Interrater reliability: The type of reliability or consistency in which all trainers, using the same instrument, assess trainees' behaviors the same way.

Interview: A qualitative assessment technique in which a trainer asks individual trainees a set of questions in order to determine training effectiveness and learning outcomes.

Intrapersonal conflict: Conflict within one's self.

Invite: The repeated performance of a skill or behavior in an effort to master the behavior.

Job talk: A brief demonstration of a training module that gives potential decision makers an idea of one's training style.

Just in time training: A training concept whereby trainees receive just the right amount and type of training exactly when it's needed.

Keyed response foil: A foil that correctly answers the stem of a multiple-choice exam item.

Kinesics: The study of the communicative potential and messages of movement.

Kinesthetic learners: Those who learn by touching and doing. Kinesthetically oriented learners remain tactile and prefer to be engaged in movement. They are partial to action and have a tendency to express emotion in physically exuberant ways.

Knowledge: Organized information. Information consists of assorted facts and data. Once organized in a manner that fits trainees' schema, then information becomes knowledge.

Law of association: This general law suggests that every new fact, idea, concept, or behavior is best learned if trainees can relate it to or with something they already know.

Law of effect: This general law suggests that trainees learn best under pleasant and rewarding conditions.

Law of frequency: This general law suggests that the more often trainees practice a trained behavior, the more likely they are to continue using the desired behavior accurately.

Law of learning: A statement that describes the conditions that must be met in order for trainees to learn.

Learning: A change in individuals, due to the interaction of the individuals and their environment, which fills a need and makes them more capable of dealing adequately with their environment.

Learning style: The way an individual perceives, organizes, processes, and remembers information.

Lecture: A training method whereby the trainer uses oral messages to impart large amounts of prepared information to trainees using one-way communication. The lecture contains information that is presented in a logical or sequential order.

Likert scale: A five-item scale that seeks to gauge a respondent's attitude toward something with choices of strongly agree, agree, undecided, disagree, and strongly disagree.

Matching: A type of exam item that challenges trainees to connect or attach two words and/or phrases together; also, an approach to training where trainers adapt their instruction to fit the trainee's learning style.

Maturity: The degree of experience rather than age that a trainee brings to the training classroom. Not all young adults are inexperienced or immature, and not all adults are experienced and mature.

Media specialist: The training job that works closely with the program designer in selecting and/or designing audio and visual media to complement and support a training program.

Meeting agenda: A schedule of events or topics to be discussed at a meeting.

Misbehaviors: Actions and communication by instructors or students that are unacceptable and detract from the learning environment.

Mnemonic: A memory aid or a memory shortcut, as in "TGIF," meaning "Thank God It's Friday."

Modeling: Learning by observing others; occurs when people acquire knowledge, attitudes, beliefs, and values and learn how to perform certain behaviors by observing others.

Monotone: The vocal tendency of a trainer to stay in one voice pitch area for an extended amount of time. Typically, this results in poor trainee reception of trainer material.

Multicolumn training format: A four-column approach to describing the time, content, methods, and materials needed to present a training session.

Multiple-choice: A type of exam item that challenges trainees' to choose among three to five possible answers or foils to a particular question. A multiple-choice item contains a stem, a keyed response foil, and distractor foils.

Motivation: An internal state of readiness to take action or achieve a goal.

Murphy's law: The law that states "anything that can go wrong, will go wrong."

Needs analyst: The training job responsible for identifying what learners do not yet know or the important or necessary skills that they can't yet perform.

Needs assessment: The process of identifying what learners do not yet know or the important or necessary skills that they can't yet perform.

Needs-assessment proposal: A formal document that explains to decision makers why their organization or some aspect of their organization deserves to be examined closely because of a possible deficiency.

Negative trainees: Trainees who constantly find fault in everything and tend to be pessimists.

Nonconfrontational conflict management style: Managing conflict by giving in or avoiding it.

Nonverbal channel: a category of nonverbal behavior such as appearance, eye behavior, facials, vocals, and space.

Nonverbal communication: Meaning stimulated in trainees' minds via trainer use of eye contact, vocals, and gestures.

Nonverbal intimacy: Immediacy promoted by nonverbal behaviors such as eye contact and vocals.

On-the-job training: An experientially based training method in which trainees receive individualized training and coaching that is job specific while performing the actual job.

Open (or open-ended) question: A question in which no specific structure is offered to frame the respondent's response; may be ambiguous and usually doesn't have correct and incorrect responses.

Opinion leader: An informal role within an organization that people look to in order to understand how they should interpret certain information.

Organization culture: The norms, rules, customs, values, history, and characteristics of an organization.

Outline training format: An organized, structured description of all training content and methods presented in traditional outline form.

Overhead projector: A projection device that shines a light through a transparent plastic sheet (generally $8 \frac{1}{2} \times 11$ inches in size) and projects images or words up on a screen.

Paraphrasing: Saying the same thing in a different way with different but similar words.

Parroting: Saying back to people exactly what you heard them say.

Participant's guide: The workbook or handout materials that are given to each trainee; it includes training content and all material needed by the trainees to participate in the training session.

Part–whole learners: Learners who prefer examining the parts rather than the whole or the big picture.

Pedagogy: The science and art of teaching children. A pedagogical approach to teaching and learning is teacher-directed rather than self-directed.

Periodicals: Magazines and journals that are published once to several times per year.

Personal thought inventory (PTI): An engagement and assessment strategy where trainees respond in writing to three questions: "What is it?" "Why is it important?" and "How do you do it or use it?"

Physical barriers to listening: Factors like noise that interfere with the accuracy and effectiveness of listening.

Physical environment: Typically the physical surroundings for a training session, including things such as room, furniture, presentation screens, temperature, and background noise.

Physiological needs: Individuals' needs for air, water, shelter, food, and the like, according to Maslow's Need Model.

Pilot test: A trial run or test of a training program that can then be used to assess the quality of the training program before it is presented to others.

Plagiarism: Using the work or writing of another and claiming it as your own.

Plus-one technique: Training technique used when training others in how to perform a complicated behavior, skill, or process. The behavior is divided into smaller components, and others are trained one step at a time. After a trainee has mastered a single step or component of the larger process, a new step is added (plus one) and mastered. This process continues until the entire behavioral process has been mastered.

Posture: How an individual stands or positions him- or herself (e.g., slumping, standing up straight with shoulders back).

Pre/post-test design: A measuring design whereby trainers measure trainees' affective, cognitive, and behavioral learning before and again immediately following a training program to determine learning gains or losses.

Presentational aids: Images and sounds that are used to enhance a presentation.

Presenter: One who delivers the training program to trainees.

Preview: A message that informs trainees of what is to come next in a lecture or presentation.

Process consulting model: Model in which a consultant is hired to work with an individual or organization in all aspects of organizational development, diagnosis, and delivery of intervention strategy.

Program designer: The training job that translates needs into learning objectives, develops training curricula, selects appropriate training methods, and develops lesson plans.

Project-based learning: Learning that occurs from trainees processing actual work-based problems rather than hypothetical case studies or simulations.

Proposal: A formal document that sells a program of training to organizational decision makers.

Prosocial BATs: Compliance-gaining strategies that are positive and relational in nature.

Proxemics: The study of the communicative potential and messages of space.

Psychological barriers to listening: Mental states or processes that interfere with the accuracy and effectiveness of listening.

Psychological environment: The organizational culture, recent events, and employee mindset and attitudes that frame and surround the training sessions.

Purchase consulting model: Model in which a consultant is hired to provide agreed-upon service, such as training, performed for an individual or organization.

Qualitative assessment: A type of assessment that describes learning outcomes using personal statements and reflections from trainees.

Quantitative assessment: A type of assessment that measures learning outcomes using numbers and statistics.

Questionnaire: Another term for survey.

Quiet trainees: Trainees who rarely talk, for whatever reason.

Reflective learners: Learners who take time to process information. Reflective learners tend to work carefully and with precision.

Reiteration: Restating content using different words, word order, and/or examples.

Relational power: Power that is based on the relationship and positive respect you have for the person asking you to do something.

Repeating: Restating content in the same exact way using the same words and word order.

Retention: How much a trainee can remember after the training session is over. Generally, the more of this, the better.

Return on investment: An economic concept that suggests that in order for an expense or an investment to be considered of value, it should provide some type of a return that is greater than the initial investment.

Review: A message that summarizes a lecture or presentation for a trainee.

Rhetorical questions: Questions that don't require answers.

Role conflict: When an individual holds two roles simultaneously that have competing functions or needs.

Role play: An experiential activity where trainees are encouraged to act out a particular part in a communication transaction. Most simulations include role plays.

Round robin: A facilitation technique where the group leader asks a question and then goes around the group asking each member for his or her response to the question.

Scan: To maintain eye contact by sweeping the room from one side to the other with one's eye gaze.

Schema: A mental "box" where you can classify and categorize and file concepts. A frame of reference for concepts and experiences one has. A mental system of understanding, interpreting, and storing cognitive or experiential input.

Semantic barriers to listening: Problems in understanding of word meanings that interfere with the listening process.

Semantic differential: A scale that measures attitudes by asking people to choose between two opposite positions or bipolar adjectives, for example, good and bad or liked and disliked.

Server: A computer in a network of computers that stores application programs and files. These programs and files can be accessed by computers at remote locations as long as they are linked to this central computer.

Set induction: A training technique that helps get trainees ready to learn by gaining their attention and motivating them to learn the information or skill.

Show: To model or demonstrate how a behavior should be performed.

Signpost: A message that helps trainees know where they are within a lecture or presentation.

Simulation: An experiential activity where trainees are given a set of circumstances and are asked to role-play or enact certain roles in order to resolve a communication-related problem.

Skill: The ability to appropriately perform a task or behavior.

Skill criteria: Skill criteria describe, in behavioral terms, what each skill rating means to the trainer who is measuring the behavioral learning outcome.

Skill ratings: A series of numbers or a scale that measures the level or quality of performance for each of the behavioral items. A common skill rating includes a 1 to 5 point scale where 1 = very poor, 2 = poor, 3 = fair, 4 = good, and 5 = very good.

Spot grid: A method of maintaining eye contact by systematically looking at specific zones in the room.

Stem: The question or incomplete statement that you want your trainees to answer or complete.

Stimulus: Using media and/or trigger questions to provoke a reaction in trainees.

Stimulus prompt: A partial statement or question that requires trainees to complete the statement or answer the question.

Stimulus variation: The training technique of using a variety of methods and strategies to teach skills and information.

Style-flexing: An approach to training where trainers accommodate and challenge their trainees'

learning styles. Trainees learn not only the training content but also how to learn in ways that are different from their preferred learning styles.

Survey: A series of written questions or statements designed to illicit information about knowledge, attitudes, or behavior.

Talkative trainees: Trainees who are seen as "talk-a-holics" and who have a tendency to dominate training sessions.

Task analysis: An outline that describes the step-by-step procedures for performing a specific behavior, skill, or task.

Task analyst: The training job responsible for taking the skills identified by the needs analyst and breaking them down into step-by-step outlines. Trainers will use this step-by-step outline to teach others in how to perform the skill.

Taxonomy: A way to classify information.

Teleconferencing: Using two-way audio and video technology in order to conduct a conference. This technology allows people to participate in meetings without being in the same physical location.

Teletraining: Training broadcasted from a studio to others in remote or distant training locations using two-way audio and video interactive television technology.

Tell: To present information in a lecture or expository way.

Threaded discussion: A facilitation technique where the group leader asks a question and then integrates carefully all responses and additional follow-up questions into a meaningful and coherent conversation.

360 survey method: An approach to seeking information from a broad range of individuals (supervisor, colleagues, self-report) to assess an individual's level of performance.

Toolbar: The row of computer icons on a computer screen. Clicking on any one of these icons causes the computer to enact a certain command (e.g., save, copy, or cut).

Total quality management: A management philosophy that advocates that doing a job right is more important than doing a job quickly. All barriers that may prevent employees from doing their best work are removed.

Training: The process of developing skills in order to more effectively perform a specific job or task.

Training and development administrator: The training job responsible for working closely with the manager to insure that the facilities, equipment, materials, participants, and other components of a learning event are present and that training programs run smoothly.

Training and development manager: The training job responsible for planning, organizing, staffing, controlling training and development operations, and bridging the operations of the departments with other units within an organization to insure that the organization's training and development needs are met.

Training assessment: A systematic process of evaluating training programs to ensure that they meet the needs of the trainees and organization.

Training budget: A formal document that outlines all of the anticipated costs needed to develop, present, and assess a training program.

Training content: The information, definitions, descriptions, concepts, and skills that are presented to trainees during a training session.

Training generalist: A training practitioner who performs all different types of training jobs and tasks, including needs assessment, writing learning objectives, developing training curricula, presenting training content, and assessing learning outcomes.

Training goal: A general statement of training outcomes.

Training methods: The procedures and strategies used to present information and help trainees achieve the training objectives.

Training module: A specific block of training time that is focused on a skill or concept without a break.

Training objective: A concise statement that describes what the trainee should be able to do at the end of a training session.

Training plan: A written description of all elements of a training session. It includes the objectives, a description of the training content, training methods, and the audiovisual training resources needed to conduct the training.

Training proposal: A formal document that outlines the training program in detail, including length of program, training content, strategies, materials, assessment plan, and training budget.

Training specialist: A training practitioner who performs only a limited number of jobs and tasks related to training and development, such as an assessment specialist who focuses only on assessing training effectiveness.

Triangulation: Assessing training effectiveness and learning outcomes by using both quantitative measuring designs (i.e., pre/post-tests) and qualitative descriptive methods (focus groups or interviews).

Trigger questions: Questions used to simulate group discussion that remain controversial and that deal with claims of value—what is right and wrong, good and bad, and why.

Tripod: A three-legged stand used for holding posters or flipcharts in a presentation.

Verbal intimacy: Immediacy conveyed by the words a trainer uses.

Visual learners: Those who learn by reading and viewing. Visually orientated learners need to see what they are learning.

Vocal cues: The volume, articulation, dialect, pitch, and inflection of the speaker's voice.

Web-based training specialist: A person who develops and designs training programs for delivery through the Internet.

Whole–part learners: Learners who prefer having the big picture before moving into the details of the concept or idea.

INDEX